NATIVE AMERICANS

THE MAGILL BIBLIOGRAPHIES

Other Magill Bibliographies:

America in Space—Russell R. Tobias
The American Presidents—Norman S. Cohen
The American Constitution—Robert J. Janosik
Black American Women Novelists—Craig Werner
Contemporary Latin American Fiction—Keith H. Brower
Ethics—John K. Roth
Masters of Mystery and Detective Fiction—J. Randolph Cox
The Modern American Novel—Steven G. Kellman
Nineteenth Century American Poetry—Philip K. Jason
The Victorian Novel—Laurence W. Mazzeno
Women's Issues—Laura Stempel Mumford

NATIVE AMERICANS

An Annotated Bibliography

Frederick E. Hoxie
and
Harvey Markowitz

D'Arcy McNickle Center for the History of the American Indian

SALEM PRESS
Pasadena, California Englewood Cliffs, New Jersey

∞ The paper used in these volumes conforms to the American National Standard for Permanence of Paper for Printed Library Materials, Z39.48-1984.

Library of Congress Cataloging-in-Publication Data

Hoxie, Frederick E., 1947-
Native Americans / Frederick E. Hoxie and Harvey Markowitz
p. c.m.—(Magill bibliographies)
Includes bibliographical references and index.
ISBN 0-89356-670-5
1. Indians of North America—Bibliography I.Markowitz, Harvey. II. Title. III. Series
Z1209.2.N67H68 1991
[E77] 91-16427
016.970004'91—dc20 CIP

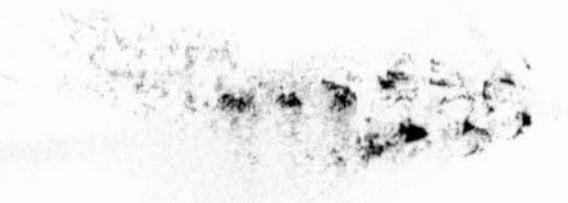

For our parents

EDITORIAL STAFF

Publisher
FRANK N. MAGILL

Advisory Board
KENNETH T. BURLES
DAWN P. DAWSON

Series Editor
JOHN WILSON

Production Manager
KATHY HIX

Copy Editor
LOIS SMITH

Contents

ACKNOWLEDGMENTS

We wish to thank the following fellows and staff of the Newberry Library for their suggestions and encouragement: Jay Miller, Father Peter Powell, Richard Sattler, R. David Edmunds, Ruth Hamilton, Martha Knack, Olive Dickason, Helen Hornbeck Tanner, John Aubrey, Raymond Fogelson, Marge Curtis, Robert Karrow, Margaret Kulis, Hilah Geer, Stephanie Karamitsos, Michael Kaplan, Christine Spencer, and Pat Morris.

NATIVE AMERICANS

INTRODUCTION

Traditionally, Native American people did not employ written records to keep track of their histories or to catalogue their customs. For centuries, knowledge was entrusted to particular individuals, who stored it in their memories, shared it in their oratory, and celebrated it in ceremonies and public performances. Many communities in North America used paintings, picture writing, and other devices to record particular elements of their cultural life, but these were intended as tools to assist the individuals charged with remembering and passing on what they had been taught. Thus, in 1492, when sustained contact between the Americas and the rest of the world was initiated by the Columbus voyages, books such as the ones then being produced in Asia and Europe did not exist north of the Rio Grande.

Writing about native North Americans began with descriptions penned by outsiders. From the outset, this separation of observer and observed produced misunderstandings. Impressed by written laws and Scripture, Europeans interpreted the absence of both in North America as a sign that the continent's indigenous communities were backward and simple. Early explorers assumed, therefore, that they could describe and understand the communities they encountered even if they did not speak the native languages. Separated by language and custom, the Europeans were also tempted to read a variety of imagined motives into their hosts' behavior. As a consequence, early European travelers sent home fanciful and distorted profiles of the Indians. Columbus, for example, believed that he had encountered people so naïve and generous that they were models of human conduct. John Smith, on the other hand, believed that the native people of the Virginia tidewater were warlike and irresponsible. Cotton Mather was convinced that the Native Americans of New England worshipped the devil. Latter-day counterparts of these early chroniclers imagined the Indians to be remnants of the lost tribes of Israel, hunters so swift they could run down a deer, or warriors so devoted to conflict that they would simply die if forced to abandon their old ways.

The distortions of the past cast a continuing shadow over books about Native Americans. In an age when teams called "Redskins" capture wide support and popular national leaders declare that the United States was founded on "virgin land," we should not be surprised that much of what is written about Indian life is insensitive or downright wrong. Unfortunately, the literature available on native people has not escaped the misunderstandings that began half a millennium ago. Books such as the ones described in this bibliography are certainly an antidote to such ignorance, but even these must be approached with caution. After all, it was barely 150 years ago that the first scholarly study of a single tribe, Lewis Henry Morgan's *League of the Iroquois*, was published. It was only a century ago that the first serious exhibits of Native American artifacts were mounted in museums for public study. And it was only within the last half century that the great length of human occupation in the Americas became widely accepted. For most scholars and students, the broad outlines of the aboriginal American experience are as new and full of surprises as the geography of the moon.

Unlike the moon, however, Native America has indigenous inhabitants. These people have not retreated into silence during the past five centuries but have struggled with increasing energy to articulate and record their own experiences. Overcoming barriers of language and social custom, thousands of Indian people have written and catalogued the beliefs of their own communities or assisted non-Indians who wished to develop an accurate picture of Indian cultures. This process began long ago, but in the last decades of the twentieth century, the effort has intensified. Multiplying numbers of Native Americans have become involved in both academic scholarship and national politics, while shifts in the racial atmosphere of both the United States and Canada have facilitated the access of these individuals to podiums and publishers. The result has been an ever-stronger native voice in the materials that describe Indian life and discuss Indian affairs.

The items listed in this bibliography reflect the trend toward ever more careful scholarship regarding Native Americans as well as the expanding Indian role in the production of that scholarship. The list includes dozens of "classic" descriptions from decades ago, but a much larger percentage is drawn from the five hundred or more English-language books and scholarly articles on Indian history and culture which now appear annually. The bulk of our citations were published in the past twenty-five years. (In most cases we have cited the original date of publication for an item; we have listed later editions only when the publication was revised.) We have also balanced our desire to list the best and most recent material with a wish to provide readers with a usable bibliography. Thus, we have emphasized books over articles published in hard-to-get scholarly journals and have avoided limited-circulation publications whenever possible. We have also concentrated on published works, avoiding most government documents, transcripts of hearings, and legislative reports. Our goal has been to produce a list of publications that is accurate, current, and accessible.

The bibliography contains four major sections: general studies and references, history, specific culture areas, and contemporary life. The sections describing general studies and references, history, and contemporary life are roughly equal in length, but the section on individual culture areas is much longer. This section, which contains subsections on each major culture area in North America, conveys the immense diversity of Indian life. Because the concept of a "culture area" is not Native American in origin, the eight regional divisions in this section are somewhat arbitrary. We have generally followed those used in the Smithsonian Institution's *Handbook of North American Indians*, as follows: Northeast, Southeast, Southwest, California, Great Basin, Plains, Northwest and Plateau, and Arctic and Subarctic.

Because the bibliography is annotated and emphasizes recent scholarship, it is far from exhaustive. Our goal in each section has been to provide readers with references to enough bibliographies, guides, and examples of outstanding writing that they will be able to understand the variety of material within each topic and to discover additional sources for further study. We have attempted to produce a "browsable" bibliography that will stimulate and assist further digging. This is a book of first, rather than last, resort.

General Studies and Reference Works

This section has two parts. The first, one of the largest in the volume, contains more than 150 books that address some aspect of Indian life across more than one culture area or period. It contains many of the "classics" of the field, such as Franz Boas' *Race, Language, and Culture*, John Collier's *Indians of the Americas*, and essays by the pioneering linguist Edward Sapir. Also included here are surveys of Indian life, such as Harold Driver's comprehensive *Indians of North America* and Alice Kehoe's more recent *North American Indians: A Comparative Account*. Finally, this section contains dozens of books on special topics, including canoes, astronomy, literature, dance, languages, medicine, plant use, political leadership, architecture, and sports.

The second part contains a list of more than one hundred reference books, including both general and critical bibliographies, research guides, directories, atlases, encyclopedias, compilations of historical documents, and directories of people and places. The books in this section attempt to cover more than a single region or tribe, even though they may describe only one data source (such as the National Archives) or topic (such as treaties). Perhaps the handiest sources in this list for beginning a research project are the bibliographies by Francis Paul Prucha (*A Bibliographical Guide to the History of Indian-White Relations in the United States* and its supplement) and George Peter Murdock and Timothy J. O'Leary (*Ethnographic Bibliography of North America*).

History

This section contains more than 150 items whose primary focus is the history of a particular era in the native past since 1492. In conformity with academic conventions, we have included Indian history *prior* to 1492 either with general studies of archaeology in the preceding section, or with the subsections on archaeology in the various regional lists in the section entitled "Culture Areas." Most historical studies of individual tribes covering periods after 1492 are listed with the appropriate culture area in the latter section. Works that bridge our division between the colonial and national periods in the United States have been placed where the emphasis of the particular book seems to lie. (We define the national era as beginning with the Revolutionary War; anything that addresses "American" issues will be in the section on Indians in the United States.) Great works of history do not follow such simple categories, and so we urge readers to consult both the index and collateral sections.

The nearly fifty books listed in the section on Indians in colonial North America will give readers a taste of the various approaches and topics that have interested scholars of this period. Careful students will note that many subjects remain to be explored, including the shifting status of Indian women, the role of law in native life, and the experience of Pacific Coast tribes in the seventeenth and eighteenth centuries. Not surprisingly, the tribes that engaged themselves most forcefully with Europeans are most heavily represented: the Cherokees, the Iroquois, and the tribes of New England.

Of the seventy-six entries for the section on Indians in the United States, barely 25 percent were published before 1970. This selection reflects our desire to emphasize recent scholarship, but it is also an indication of the explosion of interest in this field in the last generation. Fueled by similar growth in the areas of African-American, immigration, and women's history, students of American Indian history have turned to the many fascinating stories that had been either forgotten or ignored by their predecessors. The section contains a few of the most prominent pioneering works in the field, such as those by Annie Heloise Abel, Angie Debo, and James Mooney, but the bulk of the listings are recent monographs on federal policy, missionary activity, and the many adaptations tribal people made to the European presence.

Because most citizens of the United States equate their nation with the continent, they are not generally conscious of the second English-speaking national tradition in North America. The thirty-odd books in Canadian "History" are intended to correct this national chauvinism and to provide a profile of how another group of Americans have interacted with native people. Here the weight of recent publications is even greater than in the previous section; only two works listed here were published before 1970. This imbalance reflects the tremendous growth of interest in native studies in Canada (including a rapidly expanding tradition of scholarship by Indian people themselves), as well as the dramatic political history of the nation in recent years. Legal struggles over native land rights, as well as Canada's larger effort to establish a new national constitution, have stimulated intense concern for Indian issues, which is reflected in many of these books.

Culture Areas

The books for each culture area are divided into eight subsections. Although the titles are self-explanatory, readers should be aware that each category is designed to encompass one sphere of life in any culture. "Folklore, Sacred Narrative, Religious Belief and Practice" encompasses the many kinds of writing that portray Native American spiritual life in a particular area. "Subsistence and Land Use" is meant to encompass economic relations with non-Indians as well as native patterns of subsistence. "Family and Society" contains titles from the large literature on native social relations, kinship, and domestic life, and "Material Culture and the Arts" is meant to capture the broad range of titles that present information on material expression—what non-Indians often subdivide into art, handicrafts, and decoration. Studies grouped under "Tribal Life" include the tribal histories and profiles that have formed the basis for ethnography in the twentieth century. Finally, while we have attempted to include as many Native American authors as possible in all categories, "Biography and Autobiography" is meant to highlight individual Indians and to give readers access to their voices.

Northeast

The Northeast encompasses all of the United States and southern Canada east of the arid plains and north of the Mason-Dixon line. The general studies section contains the landmark *Atlas of Great Lakes Indian History* as well as the Northeast volume of the Smithsonian Institution's *Handbook of North American Indians* and more than two dozen topical studies and bibliographies.

The subsections in the Northeast section reflect the rich tradition of academic scholarship on the Indians of this region. For example, the archaeology section is one of the largest of all the culture areas, and the studies listed in "Tribal Life" include pioneering works by Frances Densmore, Felix M. Keesing, Lewis Henry Morgan, and Frank G. Speck. In addition, "Folklore, Sacred Narrative, Religious Belief and Practice" contains descriptions of native mythology (for example, William S. Simmons, *Spirit of the New England Tribes*), ceremonies (for instance, Elisabeth Tooker's study of the Iroquois midwinter ceremonies), and religious history. A classic among the latter category for all of North America is Anthony F. C. Wallace's *Death and Rebirth of the Seneca*.

Southeast

Home of the Creeks, Cherokees, and other heavily studied tribes and site of European exploration and settlement since the early sixteenth century, the Southeast has spawned a rich literature on Native Americans. This section covers all of the eastern United States not covered by the Northeast; we have not included works on the Caribbean. In addition to bibliographies and specialized works, "General Studies and References" includes three important syntheses: John R. Swanton's early overview, *The Indians of the Southeastern United States*; Charles M. Hudson's more recent *The Southeastern Indians*; and J. Leitch Wright Jr.'s historical survey, *The Only Land They Knew*.

In other subsections, works by Marvin T. Smith, Jerald T. Milanich, and John A. Walthall illustrate the intense interest in southeastern archaeology in recent years, whereas the subsection on folklore and religion contains some early classics: James Mooney's *Myths of the Cherokees* and John Swanton's *Myths and Tales of the Southeastern Indians*. "Tribal Life" contains several works that have taken advantage of the relatively long historical record available in this region. Models of this genre are works by James H. Merrell and Karen I. Blu. Also notable in the southeastern region is the relative paucity of published work on Native American subsistence patterns and the relatively small number of Indian biographies and autobiographies.

Southwest

Because the Southwest, which for our purposes encompasses the high deserts and arroyos of the Rio Grande and Colorado River drainages, was historically isolated from centers of national power in Mexico City and Washington, D.C., the native peoples of the area were often able to avoid the worst aspects of European expansion. Ruled from the south before 1848 and from the northeast afterward, this arid and sparsely populated area experienced waves of disruption from the outside but sustained its essentially Indian character until well into the twentieth century. As a consequence, the indigenous cultures of the Southwest have attracted the attention of generations of serious writers, art collectors, and tourists. The result is an impressive array of scholarship.

Two volumes of the Smithsonian Institution's *Handbook of North American Indians*, both edited by the Tewa anthropologist Alfonso Ortiz, highlight the many general studies listed in this section. Also notable is the general introduction to pueblo life by Santa Clara Pueblo's Edward P. Dozier. Other subsections, such as "Archaeology," "Subsistence and Land Use," and "Family and Society," reflect the long record of academic interest in southwestern peoples. Some of the books listed there are early classics of ethnographic research (for example, Frank H. Cushing's *Zuni Breadstuff* and Ruth M. Underhill's *Social Organization of the Papago Indians*); others, such as *Prehistory of the Southwest* by Linda S. Cordell, are syntheses of an immense literature.

Because the Southwest contains so many communities whose lifeways appear unchanged by outside pressures, their ongoing religious and ceremonial activities have attracted substantial interest. More than two dozen books are listed in "Folklore, Sacred Narrative, Religious Belief and Practice." These range from Matilda C. Stevenson's early (and controversial) studies of the Zuni to recent works such as John R. Farella's *The Main Stalk*. Similarly, the large list in "Material Culture and the Arts" reflects high public and commercial interest in this area of cultural life.

California

Scholars have long maintained that even in the precontact world, California was a distinctive place. Home to more linguistic and cultural variety than any comparable area, the modern state encompassed a distinctive set of traditions. Whether living a hunter-gatherer existence in the inland valleys and hills or clustered in fishing villages along the coast, California's native peoples avoided multivillage organization and extensive agriculture. Colonized by the Spanish in the late eighteenth century and brutally conquered by the Americans in the nineteenth, California's native people did not receive significant scholarly attention until well into the 1900's. Moreover, much of this work has been accomplished by three men: Robert F. Heizer, Alfred L. Kroeber, and Lowell J. Bean. Together they account for more than one-third of the books we list for this entire section.

In addition to being aware of the relatively brief history of scholarship on California, researchers should also be aware that both Spanish missionization and the horrors of the Gold Rush era destroyed a substantial portion of the state's native heritage. Assiduous research has produced an impressive collection of folklore and material culture studies, but the rapid destruction of native political and economic independence made it impossible for later generations to learn much in detail about individual tribal societies. In recent years, however, hard work by individual California Indian communities has produced a series of tribally sponsored publications (for example, *Our Home Forever: A Hupa Tribal History*), and the Malki Museum at the Morongo community in Banning has sponsored the publication of an impressive list of new books. For the latter, see works by Lowell Bean, David P. Barrows, Travis Hudson, and Eugene N. Anderson, Jr.

Great Basin

Like the Indians of the Southwest, the native people of the Great Basin have frequently benefitted from their isolation. The arid climate of this region, which runs south from Oregon and Idaho between the Continental Divide and the Sierra Nevada, has also preserved much of its archaeological heritage. The result is a rich literature containing detailed studies of desert land use, rock art, and religious practice. The Great Basin volume of the Smithsonian Institution's *Handbook of North American Indians* (edited by Warren d'Azevedo) and Catherine S. Fowler's bibliography of anthropological research provide excellent introductions to what has been accomplished in the region.

Among the subsections, the "Archaeology" list contains a number of studies that present the immense time depth of the Great Basin. The list describing folklore and religious life presents a number of first-hand accounts that convey the complexity of spiritual experience in communities that often appear simple and placid. The largest subsection contains nearly two dozen studies of tribal life in the region. Noteworthy among these are the four titles produced by the Intertribal Council of Nyevada and based in large part on the oral testimony of community elders.

Plains

The staple of Hollywood dramas, Plains Indians have long fascinated scholars and the general public. The dramatic confrontation between the area's tribes and the forces of "civilization" in the nineteenth century first attracted this attention, but it has been sustained by a collective sense that the native people of the region were (and are) connected to the North American landscape in a unique and powerful way. That spirit suffuses much of the work in this section.

Nearly half of the books listed in the subsection "General Studies and References" are tribal bibliographies reflecting the large but narrowly focused literature on the cultures that occupy a region stretching between the Continental Divide and the 100th meridian and running from Texas to Saskatchewan. The historical bibliography by Katherine M. Weist and Susan R. Sharrock represents an outstanding exception to this parochialism. In a similar vein, it is significant that the best general introduction to the region continues to be Robert Lowie's 1954 survey, *Indians of the Plains*.

The relatively recent engagement of scholars with the peoples of the Plains has meant that the archaeological literature listed here is somewhat limited and dominated by the many contributions of the Smithsonian Institution's Waldo

Wedel. It is also the reason that these lists contain so many ethnographic and biographical studies. The latter include a number of significant works written or dictated by Native Americans, such as *Black Elk Speaks*, Frances Densmore's compilations of tribal music, and more than a dozen autobiographies. Also represented here are a number of works by pioneers in the first-hand study of American Indian life. These include the nineteenth century artist George Catlin, as well as Alice C. Fletcher, George B. Grinnell, and James R. Walker, all of whom lived for a time with the tribes they described.

Northwest and Plateau

Comprising the northwestern quadrant of the United States and the coastal areas of Oregon, Washington, and British Columbia, this region contains cultures and peoples oriented toward the sea. Whether living along the upper reaches of the Columbia or Fraser River or inhabiting villages perched on the edge of the Pacific Ocean, the Northwest Coast and Plateau tribes were dependent on gathering the rich resources around them and maintaining the community institutions necessary for trade and cooperative labor. The most recent of the several surveys of the area is the Northwest volume of the *Handbook of North American Indians*, which appeared in 1990. Also notable are the overviews by Philip Drucker and Robert H. Ruby and John A. Brown.

Northwest ceremonial life, as well as the elaborate oral literatures of coastal peoples and the region's long tradition of shamanism, have attracted scholars. This interest is reflected in the subsection on spiritual life, as well as in the coverage of "Subsistence and Land Use," which contains works on native attitudes toward the environment, and "Family and Society," which includes studies of the famous coastal potlatch ceremony. The pervasiveness of spiritual concerns is also reflected in several of the works listed in "Tribal Life." Finally, the region has produced relatively few biographies and autobiographies but has been the inspiration for some stunning profiles of tribal life. Among the most famous of the latter category listed here are works by Franz Boas, the Nez Percé tribal historian Allen Slickpoo, and the anthropologist Elizabeth Colson.

Arctic and Subarctic

Covered by two volumes of the Smithsonian Institution's *Handbook of North American Indians* (the Arctic, edited by David Damas, and the Subarctic, by June Helm), this is easily the most extensive culture area on the continent. It covers the northern two-thirds of Canada and all of Alaska above its panhandle. Its isolation has drawn many scholars northward, but its harsh conditions have limited the size of the non-native population until the mid-twentieth century. In many parts of Alaska and the Canadian north, native people make up the majority of the population.

Listings in the "Archaeology" subsection will present historical dynamics in an area usually thought of as the "frozen north." The books listed here indicate that the so-called prehistory of the region was marked by successive migrations and technological evolutions. Also striking to beginning students is the extensive literature on the relationship between northern peoples and the animals on which they depended for survival. These relationships are touched on in several titles describing spiritual life as well as the majority of those grouped under "Subsistence and Land Use." The largest subsection, "Tribal Life," contains studies of cultural traditions (such as three works by the Canadian scholar Diamond Jenness), as well as of those traditions' responses to the dramatic changes that overcame the North in the late twentieth century.

Contemporary Life

Our object in this final section is to introduce readers to the broad variety of subjects that have interested students of modern Native American life. It should not be surprising that this literature is diverse. After all, Indian people are a living, articulate presence in the life of the United States and Canada, and they are engaged in as broad a range of activities as any other racial or ethnic group, from fine art to coal mining. The books in this section present readers with sources for describing the range, vitality, and complexity of contemporary Indian life.

In each subsection we have included only works that address contemporary affairs. Thus, for example, our lists on the family and religion avoid descriptions of traditional kinship or spiritual beliefs (those are included in other sections) and focus only on topics of current concern, such as aging or child welfare. Similarly, the subsection on "Resources and Economic Development" addresses business affairs in the present (for example, Marjane Ambler's *Breaking the Iron Bonds*) rather than traditional land use practices.

Indian people are properly resentful of journalists who sensationalize their social problems. We share this resentment, but we believe that readers should be aware of the disturbing literature on Indian health and alcoholism and the many problems and opportunities that confront Indian education. Similarly, both "Law and Government" and "Images, Self-Identity, and Protest" contain works on political problems and the often difficult relationship between Native Americans and the continent's non-Indian majority. Finally, two areas of contemporary life that are frequently overlooked by social scientists and students deserve their own categories. "Urban Indians" contains titles describing the outlines of the native communities that now account for half of all Indian people, and "Art and Literature" presents the breathtaking achievements of artists who have won prestigious fellowships, the recognition of major museums, and the highest literary awards.

Anyone using this bibliography should keep in mind the distortions and difficulties that are endemic to writing about Native American life. That reminder suggests caution, but it also serves as a dramatic backdrop to the remarkable literature represented here and the many achievements these books record.

GENERAL STUDIES AND REFERENCES

General Studies

Adney, Edwin T., and Howard I. Chapelle. *The Bark Canoes and Skin Boats of North America*. Washington, D.C.: U.S. Government Printing Office, 1964.

A study of the history, construction, and distribution of North American Indian bark and skin watercrafts. Chapter 1 summarizes information on Indian bark canoes found in the reports of early explorers, churchmen, and travelers. Chapter 2 describes the materials and technology of bark canoe building. Chapter 3 documents the various forms such canoes take. Chapters 4 through 6 offer detailed accounts of the fabrication and use of bark canoes by tribes in the following areas: Eastern Maritime Region, Central Canada, and Northwestern Canada. The last two chapters concern Arctic skin boats and temporary watercrafts, respectively. One appendix. Bibliography. Black-and-white photographs and drawings.

Allen, Paula Gunn, ed. *Studies in Native American Literature: Critical Essays and Course Designs*. New York: Modern Language Association of America, 1983.

A collection of critical essays and course designs intended to present a coherent framework for the study and instruction of Native American literature. Subjects treated include oral literature; personal narrative, autobiography, and intermediate forms between oral and written literature; American Indian women's literature; modern and contemporary American Indian literature; and the Indian in American literature. A concluding section on resources offers an extended discussion of relevant anthologies, texts, and research; listings of periodicals and small presses that regularly publish works by Indian authors or on Native American literature; and special issues of periodicals that concern Indian literature.

American Indian Historical Society. *Indian Voices: The Native American Today*. San Francisco: Indian Historian Press, 1974.

Eight papers and panel discussions from the second Convocation of American Indian Scholars held in 1972. Topics include Indian water rights, American Indian education, land use and economy on Indian reservations, health professions and the American Indian, Indian museums, and the procedures and decisions of the Indian Claims Commission. The editors characterize their anthology as "a means of communicating what Indians themselves think about many of the issues confronting [them] today."

Appleton, Le Roy H. *Indian Art of the Americas*. New York: Charles Scribner's Sons, 1950.

Reviews the diversity of art forms and styles found in seven culture areas of North, Central, and South America. An extended introduction presents the distribution, stylistic variations, tools, and materials associated with the following categories of Native American art: basket making, weaving, pottery, sculpting and carving, metalworking, lapidary, painting, building, and storytelling. Areal chapters contain oral traditions and songs pertinent to an understanding of Indian designs. More than seven hundred drawings and color plates illustrate the text. Bibliography.

Armstrong, Virginia Irving. *I Have Spoken: American History Through the Voices of the Indians*. Athens, Ohio: Swallow Press, 1971.

An anthology of more than two hundred statements and speeches dating from the early seventeenth century to 1970 which demonstrates both the rhetorical skills of Native Americans and their perspectives on Indian-white relations. Among the orators are Powhatan, Pontiac, Cornstalk, Joseph Brant, Little Turtle, Handsome Lake, Tecumseh, Black Hawk, Little Crow, Red Jacket, Seattle, Red Cloud, Sitting Bull, Wovoka, and Black Elk. Includes a few speeches by white men "as a muted counterpoint." An introduction by Frederick W. Turner III identifies themes and elements common to the speeches. Bibliography.

Aveni, Anthony F. *Native American Astronomy*. Austin: University of Texas Press, 1977.

A collection of essays by specialists in the archaeoastronomy of Central and North America. Contains five papers of particular interest to students of Native North American astronomy, including the astronomy of the Plains Caddoans, the role of medicine wheels in Plains Indian astronomy, rock art representations of the A.D. 1054 supernova, Miller's hypothesis concerning these rock art representations, and Anasazi solar observatories. Black-and-white photographs and line drawings of sites discussed in the articles.

Bahr, Howard M., et al. *Native Americans Today: Sociological Perspectives*. New York: Harper & Row, 1972.

An anthology of previously published articles of interest to those teaching or pursuing research in the sociology of Indian-white relations. The first set of papers seeks to establish a baseline of theories and issues for the more specialized essays of later chapters. Chapter 2 contains articles concerned with patterns of prejudice and discrimination against Indians. The next three chapters deal with the issues of Indian education, acculturation and identity, and crime and deviant behavior, respectively. Chapter 6 presents essays concerned with the patterns and problems of urban Indian life. Concludes with a chapter on recent Indian activism.

Bataille, Gretchen M., and Kathleen M. Sands. *American Indian Women Telling Their Lives*. Lincoln: University of Nebraska Press, 1984.

Essays explore the production, themes, and styles of American Indian women's autobiographies. An introductory chapter presents a historical overview and typology of the literature. Among the types identified are several varieties of the ethnographic autobiography, the "as-told-to" autobiography, and the written autobiography. Subsequent analyses of individual works serve to indicate "the movement from oral toward written autobiography and . . . the growing sophistication in methodology and literary expression within the genre." Selected, annotated bibliography.

Benedict, Ruth. *Patterns of Culture*. Boston: Houghton Mifflin, 1934.

Views cultures as "personalities writ large," integrated around certain basic values and displaying more or less consistent patterns of thought and action. Applies this perspective to the Kwakiutl people of North America's Northwest Coast and the Pueblo tribes of the American Southwest. Argues that the personality type of Kwakiutl culture is paranoid/megalomaniac, featuring institutions that stress self-aggrandizement and competition. The culture of the Pueblos, by contrast, is portrayed as emphasizing moderation, cooperation, and harmony. A classic of anthropology which set the groundwork for many culture and personality studies that followed.

Bierhorst, John. *The Mythology of North America*. New York: William Morrow, 1985.

Constructs a framework of mythic themes and myth types from narratives found in eleven culture areas of Native North America. Considers how myths both reflect and influence the lives of the peoples of these areas. The surveyed regions include the Northwest Coast, Arctic, Subarctic Athapaskan, Southwest, California, Great Basin, Coast Plateau, Plains, Southeast, Northeast, and Midwest. Among the characteristic themes and types identified are the transformer, the trickster, the culture hero and heroine, originator myths, dying god, clan myths, animal myths, and migration legends. Black-and-white illustrations. Contains an excellent bibliography subdivided by culture area.

Boas, Franz. *Race, Language, and Culture*. New York: Macmillan, 1940.

Seminal essays on physical anthropology, linguistics, and ethnology by the "father" of American anthropology. Of particular importance to students of Native North American history and culture are "Modern Populations of America"; "The Half Blood Indian"; "Introduction to *International Journal of American Linguistics*"; "The Classification of American Languages"; "Classification of American Indian Languages"; "Some Traits of the Dakota Language"; "The History of the American Race"; "Ethnological Problems in Canada"; "Relationships Between North-West America and North-East Asia"; "The Social Organization of the Kwakiutl"; "The Social Organization of the Tribes of the North Pacific Coast"; "The Growth of the Secret Societies of the Kwakiutl"; "Introduction to James Teit, 'The Traditions of the Thompson Indians of British Columbia'"; "The Growth of Indian Mythologies"; "Dissemination of Tales Among the Natives of North America"; "Review of G. W. Locher, 'The Serpent in Kwakiutl Religion: A Study in Primitive Culture' "; "Mythology and Folk-Tales of the North American Indians"; "The Folk-Lore of the Eskimo"; "Romance Folk-Lore Among American Indians"; "Some Problems in North American Archaeology"; "The Decorative Art of the North American Indians"; "Decorative Designs of Alaskan Needlecases"; "The Relationships of the Eskimo of East Greenland"; and "Religious Terminology of the Kwakiutl."

Bowden, Henry Warner. *American Indians and Christian Missions*. Chicago: University of Chicago Press, 1981.

An ethnological and historical survey of the prolonged conflict of culture between Christian missionaries and Native Americans. Attempts to portray the assumptions of Indian and Euro-American cultures which underlay the significant episodes of this conflict. Chapter 1 offers a broad overview of the cultures and religions of prehistoric North Americans. Chapters 2 through 4 begin with brief analyses of the socioreligious patterns of selected southwestern and northeastern peoples, then describe the attempts of Spanish, French, and English missionaries to convert these groups to various forms of Christianity. The concluding three chapters present the history of eighteenth, nineteenth, and twentieth century missions, respectively. An extended bibliographic essay concludes the book. Three maps.

Boxberger, Daniel L., ed. *Native North Americans: An Ethnohistorical Approach.* Dubuque, Iowa: Kendall/Hunt, 1990.

Ethnohistorical summaries of ten culture areas accompanied by essays on North American prehistory and Native North Americans in contemporary society. The culture areas surveyed include Arctic, Subarctic, Northeast, Southeast, Plains, Southwest, California, Great Basin, Plateau, and Northwest Coast. The chapters vary in format; however, each supplies information on regional prehistory and physiography; the techno-economic adaptations of Indian groups to their environments; patterns of kinship and society; languages; and belief systems. Each chapter contains a map that locates most of the groups discussed. Tables and black-and-white photographs.

Bruchac, Joseph. *Survival This Way: Interviews with American Indian Poets.* Tucson: University of Arizona Press, 1987.

Includes twenty-one interviews with contemporary Native American poets which "all speak to central themes of continuance and renewal, even as they present diverse, talented, eloquent writers." Among the poets interviewed are Paula Gunn Allen, Peter Blue Cloud, Diane Burns, Elizabeth Cook-Lynn, Louise Erdrich, Joy Harjo, Lance Henson, Linda Hogan, Karoniaktatie, Maurice Kenny, Harold Littlebird, N. Scott Momaday, Duane Niatum, Simon Ortiz, Carter Revard, Wendy Rose, Luci Tapahonso, Gerald Vizenor, Roberta Hill Whiteman, and Ray Young Bear. Preceding each interview is a poem by the featured artist. Bibliography and a list of the publishers of cited works.

Calloway, Colin G., ed. *New Directions in American Indian History.* Norman: University of Oklahoma Press, 1988.

A critical review of contemporary scholarship in Native North American history. Part 1 presents six essays on fields and approaches to Indian history that have recently generated a considerable amount of research. These include the use of quantitative methods, feminism, Métis history, history of the Southern Plains, Indians and the law, scholars, and twentieth-century Indians. The three papers in part 2 concern three neglected areas of Native histories: linguistics, economics, and religion.

Campbell, Lyle, and Marianne Mithune, eds. *The Languages of Native America: Historical and Comparative Assessment.* Austin: University of Texas Press, 1979.

An anthology of essays which reviews past and contemporary work on the linguistic areas, families, and languages of Native North and Middle America. The editors also provide an up-to-date classification of language families and isolates. An introduction summarizes the historical and methodological heritage of American Indian linguistics. The studies that follow treat comparative Algonquian; Iroquoian; Caddoan; Siouan; southeastern languages; Timucua and Yuchi; the languages of South Texas and the lower Rio Grande; Kiowa-Tanoan, Keresan, and Zuni languages; Uto-Aztecan; Hokan Inter-Branch comparisons; Penutian; Salishan and the Northwest; Wakashan comparative studies; Chimakuan comparative studies; Na-Dene and Eskimo-Aleut; and Middle American languages. A conclusion speculates on future directions in the field. Bibliographies accompany each paper.

Champagne, Duane. *American Indian Societies: Strategies and Conditions of Political and Cultural Survival*. Cambridge, Mass.: Cultural Survival, 1989.

Develops a multidimensional model to explain how indigenous societies change under various conditions of contact with colonial/Western powers. The primary variables of the model include the circumstances of the geopolitical environment, the types of markets available, the degree of interpenetration of Western culture and normative order, the continuity of subsistence economy, the degree and form of social and political solidarity, the configuration of societal differentiation, and the worldview and major cultural orientations of the society. Applies this model to selected tribes in the Northeast (Delaware, Iroquois), Southeast (Cherokee, Choctaw, Chickasaw, Creek), Plains (Northern Cheyenne, Crow, Northern Arapaho), Southwest (Navajo, Quechan), and Pacific Northwest (Tlingit). Bibliography.

Clifton, James. *Being and Becoming Indian: Biographical Studies of North American Frontiers*. Homewood, Ill.: Dorsey Press, 1989.

Contains fourteen biographical essays centered on the theme of how individuals living in contact with both the Indian and white worlds constructed their identities and lives. An introduction by the editor describes the social and psychological dynamics that he believes the biographies display. Papers on Simon Girty (a white abducted as a youth by Delaware Indians), Joseph Renville (a Dakota mixed blood), Augustin Hamlin, Jr. (Métis-Ottawa), Eleazor Williams (Anglo-Mohawk), Susette and Susan La Flesche (Métis-Omaha), Mourning Dove (Salish), Sylvester Long/Chief Buffalo Child Long Lance (Eastern Cherokee), Chief William Berens (Saulteaux), Dan Raincloud (Ojibwa), Maud L. Cairmont (Anglo-Shoshone), Joe True (white, affiliated Kiowa), and Ooleepeeka and Mina (Inuit). Black-and-white photographs, drawings, and maps.

Coffer, William E. (Koi Hosh). *Spirits of the Sacred Mountains: Creation Stories of the American Indian*. New York: Van Nostrand Reinhold, 1978.

A selection of traditional Native North American creation narratives. Chapters 1 through 3 present various non-Indian perspectives on human origins, Indian ancestry, and "Old World" visitors to America. Chapter 4 contains the creation stories of the Choctaw, Cherokee, Delaware (Lenape), Hopi, Navajo, Jicarilla Apache, Paiute, Omaha, Natchez, Klamath, Miwok, Gabrielino, Papago, North Pacific Coast Tribes, Modoc, Miccosukee, Cahuilla, Wintu, Yakima, Ojibwa, Winnebago, Cheyenne, Seneca, Spokane, Kansa, Shawnee, Acoma, Comanche, Blackfoot, Kiowa, and other tribes. Bibliography.

Collier, John. *Indians of the Americas*. New York: W. W. Norton, 1947.
An introduction to Native American history and culture by a former commissioner of Indian Affairs and main architect of the Indian Reorganization Act (IRA) of 1934. Part 1 begins with a sketch of the author's transformative experiences among the Pueblo Indians and his belief that Indian values offer a remedy for the materialism and depersonalization afflicting Western society. It then overviews Native American prehistory. Part 2, "South of the Rio Grande," describes the empires of the Incas and Aztecs, the Spanish conquest of Mesoamerica and South America, and Indian-white relations under Spanish and Mexican rule. Part 3, "North of the Rio Grande," first summarizes the spiritual achievements of traditional Indian life, then discusses the white colonization and conquest of the continent. A survey of federal Indian relations up to the IRA concludes the section. Closes with a summary of and prediction for Native American life in the United States. Suggested readings. Black-and-white photographs. Maps for culture areas and tribes of North and South America on the inside covers.

Costo, Rupert, and Jeannette Henry. *Indian Treaties: Two Centuries of Dishonor*. San Francisco: Indian Historian Press, 1977.
The fifth in a series entitled *The American Indian Reader*. Presents information on Indian treaties as they affect such issues as self-determination, economy, tribal jurisdiction, taxation, and water and resources. The authors see the purpose of the book as a compilation of facts to prepare people against a new Indian war that "has as its main target the destruction of the Indian treaties, and thus the destruction of the Native Americans as a people, as a race, as the original owners of the land and the source of its democratic thought.

Council on Interracial Books for Children. *Chronicles of American Indian Protest*. Greenwich, Conn.: Fawcett, 1971.
An anthology of speeches and statements by Native Americans which seeks to redress the distorted image of Indian-white relations presented in most history texts. Included are the words of King Philip, Pontiac, Tecumseh, Black Hawk, John Ross, Geronimo, Red Cloud, Sitting Bull, Chief Joseph, Akwasasne Notes, and the Association on American Indian Affairs. Each document is preceded by a short discussion of its origins and consequences.

Cox, Bruce, ed. *Cultural Ecology: Readings on the Canadian Indians and Eskimo*. Toronto: McClelland and Stewart, 1973.
A collection of essays, mostly from the 1960's, that concerns the relationship between the natural settings of selected Indian and Eskimo groups and their social and cultural institutions. Organized around the thesis that "groups adjust to such settings in part through the development of appropriate customs, beliefs,

and social arrangements, and further that human groups comprise parts of each others' environments." An introductory essay suggests a resemblance between the explanatory strategies of contemporary cultural ecologists and the theories of Karl Marx. The anthologized essays are grouped according to the following geographical areas: the Great Lakes—St. Lawrence Region, Boreal Forest, Grasslands, Pacific region, and Arctic and Barren Grounds. Concludes with suggestions for further reading.

Culin, Stewart. *Games of the North American Indians*. Bureau of American Ethnology, Annual Report 24 (1902-1903). Washington, D.C.: U.S. Government Printing Office, 1907.

Provides a typology and exhaustive discussion of the traditional games of Native North Americans. Separates these games into two major classes: games of chance and games of dexterity. Each class is further broken down into subcategories. Among the author's conclusions are that the games of North American Indians may be classified into a small number of related groups; in terms of their morphology, they are virtually identical and universal among the tribes, having a religious origin and function. Twenty-one plates, 1112 drawings, and an eight-page tabular index to tribes and games.

Curtis, Natalie. *The Indians' Book*. New York: Harper and Brothers, 1923.

A cavalcade of traditional music, lore, and drawings collected from eighteen tribes of Native North Americans. Provides the scores, lyrics, translations, and social analysis of 149 songs belonging to the Wabnaki, Dakota, Pawnee, Cheyenne, Arapaho, Kiowa, Winnebago, Kwakiutl, Pima, Apache, Yuma, Navajo, Zuni, San Juan, Acoma, Laguna, and Hopi. Supplies brief ethnographic descriptions of each people as well as a sample of their myths and legends. Illustrated with black- and-white illustrations by Indian artists and twenty-three of the author's own photographs depicting individuals and lifeways of the various tribes.

Darnell, Regna, and Michael K. Foster. *Native North American Interaction Patterns*. Quebec: Canadian Museum of Civilization, National Museums of Canada, 1988.

Presents twelve papers by anthropologists, linguists, and educators from the Conference on Native North American Interaction Patterns held at Edmonton, Alberta, in 1982. The essays focus on language use and nonverbal communication in selected American Indian societies. Among the groups discussed are the Lakota (Sioux), Iroquois, Ojibwa, Cree, Zuni, Bear Lake Athapaskans, and Navajo.

Debo, Angie. *A History of the Indians of the United States*. Norman: University of Oklahoma Press, 1970.

Based on a course originally given to teachers of Indian children in public, Indian Bureau, and mission schools. Traces the history of Native North Americans and Indian-white relations from pre-Columbian days to the contemporary era. Though containing much of the same ethnographic and historical information available in other introductory texts, this work is distinguished by the emphasis it gives to the history of Oklahoma Indians. Argues that "in many ways [their] history is an epitome of Indian history."

Denevan, William M., ed. *The Native Population of the Americas in 1492*. Madison: University of Wisconsin Press, 1976.

An anthology of theoretical and substantive papers concerned with population estimates for the Americas at the time of initial European contact. The first section contains historical and methodological overviews for the field of American aboriginal demographics. Section 2 includes seven regional studies, arranged by date of European-Indian contact: the Caribbean, Central America, and Yucatán; Mexico; South America; and North America. Glossary. Bibliography. Tables and maps.

Densmore, Frances. *The American Indians and Their Music*. New York: Womans Press, 1926.

A general account of the forms and functions of music in Native American life. The first eleven chapters briefly overview the history and lifeways of Indian peoples. The remaining sections deal with subjects specifically related to music. Among topics discussed are the social role of singing, the words of Indian songs, the songs of children, love songs, wind and percussion instruments, the characteristics of Indian music, scale, and the history and some results of the study of Indian music. Five black-and-white illustrations. Reproduces the scores and lyrics of eight songs.

Denver Art Museum. *Indian Art Leaflets*. Denver: Author, 1930-32.

A series of 171 pamphlets, many concerned with the character and distribution of Native American art forms; others with the traditional arts found among particular groups and culture areas. Attention is given to the pertinent ethnographic and historical dimensions of the arts described. Several leaflets focus on the linguistic and tribal divisions of Native American peoples. Discussions are illustrated with black-and-white photographs and drawings.

Dewdney, Selwyn. *They Shared to Survive: The Native Peoples of Canada*. Toronto: Macmillan, 1975.

A popular summary of Canadian Indian and Eskimo lifeways. Focuses on the traditional cultures of groups found in the Atlantic Coastlands, Lower Lake Regions, Canadian Shield Woodlands, Canadian Prairies, Cordilleran Interior, Pacific Coast, Taiga Northwestern Woodlands, and Arctic Coasts and Interior. Briefly discusses early Native-European contacts and the social marginalization of Canada's aboriginal population. Black-and-white illustrations by Franklin Arbuckle.

Dockstader, Frederick J. *Indian Art in America: The Arts and Crafts of the North American Indians*. Greenwich, Conn.: New York Graphics Society, 1961.

A sweeping presentation of the arts of North American Indians that seeks "to include every important region, most of the numerically preeminent tribes, and all the major techniques employed by artists" and to communicate something of the aesthetic and cultural significance of these arts for the peoples whose lives they are a part. The five chapters of part 1 define Indian art and place its styles and materials in historical context. Part 2 contains nearly 250 color and black-and-white plates. It is divided into two sections, the first displaying pieces produced before the coming of the whites; the second, containing works created during the historic period. Accompanying each plate is a brief commentary.

__________. *Weaving Arts of the North American Indian*. New York: Thomas Y. Crowell, 1978.

A general survey intended "to demonstrate the success of the Indian in mastering the art of producing woven textiles and garments so necessary to civilization, and the degree to which this knowledge was spread throughout North America." Coverage includes all of the United States and Canada (excluding the Arctic Eskimo) from prehistoric times to the present day. Begins with a historical overview of Native American weaving, then discusses the method and manner of weaving; effects of weaving on Indian life; trade and commerce; textile production by region; influences, personalities, and markets today; and how to care for woven textiles. Bibliography. Contains hundreds of illustrations, sixty-four in color.

Drennan, Robert D., and Carlos A. Uribe, eds. *Chiefdoms in the Americas*. Washington, D.C.: University Press of America, 1987.

A collection of essays by New World archaeologists concerned with prehistoric North, Central, and South American societies that attained a chiefdom level of sociopolitical complexity. The first three chapters discuss selected chiefdoms of North America. Chapter 1 presents a hypothesis concerning the relationship between social and nutritional status in the Dallas culture of Tennessee based on remains found in burial sites. Chapter 2 reconstructs the development and decline of the Mississippian center of Moundville. The third chapter addresses the controversial thesis that chiefdom-level societies existed in North America's prehistoric Southwest. Tables and maps. A bibliography accompanies each article.

Driver, Harold. *Indians of North America*. Chicago: University of Chicago Press, 1975.

Surveys the characteristic forms of subsistence, kinship, government, housing, clothing, art, and other major aspects of culture for the peoples of thirteen "culture areas" in aboriginal North America, and Mesoamerica. An appendix containing forty-five maps graphically summarizes the contents of the chapters and locates the continent's principal Indian tribes before their displacement and (in some cases) destruction by Euro-American forces. Also contains essays on history and culture change in Mexico, the United States, Canada, Alaska, and Greenland; Indian-white relations in the United States; and the achievement and contribution of Native Americans. Good references and bibliography; sparsely illustrated with pen-and-ink drawings and a few black-and-white photographs.

Edmunds, R. David, ed. *American Indian Leaders: Studies in Diversity*. Lincoln: University of Nebraska Press, 1981.

Biographical essays on twelve Native American leaders from different tribes and periods intended to illustrate the great variety in their methods of Indian leadership. The subjects include Old Briton (Miami), Joseph Brant (Mohawk), Alexander McGillivray (Creek), Red Bird (Winnebago), John Ross (Cherokee), Satanta (Kiowa), Washakie (Shoshoni), Sitting Bull (Sioux), Quanah Parker (Comanche), Dennis Bushyhead (Cherokee), Carlos Montezuma (Yavapai), and Peter MacDonald (Navajo). Black-and-white portraits of the leaders discussed. Eleven maps.

Eggan, Fred, ed. *Social Anthropology of North American Tribes*. Chicago: University of Chicago Press, 1966.

A classic collection of anthropological studies on the structure and function of Native American societies. An introductory essay briefly discusses basic principles and problems of social anthropology. The next seven papers present social analyses of the traditional institutions of selected tribes. Included are the Cheyenne, Arapaho, Kiowa-Apache, Chiricahua Apache, Fox, Eastern Cherokee, Plains Indians, and Klamath. The concluding chapters outline the history of the study of social organization and the methods and results of social anthropology, respectively. Bibliography.

Erdoes, Richard, and Alfonso Ortiz, eds. *American Indian Myths and Legends*. New York: Pantheon Books, 1984.

A collection of 166 legends that offers insight into the cosmologies and worldviews of Native North Americans. Categorizes the legends under ten headings: tales of human creation; tales of world creation; tales of the sun, moon, and stars; monsters and monster slayers; war and the warrior code; tales of love and lust; trickster tales; stories of animals and other people; ghosts and the spirit world; and visions of the end. A brief introduction explains the function of myths and legends in Indian society. Illustrated with pen-and-ink drawings by Erdoes.

Fagan, Brian. *The Great Journey: The Peopling of Ancient America*. New York: Thames and Hudson, 1987.

A panoramic overview of the origins and lifeways of America's prehistoric peoples. Part 1 discusses early theories concerning the ancestry of Native Americans, the controversies surrounding mounds and mound builders, and the development of North American archaeology. Part 2 provides a brief discussion of human evolution and the peopling of Europe and Asia. Parts 3 and 4 evaluate competing accounts of when and how prehistoric groups made their way onto the continent as well as who were America's earliest settlers. In part 5 the adaptation of prehistoric populations to North America's various environments is explored. Black-and-white photographs and drawings. An extended bibliographical essay concludes the book.

Farber, Joseph C., and Michael Dorris. *Native Americans: 500 Years After*. New York: Thomas Y. Crowell, 1975.

Uses hundreds of black-and-white photographs to portray the diversity and vibrance of contemporary Native American life. Organized by seven geographical areas: Alaska, the Far West, the Southwest, the Plains, the Lakes, the Northeast, and the Southeast. The brief commentary that precedes each section is intended to place the photographs "in a factual yet optimistic context and to take the long-term rather than short-term historical view." Selected bibliography.

Feest, Christian F. *Indians and Europe: An Interdisciplinary Collection of Essays*. Aachen, West Germany: Ed. Herodot, 1987.

A multidisciplinary collection of essays which examines Europe's five hundred-year fascination and experience with Native Americans. Among the subjects addressed by the thirty-three papers are the presuppositions underlying European depictions of Indian peoples, interactions of Indians and whites both in America and in Europe, and the effects of these interactions on European theories and images of Native Americans. An editor's postscript offers generalizations concerning the nature of European images and relations with Indians. Profusely illustrated with black-and-white reproductions of woodcuts, paintings, and photographs. A bibliography follows each paper.

__________. *Native Arts of North America*. New York: Oxford University Press, 1980.

A historical survey of the styles and technologies of North American Indian arts. Part 1 includes discussions of theoretical and methodological problems associated with the study of Indian arts and the geographical, historical, and cultural factors vital to their interpretation. Part 2 offers a sweeping narrative of artistic techniques and styles, with separate chapters on painting and engraving, textiles, and sculpture. Concludes with a detailed bibliographical essay that covers all the major issues and areas touched on by the text. Includes 173 black-and-white and 20 color plates.

Fiedel, Stuart J. *Prehistory of the Americas*. Cambridge, England: Cambridge University Press, 1987.

Describes and analyzes the evolution of pre-Columbian societies in the Americas. Stresses the complexity of determinants underlying this evolution. Chapter 1 presents an overview of the history and techniques of American archaeology. Chapters 2 and 3 trace the migrations of early man from Africa to Siberia and then to the "New World." Chapters 3 through 6 detail the lifeways of Paleo-Indians; the social patterns of Archaic, post-Pleistocene foragers; the origins of agriculture and village life; and the rise of chiefdoms and states. Concludes with a theoretical discussion of parallels and divergences between the evolution of society in the "old" and "new" worlds. 113 black-and-white drawings and maps illustrate the text. Includes an extensive bibliography.

Fletcher, Alice C. *Indian Games and Dances with Native Songs*. Boston: C. C., Birchard, 1915.

Part 1 presents a sampling of the ceremonial songs and dances of Native North American tribes. An introductory note accompanies each selection, followed by a description of its props, performance, and (translated) lyrics. Part 2 contains an overview of Indian games classified according to hazard games, guessing games, and ball games. Part 3 concerns the cultural and ritual significance of Indian names.

Forbes, Jack D. *The Indian in America's Past*. Englewood Cliffs, N.J.: Prentice-Hall, 1964.

Uses nearly two hundred documents to examine the dynamics of European-African-Indian relationships in North America. Section 1 first presents evidence for ancient Asian contacts with Native Americans, then describes early Norse and Spanish settlements in the New World. The documents in section 2 illustrate European and Euro-American images of Native Americans. Section 3 offers selections on the history of Indian resistance to white expansion and domination. Native perspectives on Indian-white relations is the theme of section 4. Section 5 depicts the various effects of white conquest on Native Americans. The use of Indians as slaves is documented in section 6. The texts in sections 7 and 8 exemplify important themes in the history of federal Indian policy. Section 9 is concerned with the intermixing of white, Indian, and African ethnics in the United States. The concluding section provides sources on the status of contemporary Native Americans.

Ford, Richard I., ed. *An Ethnobiology Source Book: The Uses of Plants and Animals by American Indians*. New York: Garland, 1986.

An anthology of twenty-one reprinted essays on the science of ethnobiology and its application to selected Native American peoples. Defines ethnobiology as "the study of the direct interrelationships between human populations and the plants and animals in their environment, including their use and cultural beliefs about them." Includes papers on the Keresan Pueblo Indians, Chippewas, the Eskimos of northern Bering Sea and Arctic regions, the Klamath Indians, and the Cherokees.

Foreman, Carolyn. *Indian Women Chiefs*. Muskogee, Okla., n.p., 1954.

An early attempt to combat the stereotype of Indian women as slaves and drudges. Argues that throughout the history of many Indian groups, women have occupied positions of authority uncontested by the males of these societies. Documents this thesis with ethnographic information drawn from various North American tribes.

Gibson, Arrell M. *The American Indian: Prehistory to Present*. Lexington, Mass: D. C. Heath, 1980.

Attempts to portray the traditionally neglected role of Native Americans in U.S. history. The first four chapters overview the origins and prehistory of Indian peoples. Chapters 5 through 10 examine the history of Indian-white relations in colonial North America. The remainder of the book discusses various phases of U.S. policy. A list of selected sources concludes each chapter. Glossary. Bibliography. Black-and-white reproductions and photographs. Maps and tables.

Gill, Sam D. *Native American Religions: An Introduction*. Belmont, Calif.: Wadsworth, 1982.

An introductory survey that strives to document the diversity and complexity of Native North American religions. The first three chapters investigate the cultural components that constitute and shape Native American belief and ritual. The next three chapters examine the varieties of religious phenomena typically found in Native American religions. Specific examples are used to illustrate the discussion. Bibliographic essays for each chapter. Black-and-white drawings.

__________. *Native American Traditions: Sources and Interpretations*. Belmont, Calif.: Wadsworth, 1983.

An anthology of readings on Native American religions authored both by practitioners of those traditions as well as their non-Indian observers. Headings for readings include white images of and attitudes toward Indian religions, religious worldview, religious language and oral traditions, sacred objects and ritual, religion and the life cycle, the sacral character of life-sustaining labors, and new religions among Indians. Each section begins with an introductory commentary on the highlighted theme. Endnotes provide bibliographic information. Concludes with a discussion of available audiovisual materials.

Grant, Campbell. *The Rock Art of the North American Indians: The Imprint of Man*. New York: Thomas Y. Crowell, 1967.

Applies the approaches of anthropology and art history to the study of prehistoric North American rock art. Part 1 presents the descriptive and analytic categories essential to the understanding and aesthetic appreciation of this art form. Includes discussions of the techniques, styles, and important motifs of rock art as well as methods of its interpretation, dating, and recording. Part 2 identifies the continent's nine rock art areas. Concludes that prehistoric North American Indians "developed an extraordinary diversity of styles, techniques, and subjects" and that different cultures developed their rock art forms in unique ways. Lavishly illustrated with black-and-white photographs, line drawings, color plates, maps, and tables. Bibliography.

Grant, John W. *Moon of Wintertime: Missionaries and the Indians of Canada in Encounter Since 1534*. Toronto: University of Toronto Press, 1984.

Traces the relationship between Christian missionaries and Canadian Indians from their first encounter at Gaspe in 1534 through the late 1970's. Focuses on the activities of various denominations among specific Native groups; the major loci of missionary activity during different periods in the nation's history; the assumptions, practices, and goals of Indian missionization; the evolution of a "classical" pattern of mission during the nineteenth century; Indian responses to missionary presence; and the effects of Christianity on Indian life. Black-and-white reproductions and photographs. One map.

Gridley, Marion E. *American Indian Women*. New York: Hawthorn Books, 1974.

Biographical sketches of eighteen historic and contemporary Native American women of note. Includes pieces on Wetamoo (a Wampanoag woman sachem); Pocahontas (the Algonquian savior of Jamestown); Mary Musgrove Matthews Bosomworth (Creek Indian empress); Nancy Ward (beloved woman of the Cherokee); Sacajawea (Shoshoni girl guide); Sarah Winnemucca (Paiute Army scout); Winema (Modoc peacemaker); E. Pauline Johnson (Mohawk poet); Susan La Flesche Picotte (Omaha physician); Gertrude Simmons Bonnin (Sioux modern progressive); Roberta Campbell Lawson (Delaware-Wyandot women's leader); Pablita Velarde (Santa Clara Pueblo artist); Maria Montoya Martinez

(San Ildejonso Pueblo potter); Annie Dodge Wauneka (Navajo modern crusader); Esther Burnett Horne (Sacajawea's great-great granddaughter); the Tallchief sisters (Osage ballerinas); Wilma L. Victor (Choctaw educator in government); and Elaine Abraham Ramos (Tlingit college vice-president). Bibliography. Black-and-white portrait of each subject.

__________. *Contemporary American Indian Leaders*. New York: Dodd, Mead, 1972.

A collection of biographies of notable contemporary Indians which seeks to "present a wide variety of viewpoints and a cross section of vocations." Among the twenty-six individuals featured are Robert L. Bennett (Oneida commissioner of Indian Affairs under Lyndon Johnson); Jarrett Blythe (principal chief of the eastern band of Cherokee); Vine Deloria, Jr. (Sioux historian and political philosopher); LaDonna Harris (Comanche activist); Peter MacDonald (chairman of the Navajo Tribal Council); N. Scott Momaday (Kiowa-Cherokee, Pulitzer Prize-winning novelist); and Ben Reifel (Sioux U.S. congressman). Black-and-white photographs of the leaders.

Haas, Mary R. *Language, Culture, and History: Essays by Mary R. Haas*. Stanford, Calif.: Stanford University Press, 1978.

A collection of twenty-eight previously published essays by an eminent anthropological linguist. Most of the papers treat topics in the history of Native American language science; others concern historical and areal linguistics in North America. Among the more notable entries are "The Study of American Indian Languages: A Brief Historical Sketch," "The Problem of Classifying American Indian Languages: From Duponceau to Powell," "Historical Linguistics and the Genetic Relationship of Languages," and "The Northern Californian Linguistic Area." Includes a bibliography of the author's works.

Hamilton, Charles, ed. *Cry of the Thunderbird*. Norman: University of Oklahoma Press, 1972.

An anthology of excerpts from Indian sources that present Native American images of their own and Euro-American cultures. Includes discussions of childhood and education, family, hunting, war, religion, songs, and oral tradition. Illustrated with paintings by George Catlin and American Indian artists. Bibliography lists books written or dictated by American Indians.

Hamilton, T. M. *Native American Bows*, edited by Nancy Bagby. York, Pa.: George Shumway Publishers, 1972.

An analysis of the construction and accuracy of Native American bows. Chapter 1 provides the following classification of Indian bows: the self bow, the reinforced bow, and the composite bow. Subsequent chapters describe the manufacture and use of each bow type as well as various peoples among which it was found. Includes a tabular analysis of bow performance. Glossary. Bibliography. Black-and-white photographs and drawings.

Henry, Jeannette, ed. *The American Indian Reader, Vol. 1: Anthropology*. San Francisco: Indian Historian Press, 1972.

Responses of four Anglo and two Native American anthropologists to the powerful critique of anthropology contained in Vine Deloria, Jr.'s *Custer Died for Your Sins*. The first series of papers examines the role anthropologists have played in formulating federal policies and programs affecting American Indian communities. The second set of presentations addresses the ambivalent feelings of Native Americans toward anthropological research. The reactions of Native American panelists to the papers is included. Concludes with criticisms and suggestions by Deloria. Bibliography of cited sources.

Highwater, Jamake. *Arts of the Indian Americas*. New York: Harper & Row, 1983.

A richly illustrated introduction to the aboriginal arts of North, Central, and South America. Preliminary chapters provide aesthetic, cultural, and historical summaries of the artistic achievements of American Indians. Chapter 3 discusses Native American art forms, iconography, media, and technology. The remainder of the book offers descriptions and analyses of the following arts: basketry, textiles, skinwork, featherwork, beadwork, pottery, carving and sculpture, metalwork, architecture, mosaics, shellwork, cutouts, painting, oral and written literature, music, dance, and ritual. Contains a glossary and selected bibliography. Illustrated with hundreds of black-and-white and color plates.

Hoijer, Harry, et al. *Linguistic Structures of Native America*. Viking Fund Publications in Anthropology, 6. New York: Viking Fund, 1946.

An anthology of fourteen seminal essays on American Indian languages. An introductory article provides a historical overview of classificatory systems proposed for the aboriginal tongues of North, Central, and South America. The papers that follow discuss the linguistic features of the following languages and language families: South Greenlandic, Chiricahua Apache, Algonquian, Delaware, Hopi, Taos, Yawelmani Yokuts, Yuma, Tonkowa, Chitimucha, Tunica, Milpa Alta Aztec, and Chipewyan.

Hoxie, Frederick E., ed. *Indians in American History: An Introduction*. Arlington Heights, Ill.: Harlan Davidson, Inc., 1988.

A collection of thirteen chronologically arranged essays by specialists in different fields of Native American studies. The papers are intended to provide the Indian side of the narrative usually found in textbooks on U.S. history. Topics of the articles include pre-Columbian America, Indians in the colonial Spanish borderlands, Indian participation in the American Revolution, Indian tribes and the American Constitution, Native Americans in southern history, an Indian perspective on national expansion, nineteenth century reformers and the Indians, and the struggle for Indian civil rights. A bibliographical essay accompanies each article. Black-and-white photographs and reproductions drawn mostly from the collections of the Newberry Library.

Hultkrantz, Ake. *The Religions of the American Indians*. Translated by Monica Setterwall. Berkeley: University of California Press, 1967.

Designed "to give a comprehensive survey of indigenous American religions." The first of the book's two parts provides an overview of the characteristic beliefs and rituals of America's "tribal" religions; the features of these religions which have been of special concern to ethnologists, folklorists, sociologists, and historians of religions; and the major lines of aboriginal tribal development. The second part presents a detailed discussion of the pre-Columbian Mayan, Aztec, and Incan religions attending to the cultural, social, and ecological contexts of each. Thirty-four black-and-white plates illustrate the text. Includes an extended bibliography.

Hurt, R. Douglas. *Indian Agriculture in America: Prehistory to the Present.* Lawrence: University Press of Kansas, 1987.

Summarizes current archaeological, historical, botanical, and anthropological scholarship on the evolution of Native American agriculture from prehistoric times to modern day. Chapters are arranged chronologically with subdivisions for region and topic. Begins with a discussion of the Mesoamerican origins and prehistory of Indian agriculture. Subsequent sections describe farming by eastern tribes at the time of European contact, agriculture in the trans-Mississippi West, Native American concepts of land tenure in relation to farming, and the effects of successive stages of federal Indian policy on Native American agriculture. Black-and-white photographs. Bibliography.

Hymes, Dell. *"In Vain I Tried to Tell You": Essays in Native American Ethnopoetics*. Philadelphia: University of Pennsylvania Press, 1981.

Essays examine "the surprising facts of device, design, and performance inherent in the words of . . . texts," that are important to their interpretation yet which have often been ignored by translators. The majority of analyses treat song, narrative, and speech texts and events of selected Northwest Coast Indian peoples. Bibliography. Tables.

Jenness, Diamond. *The Indians of Canada*. Ottawa: F. A. Acland, 1932.

A detailed overview of the Indian and Eskimo peoples of Canada. Part 1 broadly portrays the major aspects of aboriginal Canadian lifeways. Among the features described are languages, economic conditions, food resources, hunting and fishing, dress and adornment, dwellings, travel and transportation, social and political organization, social life, religion, folklore and traditions, oratory and drama, and music and art. There are also brief discussions of the origins and prehistory of Canadian natives as well as their interactions with whites. The presentation in part 2 is organized by culture area and includes migratory tribes of the Eastern Woodlands, agricultural tribes of the Eastern Woodlands, Plains tribes, tribes of the Pacific Coast, tribes of Cordillera, tribes of the Mackenzie and Yukon River Basins, and the Eskimo. A sketch of the physiography of each area is first provided, followed by the principal characteristics of its major tribes and a summary of their postcontact histories. Appendices. Notes on linguistic map. Bibliography. Superbly illustrated with hundreds of black-and-white and color plates.

Jennings, Jesse D. *Prehistory of North America*. Mountain View, Calif.: Mayfield Press, 1989.

Seeks to describe and interpret regional cultural variation and evolution in prehistoric North America. Chapter 1 presents the assumptions, definitions, methodologies, techniques, and uses of archaeological science. The book offers a chronological sequence and analysis of the continent's prehistory, beginning with the arrival of its earliest inhabitants through representative communities of the Archaic, Woodlands, and Mississippian traditions. Profusely illustrated with black-and-white drawings of artifacts described. Maps. A short bibliography follows each chapter.

Joe, Jennie, ed. *American Indian Policy and Cultural Values: Conflict and Accommodation*. Los Angeles: American Indian Studies Center, University of California, Los Angeles, 1986.

A collection of essays from the Eighth Annual Conference on Contemporary American Indian Issues which examines "some of the consequences of an ever-changing American Indian policy and its impact on the lives and cultural values of American Indians." An editor's introduction briefly sets forth the alternating currents in twentieth century federal Indian relations. The first four papers focus on periods and themes in Indian policy from the 1930's to the 1980's. The remaining contributions discuss issues pertaining to religion, economic development, education, social policy, and planning for aging American Indians. Charts.

Josephy, Alvin M., Jr. *The Patriot Chiefs: A Chronicle of American Indian Leadership*. New York: Viking Press, 1961.

Chronologically arranged biographies of nine Native American heroes. Subjects were chosen with an eye to the "variety in Indian backgrounds and cultures, geographical area and historical period, and particular large scale problems that led to crises and conflicts." Patriots include Hiawatha, King Philip, Pope, Pontiac, Tecumseh, Osceola, Black Hawk, Crazy Horse, and Chief Joseph. Black-and-white photographs and reproductions of paintings. Bibliography.

Josephy, Alvin M., Jr., ed., and William Brandon. *The American Heritage Book of Indians*. New York: American Heritage, 1961.

A panoramic history of the more than 20,000 years of Indian presence in North, Central, and South America. Though containing information on the prehistory and ethnography of Native American societies, the book is primarily concerned with the interaction between Indians and whites, from the time of Columbus through the midtwentieth century. Insets that highlight critical junctures in this interaction as well as the cultural traditions of particular peoples or culture areas punctuate a clearly written text of fifteen chapters. Maps, tables, and black-and-white and color plates.

Kehoe, Alice. *North American Indians: A Comparative Account*. Englewood Cliffs, N.J.: Prentice-Hall, 1981.

A region-by-region examination of the histories of Native North Americans. Chapters for the Southwest, Southeast, Northeast, Prairie-Plains, Intermontane West and California, Northwest Coast, Arctic, and Subarctic. Information on the prehistory, cultural traditions, and postcontact histories is provided for selected peoples of each area. Chapters conclude with summaries and lists of recommended readings. Two introductory chapters provide a general overview of

American prehistory and the rise and fall of Mexico's Indian nations. The final chapter raises issues concerning the future of Native American peoples. Black-and-white photographs, maps, chronological tables. Bibliography.

Kickingbird, Kirke, and Karen Ducheneaux. *One Hundred Million Acres*. New York: Macmillan, 1973.

Describes how Indians in the United States have been systematically divested of the majority of their territories. Focuses on specific examples of land confiscation, the ways in which Native Americans have managed to retain tenure over the slightly less than one hundred million acres that remains to them, and cases in which tribes are petitioning Congress or the president for the return of their estates. Concludes with a new formulation of federal Indian policy for Indians and Indian lands. Bibliography.

Kroeber, Alfred L. *Cultural and Natural Areas of Native North America*. University of California Publications in American Archaeology and Ethnology 38. Berkeley: University of California Press, 1939.

Sets two objectives: to review the environmental relations of the native cultures of North America and to examine the historic relations of culture areas, or geographical units of culture. Views the culture area concept as an important mechanism for reconstructing the growth of cultures for which little documentary evidence exists. A classic of American anthropology which established the theoretical foundations for decades of American Indian ethnography. Tables and maps.

Kroeber, Karl, ed. *Traditional Literatures of the American Indian: Texts and Interpretations*. Lincoln: University of Nebraska Press, 1981.

An anthology of five essays intended to introduce nonspecialists to the artistry of Native American literatures. Each essay includes the text and translation of one or more traditional narratives plus an analysis to aid in their appreciation. Among the represented tribes are the Kato, Creek, Nez Percé, Wishram, Clackamas, Zuni, and Navajo.

Krupat, Arnold. *For Those Who Come After: A Study of Native American Autobiography*. Berkeley: University of California Press, 1985.

Argues for the necessity of viewing Native American autobiographies from a literary perspective. Chapter 1 presents an interpretive model for Native American literature. Chapter 2 discusses the origin, types, and functions of Indian autobiographies. Chapters 3, 4, and 5 analyze the autobiographies of Geronimo, Crashing Thunder, Yellow Wolf, and Black Elk with an eye to "1) their relation to their historical period, 2) their relation to the discursive categories of history, science, and art (literature), and 3) their relation to the four modes of employment—romance, tragedy, comedy, and irony—by which Western authors (or editors) must structure narrative." Selected bibliography.

Kupferer, Harriet J. *Ancient Drums, Other Moccasins: Native American Cultural Adaptations*. Englewood Cliffs, N.J.: Prentice-Hall, 1988.

Examines the cultural adaptations of selected North American tribes to their natural environments. Uses major modes of subsistence as a way of organizing the case studies that make up the body of the book. Analysis is based on a holistic, ecological model that stresses the interaction of natural resources, technology, social organization, and ideology. Part 1, "Foragers," includes descriptions of the Netsilik Eskimo, the Cree, and the Washo. In part 2, "Part-Time Gardeners," the adaptations of the Havasupai, the Western Apache, and the Mandan are analyzed. Chapters examine the Cheyenne and Nootka, classified as "Affluent Hunters and Fishermen," respectively. The final section covers groups of "Intensive Farmers," including the Cherokee and the Santo Domingo Pueblo of the Rio Grande. Bibliography.

Larson, Charles R. *American Indian Fiction.* Albuquerque: University of New Mexico Press, 1978.

Proposes a four-phase evolution of Native American fiction. In the first, "assimilationist" era, little difference existed between novels by Indian authors and those of their Euro-American contemporaries. During the second, "reactionary" period, there appeared several Native American authors whose writings expressed a distinct ethnic consciousness and concern with Indian issues. In the next, "revisionist" stage, the theme of the collective tragedies of Indian peoples and their attempts to adapt to contemporary circumstances characterized much Native fiction. In its present stage, Indian literature tends to be less politically oriented and more concerned with the immediate world of its characters. Bibliography.

Laubin, Reginald, and Gladys Laubin. *Indian Dances of North America.* Norman: University of Oklahoma Press, 1977.

A detailed discussion of selected dances of North American Indians. Part 1 provides a historical overview of early reports on Indian dances, a description of the Ghost Dance, and changes in white attitudes toward Indian dancing. Part 2 describes the singing, musical instruments, masks, and paint associated with Native American dance. Parts 3 and 4 focus on traditional forms and occasions of dance. Among these are dances of the life cycle, the war dance, victory and scalp dances, the Green Corn Dance; Calumet and Eagle Dances, the Sun Dance of the Teton Sioux and other tribes, society dances, bird and animal dances, dances of the Pacific Coast, and dances of the Southwest. Part 5 examines contemporary Indian dances. Illustrated with black-and-white drawings, photographs, and color plates.

__________. *The Indian Tipi: Its History, Construction, and Use.* Norman: University of Oklahoma Press, 1977.

Presents both a historical study of movable shelters known as "tipis" and a practical guide for their construction and use. Begins with an analysis of the tipi's history by Stanley Vestal. Following are chapters on the utility and beauty of this form of architecture; the materials of the Sioux tipi; instructions on pitching the tipi; the furnishings, sociology, and culture of tipi life; tribal and functional varieties of tipis, including those made by the Shoshoni, Cheyenne, Crow, Blackfeet, Yakima, and Cree and those used as sweat baths, for council meetings, for burial, and in religious ceremonies; symbolism of Sioux and

Cheyenne tipi designs; transportation of tipis; the structure of camp circles; modern Indian camps; and animals that are likely to visit one's tipi. Illustrated with black-and-white photographs, drawings, and color plates. Bibliography.

Leacock, Eleanor Burke, and Nancy O. Lurie, eds. *North American Indians in Historical Perspective*. Prospect Heights, Ill.: Waveland Press, 1988.

An anthology of essays which focuses on the ways Indian peoples from nine culture areas have maintained and transformed their traditions in the face of contact with European and Euro-American societies. Chapters on the Coastal Algonquian, Creek/Seminole, Iroquois, Chippewa, Tlingit, Ute, and Paiute and tribes of the Plains, Southwest, California, and the Canadian Subarctic. An introduction by Leacock identifies five phases in Indian-white contact and discusses trends in Indian social history. Lurie's conclusion concentrates on attempts by contemporary Indian communities to find an option other than economic marginality and prosperity through individual assimilation. Black-and-white photographs, maps, and tables. A bibliography accompanies each essay.

Levernier, James, and Hennig Cohen, eds. and comps. *The Indians and Their Captives*. Westport, Conn.: Greenwood Press, 1977.

A collection of captivity narratives arranged to portray the historical transformations that occurred in the "details of their subject matter, style, literary forms, attitudes toward Indian culture, and the purposes to which they were applied." Organizes the narratives under five chronological phases: the discovery of the Indians, religious interpretations of captivity, rationalizations for usurping Native lands, nineteenth century enhancements of the historic heritage and socialization process, and the captivity theme as structure and metaphor for complex, pretentious art forms. Bibliographical note. Black-and-white reproductions.

Levine, Stuart, and Nancy O. Lurie, eds. *The American Indian Today*. Baltimore: Penguin Books, 1970.

Contains thirteen essays that address issues pertinent to contemporary Native North Americans. Seeks first to provide some basic information on Indian history and the evolution of federal relations; second, to discuss various concerns facing present-day Indian peoples; and, third, to present case studies that document the situation and problems of specific groups in various parts of the United States. Bibliography. Black-and-white photographs. Map.

Liberty, Margot, ed. *American Indian Intellectuals*. St. Paul, Minn.: West, 1978.

A collection of biographical sketches of Native North Americans who shared an awareness that the unique traditions of their peoples were vanishing and a commitment to preserving at least part of them for future generations. Submits that this commitment was born in part from sadness and in part from a new perspective achieved through association with the non-Indian world. Among those profiled are Ely S. Parker (Seneca), Sarah Winnemucca (Northern Paiute), Francis La Flesche (Omaha), Charles Alexander Eastman (Santee Sioux), James R. Murie (Pawnee), George Bushotter (Teton Sioux), Emmet Starr (Cherokee), Richard Sanderville (Blackfoot), Arthur C. Parker (Seneca), William Beyon (Tsimshian), Alexander General (Deskahe, Cayuga-Oneida), Jesse Cornplanter

(Seneca), Long Lance (Catawba-Cherokee and adopted Blackfoot), John Joseph Mathews (Osage), Flora Zuni (Zuni), and Bill Shakespeare (northern Arapaho). Appendix: "Prospectus for a Collection of Studies on Anthropology by North American Indians." A photograph of the subject accompanies each essay.

Lincoln, Kenneth. *Native American Renaissance*. Berkeley: University of California Press, 1983.

A multidisciplinary study of American Indian literature focusing on issues pertinent to an appreciation of such writings and the works of selected Native American authors. Among the issues discussed are the problem of translation and the nature and power of Indian oral traditions. The artists reviewed include N. Scott Momaday, Leslie Silko, Simon Ortiz, and James Welch. The author views the renaissance of Native American literature as "a written renewal of oral traditions translated into western literary forms. Contemporary Indian literature is not so much new, then, as regenerate and transitional continuities emerging from the old." Selected bibliography.

Macfarlan, Allan A., ed. *American Indian Legends*. Los Angeles: Ward Ritchie Press, 1968.

An anthology of Native American narratives drawn form the writings of Henry R. Schoolcraft, George Bird Grinnell, Franz Boas, and others. An introduction briefly summarizes the motifs commonly found in these narratives. Among such motifs are repetition for suspense and clarification; a boy or girl living with an aged grandparent or uncle; the transformation of individuals into animals or natural features by tricksters or enemies; disguised heroes and villains; invisibility; contests and games of challenge; dangerous missions resulting from dreams and unpopularity; numskulls; endurance and fortitude; taboos; resurrection; rejuvenation, and becoming beautiful; advice from enchanted objects; death caused by pointing; mind reading; the power of thought; superhuman feats; and magic weapons. Narratives are grouped by the following subjects: when the world was young; hero and culture hero tales; legends of the little people, giants, and monsters; mystery, medicine, and magic; romance, adventure, and enchantment; spirits and the supernatural; sorcery and witchcraft; trickster and transformer legends; legends of animals and birds, and bird-and-animal people; Indian "how," "why," and origin legends; and tales influenced by European fairy tales and folk tales. Illustrated with color drawings by Everett Gee Jackson.

McMillan, Allan D. *Native Peoples and Cultures of Canada*. Vancouver: Douglas and McIntyre, 1988.

An overview of Canadian Native peoples, past and present. The first two chapters briefly describe the Native language families found in Canada, the scope of anthropological research on Canada's aboriginal populations, and Canadian prehistory. The bulk of the book's remaining sections examine the history and lifeways of natives in the following culture areas: the Atlantic provinces, eastern Woodlands, Plains, Plateau, Northwest Coast, western Subarctic, and Arctic. Each section includes information on the pre- and postcontact history, cultures, and contemporary status of the Natives of its area. The final two chapters concern the Métis and major issues confronting contemporary Native Canadians. Extensive bibliographies for each chapter. Black-and-white reproductions, photographs, maps.

McNickle, D'Arcy. *Native American Tribalism: Indian Survivals and Renewals*. New York: Oxford University Press, 1973.

Examines the manner in which Indian peoples of the United States and Canada have managed to retain their ethnic and cultural identities in the face of ethnocidal agendas of white governments. Pays particular attention to the diminution of Indian lands from colonial times through the beginning of the twentieth century. Appendix. Bibliography. Black-and-white photographs. Maps.

__________. *They Came Here First: The Epic of the American Indian*. Rev. ed. New York: Farrar, Straus & Giroux, 1975.

Traces the history of Indian North America from archaic times to the early 1970's. Part 1 first summarizes what is known about the origins and lifeways of the continent's prehistoric inhabitants, then overviews the languages, religious beliefs, social forms, laws, and arts of various tribes. Part 2 traces the history of colonial America from Columbus to the Revolutionary War. Part 3 discusses the subjugation of Indian tribes and the different phases of federal Indian policy. The book concludes with a description of recent Indian activism and a retrospective.

Marriott, Alice Lee, and Carol Rachlin. *American Indian Mythology*. New York: Thomas Y. Crowell, 1964.

Presents selections from the oral literature of various tribes with the hope that "there will emerge a clearer understanding of the patterns of North American Indian religions and their mythologies, and of the philosophies which myths and legends embody." An introduction scans the origins and precontact history of Native Americans, central themes in colonial Indian-white relations, the importance of oral traditions among Indian peoples, certain elements these traditions share in common, and some anthropologists and folklorists who worked tirelessly to collect them. The narratives are organized according to the following themes: the world beyond ours, the world around us, the world we live in now, and the world we go to. Represented are the Cheyenne, Modoc, Cherokee, Iroquois, Kiowa, Musquakie (Fox), Tewa, Choctaw and Chickasaw, Navajo, Zuni, Mikasuki, Jicarilla Apache, Comanche, Arapaho, Ponca, Hopi, and Sauk. Black-and-white photographs. Bibliography.

Martin, Calvin, ed. *The American Indian and the Problem of History*. New York: Oxford University Press, 1987.

Essays loosely structured around the theme of Indian and white conceptions of time and history. Introduction questions the adequacy of Western treatments of Native American history. Eighteen papers treat a wide range of subjects, including the "new" Indian history, early Canadian contact, demographics, history versus moral philosophy and public advocacy, and tribal dancing. Concludes with an essay entitled "Time and the American Indian." Bibliography.

Mason, Otis T. *Indian Basketry: Studies in a Textile Art Without Machinery*. 2 vols. New York: Doubleday, Page, 1904.

A highly detailed study of Native American basket making. An introductory chapter provides a definition of this art and a glossary of terms applied to its description and analysis. Subsequent discussion on the materials used for basketry; the steps entailed in basket construction; ornamentation on basketry; symbolism and meaning (or their absence); uses of baskets; ethnic varieties in basketry, including those found among tribes in the eastern region (Canada, eastern states, southern states, western states), Alaskan region (Interior Alaska, Arctic Alaska, Aleutian Chain, southeastern Alaska, Queen Charlotte Archipelago), Fraser-Columbia region (Fraser drainage, Columbia drainage), Oregon-California region (southern Oregon, California), interior basin region (between Rocky Mountains and Sierras), Middle and South American region (Mexico, Central America, eastern and western South America); public and private collections. Bibliography. Includes 248 color and black-and-white plates, 212 drawings.

Monkman, Leslie. *A Native Heritage: Images of the Indian in English-Canadian Literature*. Toronto: University of Toronto Press, 1981.

Seeks to dispel the myth that the Indian has played a negligible role in the literary tradition of English-speaking Canada. Examines the various ways English-Canadian authors have understood the Indian and how these understandings have appeared as persistent themes in their works. Chapters on the image of the Indian as savage antagonist and idealized primitive; the white destruction of Indian culture; and the incorporation of Indian heroes and oral tradition into literary narratives.

Moquin, Wayne, and Charles Van Doren, eds. *Great Documents in American Indian History*. New York: Praeger, 1973.

Seeks to help rectify the wrongs committed against Indians by presenting "a survey of Indian life and history in the words of Indians of many tribes from all areas of the country." Part 1, "The Indian Way," contains selections that portray the range of traditional Native American lifeways. Part 2, "Captive Nations," provides documents demonstrating the gradual destruction and marginalization of Indian peoples during the course of nearly three centuries. Part 3, "Heading Toward the Mainstream," presents materials on issues faced by twentieth century American Indians. Each section begins with an epigraph that characterizes the thrust of Indian-white relations during the period it covers. Glossary of tribes. List of recommended readings. Black-and-white illustrations.

Morrison, R. Bruce, and C. Roderick Wilson. *Native Peoples: The Canadian Experience*. Toronto: McClelland and Stewart, 1986.

Contains twenty-six essays that examine the culture history, traditional lifeways, and contemporary situation of native groups representing seven cultural areas in Canada. Part 1 provides general discussions of the languages and prehistory of Canadian native peoples. Parts 2 through 8 present regional overviews and specialized treatments of the Eskaleuts, Eastern Subarctic, Western Subarctic,

Eastern Woodlands, Plains, Plateau, and the Northwest Coast. Among the peoples described are the Caribou Inuit, Montagnais-Naskapi, James Bay Cree, Bear Lake Indians, the Slavey, Iroquois, Micmac, Plains Métis, Blackfoot, Okanagan, Tsimshian, and Kwakiutl. Concludes with a chapter on legacies and prospects. Black-and-white photographs, maps. A list of recommended readings follows most essays.

Moses, L. G., and Raymond Wilson, eds. *Indian Lives*. Albuquerque: University of New Mexico Press, 1985.

An anthology of Native American biographies centered on the theme of "maintaining Indian identity—being an Indian—during times when it proved difficult to do so, from the early nineteenth century down to the present." Explores how each of its eight subjects struggled to affirm his or her ethnicity in a world that little valued Indian peoples and cultures. Included are Maris Bryant Pierce (Seneca), Minnie Kellogg (Oneida), Charles Curtis (Kaw-Osage), Susan La Flesche Picotte (Omaha), Luther Standing Bear (Sioux), Nampeyo (Hopi), Henry Chee Dodge (Navajo), and Peterson Zah (Navajo). Black-and-white photographs of each subject.

Nabokov, Peter. *Native American Testimony*. New York: Harper & Row, 1979.

A documentary history of Indian-white relations which focuses on the Indian interpretations of Europeans and Euro-Americans. Topics include early encounters between Indians and whites, Native American responses to white goods and commerce, reactions to Christian missionaries, the experience of tribes on the outskirts of white communities, resistance to white incursions on Indian lands, Indian perceptions of the treaty- making process, exile from traditional homelands, and revitalization of the Native American spirit. A brief essay by the editor introduces each section. Black-and-white photographs and maps.

Nabokov, Peter, and Robert Easton. *Native American Architecture*. New York: Oxford University Press, 1989.

Documents how the architecture of various tribes was as much a response to the central values of their cultures as to the natural environments in which they lived. First describes the way in which technology, climate, economics, social organization, religion, and history acted as the paramount determinants of Indian dwellings, then applies these determinants to an analysis of the Indian architecture found in nine culture areas. Illustrated with color plates, black-and-white photographs, line drawings, and maps. Bibliography reviews the history of the interest in Native American architecture, then offers key references.

Nichols, Roger L., ed. *The American Indian: Past and Present*. New York: John Wiley & Sons, 1981.

A selection of previously published articles by twenty-four scholars of American Indian history and cultures. Seeks to demonstrate several important themes: the political transformation of Native Americans from independent to subject peoples, the influence of Indians and Euro-Americans on each other's cultures, competition among Indian tribes, the changing status of Native Americans in the course of U.S. social evolution, competition with non-Indians for land and resources, recurrent attempts to forcibly assimilate Indians into the national mainstream, and Indian claims to sovereignty and self-determination. A list of supplementary readings is provided for each essay.

Niethammer, Carolyn. *Daughters of the Earth: The Lives and Legends of American Indian Women*. New York: Macmillan, 1977.

A wide-ranging treatment of the many dimensions of traditional Indian Native American womanhood. Chapters are arranged according to the periods of the female life cycle as well as by roles typically performed by women. The subjects covered include childbirth; childhood; the onset of womanhood to menopause; courtship through widowhood; woman's economic role; leaders, doctors, and witches; helpers, fighters, victors, and vanquished; crafts and recreation; sexual patterns; religion and spirituality; and old age and death. Each chapter illustrates its theme with information drawn from lifeways of different tribes. An brief annotated bibliography of theoretical treatments of women's status and role. An unannotated general bibliography. Black-and-white photographs.

Olson, James S., and Raymond Wilson. *Native Americans in the Twentieth Century*. Provo, Utah: Brigham Young University Press, 1984.

Addresses the need for a Native American history that is primarily concerned with twentieth century themes and problems. Begins with a brief overview of Native American traditions and Indian-white relations up to the present. Chapters 2 and 3 focus on government Indian policy to the end of the nineteenth century. Subsequent chapters examine the late nineteenth and early twentieth century reform of Indian policy, Collier's Indian New Deal, the post-World War II policies of termination and relocation, modern Indian militancy, and change and continuity in America's treatment of Indians. An epilogue concludes with the observation that "after hundreds of years of conflict and competition with the values of an alien way of life, Native America perseveres." Black-and-white photographs. Maps of Native American tribal areas and Native American reservations and groups as of 1980. Bibliography.

Orchard, William C. *Beads and Beadwork of the American Indian*. New York: Museum of the American Indian, Heye Foundation, 1929.

Surveys the history, techniques, and uses of American Indian beadwork before and after white contact. The opening sections describe beads of Indian manufacture, including those made from shells, pearl, bone, stone, metals, and "odd forms and materials" (for example, dried otter's liver). Also includes a section on the aboriginal drilling of beads and an extended discussion of wampum. Presented next is the history, manufacture, and varieties of beads traded by whites to Indians. Subsequent chapters distinguish various forms of beadworking. Includes 31 plates, 136 drawings.

__________. *The Technique of Porcupine-Quill Decoration Among the North American Indians*. New York: Museum of the American Indian, Heye Foundation, 1971.

Overviews the history, distribution, and practice of porcupine quill work among Native North Americans. Topics include early accounts of the use of porcupine quill, the preparation and coloring of quills, implements and techniques of quill decoration, and the materials on which quill work is applied. Brief discussion of the art and distribution of bird quillwork. 25 plates, 61 drawings. Fold-out map showing the habitat of the porcupine and tribes that produced porcupine quill work though not living in parts of the country where porcupine might be found.

Oswalt, Wendell H. *This Land Was Theirs: A Study of the North American Indian.* New York: John Wiley & Sons, 1973.

An overview of the great diversity in lifeways that flourished in pre-Columbian North America. The introduction uses a culture area approach to present the major variations that existed among Indian cultures at the time of white contact. The body of the text further illustrates these differences through the case studies of 10 peoples: the Chipewyan: hunters and fishermen of the Subarctic; the Beothuk: hunters of the Subarctic forests; the Kuskowagamiut: riverine fishermen; the Cahuilla: gatherers in the desert; the Fox: fighters and farmers of the woodland fringe; the Pawnee: horsemen and farmers of the western prairies; the Tlingit: salmon fishermen of the Northwest; the Hopi: farmers of the desert; the Iroquois: warriors and farmers of the eastern woodlands; and the Natchez: sophisticated farmers of the Deep South. Bibliography. Black-and-white illustrations and maps.

Oxendine, Joseph B. *American Indian Sports Heritage.* Champaign, Ill.: Human Kinetics Books, 1988.

Argues that the history of Native American sports displays three phases, each with its own characteristics. The first six chapters present concepts and examples of traditional Indian sport. Described are various forms of ball games, foot racing, children's play, and games of chance. The next five chapters examine phase two, the "heyday of Indian sports," which began in the late nineteenth century and lasted until 1930. Discussed are the emergence of Indian participation in such Western sports as football, baseball, and basketball; thirty-three prominent Indian athletes of the period; and the areer of Jim Thorpe. Chapter 13 portrays the diminishing participation of Indians in athletics after 1930 (phase three). Concludes by highlighting promising signs for Indians in sports.

Paper, Jordan. *Offering Smoke: The Sacred Pipe and Native American Religion.* Moscow: University of Idaho Press, 1988.

A multidisciplinary examination of the ceremonial and symbolic importance of the Sacred Pipe in many Native American traditions. The first four chapters offer analyses of the ritual, myth, and symbolism of the Sacred Pipe religion as well as descriptions of various types of pipes other than and including the Sacred Pipe. A chapter on geography and history examines the distribution and antiquity of the pipe ritual among Native Americans. An epilogue discusses the continuity and change in the beliefs and practices associated with the Sacred Pipe. Includes two appendices: the first concerning issues of methodology; the second listing data on pipes housed in nineteen museums. Frontispiece, seven black-and-white drawings, and sixteen color plates. Bibliography.

Parsons, Elsie C., ed. *American Indian Life*. New York: B. W. Huebsch, 1922.
Fictionalized accounts of the lifeways of selected Native American peoples by twenty-five noted anthropologists. The authors plot their portrayals of Indian cultures around imaginary heroes and heroines, much as would the creator of a historical novel. Among the tribes depicted are the Crow, Blackfoot, Menominee, Winnebago, Sauk-Fox, Montagnais, Iroquois, Lenape (Delaware), Lower Creeks, Apache, Zuni, Navajo, Havasupai, Mojave, Yurok, Shell Mound People, Klamath, Nootka, Chipewyan, Ten'a, and Eskimo. An introduction by the famed ethnologist Alfred L. Kroeber comments on the strengths and weaknesses of the collection. Color or black-and-white drawings introduce each selection.

Peyer, Bernd C., ed. *The Elders Wrote*. Berlin: Dietrich Reimer Verlag, 1982.
An anthology of prose written in English by Native North Americans between 1768 and 1931. Includes addresses, articles, autobiographical sketches, letters, and short monographs that reflect the experience of individuals whose Indian heritage and white education made them insiders and outsiders to both traditions. Among the twenty-three authors anthologized are Samsom Occom (Mohegan), John Ross (Iroquois), Maungwudaus (Chippewa), Sarah Winnemucca (Paiute), and Gertrude Bonnin (Sioux). Bibliography. Black-and-white photographs.

Pferd, William, III. *Dogs of the American Indians*, edited by William W. Denlinger and R. Annabel Rathman. Fairfax, Va.: Denlinger's Publishers, 1987.
Draws on data from archaeology, ethnography, documentary literature, and works of art to construct the history of American Indian dogs from prehistoric times to the late nineteenth century. Most of the chapters treat the types or breeds of Indian dogs found in the following culture areas: Great Plains, Arctic, Subarctic, Northwest Coast, Southwest, and Inca and southern South America. Bibliography. Black-and-white reproductions and photographs.

Porter, Frank W., III, ed. *The Art of Native American Basketry: A Living Legacy*. Westport, Conn.: Greenwood Press, 1990.
An anthology of essays that documents, first, the many-fold functions of basketry in the material and ideational culture of Native North Americans; second, the great differences of technology, style, design, and use associated with Indian basketry; and, third, the similar ways Indian basket makers have adapted their art after prolonged contact with non-Indians. Many of the papers focus on particular tribes; others concern entire culture areas. The tribes discussed are Micmac, Washo, Patwin, Cahuilla, Hupa, Karok, Yurok, Tlingit, Baleen, Attu, and Aleut; culture areas include Northeast, Middle Atlantic, Southeast, Plains, northwestern Plateau, Southwest, western Washington, and Northwest Coast. Includes eighty black-and-white illustrations.

Price, John A. *Indians of Canada: Cultural Dynamics*. Scarborough, Ontario: Prentice-Hall, 1979.

A survey of Canadian Indians focusing on their ecological adaptations, historical persistence and acculturation, cultural evolution, and contemporary relations with whites. The first three chapters present archaeological, linguistic, and cultural summaries for Indian Canada as a whole. Each of the five central chapters concentrates on a specific culture area, sketching one or two of its major groups and prominent areas of research. Uses an evolutionary framework of political complexity (bands, tribes, chiefdoms) to arrange the regional chapters. A final chapter discusses such topics as current anti-Indian racism, urban adaptations, and voluntary associations. Bibliography. Twenty-three sepia-toned renderings of famous paintings and photographs.

__________. *Native Studies: American and Canadian Indians*. Toronto: McGraw-Hill Ryerson Ltd., 1978.

A survey of some of the major themes and issues addressed by Native American studies. An introductory chapter summarizes the recent emergence of Native studies as an interdisciplinary field of inquiry. The next seven chapters examine various aspects of Indian history and traditional cultures. Following are chapters that focus on the dynamics and institutions of urban Indians. The book then addresses such contemporary problems as drinking, stereotyping, militancy, education, and access to political and economic resources. Bibliography. Illustrated with tables and maps.

Prucha, Francis Paul, ed. *Documents of United States Indian Policy*. 2d ed., expanded. Lincoln: University of Nebraska Press, 1990.

A compilation of 199 official and quasi-official records representing important formulations of U.S. Indian policy. The documents, which are arranged chronologically, date from the nation's founding to the late 1980's. Prefacing each is a brief history of the circumstances surrounding its origins and purposes. Among the issues addressed are treaty making, Indian sovereignty, utilization of water and natural resources, and civil rights and education. Documents include the various Trade and Intercourse Acts of the late nineteenth and early twentieth centuries, Civilization Fund Act (1819), Indian Removal Act (1830), *Worcester v. Georgia* (1832), Transfer of Indian Affairs to the Department of the Interior (1849), Abolition of Treaty Making (1871), Major Crimes Act (1885), *Lone Wolf v. Hitchcock* (1903), Indian Citizen Act (1924), Wheeler-Howard Act (1934), Indian Education Act (1972), and Indian Child Welfare Act (1978). Selected bibliography.

__________. *Indian Policy in the United States: Historical Essays*. Lincoln: University of Nebraska Press, 1981.

A collection of essays on selected topics in nineteenth century Indian affairs which attempts to "understand, not judge, the past and to investigate thoroughly the sources of the past with as few preconceptions and prejudgments as possible." Papers include "Doing Indian History; New Approaches to the Study of the Administration of Indian Policy"; "Federal Indian Policy in United States History"; "The Dawning of a New Era: The Spirit of Reform and American Indian Policy"; "The Image of the Indian in Pre-Civil War America"; "The

United States Army and the Fur Trade"; "Lewis Cass and American Indian Policy"; "Indian Removal and the Great American Desert"; "Thomas L. McKenney and the New York Indian Board"; "Andrew Jackson's Indian Policy: A Reassessment"; "American Indian Policy in the 1840's: Visions of Reform"; "Scientific Racism and Indian Policy"; "The Board of Indian Commissioners and the Delegates of the Five Tribes"; "A 'Friend of the Indians' in Milwaukee: Mrs. O. J. Hiles and the Wisconsin Indian Association"; "Indian Policy Reform and American Protestantism, 1880-1900"; and "The Decline of the Christian Reformers."

Reyhner, Jon, and Jeanne Eder. *A History of Indian Education.* Billings: Eastern Montana State College, 1989.

Describes the role of Indian schools in European and Euro-American efforts to assimilate Native Americans and patterns of Indian resistance and cooperation with these efforts. The book begins with a historical overview. Next are chapters based on the following periodization and themes of Indian-white relations: 1492-1776: colonial missionaries; 1776-1867: western removal; 1867-1924: government control, mission schools, government boarding schools; 1924-1944: a new deal; 1944-1969: termination; and 1969-1989: self-determination. An appendix presents demographic and education statistics for contemporary Native Americans. Bibliography.

Rosenstiel, Annette. *Red and White: Indian Views of the White Man, 1492-1982.* New York: Universe Books, 1983.

Native American perspectives on encounters with whites from 1511 to 1982. Each of the five chapters begins with an overview of Indian-white relations during a specified century. Following this summary are twenty statements or speeches in which Indians express their impressions of European/Euro-American culture and conduct. The narratives are preceded by explanatory notes that give information concerning the circumstances that occasioned them. One hundred reproductions of woodcuts, drawings, and photographs illustrate the text.

Rostlund, Erhard. *Freshwater Fish and Fishing in Native North America.* University of California Publications in Geography 9. Berkeley: University of California Press, 1952.

Seeks to distinguish and explain regional and seasonal differences in fish fauna, to provide a quantative assessment of fishing opportunity, and to evaluate regional variations in the importance of Indian freshwater fishing. Part 1 examines different aspects of freshwater fish as a resource, including their food value, principal species, and productivity. It also provides a resumé of the fish resource by region. Part 2 contains a detailed description of aboriginal fishing methods. The book closes with a summary of cultural-historical inferences that can be made on the basis of the data provided. Bibliography of references cited. Maps and tables.

Sapir, Edward. *Selected Writings of Edward Sapir in Language, Culture, and Personality*, edited by David G. Mandelbaum. Berkeley: University of California Press, 1949.

Assembles fifty-one previously published articles and reviews by one of America's foremost cultural anthropologists. The writings are divided into three sections, according to the themes of language, culture, and personality. The sections on language and culture include important studies in American Indian linguistics, social organization, and lifeways. Two of the more notable of these are an essay on the classification of Central and North American languages and a paper concerned with the social organization of the West Coast tribes. Closes with a bibliography of the author's scientific papers, prose writings, and poems. Tables.

Savage, William W., Jr., ed. *Indian Life: Transforming an American Myth.* Norman: University of Oklahoma Press, 1978.

A collection of thirteen essays by influential spokespersons for Indian-white relations in the late nineteenth and early twentieth centuries. Argues that the images portrayed in these essays served to rationalize divesting Plains Indians of their lands during the post-Civil War period. Among the authors included are Richard Dodge, John F. Finerty, Helen Hunt Jackson, and James Willard Schultz. Meant to be read as a companion piece to the author's *Cowboy Life: Reconstructing an American Myth.* Beautifully illustrated with sepia-toned photographs housed in the Western History Collections of the University of Oklahoma Library.

Schusky, Ernest L., ed. *Political Organization of Native North Americans.* Washington, D.C.: University of America Press, 1980.

Eleven essays that consider the effects of Euro-American contact and domination on the political organization of Native American tribes. The papers in part 1 explore the responses of various tribes to the shifting power relations between Indian and white as mirrored in the federal policy of different eras. Part 2 contains articles that examine the political actions among contemporary groups including the Seminole of Florida, Crow, Cree, and Indians in Canada's Northwest territories. A final chapter overviews Indian-white relations in a changing world.

Sebeok, Thomas, ed. *North America. Vol. 1 in Native Languages of the Americas.* New York: Plenum Press, 1976.

An anthology of papers on Native North American languages by fourteen eminent scholars. Part 1 contains general discussions on the history of American Indian linguistics; North American Indian language contact; philological approaches to the study of North American Indian languages; and a linguistic overview of Native North America. Part 2 presents papers concerned with areal analyses and groupings. These include an overview of areal linguistics in North America; Eskimo-Aleut; Na-Dene; the Northwest; California; Southwestern and Great Basin languages; Algonquian, Siouan, Iroquoian, and Caddoan; and the Southeast.

Sherzer, Joel. *An Areal-Typological Study of American Indian Languages North of Mexico.* New York: North-Holland, 1976.

Presents a detailed investigation of selected characteristics of Native North

American languages. Seeks to discover "to what degree phonological and morphological traits have diffused in North America, to delimit linguistic areas, and to compare the linguistic areas that have been posited by anthropologists on the basis of non-linguistic culture." Begins with a historical overview of language area studies in North America. Next provides a framework for the areal investigation of phonological and morphological features of Indian languages north of Mexico. Chapters 3 through 13 apply this framework to the following areas: Arctic, western Subarctic, eastern Subarctic, Northwest Coast, Plateau, California, Southwest, Great Basin, Plains, Northeast, and Southeast. Chapter 14 compares the culture areas established for North America with the linguistic areas determined by the present study. The final chapter discusses the relevance of Native North American linguistic data to the problem of linguistic universals.

Smith, Jane F., and Robert M. Kvasnicka, eds. *Indian-White Relations: A Persistent Paradox*. Washington, D.C.: Howard University Press, 1976.

A collection of ten papers originally presented at the National Archives Conference on Research in the History of Indian-White Relations in 1972. Section headings include the history, use, and potential of Indian- related records in the National Archives; aspects of Indian assimilation in the nineteenth century; Indian collections outside the National Archives and Records Service; the role of the military; recent research on Indian reservation policy; and topics in twentieth century Indian policy. The essays in most sections are preceded by an introduction and followed by a commentary. Includes an introductory paper by Francis Paul Prucha entitled "Doing Indian History." Black-and-white illustrations.

Snipp, C. Mathew. *American Indians: The First of This Land*. New York: Russell Sage Foundation, 1989.

Part of a series of volumes "aimed at converting the vast statistical yield of the 1980 census into authoritative analyses of major changes and trends in American life." Topics include American Indian demography in historical perspective, varying standards of determining Indian identity, the distribution of the nation's Indian peoples, housing, family and household structure, language and education, labor force participation, occupation and income, migration, and projections concerning social and economic conditions.

Snow, Dean R. *The American Indians: Their Archaeology and Prehistory*. New York: Thames and Hudson, 1976.

Seeks to document the achievements of pre-Columbian Americans using a minimum of specialist jargon and theoretical impositions. An introduction discusses who archaeologists are and what they do, the migration of the earliest peoples to the Americas, and the lifeways of Paleo-Indians. Chapters on the Eastern Woodlands, Great Plains, Desert West, Far West, and the Arctic and Subarctic begin by describing the environmental features of each area, then uses archaeological data to reconstruct the sociocultural patterns of its inhabitants. Closes with two extremely helpful chronologies presenting the key cultural traditions and events for areas discussed. Wonderfully illustrated with maps, black-and-white photographs, and color plates.

Spencer, Robert F., Jesse D. Jennings, et al. *The Native Americans*. New York: Harper & Row, 1977.

Begins with a short presentation of the methods and findings of New World archaeology; next provides a series of chapters that overview the environment, prehistory, languages, and tribal groupings of eleven North American and Mesoamerican "culture areas"; then details the lifeways of a number of societies within these areas. Concludes with essays on the American Indian heritage and urban Native Americans. The list of suggested readings at the end of each chapter and an extended bibliography are particularly useful to beginners in Native American studies. Profusely illustrated.

Spicer, Edward H. *Perspectives in American Indian Culture Change*. Chicago: University of Chicago Press, 1961.

A collection of six essays concerned with the acculturation of selected tribes of Native North Americans. Seeks to discern whether "any fundamental similarities exist in the responses of the different Indian groups to similar conditions of contact." Features discussions of the Yaqui, Rio Grande Pueblos, Mandan, Navajo, Wasco-Wishram, and Kwakiutl. An editor's conclusion provides generalizations regarding types of acculturative change and contact conditions through a comparison of the case studies presented. Bibliography. Illustrated with twelve maps, one diagram, and ten tables.

Stewart, Omer C. *Peyote Religion: A History*. Norman: University of Oklahoma Press, 1987.

Examines the origins and diffusion of peyote religion among Native North Americans. Part 1 contains chapters on the biological characteristics and natural growth range of peyote, peyote in Mexico, and Mexican and American peyote ceremonies in the late nineteenth century. Part 2 treats the beginnings of peyotism in the United States, 1885-1918. Part 3 offers a history of the periodic attempts to pass federal legislation against peyote use. Next examines the further spread of peyotism after the incorporation of the Native American Church, the development of peyotism in the far West, the history of peyote religion among the Navajo, and peyotism today. Three appendices: "Peyote Ritual"; "Program of the Native American Church State Convention, Allen, South Dakota, July 3-7, 1948"; "Church Canons for the Native American Church of South Dakota, 1948." Bibliography. Black-and-white photographs. Tables and maps.

Sullivan, Lawrence E., ed. *Native American Religions: North America*. New York: Macmillan, 1987.

A compilation of twenty-four essays on Native American religions drawn from *The Encyclopedia of Religion*. An introduction underscores the complexity of Indian religions and the importance of their study. Part 1 begins with an overview of religious life in Native North America. It next presents essays summarizing patterns of belief and ceremony for particular areas (Plains, Southwest, California and the Intermountain region, Northwest Coast, Far

North, Southeast Woodlands) and peoples (Blackfeet, Apache, Navajo, Inuit, Iroquois). Concludes with a summary of religious studies. Part 2 contains essays on Indian religious expression (mythic themes, tricksters, drama, iconography, music, Sun Dance, Ghost Dance, potlatch, modern religious movements). One map locates the culture areas discussed. Sparsely illustrated with black-and-white drawings. Bibliographies accompany each essay.

Svensson, Frances. *The Ethnics in American Politics: American Indians*. Minneapolis: Burgess, 1973.

A chronological discussion of key legislation, groups, and movements in the history of U.S. Indian relations. Begins with a discussion of criteria commonly used to classify individuals as Indians. Section 2, "The Indian in U.S. Politics," contains short descriptions of acts, laws, and organizations that have been instrumental in determining the political status of American Indians. Concludes with a list of recommended readings and a series of review questions (seemingly) for classroom use.

Swann, Brian. *Smoothing the Ground: Essays on Native American Oral Literature*. Berkeley: University of California Press, 1983.

A collection of twenty essays dedicated to winning a place for Native American literature within the U.S. literary canon. The topics of the papers include an overview of Native American literature, commentaries and critiques of particular authors and forms, and analyses of continuity and change in literary styles.

Swann, Brian, and Arnold Krupat, eds. *I Tell You Now: Autobiographical Essays by Native American Writers*. Lincoln: University of Nebraska Press, 1987.

Autobiographical essays by eighteen Native Americans celebrated for their short stories, novels, nonfiction, poems, and folk and popular music. Contributions by Mary Tall Mountain (Koyukon Athapascan), Ralph Salisbury (Cherokee), Maurice Kenny (Mohawk), Elizabeth Cook-Lynn (Crow-Creek-Sioux), Carter Revard (Osage), Jim Barnes (Choctaw), Gerald Vizenor (Minnesota Chippewa), Jack Forbes (Powhatan-Delaware-Saponi), Duane Niatum (Klallum), Paula Gunn Allen (Laguna Pueblo), Jimmie Durham (Wolf Clan Cherokee), Diane Glancy (Cherokee), Simon J. Ortiz (Acoma Pueblo), Joseph Bruchac (Abnaki), Barney Bush (Shawnee), Linda Hogan (Chickasaw), Wendy Rose (Hopi-Miwok), and Joy Harjo (Creek). Editors' introduction explores some of the assumptions of the collection as well as the problems they encountered in soliciting the autobiographies. Lists of suggested readings and the small presses that publish Native American writers.

Symington, Fraser. *The Canadian Indian: The Illustrated History of the Great Tribes of Canada*. Toronto: McClelland and Stewart, 1969.

A "coffee-table" overview of the history and cultures of Canada's aboriginal peoples. Section 1 rehearses the Asiatic origins and prehistory of Canadian Indians, Aleuts, and Eskimos. Section 2 is a broadly based areal presentation of fifty Canadian tribes. The third section informs the reader of the crucial periods and events in Indian-white relations. Filled with beautifully rendered color plates, black-and-white illustrations, and maps.

Taylor, Theodore W. *American Indian Policy*. Mt. Airy, Md.: Lomond, 1983.
Intended as a "comprehensive overview and description of programs and participants uniquely related to American Indians, and to serve as a reference source to identify specific *roles* of Federal and state and local governments and of major interest groups." Seeks also to provide a base for understanding how Indian policy is formulated. Chapter 1 summarizes selected aspects of contemporary Native American life. Chapter 2 presents case studies from Alaska, Maine, western Washington, and South Dakota. Chapters 3 and 4 describe federal government services for Native Americans and state and local government Indian services, respectively. In chapter 5 a variety of Indian interest groups and voluntary associations are discussed. The concluding chapter offers some thoughts on the future of Indian policy. Bibliography. Four appendices: "Map of Indian Lands and Communities"; "Resident Indian Population by Bureau of Indian Affairs Area Office, State, and Bureau of Indian Affairs Reservation Agency"; "Status of Nonintercourse Act Claims"; "Statement by Bradley H. Patterson on the Irony of the Trail of Broken Treaties." Two indexes: Indian tribes, groups, and reservations; names and subjects. Tables and figures.

__________. *The Bureau of Indian Affairs*. Boulder, Colo.: Westview Press, 1984.
Attempts a balanced account of the history and functioning of the Bureau of Indian Affairs (BIA) with the objective of raising questions and exploring options for possible improvement. Part 1 begins with a historical overview of government Indian policy from colonial times to the present. Continues with a brief organizational history of the bureau, the contemporary departments and services of the BIA, and the structure and role of tribal government. Part 2 examines the interrelationships of various participants in the Indian policy milieu. Included is a case study of the resolution of a policy issue involving the Indians of Maine. Part 3 highlights trends likely to shape the future of federal Indian policy. Three appendices: "Indian Service Population and Labor Force Estimates," "Tourism Projects," and "Status of Nonintercourse Act Land Claims." Selected bibliography. Two indexes: names and subjects; Indian tribes and groups.

Tedlock, Dennis, and Barbara Tedlock, eds. *Teachings from the American Earth: Indian Religion and Philosophy*. New York: Liveright Press, 1975.
An anthology of writings on Indian religions and philosophies by "Indians who have tried to make themselves heard, or whites who have tried to hear Indians and were changed by this experience." An introduction by the editors briefly describes some important aspects of Indian religious experience and compares and contrasts Indian and white cosmologies. Includes statements by Gitksan and Sioux medicine men Isaac Tens and Black Elk; J. S. Slotkin on the Peyote Way; a section from James Mooney's report on the ghost dance; and Alfonso Ortiz on the Tewa worldview.

Thornton, Russell. *American Indian Holocaust and Survival: A Population History Since 1492*. Norman: University of Oklahoma Press, 1987.
An investigation of the demographic effects of the Columbian encounter on the

aboriginal occupants of North America. Chapter 1 begins with a summary of Indian prehistory and population movements, then considers the relatively recent arrivals of European explorers and colonists. Chapters 2 through 7 present population estimates for the American Indian population prior to Columbus' landing and the primary causes of its destruction in the centuries that followed. Chapters 8 and 9 describe the demographic and nondemographic causes of the population growth among contemporary Native Americans. Chapter 9 discusses the urbanization of a great percentage of Indian people. Black-and-white photographs, maps, tables.

Turner, Frederick W., III, ed., *The Portable North American Indian Reader*. New York: Viking Press, 1974.

Proposes "to introduce the general American reader to the traditions and the historical realities of the North American Indian." Begins with a selection of myths and legends belonging to various groups. Next presents examples of Indian poems, songs, and oratory. Continues with excerpts from writings that characterize the responses of Indian and white to situations of culture contact. Concludes with conflicting images of Native Americans found in literature written by Indians and whites. A general introduction serves to dispel some common misconceptions regarding Native Americans. Each section begins with an editor's note describing key features of the type of literature to be surveyed.

Tyler, Daniel, ed. *Red Men and Hat Wearers: Viewpoints in Indian History*. Boulder, Colo.: Pruett, 1976.

A selection of papers from the Colorado State University Conference on Indian History held in 1974. Speakers consider whether Indians and whites are polarized over the meaning and function of historical research. Part 1 contains discussions of Indian-white relations based on resources and modes of interpretation traditionally employed by Western historians. The papers in part 2 address these relations from an Indian perspective.

Tyler, S. Lyman. *A History of Indian Policy*. Washington, D.C.: U.S. Department of the Interior, Bureau of Indian Affairs, 1973.

A historical summary of federal Indian policy intended for use by students, teachers, government employees, and the general public. An introduction defines Indian policy, presents an overview of its historical structure and dynamics, and briefly describes the approaches of various colonial powers to Indian-white relations. Chapter 2 deals with treaties and Indian trade. Subsequent sections concern tribal removal, reservations, allotment, Indian reorganization, relocation, Indian policy in the 1960's, self-determination through Indian leadership, and policy goals for the early 1970's. Black-and-white drawings and photographs; foldout maps of culture areas, Indian population by county (circa 1970), and contemporary reservations. Appendices listing dates significant in the development of Indian policy and administrators of U.S. Indian policy, 1789 to the present. Bibliography of general references, unpublished materials, government documents, and newspaper and periodical literature.

Umiker-Sebeok, D. Jean, and Thomas Sebeok, eds. *Aboriginal Sign Languages of the Americas and Australia.* 2 vols. New York: Plenum Press, 1978.

A collection of early and recent analyses of the conventional gesture systems of selected American and Australian tribes. Volume 1 contains three important papers by Colonel Garrick Mallery originally published in the late nineteenth century: "Introduction to the Study of Sign Language Among the North American Indians as Illustrating the Gesture Speech of Mankind"; "A Collection of Gesture-Signs and Signals of the North American Indians with Some Comparison"; and "The Gesture Speech of Man." The first section of volume 2 presents eighteen essays on Native North American sign language by such noted scholars as Franz Boas, Alfred L. Kroeber, Carl Voegelin, James A. Teit, and Richard I. Dodge. The original photographs, drawings, and maps that accompanied the articles are reproduced.

Underhill, Ruth M. *Red Man's Religion.* Chicago: University of Chicago Press, 1965.

Surveys selected categories of religious belief and practice among Native Americans north of Mexico. Chapters 1 and 2 provide general discussions of the characteristic elements, geography, and history of Indian religions. The remaining twenty-one chapters investigate expressions of religious life either universal to Indian groups (for example, cosmogenetic narratives, beliefs in spirits, attitudes toward the dead, presence of religious specialists) or limited to one or a few culture area (for example, Sun Dance, planting ceremonies). Intended as a companion to the author's *Red Man's America.* A few black-and-white reproductions and photographs illustrate the discussions.

Utley, Robert M., and Wilcomb B. Washburn. *The American Heritage History of the Indian Wars.* New York: American Heritage, 1977.

A history of the conflicts between Indians and whites from the early seventeenth to the late nineteenth century. Part 1 examines the failed attempts by tribes east of the Mississippi to combat white domination of their lands and their lives. Also explores the entanglement of various Indian peoples in the colonial ambitions of the English and French.

Vecsey, Christopher. *Imagine Ourselves Richly: Mythic Narratives of North American Indians.* New York: Crossroad, 1988.

Provides a multidisciplinary approach to the analysis of selected Native American narratives and rituals. Argues that through their myths, "Indians have examined their lives in a way at least as valid as the discursive methods of academics." Analyzed are the Hopi myth of emergence and clan migration; the Ojibwa creation myth; the Iroquois version of their confederacy's origin; a Navajo hero myth; myths of the origins of peyotism; and a contemporary southeastern sweat lodge ceremony. Three pen-and-ink drawings and two maps. An extensive and very useful bibliography.

Velie, Alan R. *Four American Indian Literary Masters: N. Scott Momaday, James Welch, Leslie Marmon Silko, and Gerald Vizenor.* Norman: University of Oklahoma Press, 1982.

Seeks to introduce teachers of Indian literature and the interested lay reader to the works of N. Scott Momaday, James Welch, Leslie Marmon Silko, and Gerald Vizenor. An introduction describes the traditional forms of Indian literature and addresses some fundamental misconceptions held by non-Indians concerning such works. Following are chapters on Momaday's autobiographical writings, poems, and novel *The House Made of Dawn*. Next examines the poetry of Welch and his novel *A Winter in the Blood*. Discussion then turns to Silko's novel *Ceremony*. The final chapter analyzes the postmodern fiction of Vizenor. Black-and-white photographs of each author.

Velie, Alan R., and Robert W. Venables, eds. *American Indian Environments: Ecological Issues in Native American History*. Syracuse, N.Y.: Syracuse University Press, 1980.

Ten essays that examine the relationship between historical and present-day Native Americans and the natural environment. Seeks to provide an overview of how this relationship has continued and been transformed in the face of white colonialism; the continuing competition with non-Indians for land use and resources; and contrasting Indian and white assumptions concerning the environment, subsistence techniques, and land-based sovereignty. Papers include "American Indian Environmental Religions"; "Subarctic Indians and Wildlife"; "Indians as Ecologists and Other Environmental Themes in American Frontier History"; "Justifying Dispossession of the Indian (The Land Utilization Argument)"; "Iroquois Environments and 'We the People of the United States'"; "Refugee Havens: The Iroquois Villages of the Eighteenth Century"; "Victim Versus Victim: The Irony of the New York Indians' Removal to Wisconsin"; "A Report to the People of Grassy Narrows, Navajo Natural Resources"; "An Iroquois Perspective." Black-and-white illustrations.

Vogel, Virgil. *American Indian Medicine*. Norman: University of Oklahoma Press, 1970.

A detailed discussion of Native American treatments for disease and injury. The opening chapter acknowledges the Indian origins of many Western pharmaceuticals. Chapter 2 explores Indian theories of disease and shamanistic practices offering a culturally appropriate definition of medicine as well as descriptions of the equipment, methods, and results of Native treatments. The next four chapters provide early evaluations by whites of Indian medicine; instances of Indian doctors servicing whites; the influence of Indian medicine on folk medicine, irregular practitioners, and patent medicines; and patterns of Indian health and disease. Chapter 7 presents an extended description of Indian curing methods, including the drug and drugless treatments of internal and external injuries, obstetrics, dentistry, and hygienic and sanitary practices. An appendix cites American Indian contributions to pharmacology. Index of botanical names. Bibliography.

__________. *This Country Was Ours: A Documentary History of the American Indian*. New York: Harper & Row, 1972.

A documentary history of Indian-white relations intended to counteract the distorted presentations found in most textbooks. Develops a fourfold periodization of United States Indian history before Columbus (prehistory); from discovery and settlement to the Revolutionary War, 1492-1775; from the Revolutionary War to the Civil War, 1775-1860; and from the Civil War to the present, 1861-1972. First, summarizes the role of Indians in each of these periods. Next, presents documents illustrative of events and conditions affecting Indian life.

Washburn, Wilcomb E., comp. and ed. *The American Indian and the United States*. 4 vols. New York: Random House, 1973.

A compendium of documents that illustrates the evolution of federal Indian relations. Documents were selected from five principal sources: reports of the commissioners of Indian Affairs, congressional debates, judicial decisions, treaties, and acts of Congress. The documents of each category are segregated into separate sections and arranged in chronological order. A brief introduction precedes each section.

__________. *The Indian in America*. New York: Harper & Row, Publishers, 1975.

Proposes to isolate and describe unifying and consistent patterns in precontact Indian personality and culture, and to demonstrate how pressures outside Indian life wrought changes in these patterns. Chapters 1 through 3 explore the origins of American Indians, Indian personality, and Indian social structure. The remaining nine chapters trace the history of Indian-white relations, concentrating on its repercussions for Native American society and identity. A concluding essay evaluates selected bibliographies, journals, reference works, general works by anthropologists and historians, tribal ethnographies and histories, specialized anthropological works, books on government policy, literary works, and monographs on the contemporary Indian.

__________. *Red Man's Land, White Man's Law: A Study of the Past and Present Status of the American Indian*. New York: Charles Scribner's Sons, 1971.

A historical investigation of the legal status of Native North Americans. Part 1 documents how classical assumptions concerning human nature and the theology of Christian mission conditioned Spanish views on the legal and moral rights of Indians. Part 2 summarizes the continuities and changes in four hundred years of Anglo-American Indian policy. Parts 3 and 4 examine the political status of Indian lands and peoples as of the early 1970's.

Weeks, Philip. *The American Indian Experience: A Profile, 1524 to the Present*. Arlington Heights, Ill.: Forum Press, 1988.

Provides a synthesis of contemporary scholarship on Indian-white relations from the early sixteenth century to the present. Part 1 contains essays on Indian-white relations in New France and New England from 1524 to 1701; European-Indian relations in the greater Southwest; Indian-white relations in British America, 1701-1763; Indians and the American Revolution; retreat of the western tribes; and the removal of the southern Indians. Part 2 features articles on the impact of the Civil War on Indian tribes in the trans-Mississippi West; the Plains wars;

western Indian reservation life; Indian policy under the Hayes administration; and the liquidation of the five Indian republics. Part 3 presents papers on reform policy of the late nineteenth century, attempts at Indian assimilation through education, the Indian New Deal, termination and relocation, urban Indians, and Indians since World War II. Each essay contains a list of suggested readings.

Wilkinson, Charles F. *American Indians, Time and Law: Native Societies in a Modern Constitutional Democracy*. New Haven, Conn.: Yale University Press, 1987.

Identifies four "zones of time" in Indian history, law, and politics: the pre-Columbian era of aboriginal culture and sovereignty; the period of confining Indians to reservations; the period of imposing assimilationist policies on Indians; and recent attempts of tribes to reestablish sovereignty. Attempts to understand each of these zones and their relationships to one another and to the egalitarian laws and traditions of the majority society. Argues that court decisions have tended to enforce "laws of another age in the face of compelling, pragmatic arguments that tribalism is anachronistic, antiegalitarian, and unworkable in the context of contemporary American society." Concludes by examining issues central to the constitutional status of tribes: the institutional place of tribal governments within the federal system; the implications of tribalism for the application of due process and equal protection to Indian peoples; and the tension between the promise of separate, tribally governed lands and constitutional safeguards for non-Indian peoples who lawfully enter Indian lands. Appendix: "Supreme Court Cases during the Modern Era, 1959-1986."

Willey, Gordon R., and J. A. Saboloff. *A History of American Archaeology*. San Francisco: W. H. Freeman, 1974.

Provides a history of the theory and practice of American archaeology. Identifies five major phases in this history: the Speculative Period (1492-1840), dominated by armchair thinking about the origins of the American Indian; the Classificatory-Descriptive Period (1840-1914), characterized by an emphasis on the description of archaeological materials and their rudimentary classification; the Classificatory-Historical Period (1914-1940), in which the problem of chronology took precedence; the Classificatory-Historical Period (1940-1960), which combined a new concern for the social context and function of artifacts with an interest in chronological ordering; and the Explanatory Period (1960-), marked by the emergence of the "New Archaeology" with its application of systems theory and neoevolutionism to archaeological problems and materials. Black-and-white reproductions, photographs, drawings, tables, and maps. Bibliography.

Williams, Walter L., ed. *Indian Leadership*. Manhattan, Kans.: Sunflower University Press, 1984.

A collection of case studies and overviews of twentieth century Indian leaders and leadership. The essays portray the variety of circumstances in which leaders arose, the goals toward which they strove, and the various skills underlying their influence. An editor's introduction summarizes the main themes of the volume.

Subsequent papers feature Dr. Charles Eastman (Dakota); Chief Fred Lookout (Osage); Melford Williams (Caddo); Gertrude Bonnin (Sioux); Ruth Muskrat Bronson (Cherokee); Ella Deloria (Sioux); Bob Yellow Bird (Sioux); Chippewa leaders on the White Earth reservation, 1906-1949; and Crow leadership in the late nineteenth and early twentieth centuries. The volume concludes with an extended bibliographical essay.

__________. *The Spirit and the Flesh: Sexual Diversity in American Indian Culture.* Boston: Beacon Press, 1986.

An anthropological and historical discussion of the berdache: the Native American man whose sexually ambiguous behavior and dress sets him apart from other males in his society. Part 1 describes traditional Indian perspectives on the origins, nature, and social status of the berdache. Part 2 explores changes in the berdache tradition since the coming of the European, attributing its decline to the forces of white acculturation and repression. The author nonetheless notes that not only has that tradition survived, "but knowledge of it has had a significant impact on the rise of the gay liberation movement in Western culture . . . [which] has in turn had an impact on younger contemporary Indians." Part 3 argues for a new understanding of gender and sexual variance based on berdachism and similar institutions. Bibliography. Black-and-white photographs.

Williamson, Ray A. *The Living Sky.* Boston: Houghton Mifflin, 1984.

Draws on the findings of archaeology, astronomy, ethnology, folklore, and history to portray how most Native Americans "directly associated their lives, indeed their very beings, to the sky, and to the earth." Among the subjects presented are the calendrical systems of selected tribes; the importance of the sun in Pueblo religious, social, and economic belief and practice; sun observatories of the Southwest; the astronomical significance of Plains medicine wheels; the Pawnee Ceremony of the Morning Star; sun worship among tribes in eastern North America; and astronomy and ritual among California Indians. Color and black-and-white photographs; line drawings by Snowden Hodges.

Worcester, Donald E., ed. *Forked Tongues and Broken Treaties.* Caldwell, Idaho: Caxton, 1975.

Documents how the policies of imposed treaty making, assimilationism, and termination acted to divest North American Indians of most of their homelands. Provides case studies on the Choctaw, Cherokee, Creek, Southern Cheyenne, Comanche, Teton Sioux, Blackfeet, Omaha, Klamath, Nez Percé, Apache, and eastern Pueblos. Most chapters feature maps detailing the progressive erosion of the Indian estate. A list of suggested readings accompanies each paper. More than 175 black-and-white illustrations.

Yarrow, H. C. *Introduction to the Study of Mortuary Customs Among the North American Indians.* Bureau of American Ethnology. Washington, D.C.: U.S. Government Printing Office, 1881.

Surveys the wide variety of burial observances practiced by Native North Americans. Forms described are inhumation (interment in the ground), burial in stone graves and cistern, burial in mounds and in caves, mummification, partial and full cremation, scaffold burials, burial in boxes and canoes; and aquatic burial. A number of rites accompanying burials are also discussed.

References

Abler, Thomas S., and Sally M. Weaver. *A Canadian Indian Bibliography, 1960-1970*. Toronto: University of Toronto Press, 1974.

An annotated listing of resources pertaining to Canadian Indians and Métis. Part 1 surveys materials on Native society and culture published between 1960 and 1970. Subject areas include bibliographies, general and comparative studies, legislation (bills and acts), Indian administration and government policy, history, demography, material culture, education, economics, social organization, politics and law, medicine, religion, oral tradition and folklore, music and dance, and urban. Part 2 features a case law digest covering the period 1867 to 1972. Organized by the culture areas of Subarctic, Northwest Coast, Plateau, Plains, Eastern Woodlands, and Métis, with subheadings for different bands. Indexes for the bibliography and case law digest. Two maps.

Allen, Robert S. *Native Studies in Canada: A Research Guide*. Ottawa: Treaties and Historical Research Center, 1989.

Intended for use by students, researchers, and others engaged in studies related to Canada's native peoples. Chapter 1 presents a province-by-province listing of universities offering Canadian Native studies programs and courses. Chapter 2 provides brief descriptions of five major Canadian Native associations: Assembly of First Nations, Native Council of Canada, Inuit Tapirisat of Canada, Native Women's Association of Canada, and National Association of Friendship Centres. Chapter 3 lists many of Canada's Native studies-related resource centers. Contained in chapters 4 and 5 are select bibliographies on Canadian Native peoples and comparative Native studies.

American Indian Historical Society. *Textbooks and the American Indian*. San Francisco: Indian Historian Press, 1970.

Presents the assessments of thirty-two Indian scholars on the portrayal of Native American history and cultures contained in more than three hundred primary and high school textbooks. The categories of texts reviewed include American history and geography, state and regional history, government and citizenship, American Indians, and world history and geography. Evaluations of the books in each category were based on nine general criteria as well as varying numbers of category-specific standards. Conclusions: "Not one [of the textbooks] could be approved as a dependable source of knowledge about the history and culture of Indian people in America. Most of the books were, in one way or another, derogatory to the Native Americans. Most contained misinformation, distortions, or omissions of important history." Bibliography.

Bantin, Philip C. *Guide to Catholic Indian Mission and School Records in Midwest Repositories*. Milwaukee: Marquette University Press, 1984.

Surveys the unpublished records of Catholic Indian missions and schools found in 277 institutions in twelve midwestern states. Entries are arranged alphabetically first by state, then city, and finally by the name of the institution or religious order. Each citation includes a chronology of a specified mission, school, or religious community; a description and analysis of its holdings; and its address, telephone number, hours, use policy, and copying facilities. Index.

Barrow, Mark V., et al., comps. *Health and Disease of American Indians North of Mexico: A Bibliography, 1800-1969*. Gainesville: University of Florida Press, 1972.

A listing of nearly 1500 publications on issues related to health and disease among Native North Americans, including those living in Canada and the Arctic. Entries are arranged chronologically under twenty-two categories. Indexed by author, disease subject, and tribe.

Bataille, Gretchen M., and Charles L. P. Silet. *Images of American Indians on Film: An Annotated Bibliography*. New York: Garland, 1985.

Seeks to aid research on how the movie industry portrays Native American peoples. The bibliographical entries are listed under four sections. The first cites books and articles concerned with the dominant culture's understanding of Indian peoples. Section 2 includes general studies on the image of Indians in film. The third section contains reviews and essays of selected movies. Section 4 lists titles, dates, running times, directors, and casts of films in which Indians are among the major characters. A historical introduction overviews and assesses how films have depicted Indians. Illustrated with black-and-white movie stills.

Beaver, R. Pierce. *The Native American Church Community: A Directory of Indian, Aleut, and Eskimo Churches*. Monrovia, Calif.: Mission Advanced Residence and Communications Center, 1979.

Provides information on the number and distribution of Indian, Aleut, and Eskimo Christian communities in the United States and Canada. Begins with a summary of the historical, social, political, and demographic factors important to an understanding of Native Christian communities in the 1970's. Next lists the denominational and nondenominational agencies, ministries, societies, and churches active among North American native groups. Listings include addresses, telephone numbers, membership, and affiliations of organizations as relevant. Additional chapters on Native American urban churches; councils, service organizations, and educational ministries; and church population reports. Tables.

Boas, Franz. *Handbook for American Indian Languages*. 3 pts. Bureau of American Ethnology, Bulletin 40. Washington, D.C.: U.S. Government Printing Office, 1911.

An early survey of Native American languages. An extended introduction by Boas presents the theoretical and methodological principles underlying his approach to anthropological linguistics. He also suggests some of the defining characteristics of American Indian languages. Subsequent chapters feature analyses by various experts on particular languages or language families. These include Athapaskan, Tlingit, Haida, Tsimshian, Kwakiutl, Chinook, Maidu, Algonquian (Fox), Siouan, Eskimo, Takelma, Coos, Siuslawan, Chukchee, Tonkowa, Quileute, Yuchi, Zuni, and Coeur d'Alene.

Brigham Young University. *Bibliography of Nonprint Instructional Materials on the American Indian*. Provo, Utah: Brigham Young University Printing Service, 1972.

Nearly fifteen hundred annotated entries for nontext educational materials on Native American history and culture. Includes listings for 16-millimeter motion pictures, 8-millimeter film loops, filmstrips, 35-millimeter slides, overhead transparencies, study prints, maps, charts, audio recordings, and multimedia kits. Citations are alphabetically arranged by title. Subject heading index, subject index, addendum, and distributors index.

Brown, George, and Ron Maguire. *Indian Treaties in Historical Perspective*. Ottawa: Research Branch, Department of Indian and Northern Affairs, 1979.

A general overview of Indian treaty activity in Canada and a resource for study. Part 1 presents a chronological sequence of significant events in Canadian Indian-white relations, 1497-1978. Part 2 lists Indian treaties and grants, 1680-1929, including dates, parties involved, and the areas affected. A concluding essay discusses the premises and historical background of treaty making, then traces treaty activity in the Canadian provinces.One chart and one map.

Brumble, H. David. *An Annotated Bibliography of American Indian and Eskimo Autobiographies*. Lincoln: University of Nebraska Press, 1981.

Lists all published first-person narratives by Native Americans and Eskimos, with some entries for autobiographical materials in manuscript and on tape. An introductory essay briefly considers theoretical issues involved in the classification and evaluation of such autobiographies. The author suggests that "whatever else the American Indian autobiographies may be, they are the record—and to some degree the means—of a people's "move from pre-literacy to an awareness that a self might, perhaps ought to, be unique." Index of editors, anthropologists, ghosts, and amanuenses; index of tribes; subject index.

Clements, William M., and Frances M. Malpezzi. *Native American Folklore, 1879-1979: An Annotated Bibliography*. Athens, Ohio: Swallow Press, 1984.

Cites and annotates more than five thousand books and articles pertaining to American Indian folklore which have appeared since the "birth" of Native American studies in 1879. Defines folklore as the texts and performance of such verbal arts as myths, legends, tales, proverbs, riddles, and ballads and songs. Except for a section on general works, the sources are categorized by tribe within the following culture areas: Northeast, Southeast, Midwest, Plains, Southwest, Great Basin, California, Northwest Coast, Plateau, Subarctic, and Arctic. The annotations tend to be brief and stress description over evaluation.

Coe, Michael, et al. *Atlas of Ancient America*. New York: Facts on File, 1986.

Offers archaeological reconstructions for the lifeways of specified culture areas and groups in prehistoric North America, Mesoamerica, and South America. Fifty-six highly detailed maps present the key environmental features, historical events, and cultural achievements for selected geographical areas. Numerous insets use colorful plates and drawings to illustrate materials from important sites. A chronological table documents the continuity and change of Indian cultures in the Americas from 20,000 B.C. through the twentieth century. An introductory section describes the migrations of Indians to the American continents, their European discovery and conquest, and the rise of New World archaeology. Concludes with a discussion of the surviving inheritance from ancient America.

Cohen, Felix. *Felix Cohen's Handbook of Federal Indian Law*. 2d ed. Charlottesville, Va.: Michie/Bobbs-Merrill, 1982.

An update of Cohen's 1942 synthesis of federal Indian law. Retains Cohen's articulation of the central principles of Indian law: "Indian tribes are political bodies with retained powers of self-government; the United States has broad authority over Indian affairs; the federal government has a trust obligation to Indians, resulting in the protection of tribal self-government from state incursions, the protection of Indian property interests, and the provision of services and programs; and Indian tribes and individuals are entitled to be free of invidious discrimination under federal and state laws." Chapter topics include the field of Indian law; a history of Indian policy; the source and scope of federal authority in Indian affairs; the source and scope of state authority in Indian affairs; jurisdiction; taxation; hunting, fishing, and gathering rights; tribal property; water rights; individual property; civil rights; government services to Indians; and special groups. Tables of statutes and cases.

Colonnese, Tom, and Louis Owens. *American Indian Novelists: An Annotated Critical Bibliography*. New York: Garland, 1985.

Attempts to include works by all novelists who "share in common the quality of both considering themselves and being considered by their communities as American Indians by heritage." Focuses primarily on novels and their criticism, though also cites a selection of the shorter works of each author. Included are Paula Gunn Allen, Denton R. Bedford, Dallas Chief Eagle, Janet Campbell Hale, Jamake Highwater, Hum-Ishu-Ma (Mourning Dove), D'Arcy McNickle, Markoosie, John Joseph Mathews, N. Scott Momaday, Nasnaga (Roger Russell), John Milton Oskison, Chief George Pierre, Simon Pokagon, Leslie Marmon Silko, Virginia Driving Hawk Sneve, Hyemeyohsts Storm, John William Tebbel, James Tucker, Gerald Vizenor, and James Welch. Supplies a brief biography of each writer. An introduction briefly describes the coming of age of the Indian novel.

Confederation of American Indians, comp. *Indian Reservations: A State and Federal Handbook*. Jefferson, N.C.: McFarland, 1986.

Descriptions, alphabetically arranged by state, of U.S. Indian reservations. Most entries provide information on the following topics: land status, history, culture(s), government, population profile, tribal economy, climate, utilities, and recreational facilities.

Danky, James P., ed., and Maureen E. Hady, comp. *Native American Periodicals and Newspapers, 1828-1982: Bibliography, Publishing Records, and Holdings.* Westport, Conn.: Greenwood Press, 1984.

A listing of nearly twelve hundred magazines and newspapers by and about American Indians. Includes serials still in publication (as of 1982) as well as those no longer in circulation.

Dawdy, Doris O., comp. *Annotated Bibliography of American Indian Painting.* Contributions from the Museum of the American Indian, Heye Foundation, vol. 21, pt. 2. New York: Museum of the American Indian, Heye Foundation, 1968.

An annotated listing of published works on contemporary Native American painters and painting. Encompasses the period since Indians discovered "that they could paint with white men's tools and materials." Entries are arranged alphabetically by author. Descriptions vary in length from one to several lines. A brief historical overview precedes the bibliography.

Dennis, Henry C., comp. and ed. *The American Indian, 1492-1976: A Chronology and Fact Book.* Dobbs Ferry, N.Y.: Oceana, 1977.

Intended as a ready reference to events significant for their effects on the lives of Native Americans and, increasingly, on the conscience of America. Each entry is dated and accompanied by a brief description. Additional sections present biographical sketches of some prominent Indian figures of the past and a random sampling of contemporary Indians and their activities. Nine appendices: "Population," "Indian Wars and Local Disturbances," "U.S. Administrators of Federal Indian Policy," "Government Appropriations for Indian Education," "Indian Museums," "A Few Indian Groups" (that is, organizations), "Some Indian Publications," "A Few Audio-Visual Suggestions," "A Reading and Research Bibliography." Index to indian tribes and prominent leaders.

Dobyns, Henry F. *Native American Historical Demography: A Critical Bibliography.* Newberry Library Center for the History of the American Indian Bibliographical Series. Bloomington: Indiana University Press, 1976.

A bibliographic essay that discusses 217 reliable sources and studies dealing with the population statistics and dynamics of Native North America. Headings include peopling the continent; proto-historic population; history of epidemics; endemic diseases, warfare, and famine; depopulation trends; population recovery; and demographic case studies. Lists of recommended works for the beginner and for a basic library collection. Items suitable for secondary school students are indicated with an asterisk.

Dockstader, Frederick J., comp. *The American Indian in Graduate Studies: A Bibliography of Theses and Dissertations.* 2d ed. Contributions from the Museum of the American Indian, Heye Foundation. vol. 25, pt. 1. New York: Museum of the American Indian, Heye Foundation, 1973.

Lists 3684 theses and dissertations on the American Indian written between 1890 and 1955 by students at 203 colleges and universities in the United States, Canada, and Mexico. Works from all academic fields are represented. Selection based solely on the inclusion of Indian subject matter in at least one chapter, either by specific section or in passim. The compiler warns that the "value of these studies varies tremendously. Some are probably worthless, either because of outdating, third-hand source material, or duplication of topic ad infinitum. Many, however, are excellent—and some contain surprising amounts of original information." Entries arranged alphabetically by author. One- or two-line annotations appear sporadically throughout the bibliography.

__________. *Great North American Indians: Profiles in Life and Leadership*. New York: Van Nostrand Reinhold, 1977.

An alphabetically arranged collection of three hundred of "the most sought-after Indian biographies from North America." Attempts to portray the importance of these individuals on the basis of Native American rather than white criteria. Includes black-and-white reproductions of painted portraits, photographs, and drawings. Bibliography.

Dockstader, Frederick J., and Alice W. Dockstader. *The American Indian in Graduate Studies: A Bibliography of Theses and Dissertations*. Contributions from the Museum of the American Indian, Heye Foundation. vol. 35, pt. 2. New York: Museum of the American Indian, Heye Foundation, 1974.

A supplement to the 1973 volume containing 3787 additional titles. Utilizes the same criteria of selection as part 1.

Ebeling, Walter. *Handbook of Indian Foods and Fibers of Arid America*. Berkeley: University of California Press, 1986.

A summary of multidisciplinary research on plants and animals that were used as sources of food and fibers by native peoples living in the arid regions of North America. Emphasis on various modes of resource exploitation, the contribution of particular plants and animals to tribal diets and cultures, and the relation of subsistence patterns to other aspects of social life. Coverage for the period predating human habitation on the continent through historic times "as long as native cultures remained relatively unchanged." Sections on the first Americans, the Great Basin, Owens Valley, California, the lower Colorado River basin, the U.S. Southwest, and Mexico. An appendix provides a tabular listing of plant species Indians used for food and/or fiber, regions in which they occurred, how they were used, and where some are illustrated in the book. Glossary. Bibliography of literature cited. Black-and-white reproductions, photographs, and drawings. Maps, charts, and tables.

Evans, G. Edward, and Jeffrey Clark. *North American Indian Language Materials, 1890-1965*. Los Angeles: American Indian Studies Center, University of California, Los Angeles, 1980.

An annotated update of the nine bibliographies that James C. Pilling compiled for the Bureau of American Ethnology. Includes "all dictionaries, grammars, orthographies, primers, readers, and the like concerning those Native American languages whose main province lay north of the Mexican border." Entries also for comparative grammars and dictionaries of stems appearing in scientific publications. Works listed in alphabetical order by author or title under primary language treated. Annotations are descriptive and offer no evaluations of the works cited.

Fenton, William N., et al. *American Indian and White Relations to 1830: Needs and Opportunities for Study*. Chapel Hill: University of North Carolina Press, 1957.

A resource intended for use by both scientists and humanists whose research concerns Indian-white relations up to the early nineteenth century. Begins with an essay by Fenton on how the methods of ethnology and history might be profitably combined to form "ethno-history." The bibliography that follows includes subheadings for references and bibliographical aids, ethnological literature, historical literature (before 1850/after 1850), serials, manuscript sources, documentary publications, and special topics (portraiture; literature, songs, and art; biography and autobiography; captivities; missions and education; government policy; the Indian in literature and thought).

Folsom, Franklin, and Mary Folsom. *America's Ancient Treasure*. 3d rev. ed. Chicago: Rand McNally, and Company, 1974.

Lists all museums of Native American prehistory and archaeological sites north of Mexico that have been prepared for public visit. Listings organized by state within the culture areas of the Southwest, Great Basin, Northwest, Great Plains, Southeast, North Central, and Northeast. Each section features an introduction to the prehistory of the area followed by insets that discuss its most significant cultural features and artifacts. Illustrated with black-and-white drawings, photographs, and reproductions of paintings and dioramas. Bibliography.

Frazier, Gregory W. *The American Indian Index: A Directory of Indian Country, USA*, edited by Randolph J. Punley. Denver, Colo.: Arrowstar, 1985.

Intended for those seeking facts on contemporary Indians and Indian country. Chapters include "Census Information"; "Federally Recognized Indian Tribes"; "Alaska Native Corporations—Regional Corporations/Village Corporations"; "Other Indian Tribes and Groups"; "Indian Interest Organizations and Groups—National Indian Organizations/Indian Special Interest Groups"; "Bureau of Indian Affairs Office—Headquarters/Area and Agency Offices"; "State Indian Commissions"; "Indian Education Projects—Indian Education Act Grantees (Title IV A)"; "Indian Boarding Schools"; "Indian Colleges"; "Indian Housing Authorities"; "Indian Employment Programs"; "Reservation Based Service Programs—Indian Alcoholism Programs, Indian Child Welfare Programs"; "Urban and Off-Reservation Service Programs—Urban Indian Social Service Projects, Urban Indian Health Contractors"; "Indian Publications"; "Museums and Cultural Centers"; "Pow-Wow and Events"; and "Arts and Crafts Directory."

Getches, David H., and Charles F. Wilkinson. *Cases and Materials on Federal Indian Law*. 2d ed. St. Paul, Minn.: West, 1986.

An overview of the legal status of Native Americans and a sourcebook of cases pertaining to various aspects of that status. Chapter 1 provides a sketch of Native Americans today and perspectives on Indian law. Chapters 2 through 13 present decisions relating to the following areas: the history of federal policy toward American Indians; the federal-tribal relationship; tribal sovereignty, federal supremacy, and states' rights; the jurisdictional framework; criminal jurisdiction; civil court jurisdiction; tax and regulatory jurisdiction; the rights of individual Indians; tribal economic development; water rights; fishing and hunting rights; and the frontiers of Indian law. The body of the book is preceded by an introduction entitled "The Study of Indian Law," a summary of contents, and a table of cases.

Green, Rayna. *Native American Women: A Contextual Bibliography*. Bloomington: Indiana University Press, 1983.

Lists and evaluates 672 books, articles, films, government reports, and dissertations by or about Native American women as members of groups or as individuals. In a lengthy introductory essay, the author comments that her review of the literature has left her "with the conviction that Native women have been neither neglected nor forgotten. They have captured hearts and minds, but, as studies of other women have demonstrated, the level and substance of most passion for them has been selective, stereotyped, and damaging." Includes a date index and a subject index.

Griffiths, Curt T., and Linda F. Weafer. *Native North Americans: Crime, Conflict, and Criminal Justice*. 2d ed. Burnaby, British Columbia: Criminology Research Centre, Simon Fraser University and the Northern Conference, 1984.

A comprehensive listing of research materials on "native Indian crime and delinquency and the extensive involvement of native Indians at all stages of the criminal justice system in Canada and the United States." Citations are arranged by subject area. Subject headings include Native American bibliographies, Native Indian organizations, Native Indian contemporary studies, Native Indian jurisdictional issues and civil rights, Native Indian crime and delinquency, Native Indians and the criminal justice system, Native Indians and the police, Native Indians and the courts, Native Indians and corrections, Native Indian adult parole and probation, Native Indian health and welfare, Native Indians and alcohol, Native Indians and drugs, Native Indian juvenile programs and services, Native Indians and suicide, and Native Indians and education. Author and year indexes.

Haas, Marilyn L. *Indians of North America: Sources for Library Research*. Hamden, Conn.: Library Professional Publications, 1983.

Provides a list of significant resources on selected areas of Native American studies. Part 1 presents the major tools and techniques of modern library research including reference works, abstracts, on-line data bases, directories, government documents and archives, catalogues, and classification systems. Part 2 contains an annotated bibliography, alphabetically arranged by subject. Subjects include agriculture, alcohol, anthropology, archaeology, art, artifacts, authors (Indian), autobiography and biography, bows and arrows, Canada, captivities, cooking, crafts, dance, education, folklore, games, genealogy, health and medicine, history, journalism, land, language, law, libraries, literature, missions, motion pictures, music, religion, sociology, treaties, urban indians, war, and women. Part 3 offers an unannotated bibliography for specific tribes.

Hargrett, Lester. *Bibliography of the Constitution and Laws of the American Indian*. Cambridge, Mass.: Harvard University Press, 1947.

Presents annotated citations for 225 publications that reproduce the constitutions, statutes, session acts, and resolutions of authorized bodies of formerly self-governing Indian peoples living in the present- day United States. According to the introduction by John Swanton, "All the documents represent efforts by, or for, the tribes in question to adjust them to those new conditions brought about by European intrusion." The resources are organized according to tribe and are introduced by brief political histories of the groups to which they pertain. Included are the Cherokee, Chickasaw, Choctaw, Creek, Nez Percé, Omaha, Osage, Ottawa, Sac and Fox, Seminole, Seneca, "State of Sequoyah," Stockbridge and Munsee, and Winnebago. Includes "Chronology of Principal Events." An appendix reproduces Thomas Jefferson's letter of January 9, 1809, to the Cherokee Deputies. Ten black-and-white plates.

Harris, R. Cole, ed. *Historical Atlas of Canada: From the Beginning to 1800*. Toronto: University of Toronto Press, 1987.

A Canadian history, in maps and text, covering the period between the late Wisconsinan glacial maximum (18,000-10,000 B.C.) and A.D. 1800. Section 1 outlines Canada's prehistory and presents a summary of Canadian populations and economies in the early historic period. Sections 2 and 3 contain regional histories of the Atlantic realm and Inland territories. Among the stated biases of the editor are an emphasis on the economic and social circumstances of ordinary life rather than geopolitical events and their consequences, more attention to Atlantic Canada and the West than is common in most general analyses of early Canada, and an attempt to give full place to native peoples. Contains more than one hundred color maps; graphs, tables, drawings.

Harvey, Cecil, comp. *Agriculture of the American Indian: A Select Bibliography*. Bibliographies and Literature of Agriculture 4. Washington, D.C.: Science and Education Administration, Technical Information Systems, Economic, Statistical, and Cooperative Services, National Economics Division, U.S. Department of Agriculture, 1979.

An update of *Bibliography on the Agriculture of the American Indians* by Everett E. Edwards and Wayne B. Rasmussen published in 1941. The first section lists historical, anthropological, and bibliographical references dealing with Native American agriculture. Section 2 cites works on the agriculture of particular culture areas. Their culture areas include Mesoamerica (Aztec-Maya); Canada; the Southwest, Northeast, Southeast, Northwest, Great Lakes, Plains, and California of the United States; and South America. Subsequent sections contain literature on Native American crops, livestock, agriculture on Indian reservations in the United States and Canada, uncultivated crops, and irrigation.

Hawthorn, Harry, ed. *A Survey of the Contemporary Indians of Canada*. 2 vols. Ottawa: Queen's Printer, 1966-1967.

An analysis and evaluation of the condition of Canadian Indians commissioned in the mid-1960's by the minister of the Department of Citizenship and Immigration. The object of the report's analysis and its recommendations is "to find courses of action which will be profitable for the Indian and to improve his position to choose and decide among them." Part 1 offers an examination of those conditions and programs that are primarily economic, political, and administrative. Part 2 treats issues of education and the internal organization of reserves. A list of recommendations addressing general considerations, economic development, federal provincial relations, welfare, and local government accompanies the report.

Heth, Charlotte, and Susan Guyette. *Issues for the Future of American Indian Studies*. Los Angeles: American Indian Center, 1984.

States as its purposes to identify graduate and undergraduate level programs (current and planned) for American Indian students; to determine the needs of American Indian/Alaskan learners for culturally appropriate educational programs; to assess Indian communities to determine the need for trained professionals; and to identify the *gaps* between the training now available and the needs of the communities in an effort to design more culturally appropriate educational programs. Part 1 presents the results of three nationwide surveys on needs assessment for American Indian higher education. Part 2 is a directory, organized by state, of American Indian studies and support programs. Bibliographical essay.

Hilger, Michael. *The American Indian in Film*. Metuchen, N.J.: Scarecrow Press, 1986.

Annotated entries for more than eight hundred films in which American Indians play a significant role in terms of character or plot. Films are arranged chronologically "to illustrate the development and sometimes strange mixture of images and themes in the historical periods." These periods include the silent films, the early sound films, films of the 1950's and 1960's, and films of the 1970's and 1980's. The annotations describe the place of Indians in the overall plots of the movies. A conclusion briefly examines film technique in relation to the fictionalized Indian of cinema. Bibliography. Name and topical indexes.

Hill, Edward E., comp. *Guide to the Records of the National Archives of the United States Relating to American Indians*. Washington, D.C.: National Archives and Records Service, 1981.

Seeks to aid the researcher in locating materials on Native Americans and Indian-white relations which are housed in the National Archives of the United States. The records described are primarily for tribes under the supervision of the Bureau of Indian Affairs or in military conflict with the federal government.

Hirschfelder, Arlene B. *American Indian and Eskimo Authors: A Comprehensive Bibliography*. New York: Association on American Indian Affairs, 1973.

An annotated list of works by nearly three hundred Indian and Eskimo writers from more than one hundred tribes. The first section groups the authors by tribal affiliation. The entries are alphabetically arranged by author. Each includes the title of the work, publisher, place and date of publication, number of pages, price, and availability in paperback edition. Lists the addresses of the publishers cited.

____________. *American Indian Stereotypes in the World of Children: A Reader and Bibliography*. Metuchen, N.J.: Scarecrow Press, 1982.

Purpose is "to try and shock adults into realizing that the world of contemporary American infants and young children is saturated with inappropriate images of Indians." Part 1, a reader, offers essays on children's stereotypes and impressions of American Indians, the Plains Indian as the symbol of the North American Indian, Indian authors for young people, misrepresentations and distortions of Native American history and culture in textbooks, and misuse of Indian images in toys and as mascots. Part 2 provides an annotated bibliography of books and articles that deal with the stereotyping of Native Americans as well as materials that can be used to combat these stereotypes. Indexes for both reader and bibliography.

____________. *Annotated Bibliography of the Literature on American Indians Published in State Historical Society Publications: New England and Middle Atlantic States*. Milwood, N.Y.: Kraus Reprint, 1982.

Contains nearly 1,200 annotated entries for primary and secondary materials by or about Native Americans found in the publications of thirteen state historical societies of the New England and Middle Atlantic regions. The societies include Connecticut Historical Society, Historical Society of Delaware, Historical Society of Pennsylvania, Maine Historical Society, Maryland Historical Society, Massachusetts Historical Society, New Hampshire Historical Society, New Jersey Historical Society, New York Historical Society, New York State Historical Association, Pennsylvania Historical Association, Rhode Island Historical Society, and Vermont Historical Society. Three indexes: subjects; person, places, and titles; and Indian nations. Three illustrations.

____________, et al. *Guide to Research on North American Indians*. Chicago: American Library Association, 1983.

Annotated citations for approximately eleven hundred written materials dealing with Native North Americans. Part 1, "Introductory Materials," contains entries for general sources and studies. Part 2, "History and Historical Sources," lists materials relating to geography and cartography, archaeology and prehistory, descriptive narratives, autobiographies and biographies, land tenure and resources, political organization, federal and state Indian relations, and histories. Part 3, "Economic and Social Aspects," carries listings for population and demography; health, medicine, and disease; subsistence patterns; economic aspects; architecture and housing; warfare patterns; social organization; urban life; physical characteristics; and language. The concluding part, "Religion, Arts, and Literature," includes works categorized under religion and philosophy, music and dance, education, arts, science, law, and literature. Each part is introduced by a bibliographical essay. Author-title and subject indexes.

Hodge, Frederick W., ed. *Handbook of American Indians North of Mexico*. 2 vols. Washington, D.C.: U.S. Government Printing Office, 1907-1910.

A classic compendium of ethnographic, archaeological, historical, linguistic, and biographical information on Native North Americans and Eskimos. Important not only for a resource on Indian cultures but for how anthropologists of the time described and analyzed these cultures. Alphabetically arranged listings. Where appropriate, bibliographies are provided. Profusely illustrated with plates and drawings. Available in reprint form.

Hodge, William, comp. *A Bibliography of Contemporary North American Indians*. New York: Interland, 1976.

Cites materials on contemporary Indian life which meet one or more of the following criteria: "1) They have not been published, e.g. state and federal reports such as committee hearings, position papers, procedural guides, tribal government documents, etc.; 2) For one or a combination of reasons, they have not been widely circulated; 3) They contain significant amounts of ethnographic data which also have immediate implications for important theoretical questions now current within the society sciences; 4) Their chief focus is upon current Indian activity." Among the twenty-seven chapter headings are "Anthropologists and Indians," "History-Overview," "Contemporary American Indian Images—Professional Indians of Various Kinds," "Material Culture," "Social Organization," "Reservation/Rural Areas as Communities," "City Living," "Linguistics," "Economics," "Formal Education," "Music-Dance," "Religion," "Health-Disease-Poverty." Provides study guides for Indian life prior to 1875 and contemporary American Indians.

Horr, David A., comp. and ed. *American Indian Ethnohistory*. 118 vols. New York: Garland, 1974.

A multivolume presentation of evidence solicited by the U.S. Indian Claims Commission between 1946 and 1978 for mediating questions of Native American land title and use. Includes volumes for tribes of California and Basin-Plateau, Northwest, Southwest, North Central and Northeastern regions, Plains, and South and Southeastern regions. Introductory materials on tribes and the commission's proceedings accompany the volumes. Maps present the location of the tribes as of 1950 as well as estimates of their original range.

Indian Historian Press. *Index to Literature on the American Indian*. 4 vols. San Francisco: Author, 1970-1973.

Entries for periodical literature, texts, and books pertaining to Native North Americans. The entries are alphabetically arranged by author and subject.

Jelks, Edward B., ed. *Historical Dictionary of North American Archaeology*. Westport, Conn.: Greenwood Press, 1988.

A compendium of more than eighteen hundred entries that provide information on the major prehistoric peoples, sites, and artifact types of North America. Most entries for sites include their locations, dates of discovery, excavation, the peoples who occupied them, and functions. Entries for cultures, traditions, phases, and so on typically include their characteristic features and spatiotemporal distributions as well as those archaeologists most important to their categorization and study. Length of entries varies from a few lines to several pages. Represents the collective effort of 151 specialists in selected areas of North American prehistory. Bibliography.

Johnson, Steven L. *Guide to American Indian Documents in the Congressional Series Set, 1817-1899*. New York: Clearwater, 1977.

Lists the more than 10,000 documents relating to American Indians found in the Congressional Serial List prior to 1900. Arranges these documents in chronological order. Each entry contains the title and date of the document; a document citation that includes the document series, the document number, the Congress and session, the volume in which the document is printed, the number of pages in the document, and the serial number of the volume in which the document is to be found; and a description of the contents. Three appendices: "Entries from Poore's Catalogue Not in the Serial Set," "The American State Papers on Indian Affairs," "Records of the War of the Rebellion." Subject index.

Kapplar, Charles. *Indian Affairs: Laws and Treaties*. 2 vols. Washington, D.C.: U.S. Government Printing Office, 1904-1941.

A compilation of treaties, laws, executive orders, and other materials relating to U.S. Indian affairs from the organization of the nation to 1938. Volume 1 contains the text of permanent general laws relating to Indian affairs, permanent acts relative to particular tribes, and executive orders relative to Indians on reserves and proclamations. Volume 2 reprints ratified treaties between the federal government and Indian tribes from 1778 to 1883.

Kelso, Dianne R., and Carolyn L. Attneave, comps. *Bibliography of North American Indian Mental Health*. Westport, Conn.: Greenwood Press, 1981.

Cites studies that explore subjects related to the mental health of North American Indians, Aleuts, Eskimos, and Métis. Defines mental health as "a continuum of states and behaviors ranging from the vigorous and healthy to the pathological." Citations for articles, unpublished research reports, government documents, doctoral dissertations, and papers from professional meetings.

Klein, Barry T., ed. *Reference Encyclopedia of the American Indian*. 2 vols. 4th ed. New York: Todd, 1986.

Volume 1 provides an alphabetically and alphageographically arranged listing for organizations, associations, government agencies, reservation and tribal councils, museums and library collections, Indian health service, Indian schools, university and college offerings, magazines and periodicals, and audiovisual material. Listings include addresses, telephone numbers, chief personnel, and other pertinent information. Also contains bibliographies arranged alphabetically by title, subject, and publisher for more than 3500 books in print about or relating to Indians of North America. Volume 2 presents an alphabetically and alphageographically arranged "Who's Who" of Indians and non-Indians prominent in organizations, areas of study, and professions related to contemporary Native American life.

Krech, Shepard, III. *Native Canadian Anthropology and History: A Selective Bibliography*. Winnipeg: Rupert's Land Research Centre, University of Winnipeg, 1986.

A listing of more than two thousand primary and secondary sources on native peoples of Canada. The entries are organized in nineteen sections grouped in three parts. Part 1 includes citations for reference materials, comparative analyses, and historical materials. Part 2 contains sections for various tribal groups. Part 3 includes headings for various topics of interest to contemporary researchers and students.

Lamar, Howard R., ed. *The Reader's Encyclopedia of the American West*. New York: Thomas Y. Crowell, 1977.

Contains 2400 alphabetically arranged entries on people, places, and themes of significance to the history of the American West. Many of the entries are specifically concerned with Indian tribes, leaders, history, and culture. Others provide information helpful for understanding the development of Indian-white relations from the sixteenth through the twentieth centuries. Black-and-white illustrations.

La Polin, Armand S., ed. *Native American Voluntary Organizations*. Westport, Conn.: Greenwood Press, 1987.

Seeks to "assist scholars and students of Native American studies in understanding the development of non-tribal organizations, including the important role that they played in the history of Anglo-American Indian relations; and to provide the general reader with current groups that serve the needs of Native Americans." An introduction supplies a historic overview of the origins, structures, and functions of Native American voluntary associations. The body of the book presents an alphabetically arranged listing of defunct and extant voluntary associations with summaries of their histories, membership, and goals. Two appendices: one classifies the associations according to their functions, the other offers a chronological list of organizations and key historical events.

Lee, Dorothy S. *Native North American Music and Oral Data*. Bloomington: Indiana University Press, 1979.

Catalogues the sound recordings of North American Indian music and oral data housed at the Indiana University Archives of Traditional Music. Citations include the following data (where applicable): collector, deposition, editor, performer; accession number; culture group; culture area; year recorded; medium of recording; recording company and issue number; degree of public access; length and quality of recording; archives tape library number; quality of documentation provided by recorder; and subject description. Indexed by culture group and subject.

Leitch, Barbara. *A Concise Dictionary of Indian Tribes of North America*. Algonac, Mich.: Reference Publications, 1979.

Includes information on the cultures, languages, religions, and ethnic and postcontact histories of nearly three hundred Native North American peoples. Maps for language groups, culture groups, Indian lands, and communities in the

United States. Regional maps of the Northeast, Southeast, Plateau-Basin-Plains, West Coast, Northwest Coast, Mackenzie-Yukon, and Arctic Coast. Introduction by Vine Deloria, Jr. Black-and-white illustrations.

Littlefield, Daniel F., Jr., and James W. Parin. *American Indian and Alaskan Native Newspapers and Periodicals, 1826-1924*. Westport, Conn.: Greenwood Press, 1984.

An alphabetically arranged listing of Native North American newspapers and periodicals, except those published in Canada. Includes both serials "edited or published by American Indians or Alaskan Natives and those whose primary purpose was to publish information about *contemporary* Indians."

__________. *A Biobibliography of Native American Writers, 1772-1924*. Metuchen, N.J.: Scarecrow Press, 1981.

Cites more than four thousand works by Native North Americans (excluding those of Canada) written in or translated into English between 1772 and 1924. Includes pieces either purposely composed for public consumption or which later found their way into print. Part 1 lists works by authors for whom there exists corroborating evidence of Indian descent. Part 2 contains writings of those known only by pen name. Part 3 presents biographical sketches of the authors.

__________. *A Biobibliography of Native American Writers, 1772-1924: Supplement*. Metuchen, N.J.: Scarecrow Press, 1981.

Utilizes the same format as the original. Supplies more than three thousand additional citations.

Lobb, Michael L., and Thomas D. Watts. *Native American Youth and Alcohol: An Annotated Bibliography*. Westport, Conn.: Greenwood Press, 1989.

Lists published works from all disciplines having relevance to the subject of alcoholism among Native American youth. Unlike the older literature, which was basically anchored in anthropology, the editors see the emerging literature on the subject as more interdisciplinary in nature. Subject headings include accidental death, biomedical factors, crime, etiology, gender, policy and prevention, reservations, sociological factors, suicide, treatment, and urban versus rural. Subject and author indexes.

Lyndon, James G. *Struggle for Empire: A Bibliography of the French and Indian War*. New York: Garland, 1986.

Lists more than fifteen hundred primary and secondary sources in English, French, and Spanish on the French and Indian War (1756-1763). The entries in part 1 are arranged by the following topics: general references; military aspects; naval aspects; diplomatic relations; government; Indian relations; military organizations; forts and topography; captivities; culture and war; religious aspects; and biographies, memoirs, letters, and papers. The listings in part 2 are organized by the following geographical divisions: New France, Maritime Provinces, New England theatre, war in New York, Pennsylvania theatre, war in the South, Florida and Louisiana, West Indian theatre. Includes citations for filmstrips, microfilms, and cassettes. Author and subject indexes.

Mail, Patricia D., and David R. McDonald, comps. *Tulapai to Tokay: A Bibliography of Alcohol Use and Abuse Among Native Americans of North America*. New Haven, Conn.: Human Relations Area File Press, 1980.

Annotated citations for nearly one thousand published and unpublished materials concerned with alcohol consumption and addiction among Native North Americans. Entries arranged alphabetically by author. An introductory essay reviews the literature on Indian alcohol use. The compilers offer the following explanation of the book's title: "Tulapai . . . was an alcoholic beverage made originally by the Apaches. Tokay, an inexpensive wine, is frequently consumed by contemporary Native Americans. The title, *Tulapai to Tokay*, symbolizes the changes that have occurred over time in the pattern of alcohol use among Native Americans, and reflects the historical range of alcohol use among them."

Marken, Jack W. *The American Indian: Language and Literature*. Arlington Heights, Ill.: AHM Publishing, 1978.

More than 3500 listings for publications by Native North American authors or about Indian languages and literatures. Entries are arranged primarily by culture area, including the Northwest Coast, Oregon and Washington Seaboard, California, Basin and Peninsula, Plateau, Plains, Midwest, Northeast, Southeast and Gulf, Southwest, Western Canada, and Eastern Canada. Within each area, materials are classified according to whether they are general in nature or pertain to the languages and literatures of specific tribes. Nongeographical headings: bibliographies, autobiographies, and general literature and general language.

__________. *The Indians and Eskimos of North America: A Bibliography of Books Printed Through 1972*. Vermillion, S.D.: Dakota Press, 1973.

A listing of predominantly nonfiction books by or about U.S. and Canadian Indians in print as of 1972. Section headings for bibliographies, handbooks, autobiographies, myths and legends, "All Other Books," and reprints in american archaeology and ethnology. Citations include price and number of pages. Indicators for paperback editions and children's literature.

Marquis, Arnold. *A Guide to America's Indians: Ceremonies, Reservations, and Museums*. Norman: University of Oklahoma Press, 1974.

Intended as an easy and accurate reference to the world of the American Indian. Part 1, "America's Indians," presents a broad overview of Native American cultures, history, and sociology. Part 2 provides some helpful hints on visiting Indian country. The final section of the book is a guide to selected tribes, reservations, campgrounds, and Indian events for Southwest, Central, Northwest, Southeast, and Northeast regions of the United States. Three appendices: "Indian Museums," "Indian Organizations," and "Tribal and Indian Interest Publications." Bibliography. Black-and-white photographs, maps and tables.

Meiklejohn, C., and D. A. Rokala, eds. *The Native Peoples of Canada: An Annotated Bibliography of Population Biology, Health, and Illness*. Canadian Museum of Civilization Mercury Series 134. Ottawa: National Museums of Canada, 1987.

A partially annotated offering of 2100 materials on the population biology, health, and illness of Canada's prehistoric, historic, and contemporary Native peoples. Entries arranged alphabetically by author. Author and subject indexes.

Morse, Bradford W., eds. *Aboriginal Peoples and the Law: Indian, Métis, and Inuit Rights in Canada*. Ottawa: Carleton University Press, 1989.

A resource containing excerpts from selected materials and original texts on the position of Indians, Métis, and Inuits in Canadian law. The chapters are organized around five themes: the importance of international law to the development of aboriginal and treaty rights, the impact of modern international law on domestic legal thinking and the "internationalization" of concerns of the world's indigenous peoples, the relation of specific laws to aboriginal and treaty rights, the impact of land rights, and the lands claims process.

Murdock, George Peter, and Timothy J. O'Leary. *Ethnographic Bibliography of North America*. 4th ed. 5 vols. New Haven, Conn.: Human Relations Area Files Press, 1975.

Provides "a basic coverage of the published literature on the Native Peoples of North America through the end of the year 1972." Volume 1 begins with area bibliographies for the Arctic Coast, Mackenzie-Yukon, Northwest Coast, Oregon Seaboard, California, Peninsula, Basin, Plateau, Plains, Midwest, Eastern Canada, Northeast, Southeast, Gulf, and Southwest. It next presents bibliographies for North America as a whole, Pan-Indianism, urban Indians, Canadian Indians, United States government relations, and Canadian government relations. Volumes 2 through 5 contain ethnic bibliographies for Arctic and Subarctic, Far West and Pacific Coast, and Eastern United States. Line drawings of culture areas designating major tribal groups appear in their appropriate volumes.

National Library of Canada. *Indian-Inuit Authors: An Annotated Bibliography*. Ottawa: Information Canada, 1974.

Citations and short descriptions of writings by Canadian Indians and Inuit. Includes sections for books/books by Native children; anthologies and collected works, poetry and songs; articles; addresses; conferences, reports, studies, theses; language; and texts. Indexes for authors and illustrators of works cited. Illustrated with pen-and-ink drawings.

Porter, Frank W., III, comp. *Native American Basketry: An Annotated Bibliography*. Westport, Conn.: Greenwood Press, 1988.

Annotated listings for more than eleven hundred works on American Indian basketry. Includes citations for books, journal articles, dissertations, theses, and selected newspaper articles. An introductory essay discusses the decline and revival of Native American basket making as well the emergence of basket collecting. Entries are listed alphabetically by author according to the following culture areas: Northeast, Southeast, Great Lakes, Plains, Great Basin, Southwest, California, Northwest, Plateau, Subarctic, and Arctic. Indexed by author and subject.

Price, John. *U.S. and Canadian Indian Periodicals*. Training Center for Community Programs in coordination with Office of Community Programs, Center for Urban and Regional Affairs. Minneapolis: University of Minnesota, 1971.

A listing of periodicals published in the U.S. and Canada intended primarily for Indian readerships. An introduction briefly characterizes the importance of these publications, observing that for Indians they are central to the process of political, social, and ideological unification, whereas for social scientists they are a major source of cultural data.

Price, Monroe, and Robert Clinton. *Law and the American Indian: Readings, Notes, and Cases*. Charlottesville, Va.: Michie Co., 1983.

Identifies as its purposes to survey the major doctrines in the field of Indian law and to inquire into the role of law and the legal process in protecting or frustrating the autonomy of various racial, cultural, religious, or national subgroups within society. Chapter 1 examines the tensions between assimilationist and separatist forces operating in Indian-white legal relations. Chapters 2 through 4 present materials on the competition among the federal government, states, and tribes over jurisdiction in various aspects of Indian affairs. Chapter 6 concerns tribal hunting, fishing, and water rights. Chapter 7 deals with the control and development of resources on Indian lands.

Prucha, Francis Paul. *A Bibliographical Guide to the History of Indian-White Relations in the United States*. Chicago: University of Chicago Press, 1977.

Cites approximately 9700 works pertaining to Indian-white relations in the United States. Part 1 lists important guides to unpublished sources, including those for materials in the National Archives, documents of the federal government, and manuscripts. Part 2 offers a classified bibliography of published works. Subject headings for Indian affairs/Indian policy, the Indian department, treaties and councils, land and the Indians, military relations, trade and traders, missions and missionaries, legal relations, Indian education, Indian health, social and economic developments, Indians and Indian groups, and special topics. Author-subject index.

__________. *Handbook for Research in American History*. Lincoln: University of Nebraska Press, 1987.

Designed primarily as a research tool for beginning historians. Part 1 describes recent guides to research materials of the following types: library catalogues and guides; general bibliographies; catalogues of books and imprints; book review indexes; guides to periodicals; manuscript guides; guides to newspapers; lists of dissertations and theses; biographical guides; oral history materials; printed documents of the federal government; the National Archives; state and local materials; guide to legal sources; atlases; maps and geographical guides; encyclopedias, dictionaries, and handbooks; and databases. Part 2, which deals with specific subjects, contains a section on American Indians. Includes entries for handbooks, guides and bibliographies, dissertations, special collections, atlases, newspapers and periodicals, biographies, and special publications.

__________. *Indian-White Relations in the United States: A Bibliography of Works Published 1975-1980*. Lincoln: University of Nebraska Press, 1982.

A five-year update of Prucha's 1977 *A Bibliographical Guide to the History of Indian-White Relations in the United States*. Contains an additional 3400 entries. Utilizes the same format as the earlier work.

__________. *United States Indian Policy: A Critical Bibliography*. Newberry Library Center for the History of the American Indian Bibliographical Series. Bloomington: Indiana University Press, 1977.

Bibliographical essay citing 175 major books and articles dealing with federal Indian policy. Assumes that "Indian history of the modern era must be understood in a context that also includes the history of the powerful intervention of non-Indians in Indian affairs." Headings for the early national period, Indian removal, Indians and the expanding West, Civil War, post-Civil War Indian reform, reversal of Indian policy: the Indian New Deal, recent history, special topics, histories of tribes, and documents. Listings of recommended works for the beginner and for a basic library collection.

Rock, Roger O., comp. *The Native American in American Literature: A Selectively Annotated Bibliography*. Westport, Conn.: Greenwood Press, 1985.

A partially annotated list of nearly sixteen hundred resources relevant to the studies of the American Indian in literature and American Indian literature. Section headings include bibliographies, the Indian in literature, and Native American literature. Author and subject indexes.

Ronda, James, and James Axtell. *Indian Missions: A Critical Bibliography*. Newberry Library Center for the History of the American Indian Bibliographical Series. Bloomington: Indiana University Press, 1978.

A bibliographical essay that discusses 211 books and articles concerning Christian missions among Native North Americans. An introduction presents continuity and change in the study of Indian missions. Headings include the missions of Anglicans and Episcopals, Baptists, Catholics, Methodists, Moravians, Mormons, and Quakers; the goals of mission; methods of conversion; and Indian responses. Lists of recommended works for the beginner and for a basic library collection.

Ruoff, A. Lavonne, and Karl Kroeber. *American Indian Literatures in the United States: A Basic Bibliography for Teachers*. New York: Association for the Study of American Indian Literature, 1983.

An annotated listing of works pertaining to the literatures of Native Americans of the U.S. that is of special interest to those teaching these literatures. Entries are organized according to the following categories: bibliographies and research tools; anthropological/linguistic backgrounds; philosophies, religions, and worldviews; Indian-white relations and images of the Indian; general literature; Native American authors—personal narratives; Native American authors—fiction, poetry, prose, drama; selected periodicals, special issues of periodicals, and small presses. Annotations are generally brief and evaluative.

Schmeiser, Douglas A., et al. *The Native Offender and the Law*. Ottawa: Information Canada, 1974.

A collection of statistical data on Canadian Indian, Métis, and Eskimo offenders, gathered mainly from the four western provinces, particularly Saskatchewan. Data are provided for the following subjects: the proportion of Native offenders in the prison population, the types of offenses committed, use of alcohol by Native offenders, sentencing, and recidivism rate. Closes with eleven general conclusions concerning the nature of Native criminality in Canada.

Shanks, Ralph, and Lisa Shanks. *North American Indian Travel Guide*. Petaluma, Calif.: Costano Books, 1986.

An alphabetical listing by state and province of sites and events important to the heritage and contemporary life of Native North Americans. Includes information on parks, cultural centers, tribal offices, Native American-owned businesses, pow-wows, and ceremonies. Four introductory chapters provide overviews of Indian and Eskimo "culture areas; "hints for preparing a trip and visiting reservations; some major trends and issues in Indian country; maps of cultural areas, U.S. Indian tribes, and Canadian Indian bands. Illustrated with numerous black-and-white photographs.

Slattery, Brian. *Canadian Native Law Cases*. 8 vols. Saskatoon: University of Saskatchewan Native Law Centre, 1980.

A comprehensive, chronologically arranged collection of cases dealing with Indians, Inuit, and Métis decided by the Canadian courts or by the Privy Council on appeal from Canada between 1763 and 1978. An index to subject matter contains headings for the major legal points of the cases and records references to statutes and executive acts relevant to Native peoples.

Smith, Dwight L., ed. *Indians of the United States and Canada: A Bibliography*. Santa Barbara, Calif.: American Bibliographical Center/Clio Press, 1974.

Contains 1687 annotated entries for articles on North American Indians which appeared between 1954 and 1972 in major historical and social science periodicals. Headings for citations include pre-Columbian Indian history; tribal history, 1492-1900; general Indian history, 1492-1900; and Indians in the twentieth century. Subdivisions based on the culture areas of Arctic, Subarctic, Northwest Coast, Plateau, Great Basin, California, Southwest, Great Plains, Northeast, and Southeast. An introduction by John C. Ewers of the Smithsonian Institution provides a historical overview of Native American research.

__________. *Indians of the United States and Canada: A Bibliography*. Vol. 2. Santa Barbara, Calif.: American Bibliographical Center/Clio Press.

A supplement to the 1974 edition.

Snodgrass, Jeanne O. *American Indian Painters: A Biographical Directory*. Contributions from the Museum of the American Indian, Heye Foundation, vol. 21, pt. 1. New York: Museum of the American Indian, Heye Foundation, 1968.

Biographical listings for nearly twelve hundred Native American artists. Entries are arranged alphabetically by artist and include the following information where applicable or available: Indian name, date and place of birth, education, marriage status, positions held, exhibitions, awards, commissions, collections displaying works, and address. Tribal index. Bibliography.

Snodgrass, Majorie P., comp. *Economic Development of American Indians and Eskimos 1930 Through 1967: A Bibliography*. Washington, D.C.: U.S. Department of the Interior Departmental Library, 1968.

Cites nearly sixteen hundred published and unpublished sources concerned with "individual and collective efforts on and off the reservations that are directed to the production of tangible income." Entries arranged alphabetically under fifteen headings including arts and crafts development; irrigation, dams, and reclamation projects; overall economic development plans; ten-year plans, tourism, and recreation development.

Snow, Dean R. *Native American Prehistory: A Critical Bibliography*. Newberry Library Center for the History of the American Indian Bibliographical Series. Bloomington: Indiana University Press, 1979.

A bibliographical essay that reviews 204 articles and books pertaining to the prehistory of Native North America. The essay is divided by five subtopics: "General Works on Archaeology," "General Works on North American Archaeology," "Mesoamerican Background," "The Earliest Americans," and "Regional Works." The regional subheading is further divided by the following five culture areas: the Eastern Woodlands, the Great Plains, the Desert West, the Far West, and the Arctic and Subarctic. Lists recommended works for the beginner and for a basic library.

Stensland, Anna Lee. *Literature by and About the American Indian: An Annotated Bibliography*. Urbana, Ill.: National Council of Teachers of English, 1973.

Intended to aid junior and senior high school teachers and students in their choices of readings on Native North Americans. Topics include myth, legend oratory, and poetry; fiction; drama; biography and autobiography; history; anthropology and archaeology; modern life and problems; music, arts, and crafts; and aids for the teacher. An introductory essay addresses the problem of stereotypes in literature and the criteria the author has used in selecting the works cited. Also includes a study guide to nine popular titles, biographies of the twenty-five most prolific American Indian writers, a list of basic books for a collection, sources for additional materials, and a directory of publishers.

Stuart, Paul. *Nations Within a Nation: Historic Statistics of American Indians*. Westport, Conn.: Greenwood Press, 1987.

Presents a variety of statistics relating to American Indian groups in the U.S. drawn from publications of the Bureau of the Census, the Bureau of Indian Affairs, the Indian Health Service, and other federal agencies. Chapter headings include "Land Base and Climate"; "Population"; "Removal, Relocation, and Urbanization"; "Vital Statistics and Health"; "Government Activities"; "Health Care and Education"; "Employment, Earnings, and Income"; and "Indian Resources and Economic Development." Statistical tables preceded by brief discussions containing relevant historical and cultural information as well as advisements regarding the shortcomings of the statistical data given.

Sturtevant, William C., gen. ed. *Handbook of North American Indians*. Washington, D.C.: U.S. Government Printing Office, 1978.

A projected twenty-volume set intended "to give an encyclopedic summary of what is known about the prehistory, history, and cultures of the aboriginal peoples of North America who live to the north of the urban civilizations of central Mexico." Volumes in print will be cited under appropriate headings of the bibliography.

Surtees, Robert J. *Canadian Indian Policy: A Critical Bibliography*. Newberry Library Center for the History of the American Indian Bibliographical Series. Bloomington: Indiana University Press, 1982.

A bibliographical essay that reviews nearly 300 books and articles on Indian policy in Canada. The essay is divided into three sections, each containing an introduction. Section 1, "The French Period: 1608-1763," includes subheadings for French-Iroquois-Huron relations, policy of "Francization," French imperialism and the Indian, and Acadia. Section 2, "The British Period: 1763-1867," cites resources on land policy, military policy, the reserve policy, and the Maritime colonies. The final section, "The Canadian Period: 1867 to the Present," presents works dealing with western Canada, British Columbia, and the White Paper. Lists recommended works for the beginner and for a basic library collection.

Sutton, Imre. *Indian Land Tenure: Bibliographical Essays and a Guide to the Literature*. New York: Clearwater, 1975.

A synthesis and critical review of the literature on Indian land organized around a complex typology of interlocking historical themes. Three major themes—aboriginal occupancy and territoriality, land cessions and the establishment of reservations, and land administration and land utilization—serve as the topics of the book's first part. The four topics in part 2 derive from an overlapping of the three major themes: original title and land claims; title clarification and change; tenure and jurisdiction; and tenure and culture change. An extensive bibliography of sources reviewed concludes the book. Seven maps.

Swagerty, William R. *Scholars and the Indian Experience*. Bloomington: Indiana University Press, 1984.

Ten essays, each written by a specialist, review recent literature in selected areas of Native American history. Essays are accompanied by bibliographies of references cited. Topics include Native American prehistory; Native American population collapse and recovery; Spanish-Indian relations, 1513-1821; Anglo-Indian relations in Colonial North America; Indian-white relations: 1790-1900; Twentieth century federal Indian policy, contemporary American Indians; native americans and the environment; Indian tribal histories; and the Indian and the fur trade.

Terrell, John Upton. *American Indian Almanac*. Cleveland: World Publishing, 1971.

Draws on scientific and historical sources to reconstruct the lifeways of peoples who inhabited ten prehistoric cultural areas in what is now the continental United States. The areas included are Southwestern Deserts and Mesa Lands, Gulf Coasts and Tidal Swamps, Southeastern Woodlands, Northeastern Woodlands, Central Prairies and Woodlands, Northern Great Plains, Southern Great Plains, Northern Mountains and Plateaus, Great Basin, and Pacific Coast. Each section contains maps of the area described, important archaeological sites, tribes at the beginning of the historic period, vignettes of the peoples of each area, tables of the area's languages, earliest population estimates, and Indian place names. Bibliography and glossary.

Thornton, Russell, and Mary K. Gramsmick. *Bibliography of Social Science Research and Writings on American Indians*. Minneapolis: Center for Urban and Regional Affairs, University of Minnesota, 1979.

Cites articles on Native Americans published through 1976 in scholarly journals of American and ethnic studies, economics, geography, history, political science, sociology, and interdisciplinary social science. Omits anthropological references because of their large number and adequate coverage in other bibliographies. Separate sections for each of the social sciences include citations and a listing of journals surveyed.

__________. *Sociology of American Indians: A Critical Bibliography*. Newberry Library Center for the History of the American Indian Bibliographical Series. Bloomington: Indiana University Press, 1980.

A bibliographical essay reviewing 331 books and articles that approach Native Americans from a sociological point of view. Headings for historical and contemporary Indian populations, overviews and types of sociocultural change and response found among Native Americans, religion and religious movements, relations with majority and minority groups, social stratification, economics and economic concerns, politics and political movements, social control and the judicial system, Indian family, Indian education, social psychology, and urbanization. Recommends works for beginners and for a basic library collection.

__________, et al. *The Urbanization of American Indians: A Critical Bibliography*. Newberry Library Center for the History of the American Indian Bibliographical Series. Bloomington: Indiana University Press, 1982.

A bibliographical essay reviewing 198 books and articles that pertain to various aspects of Native American life in urban centers. The essay is divided into two parts. The first part, entitled "American Indian Cities, Towns and Villages" discusses significant research on the cities of pre-Columbian Middle and South America as well as those of pre- and post-Columbian North America; part 2 concerns twentieth century urbanization and includes such topics as the trend toward urbanization; the determinants of rural-to-urban migration; demographic trends; urbanization and economic status; the kinship system in an urban context; alcohol consumption, crimes, and mental health; the continuing assimilation and adaptation of Native Americans to city life. Recommends works for beginners and for a basic library collection.

Turner, Harold W. *North America. Bibliography of New Religious Movements in Primal Societies*. Vol. 2. Boston: G. K. Hall, 1978.

The second in a series of four bibliographies that treats religious movements "which arise in the interaction of a primal society with another society where there is a great disparity of power or sophistication." Includes resources on selected groups of Native Americans from northern Mexico, the United States, Canada, and Greenland. The first two sections list theoretical and historical treatments of these religious movements. Section 3 cites titles pertaining to specific peoples. Indexes of authors and sources; films, records, and tapes; and main movements and Indian individuals.

Ullom, Judith C., ed. *Folklore of the North American Indians: An Annotated Bibliography*. Washington, D.C.: Library of Congress, 1969.

Contains 152 annotated entries for books about or containing the sacred narratives and folktales of Native North Americans. Part 1 lists general studies of folklore in non-Western societies, stylistic characteristics of Indian literature, comparisons of Old World and New World literary forms, relationships between myth and culture. Part 2 cites collections of folklore from eleven different culture areas. Editions for children follow each section. Author-subject index. Black-and-white photographs and drawings.

Waldman, Carl. *Atlas of the North American Indians*. New York: Facts on File, 1985.

A resource on the cultures, tribal histories, migrations, and locations of Indian peoples of North and Central America from prehistoric times to the present. Seven chapters discuss ancient Indians, ancient civilizations, Indian lifeways, Indians and explorers, Indian wars, Indian land cessions, and contemporary Indians. Six appendices: "Chronology of North American Indian History"; "The Indian Tribes of the United States and Canada with Historical and Contemporary Locations"; "Federal and State Indian Reservations, Trust Areas, and Native Villages in the United States"; "Indian Bands in Canada"; "Major Indian Place Names in the United States and Canada"; and "Museums, Historical Societies, Reconstructed Villages, and Archaeological Sites Pertaining to Indians in the United States and Canada." Nearly 100 maps. Black-and-white drawings and illustrations.

__________. *Encyclopedia of Native American Tribes*. New York: Facts on File, 1988.

Alphabetically arranged descriptions of Native North and Mesoamerican peoples and cultures. Entries for specific tribes (for example, "Sioux," "Zuni"); more general cultural names ("Prehistoric Indians," "Cliff Dwellers," etc.); entire civilizations ("Maya," "Toltec," etc.); language families ("Algonquian," "Athapaskan," etc.); and culture areas ("Northwest Coast," "Southeast," etc.). Watercolors (by Molly Braun) illustrate sites, artifacts, and scenes from past and contemporary Indian life. More than 150 entries. Includes a glossary of important terms and an extensive bibliography.

__________. *Who Was Who in Native American History: Indians and Non-Indians from First Contacts Through 1900*. New York: Facts on File, 1990.

An elementary introduction to personalities of note in Indian-white relations from the late fifteenth through the nineteenth century. Each of the more than one thousand alphabetically arranged entries provides a biographical sketch that places particular stress on its subject's role in crucial interactions between Native Americans and whites. Liberally illustrated with black-and-white reproductions and photographs. An appendix lists Native Americans by tribes and non-Indians by their most relevant contributions to Native American history. Black-and-white photographs.

Waldman, Harry, et al., eds. *Dictionary of Indians of North America*. 3 vols. St. Clair Shores, Mich.: Scholarly Press, 1978.

A "Who's Who" of historical and contemporary Native Americans. Biographical sketches range from a few lines to several pages. Illustrated with black-and-white drawings and photographs of many of the individuals discussed.

Washburn, Wilcomb E. *History of Indian-White Relations*. Vol.4 in *Handbook of North American Indians*. Washington, D.C.: U.S. Government Printing Office, 1988.

Essays on various themes and periods in the history of Indian-white relations by fifty-seven experts in the field. The papers are divided according to the following categories: national policies, military situation, political relations, economic relations, religious relations, and conceptual relations/effects of Indians on non-Indian cultures. Contributions treat the history of Indian-white relations "from the perspective of the institutions and policies of the intruding societies, in response to which the Native cultures changed" while also considering ". . . each European and Europe-derived nation differed from others in extending its authority and culture over North America." An extensive bibliography concludes the volume. Illustrated with numerous black-and-white reproductions, photographs, and maps.

Weatherford, Elizabeth, and Emelia Seubert. *Native Americans on Film and Video*. New York: Museum of the American Indian, Heye Foundation, 1981.

Describes approximately four hundred films and videotapes about Native Americans, most made between 1970 and 1980. Selected on the basis of "their clarity of viewpoint, the input of Native Americans, technical quality and documentation of critical issues and of information formerly unavailable on film or videotape." Includes ethnographic documentaries, films on the structure of Native society, archaeology, social and political issues, and individuals. Includes some "fictional" films. Lists many media organizations and programs initiated by American Indians to meet their needs, collections of Native American films and videotapes, and film distributors. Subject index and bibliography of general readings and film catalogues.

Whiteside, Don (sin a paw). *Aboriginal People: A Selected Bibliography Concerning Canada's First People.* Ottawa: National Indian Brotherhood, 1973.
Lists unpublished materials from various conferences, pertinent newspaper articles, and works that represent the viewpoints of Canadian Native peoples. Chapter headings for general (works); history of Native people—specific cultural and linguistic groups; population distribution; values, traditions, tales, crafts, and biographies; religious beliefs, experiences, and ceremonies; aboriginal rights and treaties; the Indian acts; discussion of Indian administration; prejudice and discrimination; aboriginal association (formal), and conferences not listed elsewhere; resistance; community development and internal organization; economic development; other social and cultural changes; urbanization; formal education; health, housing, welfare—poverty; crime and other legal matters (excepting treaties); and aboriginal people in other than North American countries. Indexes by name of principal author and by subject.

HISTORY

Indians in Colonial America

Aquila, Richard. *The Iroquois Restoration: Iroquois Diplomacy on the Colonial Frontier, 1701-1754*. Detroit: Wayne State University Press, 1983.

Argues that from the early to mid-eighteenth century, the five Iroquois nations of New York devised a program to regain the economic, political, and military power they held prior to King William's War. The four major strategies in this policy of restoration were neutrality toward English and French powers tempered with a pragmatic use of each to further their own ends; a rapprochement with tribes of the upper Great Lakes and Canada; amiable relations with the government of Pennsylvania; and warfare with the southern tribes. Bibliography. Black-and-white reproductions and photographs. Maps.

Axtell, James. *After Columbus: Essays in the Ethnohistory of Colonial North America*. New York: Oxford University Press, 1988.

A collection of eleven original and previously published studies on various aspects of Indian-white encounters in colonial North America. The first two essays examine the legitimacy of moral evaluations in the writing of Indian ethnohistory. The second group of papers deals with the interactions of missionaries and Native Americans. The anthology concludes with articles concerning early Indian views of Europeans; trading in the sixteenth century; the rise and fall of the Powhatan empire; the importance of the role of Indians in American history. An afterword considers the scholar's obligations to Native peoples. Black-and-white reproductions and photographs. Maps.

__________. *The European and the Indian: Essays in the Ethnohistory of Colonial North America*. New York: Oxford University Press, 1981.

Ten essays that present an ethnohistorical perspective "on the social and cultural interactions of the various peoples who inhabited the greater northeastern quadrant of colonial North America, particularly the French, English and the Indians." The themes of the chapters include the methodology of ethnohistory, assimilation and acculturation of Native Americans, white Indians, the English colonial impact on Indian culture, the Indian impact on English colonial culture, and the institution of scalping.

__________. *The Invasion Within: The Contest of Cultures in Colonial North America*. New York: Oxford University Press, 1985.

An ethnohistorical examination of the educational and cultural interactions of colonial French, English, and Indian populations of eastern North America. The six chapters of part I focus on Catholic missionary activities and Indian responses in New France. Part 2 details attempts by English colonists to Christianize and "civilize" the Native inhabitants surrounding their settlements. In the final section, the phenomenon of social and religious crossover by English, French, and Indians is discussed.

Bailey, Alfred G. *The Conflict of European and Eastern Algonquian Cultures: A Study in Canadian Civilization*. 2d ed. Toronto: University of Toronto Press, 1969. Reprint. Sackeville, New Brunswick: Tribune Press, 1937.
Examines the cultural contacts between the eastern Algonquian tribes of New France and French traders during the sixteenth and seventeenth centuries. Argues that in many cases these contacts led to the destruction of Indian cultures; in others, however, Indians adapted to the new conditions imposed on them by European invaders. Often a fusion of Indian and European elements occurred, resulting in a new, "Canadian," culture. The narrative is partially chronological and partially topical. Bibliography.

Brandon, William. *New Worlds for Old: Reports from the New World and Their Effects on the Development of Social Thought in Europe, 1500-1800*. Athens: University of Georgia Press, 1986.
Documents the various ways in which Native American alternatives to Old World institutions influenced the evolution of European social and political thought from the sixteenth to the nineteenth century. Contends that reports on the "Otherness" of New World peoples and cultures both shaped the ideas of Europe's leading social philosophers and contributed to the formation of competing political ideologies still operative in Western civilization.

Bridenbaugh, Carl. *Jamestown: 1544-1699*. New York: Oxford University Press, 1980.
A brief, unsentimental, and imaginative reconstruction of life in England's first permanent North American colony. Sees the settlement's history as "a somber chronicle, one unrelieved by either merriment or an attitude of warm humanity." The opening chapters portray the ever- escalating mistrust between the early settlers and the surrounding Algonquian tribes led by Powhatan and his brother Openchancanough. This escalation climaxed in the "Massacres" of 1622 and 1644. Three appendices: "Jamestown Chronology: 1544-1699" subdivided into Indian, French, and English periods; "A Note on Archaeology and Restoration at Jamestown"; "Suggestions for Further Reading." Four black-and-white illustrations.

Corkran, David H. *The Cherokee Frontier: Conflict and Survival, 1740-62*. Norman: University of Oklahoma Press, 1962.
Examines the relationship among the Lower, Middle, and Overhill divisions of the Cherokee people during the mid-eighteenth century and their participation in colonial rivalries between England and France. Bibliography. Black-and-white reproductions. Maps.

__________. *The Creek Frontier, 1540-1783*. Norman: University of Oklahoma Press, 1967.
A history of Creek-white relations during the colonial period that gives primacy to Indian perceptions and institutions in the analysis of events. Examines the essential role the Creeks played in shaping Spanish, British, and French territorial aspirations and contests within the American Southeast. Discusses why the Creeks decided to cast their lot with the British during the Revolutionary

War and the reparations exacted upon them for having chosen the losing side. Bibliography. Black-and-white reproductions. Maps.

Crane, Verner W. *The Southern Frontier, 1670-1732*. Durham, N.C.: Duke University Press, 1929.

A history of English colonial expansion in southeastern North America. Highlights British contests with the Spaniards for dominion over Florida and with the French for control of Louisiana and the Mississippi basin. Gives careful consideration to European trade relations and alliances with the Creek, Cherokee, Choctaw, and Chickasaw Indians. Important chapters on the origins of Georgia, emphasizing the important roles played by James Oglethorpe and Reverend Thomas Bray of the Society for the Propagation of the Gospel.

Cronon, William. *Changes in the Land: Indians, Colonists, and the Ecology of New England*. New York: Hill & Wang, 1983.

Argues that the transfer from Native American to European dominance in colonial New England had important consequences for the flora and fauna of the area. Purpose is to explain why the environment changed as it did. Begins by contrasting the precolonial ecosystems of New England with those of the early nineteenth century. Next compares the theory and practice of relationship which colonials and Indians had to the land. Finally, describes the ecological changes that resulted from European settlement. Concludes with an extended bibliographical essay.

Crosby, Alfred W., Jr. *The Columbian Exchange: Biological and Cultural Consequences of 1492*. Westport, Conn.: Greenwood Press, 1972.

Argues that the most important changes brought about by the Columbian voyages involved the exchanges of plants, animals, and microorganisms. Traces the spread of such cultigens as maize, potatoes, sweet potatoes, and beans from the Americas to Europe and the counterdispersal of wheat, barely, chickens, and horses. Claims that where most of the diseases native to the New World have proven to be inexportable, numerous Old World pathogens rampaged through America's aboriginal population. Sees the Columbian exchange as having impoverished rather than enriched the world's ecology.

De Vorsey, Louis. *The Indian Boundary in the Southern Colonies, 1763-1775*. Chapel Hill: University of North Carolina Press, 1966.

Follows the process by which the southern colonies established their frontiers with the Creek and Cherokee peoples from the conclusion of the French and Indian War to the eve of the American Revolution. Provides insight into traditional Creek and Cherokee concepts of geography and boundaries as well as the active role they played in the survey and the final determination of boundary lines. Maps. Bibliography.

Dickason, Olive P. *The Myth of the Savage and the Beginnings of French Colonialism in the Americas*. Edmonton: University of Alberta Press, 1984.

Investigates the evolution and ideological functions of European concepts of American Indian savagery. Chapters 1 through 4 concern the development of Europe's beliefs about and attitudes toward Native Americans. Chapter 5 provides both a series of ethnographic sketches of selected Native cultures on the eve of European contact and some initial effects of this contact. The remaining chapters examine how European assumptions regarding Native humanity and cultures influenced Indian-white relations in colonial North America. Bibliography. Black-and-white reproductions and photographs.

Fitzhugh, William W., ed. *Cultures in Contact: The European Impact on Native Cultural Institutions in Eastern North America, A.D. 1000-1800*. Washington, D.C.: Smithsonian Institution Press, 1985.

Nine essays which bring an archaeological perspective to the study of early contacts between Native Americans and Europeans. The papers seek to relate structural changes that occurred in the primary institutions of Indian societies to various contact and acculturation phenomena. Part 1 examines Inuit responses to explorers, whalers, traders, and missionaries. Part 2 looks at land, politics, and disease in New England. The articles in part 3 investigate the effects of European contact on sociopolitical organization within the Powhatan chiefdom and patterns of Anglo-Indian aggression and accommodation along the mid-Atlantic coast. The final part concerns Spanish-Indian interaction in sixteenth century Florida and Hispaniola.

Gibson, Charles, and Howard Peckham, eds. *Attitudes of Colonial Powers Toward the American Indian*. Salt Lake City: University of Utah Press, 1969.

Six essays that examine the attitudes and policies of European nations toward the Indian peoples in their colonies. Paper topics include Indians and Spaniards in the New World, the struggle between Jesuits and white settlers over Indian rights in colonial Brazil, Dutch treatment of Indians in New Netherlands, the French and the Indians, British relations with Native Americans, and the political incorporation and culture change of Indians in New Spain.

Green, L. C., and Olive P. Dickason. *The Law of Nations and the New World*. Edmonton: University of Alberta Press, 1989.

Places in historical context the issue of tribal sovereignty for Canada's Native peoples. Part 1, "Claims to Territory in Colonial America" by L. C. Green, discusses the legal assumptions, reasoning, and practices informing the European colonization of the New World during the sixteenth and seventeenth centuries. In part 2, "Concepts of Sovereignty at the Time of First Contact," Olive Dickason analyzes competing philosophical and theological positions regarding the nature, cultures, and political status of Amerindians with reference to colonial institutions and policies in the New World.

Hanke, Lewis. *Aristotle and the American Indians*. Chicago: Henry Regnery, 1959.

Follows the confrontation between Juan de Sepulveda and Bartholome de las Casas over the application of the Aristotelian doctrine of natural slavery to the Indians of the Americas. In question was whether a respect for the human rights of the Native Americans ought to constitute a fundamental component of Spanish Indian policy. At a meeting in Valladolid in 1550, Sepulveda attempted to convince the Crown of the innate inferiority of Indians to Europeans while las Casas argued for the essential equality of whites and Native Americans. The

Crown and council found in favor of las Casas. Five black-and-white illustrations. Two appendices: one containing letters exchanged between Sepulveda and Alfonso de Castro; the other, a bibliographical essay.

Harriot, Thomas. *A Briefe and True Report of the New Found Land of Virginia*. Mineola, N.Y.: Dover, 1972.

An unabridged reproduction of the first, illustrated edition of Harriot's famous essay on the colony of Roanoke published in 1590. The first two parts survey the environmental setting of this short-lived settlement. Part 3 presents information on the material and social life of the Algonquian peoples inhabiting the surrounding area. An introduction by Paul Hulton places the report in historical context. List of suggested readings. Black-and-white reproductions.

Honour, Hugh. *The New Golden Land*. New York: Pantheon Books, 1975.

Examines the continuity and change in Europe's conception of America and Americans from the late fifteenth century to the present. The first five chapters contain much useful information concerning European attempts to make sense of Native American humanity and culture. Hundreds of color and black-and-white reproductions illustrate the text. Includes many early and rarely seen woodcuts, engravings, and paintings of American Indians as envisioned by European artists. Contains bibliographical essays for the book's ten chapters.

Huddleston, Lee Eldridge. *Origins of the American Indians: European Concepts, 1492-1729*. Austin: University of Texas Press, 1967.

Examines the theories of Amerindian origins represented in European literature from the late fifteenth to early eighteenth century. Identifies two rival traditions: the Acostan tradition, "characterized by a moderate skepticism with respect to the comparative and exegetical methodology of the day, by and adherence to geographical and faunal considerations in theorizing, and by a reluctance to produce finished origin theories . . ."; and the Garcian tradition, "marked by an uncritical acceptance of the comparative ethnological technique in determining origins and a tendency to accept trans-Atlantic migrations." Bibliography.

Jacobs, Wilbur R. *Dispossessing the American Indian: Indians and Whites on the Colonial Frontier*. New York: Charles Scribner's Sons, 1972.

A collection of eleven essays that probe the relations between Indians and whites living on the borders of the eighteenth century eastern woodlands. The selections in part 1 examine these relations as they concern trade, treaty making, and diplomacy. Part 2 contains treatments of Indian-white conflicts and the attempts by British authorities to control the encounters between Natives and colonists. Part 3 examines the attitudes and policies of the British empire toward Native Americans. It also compares the colonial histories and experiences of native peoples in North America, Australia, and New Guinea. Two appendices. Black-and-white reproductions. Maps.

__________. *Wilderness Politics and Indian Gifts: The Northern Colonial Frontier, 1748-1763*. Lincoln: University of Nebraska Press, 1966.

Explores how the French and English used the Indian custom of gift giving to secure Native friendship and alliance as they vied for dominance along the Ohio and Northwest frontiers from 1748 to 1763. Early chapters examine the traditional place of gift exchange among the Indian cultures of the Northeast, the similarities and differences in British and French systems of distributing gifts to Indians, and the types and costs of presents. Later chapters discuss the importance of winning and maintaining Indian alliances through gifts for the specific military campaigns of the period. Seven black-and-white illustrations including a foldout map of the "Old West."

Jaenen, Cornelius J. *Friend and Foe: Aspects of French-Amerindian Cultural Contact in the Sixteenth and Seventeenth Centuries*. New York: Columbia University Press, 1976.

Examines various dimensions of French-Indian relations in sixteenth and seventeenth century New France. Focuses on the assumptions shaping these relations and effects of contact on both groups. Among the topics discussed are French evaluations of Indian humanity and culture; the obstacles confronted by Jesuits in their attempts to missionize Indian populations; epidemics, alcohol abuse, and other social problems arising from situations of contact; and differences in practices of war and the treatment of captives.

Jennings, Francis. *The Ambiguous Iroquois Empire: The Covenant Chain Confederation of Indian Tribes with English Colonies from Its Beginnings to the Lancaster Treaty of 1744*. New York: W. W. Norton, 1984.

Probes the composition and functioning of the "Covenant Chain," a political, military, and economic confederation of English colonies, the Iroquois, and other tribes ". . . capable of tipping the scales of dominance in North America." Views the chain as an example of cooperation and accommodation between peoples with radically different cultures and polities. Three appendices. Bibliography. Black-and-white reproductions and drawings. Maps.

__________. *The Invasion of America*. New York: W. W. Norton, 1975.

Documents, first, the methods that Puritan New Englanders used to rationalize their armed conquest of Native American peoples and lands; and, second, how the suppositions informing this "cant of conquest" still influence the depiction of Indians and Indian-white relations in American historiography. According to the author, ". . . contemporary Europeans . . . made preparations of two sorts: guns and munitions to overpower Indian resistance and quantities of propaganda to overpower their own countrymen's scruples. The propaganda gradually took standard form as an ideology with conventional assumptions and semantics. We live with it still." Appendix. Bibliography. Black-and-white reproductions. Maps.

John, Elizabeth A. H. *Storms Brewed in Other Men's Worlds: The Confrontation of Indians, Spanish, and French in the Southwest, 1540-1795*. Lincoln: University of Nebraska Press, 1975.

Seeks to incorporate a fair understanding of Indian experiences and cultures into the colonial history of the American Southwest. The chapters move chronologically among various regions, European colonists, and Native peoples, beginning with Coronado's incursion into the Pueblo world in 1540 up to the crumbling of Spanish authority in New Mexico and Texas during the late eighteenth century. Bibliography.

Jones, Dorothy V. *License for Empire: Colonialism by Treaty in Early America.* Chicago: University of Chicago Press, 1982.

Examines how the treaty system employed by whites in their dealings with Indians helped to establish colonialism in North America. Argues that between 1763 and 1768, the treaty system functioned with reasonable success in meeting the mutual concerns of Indians and whites: peace, friendship, trade, and maintenance of an Indian-white boundary. Between 1768 and 1796, however, events, decisions, and conditions acted to transform the system into the primary vehicle by which whites divested Indians of their lands. At the basis of this transformation was an emergent disparity of power between the participants so that the "system no longer expressed mutual compromise and accommodation, but rather the domination of the Indians by the United States." Two appendices. Bibliography. Tables and graphs.

Kennedy, John H. *Jesuit and Savage in New France.* New Haven, Conn.: Yale University Press, 1950.

An examination of missionary activity in New France, focusing primarily on Jesuit work among the Huron. Presents the corporate and personal motivations underlying this ministry; the theological assumptions informing the Jesuit theory and practice of mission; missionary interpretations of Indian humanity, society, and culture; and the influence which Jesuit descriptions of American "savages" exercised on French social philosophy. Bibliographical note on guides, sources, and authorities. Foldout map of New France.

Kupperman, Karen O. *Settling with the Indians: The Meeting of English and Indian Cultures in America, 1580-1640.* Totowa, N.J.: Rowman and Littlefield, 1980.

Seeks, first, to examine how persons actually involved in the initial sixty years of the English colonization of North America assessed Indian humanity and culture; second, to compare Indian and European technologies, religious and ideational worlds, forms of society and government, and social ideals; and third, to probe the theological significance which the English attributed to their colonial efforts in North America. One appendix. Bibliography.

Leach, Douglas Edward. *Flintlock and Tomahawk: New England in King Philip's War.* New York: Macmillan, 1958.

An examination of King Philip's War, a conflict that pitted Puritans from Plymouth, Massachusetts Bay, Connecticut, and Rhode Island against neighboring Algonquian peoples during 1675 and 1676. The first chapter provides an overview of the settlements, subsistence, and social organization of the New England Indians. Subsequent chapters detail the causes of the war, its engagements, and demographic and economic consequences for both Indians and whites. Bibliography. Black-and-white reproductions. Maps.

Milanich, Jerald T., and Susan Milbruth, eds. *First Encounters: Spanish Explorations in the Caribbean and the United States, 1492-1570.* Gainesville: University of Florida Press, 1989.

An anthology of thirteen essays which treats the first century of Spain's colonial expansion in the New World. The four opening chapters describe the earliest phases of Spanish colonization. Remaining sections discuss the expanding borders of Spanish New World claims, an example of Indian response to Spanish contact, and European views on the meeting of Old World and New. Illustrations include both black-and-white and color plates. Bibliography.

Morison, Samuel Eliot. *The European Discovery of America*. 2 vols. New York: Oxford University Press, 1971, 1974.

A detailed description of European voyages to the New World prior to 1600. Volume 1, *The Northern Voyages: A.D. 500-1600*, begins with the travels of St. Brendan and the Irish. Subsequent chapters on the Norsemen and Vineland, expeditions to Newfoundland and Labrador, and the voyages of John Cabot, Jacques Cartier, Martin Forbisher, Humphrey Gilbert, John Davis, Richard Grenville, and many others. Volume 2, *The Southern Voyages: 1492-1616*, concentrates on the discoveries of Columbus, Magellan, and Drake. Bibliographies and notes accompany each chapter.

Morrison, Kenneth M. *The Embattled Northeast: The Elusive Ideal of Alliance in Abnaki-Euramerican Relations*. Berkeley: University of California Press, 1984.

Utilizes documentary, ethnographic, and oral sources to interpret the structure and dynamics of Abnaki, French, and English relations in the colonial Northeast. Emphasis is placed on the socioreligious assumptions informing Abnaki diplomacy and their ability to maintain social order by adapting to the ever-present crises of postcontact life.

Nammack, Georgiana C. *Fraud, Politics, and the Dispossession of the Indians: The Iroquois Land Frontier in the Colonial Period*. Norman: University of Oklahoma Press, 1969.

Employs a number of representative case studies to examine Iroquois-British conflicts over landownership in the New York area during the period of English control from 1664 to the American Revolution. Views the struggle for land as a three-sided affair, "with the British government in many cases playing a third role—that of protector when the natives were subjected to abuse and fraud in the purchase of lands by the colonists." One appendix. Bibliography.

Nash, Gary B. *Red, White, and Black: The Peoples of Early America*. Englewood Cliffs, N.J.: Prentice-Hall, 1974.

Compares the cultural values and interactions of Indians, Africans, and Europeans in eastern North America up to the American Revolution. Concerning Indian-European relations, the author comments that "we are best equipped to understand the pattern of interaction and conflict between [them] by appreciating that each group pursued its own interests as steadfastly as it could, limited primarily by the resources available to it and restricted partially by conditions and attitudes that predated European arrival. . . . For both, survival and the enhancement of their own culture were the paramount objectives." Bibliographical essay. Black-and-white reproductions and photographs. Maps.

Parkman, Francis. *The Jesuits in North America in the Seventeenth Century*. New York: Little, Brown, 1897.

Chronicles the short-lived Jesuit mission to the Huron Indians in New France during the first half of the seventeenth century. Describes the motivations of the Jesuits, their tactics of missionization, the various reactions of the Huron people to Catholic belief and ceremony, the structure and operation of the missionary establishment of Sainte Marie, and the warfare between the Hurons and Iroquois which contributed to the mission's demise. Based primarily on information contained in *Jesuit Relations* as filtered through the biases of a nineteenth century Protestant historian. One black-and-white photograph. One map.

Ray, Arthur J., and Donald B. Freeman. *"Give Us Good Measure": An Economic Analysis of Relations Between the Indians and the Hudson's Bay Company Before 1763*. Toronto: University of Toronto Press, 1978.

Provides a history of the Hudson's Bay fur trade company during the first century of its operation. Focuses on those institutionalized relationships and processes that allowed Indians and Europeans to maintain an extended period of trade partnerships despite radical differences in their cultures. Refutes the still widely accepted thesis that Indian participation in trade was motivated primarily by religio-political considerations rather than economic interests. One appendix. Bibliography. Black-and-white reproductions.

Reid, John R. *A Better Kind of Hatchet: Law, Trade, and Diplomacy in the Cherokee Nation During the Early Years of European Contact*. University Park: Pennsylvania State University Press, 1976.

Documents the evolution of Cherokee law, trade, and diplomacy up to 1760. Among the topics discussed are the assumptions, structure, and functioning of the tribe's law-ways; the diplomatic relationship of the Cherokee with various colonial powers; and the network of commercial transactions between Cherokee and Europeans centered on the deerskin trade.

Richter, Daniel K., and James H. Merrell. *Beyond the Covenant Chain: The Iroquois and Their Neighbors in Indian North America, 1600-1800*. Syracuse, N.Y.: Syracuse University Press, 1987.

A collection of nine essays that focuses on the relationship between the Iroquois and tribes to their north, east, and south in order to "foster a clearer sense of the Iroquois place in colonial North America and inspire a new appreciation of the importance and complexity of interactions among native peoples." The first group of papers examines the structure and dynamics of Iroquois diplomacy within the Iroquois nation. The three essays of part 2 analyze the interactions between the Iroquois and southern New England Algonquians and Ohio and Pennsylvania Indians. The concluding section describes contacts between the Six Nations and the Catawba, Cherokees, and Tuscaroras.

Salisbury, Neal. *Manitou and Providence: Indians, Europeans, and the Making of New England*. New York: Oxford University Press, 1982.

An ethnohistory of colonial New England which presents intertribal and intercultural relations during the sixteenth and early seventeenth century from the perspectives of both their Indian and European participants. Begins with a brief examination of the pre-Columbian economies, polities, and intergroup contacts of northeastern peoples. Follows with chapters on the "trader phase" of European conquest; the beginnings of English colonization; and the transformations in New England society and Indian-white relations resulting from the ever- quickening pace and quantity of English emigration. Black-and-white photographs and reproductions. Footnotes but no bibliography.

Sauer, Carl. *Sixteenth Century North America*. Berkeley: University of California Press, 1971.

Recounts the earliest European explorations of the New World. Focuses on the motives and scope of these expeditions as well as the explorers' impressions of the landscapes and native peoples they encountered. Includes discussions of the first journeys along the continent's Atlantic coast; the forays of Coronado, De Soto and other Spanish adventurers into the interior and Far West; the strategic importance of Florida as a part of New Spain; and the failed attempts of early English settlers to maintain a colony at Roanoke. Concludes with a useful summary of Europe's conceptions of North American nature and cultures and the impact of European goods, slave trade, and diseases on Indian peoples. Twenty-three black-and-white drawings and maps. Bibliography of frequently cited writings by sixteenth century explorers.

Segal, Charles M., and David A. Stineback. *Puritans, Indians, and Manifest Destiny*. New York: Putnam, 1977.

An anthology of fifty-five primary documents from the seventeenth century pertaining to the various aspects of Puritan-Indian relations. Its purpose is to introduce readers to the basic issues involved in these relations as well as to contribute a new point of view to the study of Puritan and Indian contact. Chapter headings include "Land and Trade," "Government Relations," "The Pequot War," "Christianizing the Indian," and "King Philip's War." Each chapter begins with an introduction that provides a historic context for the documents presented. All documents are preceded by an explanatory note concerning the circumstances of their origins and significance. Includes a list of significant dates in the history of Puritan and Indian relationships. A bibliographical essay concludes the work.

Sheehan, Bernard W. *Savagism and Civility: Indians and Englishmen in Colonial Virginia*. New York: Cambridge University Press, 1980.

Examines the conception of Indians which early seventeenth century Virginia colonists brought with them from Europe and how this understanding shaped their attitudes and policies toward Native Americans. Focuses on the role of the doctrine of "savagism" in structuring colonial perceptions of Native society, the imperviousness of this doctrine to English experiences of Indian humanity and culture, and its centrality in warranting colonial exploitation and subjugation of surrounding tribes. Bibliography.

Szasz, Margaret C. *Indian Education in the American Colonies, 1607-1783*. Albuquerque: University of New Mexico Press, 1988.

Examines the formal schooling of Native Americans during the seventeenth and eighteenth centuries. Views this schooling as "a single, crucial dimension of the larger process of cultural interaction" between Indian and white. The first two chapters present basic concepts and methods of American colonial education as well as aspects of Native cultures that accompanied Indian students to schools. The next eight chapters describe and analyze specific attempts by religious denominations in New England and the middle and southern colonies. Bibliography. Black-and-white reproductions. Maps.

Trelease, Allen W. *Indian Affairs in Colonial New York: The Seventeenth Century.* Ithaca, N.Y.: Cornell University Press, 1960.

An analysis of colonial Indian policy in seventeenth century New York, first under the Dutch and then under the English. Focuses on the key role which the Algonquian and Iroquois tribes played in the economy and politics of the colony and how the various aspects of colonial policy toward Native Americans shaped economic and political ends. Bibliography. Black-and-white reproductions. Maps.

Tyler, S. Lyman. *Two Worlds: The Indian Encounter with the European, 1492-1509.* Salt Lake City: University of Utah Press, 1987.

A chronologically arranged collection of texts intended to demonstrate how early Spanish colonists viewed both the aboriginal inhabitants of the New World and their fellow countrymen. Focuses on the reports of Christopher Columbus and Bartholome de las Casas, a Dominican friar who severely critiqued the brutalization of Native Americans at the hands of the Spanish colonials. An appendix, reproducing a codicil to the will of Queen Isabella, admonishes future sovereigns to treat their Indian subjects with benevolence.

Vaughan, Alden T. *New England Frontier: Puritans and Indians, 1620-1675.* Boston: Little, Brown, 1975.

A positive appraisal of Puritan attitudes and behavior toward Native Americans during the mid-seventeenth century. Examines the important interactions between New England colonists and Indians; the adaptations of social theory and practice of Puritan life on the Indian frontier; and the changes brought about in Indian society by contacts with Europeans. Finds that the New England Puritans "followed a remarkably human, considerate, and just policy in their dealings with the Indians." Based solely on Puritan sources. For a radically different interpretation, see Francis Jennings' *The Invasion of America*. Extensive bibliography.

Vaughan, Alden T., and Edward W. Clark, ed. *Puritans Among the Indians: Accounts of Captivity and Redemption, 1676-1724.* Cambridge, Mass.: The Belknap Press of Harvard University Press, 1981.

Excerpts from eight of colonial New England's most famous captivity narratives, arranged chronologically according to the dates of the incidents described. Includes selections either written by the captives themselves or reported second hand by Cotton Mather. Among those captured and redeemed are Mary Rowlandson, Quentin Stockwell, John Gyles, Hannah Swarton,

Hannah Dustan, and Elizabeth Hanson. A bibliography cites additional captivity narratives and analyses, works on New England and Canadian contexts of Puritan captivities, and on early northeastern ethnohistory.

Indians in the United States (1776-1990)

Abel, Annie H. *The Slaveholding Indians*. 3 vols. Cleveland: Arthur H. Clark, 1919-1925.

Examines the relations between the U.S. government and the slave-owning Choctaws, Chickasaws, Creeks, Cherokees, and Seminoles (the Five Civilized Tribes) before, during, and following the Civil War. Volume 1 deals with the period between the forced removal of the Civilized Tribes to Indian Territory and the start of the war. Volume 2 examines the overwhelming support which these tribes gave to the Confederacy. Volume 3 describes the terms of peace the five tribes were forced to accept following the conflict. Bibliography.

Berkhofer, Robert F., Jr. *Salvation and the Savage: An Analysis of Protestant Missions and American Indian Response 1787-1862*. Lexington: University of Kentucky Press, 1965.

Investigates the aims, operation, and Native responses to Protestant Indian missionaries from 1787 to 1862. Begins with an analysis of the missionaries' goal of propagating the Gospel and its relation to that of civilizing Native Americans. Next explores the values embedded in the theory and practice of missionization. The disagreements among missionaries concerning matters of doctrine are then discussed. Subsequent chapters cover the directed change of Indian cultures attempted by missionaries, missionary relations with traders and other whites, the treatment of Indian converts by whites and nonconverted members of their tribes; and the effects of missionization on tribes. Includes a bibliographical essay on archival materials available for the study of Protestant Indian missions.

Bodmer, Karl. *Karl Bodmer's America*. Lincoln: Joslyn Art Museum and University of Nebraska Press, 1984.

Reproduces nearly all the known watercolors and sketches that resulted from Swiss artist Karl Bodmer's participation in Prince Maximilian's expedition up the Missouri River from 1832 to 1834. Part 1 presents a summary of the mounting and itinerary of the expedition and key features of Bodmer's renderings of Sioux, Assiniboin, Blackfeet, Hidatsa, Mandan, and other Indian peoples. Part 2 contains the majority of the book's more than 350 plates, accompanied by commentaries. Part 3 provides a biography of the Swiss artist.

Brown, Dee. *Bury My Heart at Wounded Knee*. New York: Bantam Books, 1975.

A popular account of the wars of extermination that whites waged against the Western Indians from 1860 to 1890. Focuses on the struggles of the Navajo, Santee Sioux of Minnesota, Cheyenne and Arapaho, Apache, Modoc, Nez Percé, and Teton Sioux to stave off Euro-American domination. Concludes with a description of the Ghost Dance Movement and the massacre of Big Foot's band of Minneconjou Sioux at Wounded Knee, South Dakota. Bibliography. Black-and-white photographs.

Burt, Larry W. *Tribalism in Crisis: Federal Indian Policy, 1953-1961*. Albuquerque: University of New Mexico Press, 1982.

Analyzes the attempts of a coterie of conservative western congressmen in the early and middle 1950's to institute a rapid form of Indian assimilation through the termination of federal supervision and services to Native Americans. Argues that the election of Dwight D. Eisenhower and a Republican congressional majority in 1952 offered these terminationists a hospitable environment in which to mount their assault on Indian lands and tribal sovereignty. Chapters examine the events surrounding the rise and retreat of the policy of termination as well as its major proponents and opponents. Bibliography.

Cadwalader, Sandra, and Vine Deloria, Jr., eds. *The Aggressions of Civilization*. Philadelphia: Temple University Press, 1984.

Nine essays that examine different aspects of late nineteenth and twentieth century Indian policy. Topics include an appraisal of the Indian Rights Association, attempts by Protestant reformers to suppress Pueblo ceremonial dances, an overview of Indian policy since the 1880's, the evolution of the Indian Service, the course of Indian legislation, the Indian Reorganization Act, Indian litigation, Indian land rights, and the consequences of *Lone Wolf v. Hitchcock*.

Calloway, Colin G. *Crown and Calumet: British-Indian Relations, 1783-1815*. Norman: University of Oklahoma Press, 1987.

Examines British and Indian conceptions of each other and the conditions that shaped their interpretations from the Peace of Paris (1783) to the Peace of Ghent (1815). Argues that during this period, both sides tended to base their evaluations on military and commercial criteria. Begins with a discussion of the changes that the end of the American Revolution brought about for relations between Britons and Indians. Subsequent chapters concern meetings and reciprocal interpretations of British and Indian cultures, Indian and British trade and trade relations, and the military alliances between Indian tribes and Britons. Sixteen black-and-white reproductions of eighteenth and nineteenth century paintings; two maps; selected bibliography.

Carlson, Leonard A. *Indians, Bureaucrats, and Land: The Dawes Act and the Decline of Indian Farming*. Westport, Conn.: Greenwood Press, 1981.

Employs the methodology of the "new" economic history (Cliometrics) to investigate the implementation of the Dawes or General Allotment Act of 1887 and its effects on Indian agriculture. Part 1 develops alternative models to explain the order in which reservations were selected for allotment. Finds that statistical tests and literary evidence support the hypothesis that the Indian Office "chose reservations for allotment as a direct response to the interests of whites who wanted to develop reservation lands." Part 2 demonstrates that the Dawes Act actually worked against its intended function of culturally and economically assimilating Indians through farming. Statistical appendices. Selected bibliography.

Coleman, Michael C. *Presbyterian Missionary Attitudes Toward American Indians, 1837-1893*. Jackson: University Press of Mississippi, 1985.
Examines the understanding of self and Indian other held by missionaries from the Board of Foreign Missions of the Presbyterian Church. Concentrates on the rhetoric and attitudes of BFM missionaries who lived among two tribes: the Choctaw of the Oklahoma Indian Territory and the Nez Percé of Idaho. Extracts a clashing double image of Indian life in the coexisting cultural ethnocentrism and racial egalitarianism of the missionaries: "Indian forms of 'heathenism,' in the perceptions of the Presbyterians, both repressed tribal members and simultaneously allowed them anarchic freedom."

Cook, Sherburne F. *The Conflict Between the California Indian and White Civilization*. Berkeley: University of California Press, 1974.
Sets forth the similarities and differences in the physical, demographic, and behavioral responses of California Indians to competition for material resources posed by Spanish missionaries, Spanish-Mexican settlers (1770 to 1848), and American (Yankee) invaders (1848-1870). Finds that on the whole and for many reasons, there was greatest violence between settlers from the U.S. and that this "violence was reflected in greater relative population decline and in more difficult adjustment in all material respects under the American occupation." Charts.

Curtis, Edward S. *In a Sacred Manner We Live*. Barre, Mass.: Barre Publishers, 1972.
Selects 120 from the more than 2200 photographs that originally appeared in Curtis' *The North American Indian* (1907-1930). Opens with a sketch of the photographer's life and career. The sepia-toned pictures are arranged according to the following culture areas: the Plains, Southwest, Plateau, Desert West; Northern and Central California, Northwest Coast, and Eskimo. Each section is introduced by a brief characterization of the area and its Indian peoples.

Debo, Angie. *The Rise and Fall of the Choctaw Republic*. 2d ed. Norman: University of Oklahoma Press, 1967.
A political history of the Choctaw Nation. Begins with brief treatments of traditional Choctaw society and the events which climaxed in the tribe's removal to Indian Territory (present-day Oklahoma) during the early nineteenth century. Subsequent chapters trace the evolution of postremoval Choctaw Republic up to its termination in 1907 when Oklahoma became a state. Bibliography. Black-and-white photographs. Maps.

Dippie, Brian W. *The Vanishing American: White Attitudes and U.S. Indian Policy*. Middletown, Conn.: Wesleyan University Press, 1982.
Documents how the myth of the "vanishing American" manifested itself in white perceptions of the American Indian from the late eighteenth century to the middle of the present century. Submits that this myth has been a constant element in the popular conception of the Indian as well as in the formulation of

such otherwise divergent federal Indian policies as removal, assimilation, and the Indian Reorganization Act. It has served to rationalize wrongs done to Native Americans by encapsulating the latter "in a tradition reeking of inevitability." Black-and-white reproductions of works of art and editorial cartoons that help to substantiate the author's thesis.

Ellis, Richard N. *General Pope and U.S. Indian Policy*. Albuquerque: University of New Mexico Press, 1970.

Uses the career of General John Pope to explore the history of federal Indian policy during the second half of the nineteenth century. As a commander of various military divisions west of the Mississippi, Pope gained a first-hand knowledge of the Sioux, Cheyenne, Kiowa, and numerous other northern and southern Plains tribes. He also gained an insider's experience of the theoretical and practical deficiencies in federal Indian policy. Based primarily on the records of the War and Interior Departments. Bibliography.

Fixico, Donald L. *Termination and Relocation: Federal Indian Policy, 1945-1966*. Albuquerque: University of New Mexico Press, 1986.

Analyzes the brand of assimilationist Indian policy that emerged under the Truman and Eisenhower administrations. Demonstrates how both these administrations sought to dissolve federal treaty obligations with tribes and "de-Indianize" Native Americans by relocating them in urban centers. Chapters 1 through 8 describe the evolution of renewed proassimilationist sentiments and the mechanisms by which they were translated into federal Indian policy. Chapter 9 describes the disastrous social and psychological effects of termination and relaocation on Indian people. Appendices present Indian claims settlements during the 1950's, tribes that the Bureau of Indian Affairs considered ready and those it deemed not ready for termination, and an organizational flowchart for relocation from 1957. Bibliography; ten black-and-white photographs. Three maps.

Foreman, Grant. *Indian Removal: The Emigration of the Five Civilized Tribes of Indians*. Norman: University of Oklahoma Press, 1932.

Treats in detailed fashion the early nineteenth century removals of the Choctaws, Creeks, Chickasaws, Cherokees, and Seminoles—the Five Civilized Nations—from their homelands in the southeastern U.S. to Indian Territory. The book is divided into five sections, each of which presents the circumstances surrounding the displacement and relocation of a specific tribe. Bibliography. Black-and-white photographs.

Fritz, Henry. *The Movement for Indian Assimilation, 1860-1890*. Philadelphia: University of Pennsylvania Press, 1963.

Discusses the assimilationist "solution" to the crisis in post-Civil War Indian policy. Focuses on the forces of Protestant reform backing assimilationism, their influence on the shaping and execution of Grant's "Peace Policy," the reactions of the Catholic church and the military to that measure, and the culmination of reform efforts in passage of the Dawes Allotment Act of 1887. Offers balanced evaluations of both the Peace Policy and the movement for Indian assimilation as a whole. Six illustrations and three maps. Bibliography.

Graymont, Barbara. *The Iroquois in the American Revolution*. Syracuse, N.Y.: Syracuse University Press, 1972.

Provides a detailed ethnohistory of Iroquois involvement in the American Revolution. Begins by describing the cultural foundations and integration of pre-Revolutionary Iroquois life, represented at their fullest in the Six Nations Confederacy. Subsequent discussion concerns the failed attempts of the Iroquois to maintain friendly relations with both British and Americans; the stresses that colonial conflicts placed on the traditional cultural, economic, and political patterns of Iroquois society; and the factionalism and civil war to which these stresses ultimately led. Bibliography.

Green, Michael D. *The Politics of Indian Removal: Creek Government and Society in Crisis*. Lincoln: University of Nebraska Press, 1982.

A social and political history of the crisis in Creek-white relations during the two decades preceding the tribe's removal to Indian territory in the 1830. Emphasis is given the strategies that the Creek National Council employed to deal with increasing hunger of whites for the tribe's lands, how these strategies led to significant changes in traditional Creek sociopolitical organization and factionalism, and some of the reasons for the failure of the council's policies.

Gross, Emma R. *Contemporary Federal Policy Toward American Indians*. Westport, Conn.: Greenwood Press, 1989.

A public policy study which argues that during the 1970's, "a liberal shift occurred in Indian policy making so that Indian constituency interests came to be surprisingly well represented in major legislation enacted at the time." Seeks to identify the degree to which Indians benefitted from the shift, the political processes that underlay the passage of policies beneficial to Indians, and why these changes took place in the 1970's. Argues that the reasons for this shift in the government's approach to Indian relations did not derive from purely rational processes and were "varied, complex and unpredictable." Concludes with a chapter on the future of American Indian policy. Tables and figures. Three appendices: the first, a note on method; the second, listing important Indian legislation from 1970 to 1980; and the third, presenting Washington firms listing two or more American Indian clients, tribes, and/or organizations in 1983. Bibliography.

Hagan, William T. *American Indians*. Rev. ed. Chicago: University of Chicago Press, 1979.

Discusses the major periods in the history of U.S. Indian policy. Sees the patterns of this policy "already evidenced in the corruption and elimination of scores of Indian peoples during colonial days." Chapters successively examine the use of Indians as pawns in British-American war and diplomacy between 1776 and 1816, the tragedies of Indian removal, the subjugation of the Plains Indians, various attempts to assimilate the Indian forcibly, and the New Deal and after. Contains a chart of important dates in Indian-white relations from 1622 to 1978. Bibliographical essays for each chapter conclude the book. Sixteen black-and-white photographs.

__________. *The Indian Rights Association: The Herbert Welsh Years, 1882-1904*. Tucson: University of Arizona Press, 1985.

Examines the activities of the Indian Rights Association during its first twenty years of advocacy for Native American peoples. Focuses on the role of Herbert Welsh in shaping the character and agenda of the association, its interactions with various administrations, and its participation in land, resource, and educational issues pertaining to American Indians. Key chapters concern the IRA's involvement in the Sioux land problem and its efforts in behalf of the Dawes Severalty Act. Illustrated with twelve black-and-white photographs of personalities discussed in the text. Short bibliography.

Hill, Edward E. *The Office of Indian Affairs, 1824-1880: Historical Sketches*. Library of the American Indian. New York: Clearwater, 1974.

Provides historical sketches of the one hundred superintendencies and agencies that constituted the field units of the Bureau of Indian Affairs between 1824 and 1880. Also includes subject headings for "Annuity Goods": awards to tribes of materials as specified by treaties; "Centennial": Indian exhibits at the U.S. International Exhibition at Philadelphia in 1876; "Schools": missionary, tribal, and government day and boarding schools for Indians; "Stocks": securities and funds in which Indian monies were held in trust; and miscellaneous. Includes a tribal index listing the majority of native groups under the bureau's supervision during the period covered and jurisdictional index which cites the names and operating date of the field units described.

Horsman, Reginald. *Expansion and American Indian Policy, 1783-1812*. East Lansing: Michigan State University Press, 1967.

Examines the evolution of American Indian relations in the period between the nation's founding and the conclusion of the War of 1812. Concludes that during these years, the U.S. government attempted to develop a coherent policy that balanced expansion into Indian-held territories with respect for the "natural" right of tribes to these lands. Sees acquisition by purchase and early experiments in Indian assimilation as attempts rationalize expansionism.

Hoxie, Frederick E. *A Final Promise: The Campaign to Assimilate the Indians, 1880-1920*. Lincoln: University of Nebraska Press, 1984.

Investigates the changes in the theory and practice of Indian assimilation from 1880 to 1920. Proposes two distinct phases for this assimilationist campaign. During the first of these phases, there was widespread interest and optimism in transforming Indians into civilized citizens; the second phase, coinciding with the rising power of politicians in the West, was characterized by a more pessimistic assessment of Indian prospects. Bibliography.

Jackson, Helen Hunt. *A Century of Dishonor: A Sketch of the United States Government's Dealings with Some of the Indian Tribes*. New York: Harper and Brothers. 1881.

An impassioned plea for the reform of late nineteenth-century federal Indian policy. Chapters review the history of government relations with the Delawares, Cheyennes, Nez Percé, Sioux, Poncas, Winnebagos, and Cherokees. A concluding chapter presents a devastating portrait of selected massacres of Indians by whites. Concerning the record of government dealings with the Indians the author states, "every page and every year has a dark stain. The story of one tribe is the story of all, varied only by differences of time and place; but neither time nor place makes any difference in the main facts."

Keller, Robert H. *American Protestantism and United States Indian Policy, 1869-82*. Lincoln: University of Nebraska Press, 1983.

A detailed history of the Indian "Peace Policy": President Ulysses S. Grant's attempt to institute reform in Indian administration by placing it in the hands of Christian denominations. Examines the origins and instrumentation of the policy; formation of the Board of Indian Commissioners, a semiofficial body of Protestant reformers and philanthropists charged with advancing the assimilationist goals of the policy; the forces opposed to Indian reform; and the failures and eventual termination of the Peace Policy in 1882. Three appendices. Bibliography. Black-and-white photographs. Maps and tables.

Kersey, Harry A., Jr. *The Florida Seminoles and the New Deal, 1933-1942*. Boca Raton: Florida Atlantic University Press, 1989.

Examines Seminole responses to Indian Commissioner John Collier's Indian New Deal, a Depression era policy which sought to revitalize Native American cultures and economies. Concludes that as was the case among many American Indian tribes, the New Deal received a mixed reception among the Seminoles and generated both positive and negative results. According to the author, "it was definitely limited in scope, and its primary value lay in preparing the way for future change." Bibliography. Black-and-white photographs. One map.

McLoughlin, William G. *Cherokees and Missionaries, 1789-1839*. New Haven, Conn.: Yale University Press, 1984.

Discusses the relationship between various denominations of Protestant missionaries and the Cherokees during the late eighteenth and early nineteenth centuries. Primary focus is directed, first, to the specific ways in which Cherokees and missionaries of this period "looked at the need for, and means of, modifying social, institutional, familial, and individual behavior, belief, and customs," and, second, the role played by various types of Cherokee factions (regional, political, ethnic, social, and ideological) in determining the speed and extent of culture change needed to cope with internal and external pressures. Bibliography.

Mardock, Robert Winston. *The Reformers and the American Indian*. Columbia: University of Missouri Press, 1971.

Examines the influence of Christian reformers on the formulation and implementation of federal Indian policy in the latter half of the nineteenth century. Details the historical and social background of Christian reform and its application to Indian-white relations; the cultural and religious assumptions informing the reform agenda of Indian "civilization and Christianization"; and the opposition that reformers faced both within the political establishment from among Western frontiersmen. Bibliography.

Meriam, Lewis. *The Problem of Indian Administration.* Institute for Government Research, Brookings Institution. Baltimore: Johns Hopkins University Press, 1928.

The results of Lewis Meriam's 1926 survey, of social conditions of American Indians. In addition to describing the inadequate services provided Native Americans, the report offers a critique of past Indian policy and recommendations for its improvement. The Meriam Report was of fundamental importance in shaping John Collier's Indian New Deal of 1934.

Milner, Clyde A., and Floyd A. O'Neil, eds. *Churchmen and the Western Indians: 1820-1920.* Norman: University of Oklahoma Press, 1985.

Uses the careers of six missionaries from different denominations to highlight several comparative themes surrounding late nineteenth century attempts to Christianize and "civilize" American Indians. Encourages the reader "to consider both the churchmen's and the Indians' willingness to change and adapt, or their unwillingness to do so." Featured are Cyrus Byington, John Jasper Methvin, George Washington Bean, Joseph M. Cataldo, S. J., Albert K. Smiley, and Bishop Henry B. Whipple.

Miner, H. Craig. *The Corporation and the Indian: Tribal Sovereignty and Industrial Civilization in Indian Territory, 1865-1907.* Columbia: University of Missouri Press, 1976.

Examines the relationship between corporations and Native peoples in Indian Territory between the Civil War and Oklahoma's admission to statehood. Focuses on the role that railroad, coal, and oil corporations played and the strategies they used in undermining the sovereignty of the Osage, Cherokee, and Choctaw tribes.

Mooney, James. *The Ghost Dance Religion and the Sioux Outbreak of 1890*, Bureau of American Ethnology, Annual Report 14 (1892-1893). Washington, D.C.: U.S. Government Printing Office, 1896.

An exhaustive discussion of the Ghost Dance Religion of the late nineteenth century and its relation to the massacre of Big Foot's band of Minneconjou Sioux at Wounded Knee on December 29, 1890. Chapters 1 through 8 furnish information on Indian religious revivals preceding the 1890 Ghost Dance, including those of the Delaware and Shawnee prophets, Smohalla religion of the Columbia region, and the Shakers of Puget Sound. Chapters 9 through 15 describe in detail the Ghost Dance of the 1880's and 1890's placing particular emphasis on its diffusion and practice among the Sioux. Chapter 16 compares the Ghost Dance with other religious systems and cults. Includes more than 150 Ghost Dance songs of the Arapaho, Cheyenne, Comanche, Paiute, Washo, Pit River Indians, Sioux, Kiowa, Kiowa Apache, and Caddo. Bibliography. Black-and-white reproductions, photographs, and drawings.

Parker, Linda S. *Native American Estate: The Struggle over Indian and Hawaiian Lands.* Honolulu: University of Hawaii Press, 1989.

Compares and contrasts the effects of Western expansionism among Hawaiians and Native North Americans. Focuses on the processes by which these indigenous peoples have been divested of their traditional lands and their recent attempts to use political and legal means to regain territories. An introduction discusses the Western concepts and rationales that underlay the appropriations of Indian and Hawaiian lands. Chapter 2 discusses systems of Native land tenure. Chapters 3 through 6 review the means by which Indian and Hawaiian lands were appropriated. Chapters 7 and 8 examine ongoing attempts at restitution and struggles over use and access rights.

Parman, Donald L. *The Navajos and the New Deal*. New Haven, Conn.: Yale University Press, 1976.

A history and evaluation of the Navajo New Deal, one application of Indian Commissioner John Collier's Depression era program intended to revitalize Native American cultural and economic life. Particular attention is given the controversial policy of Navajo livestock reduction, pointing out how government mismanagement resulted in the demoralization of Navajo people. The author gives a mixed review to the Navajo New Deal, noting both its positive and negative aspects. Bibliography.

Perdue, Theda. *Slavery and the Evolution of Cherokee Society, 1540-1866*. Knoxville: University of Tennessee Press, 1979.

Analyzes the traditional practice of slavery among the Cherokee and how contact with whites transformed that institution from the mid-sixteenth to mid-nineteenth centuries. Chapters compare and contrast the aboriginal theory and practice of slavery with its Euro-American counterpart; examine the political, economic, and psychological forces that led a portion of the Cherokee to participate in the trade and exploitation of black slaves; detail variations in the Cherokee treatment of slaves; and describe how the Cherokee development of "plantation" slavery caused a fracturing of intratribal relationships and tensions with abolitionist missionary associations.

Peroff, Nicholas C. *Menominee Drums: Tribal Termination and Restoration, 1954-1974*. Norman: University of Oklahoma Press, 1982.

Seeks to explain the evolution of the federal Indian policy of termination, the application of this policy to the Menominees, and its eventual reversal in 1974. Discusses the place of "termination" within the context of white America's traditional attempts to assimilate Native peoples, the evolution of the Menominee Termination Act of 1954, the effect of the Termination Act on the Menominee people, and the important role the organization DRUMS (Determination of Rights and Unity for Menominee Shareholders) played in restoring the tribe's federal recognition. Bibliography. Black-and-white photographs. Maps and charts.

Phillips, George H. *Chiefs and Challengers: Indian Resistance and Cooperation in Southern California*. Berkeley: University of California Press, 1975.

Examines the responses of Luiseno, Cupeno, and Cahuilla Indians to Hispanic and Anglo-American colonization. Focuses on the importance of three leaders—Antonio Gara, Juan Antonio, and Manuelito Cota—in instrumenting the strategy of resistance or accommodation chosen by each group. Bibliography.

Philp, Kenneth R. *John Collier's Crusade for Indian Reform: 1920-1954*. Tucson: University of Arizona Press, 1977.

Examines the redirection of federal Indian policy under John Collier, President Franklin D. Roosevelt's Commissioner of Indian Affairs. Demonstrates how Collier's encouragement of Indian cultural values, economic development, and limited political sovereignty was continuous with his earlier experiments in ethnic affirmation while a social worker in New York. Describes the initiation and structure of Collier's Indian New Deal, white and Indian responses to its various programs and goals, and an assessment of the Collier legacy. Bibliographical essay. Black-and-white photographs.

Priest, Loring Benson. *Uncle Sam's Stepchildren: The Reformation of United States Indian Policy, 1865-1887*. New Brunswick, N.J.: Rutgers University Press, 1942.

Examines the evolution in U.S. Indian relations between the end of the Civil War and the passage of the Dawes Allotment Act in 1887. Concentrates on the rising tide of Christian/humanitarianism and how it set the assumptions and agenda for the reform of Indian policy, the most important supporters and opponents of reform, and the methods by which reformers proposed to transform the Indian from savage to civilized citizen. Concludes with a discussion of reform land policies, which culminated in the passage of the Dawes Severalty or Allotment Act. The author sees the allotment of Indian lands as both "an outgrowth of a desire for expansion . . . [and] the product of a sincere conviction that [Indian] emulation of whites was essential." Footnotes but no bibliography.

Prucha, Francis Paul. *American Indian Policy in Crisis: Christian Reformers and the Indian, 1865-1900*. Norman: University of Oklahoma Press, 1976.

Recounts the history of the reform movement in federal Indian policy during the last third of the nineteenth century. Considers these years "the most critical period in the whole history of Indian-white relations in the United States." Chapters describe the evolution of the reform movement; the background and aspirations of the reformers; reservations and allotments as instruments of reform; law and citizenship for the Indian; civil service reform; and the liquidation of Indian Territory. Thirty-seven black-and-white photographs and four maps. Extensive bibliography.

__________. *American Indian Policy in the Formative Years: The Indian Trade and Intercourse Acts, 1790-1834*. Cambridge, Mass.: Harvard University Press, 1962.

An analysis of federal Indian policy from colonial times to the era of removal in the early nineteenth century. Sees a basic continuity in the aims and principles of this period. This continuity may be seen in the Indian policy of the government which "took shape primarily in a series of federal laws 'to regulate trade and intercourse with Indian tribes, and to preserve peace on the frontier.'"

Chapters examine how the government sought to regulate the fur trade, control the flow of whiskey into Indian territories, punish crimes committed by one race against the other and compensate for damages, promote Indian education and civilization, and restrict whites from Indian lands.

__________, ed. *Americanizing the American Indian: Writings by the "Friends of the Indian" 1880-1900*. Cambridge, Mass.: Harvard University Press, 1973.
A collection of forty documents by advocates of the humanitarian reform of late nineteenth century Indian policy. Provides information on the reform agenda and the intensity with which the "Friends of the Indians" fought for its adoption. An introduction places the writings within a historical context and summarizes the three principal proposals in which reformers put their faith: "first, to break up the tribal relations and their reservation base and to individualize the Indian on a 160-acre homestead by the allotment of land in severalty; second, to make the Indians citizens and equal with the whites in regard to both the protection and the restraints of law; and third, to provide a universal government school system that would make good Americans out of the rising generations of Indians."

__________. *The Churches and the Indian Schools*. Norman: University of Oklahoma Press, 1979.
Discusses the conflict that erupted between the Catholic church and the Protestant-controlled Indian Bureau during the late nineteenth century over the use of treaty-granted education funds for denominationally operated Indian schools. The Indian Bureau argued that such allocations violated the separation of church and state, while Catholics countered that denying Indians the right to use these funds to finance parochial schools was an infringement of their religious freedom. Bibliography. Black-and-white photographs.

__________. *The Great Father: The United States Government and the American Indians*. Lincoln: University of Nebraska Press, 1986.
An abridgment of the author's two-volume history of federal Indian relations. Covers the two centuries from the nation's founding to 1980. Finds that throughout this period, "the controlling force in Indian-white relations has been the policy determined by the white government, not by the wishes of the Indians." While retaining the scope of the original, this abridgment contains half of the latter's text and has eliminated all of its footnotes and illustrations. Eight maps and three tables. Bibliography.

Rahill, Peter J. *The Catholic Indian Missions and Grant's Peace Policy, 1870-1884*. Washington, D.C.: Catholic University of America Press, 1953.
A history of the Bureau of Catholic Indian Missions during the era of President Grant's Peace Policy. Documents how the origins of that bureau were a direct consequence of the anti-Romanism which the American Catholic hierarchy attributed to those at the helm of federal Indian relations, the Catholic Bureau's role as official mediator between missionaries in the field and the Indian Office, and the bureau's struggles with its Protestant adversaries. Bibliography.

Riley, Glenda. *Women and Indians on the Frontier, 1825-1915*. Albuquerque: University of New Mexico Press, 1984.

Sets as its primary objective to study the initial reactions and subsequent relations of frontierswomen to Native Americans. Also provides a gender-based examination of Indian-white relations. Suggests a number of hypotheses concerning why the relations between Indians and white women "developed a pattern that contradicted the accepted image, remained distinct from that established between white men and Indians, and that has received little, if any, scholarly attention." Notes on sources. Black-and-white reproductions and photographs.

Satz, Ronald N. *American Indian Policy in the Jacksonian Era*. Lincoln: University of Nebraska Press, 1975.

An analysis of federal-Indian relations in the years during and immediately following the presidency of Andrew Jackson. Particular attention is given to the social and political events and forces leading up to congressional passage of the Removal Act of 1830, supporters and critics of Indian removal, the theory and practice of Indian expulsion from the Southeast, conditions frustrating the reinstitution of sovereignty among removed peoples, fears of settlers on the western frontiers concerning emigrating Indians, the ineffectiveness of the Indian Service during the Jacksonian era, and attempts to "civilize and Christianize" the tribes resettled in Indian Territory. Bibliography.

Searcy, Martha C. *The Georgia-Florida Contest in the American Revolution, 1776-1778*. University: University of Alabama Press, 1985.

Examines the campaigns of 1776, 1777, and 1778 waged between British loyalists and American revolutionaries for control over Georgia and east Florida. Pays particular attention to the role of the Creek Confederacy in the strategy and outcomes of these campaigns. According to the author, the "use of warriors and Indian policy in general [was] a crucial part in the military plans of both British and American leaders." Meanwhile, the Creeks used their well-honed diplomatic skills to play one side off against the other, waiting to see which party gained the advantage. Bibliography of sources cited. One map.

Sheehan, Bernard W. *Seeds of Extinction: Jeffersonian Philanthropy and the American Indian*. Chapel Hill: University of North Carolina Press, 1973.

Examines the assumptions informing the philanthropic agenda of Jeffersonian Indian policy and the various factors that resulted in the failure of this program. Argues that the Jeffersonian humanitarians failed to understand not only Indian humanity and culture but the nature of Indian-white relations. Bibliography.

Sutton, Imre, ed. *Irredeemable America: The Indians' Estate and Land Claims*. Albuquerque: University of New Mexico Press, 1985.

An anthology of fifteen papers examining the procedures and decisions of the U.S. Claims Commission, a quasi-judicial branch of Congress that considered land claims lodged by tribes against the U.S. government from 1946 to 1978. The essays and case studies in part 1 focus on the history of the commission and various aspects of the claims process. Those in part 2 primarily deal with tribes that seek restoration of their lands, in favor of the monetary settlements offered by the federal government. Three appendices: relevant laws and treaties, bibliographical note, and table of cases cited. Maps.

Svaldi, David. *Sand Creek and the Rhetoric of Extermination: A Case Study in Indian-White Relations*. Lincoln: University of Nebraska Press, 1989.
Uses the rhetoric surrounding the Sand Creek Massacre of 1864 as a case study in the discourse of Indian-white relations in the United States. Concludes that embedded in the Sand Creek rhetoric are key symbols about "enemies" and violence which whites use to rationalize their treatment of Native Americans. Applies this conclusion to America's experience in Vietnam with particular reference to the massacre at Mai Lai.

Szasz, Margaret. *Education and the American Indian: The Road to Self-Determination, 1928-1973*. Albuquerque: University of New Mexico Press, 1974.
Focuses on the shifting contexts, policies, and delivery of federal Indian education during the fifty years separating the Merriam and Kennedy reports (1928-1969). The first chapter briefly describes the assimilationist nature of Indian education during the late nineteenth and early twentieth centuries. The next section details the attempts of those instrumenting Collier's Indian New Deal to replace assimilationist schooling with that guided by principles of cultural pluralism and Indian self-determination. The subsequent three chapters track the shift away from and then return to self-determination in the period between World War II and 1969. An epilogue sketches trends in Indian education during the early 1970's.

Tatum, Lawrie. *Our Red Brothers and the Peace Policy of President Ulysses S. Grant*. Lincoln: University of Nebraska Press, 1970.
A first-hand account of the workings of the Grant Peace Policy by a Quaker agent who served on the Kiowa-Comanche reservation from 1869 to 1873. Includes sections on the history of the two tribes and their relationship with other Indian peoples and the federal government, aspects of traditional southern Plains culture, important Kiowa and Comanche personalities, and the elements and goals of the Peace Policy and humanitarian reform. An introductory essay by Richard N. Ellis places Tatum's work in the history of U.S. Indian relations and presents a sympathetic portrait of the author. Sixteen black-and-white photographs.

Taylor, Graham D. *The New Deal and American Indian Tribalism: The Administration of the Indian Reorganization Act, 1934-1945*. Lincoln: University of Nebraska Press, 1980.
An analysis of John Collier's Indian New Deal and its failure to achieve its principal goals. Focuses on those elements of the deal which Collier regarded as central, including tribal political reorganization and the development of Indian economies. Argues that the Indian New Deal was "fatally weakened by emphasis on tribal reorganization and the assumptions about contemporary Indian societies which formed the basis for the tribal ideal" and that the Collier administration's failure to revive the tribe "undermined as well the ambitious and farsighted plans for ensuring Indian economic self-sufficiency." Bibliographical essay.

Thornton, Russell. *We Shall Live Again: The 1870 and 1890 Ghost Dance Movement as Demographic Revitalization*. Cambridge, England:: Cambridge University Press, 1986.

Rejects the popular interpretation of the Ghost Dance movements as hysterical reactions to the disorganization, frustrations, and deprivations experienced by Indians during the latter half of the nineteenth century. Argues that these movements were deliberate and rational attempts on the part of Native Americans to "accomplish their demographic revitalization. In other words, they sought to assure survival as physical peoples through regaining population—bringing the dead to life—by performing the Ghost Dance ceremonies [sic]." Uses historical and statistical analyses to test the hypothesis. Eight appendices.

Trennert, Robert A., Jr. *Alternative to Extinction: Federal Indian Policy and the Beginnings of the Reservation System, 1846-51*. Philadelphia: University of Pennsylvania Press, 1975.

Proposes that the philosophical origins of the modern reservation system trace their roots to the years between 1846 and 1851. Argues that during this period, westward expansionism led to confrontations dangerous for both Indians and whites. The U.S. government thus sought a policy that would protect its citizens while guarding Native Americans from extinction. Its solution, represented in the Fort Laramie Treaty of 1851, lay in segregating Indians in restricted areas where they might slowly be assimilated into Western society. Bibliography.

Truettner, William H. *The Natural Man Observed: A Study of Catlin's Indian Gallery*. Washington, D.C.: Smithsonian Institution Press, 1979.

A critical examination of the career of artist George Catlin, whose "Gallery" of Indian sketches and paintings numbered more than 2000 pieces. The introductory chapters analyze the motives underlying Catlin's work among Native Americans, the image of the Indian it presents, and the historical and ethnographic value of his paintings. Part 2, "A Descriptive Catalogue of the Indian Gallery," cites where and when pieces were painted and includes hundreds of black-and-white and color reproductions.

Utley, Robert M. *The Indian Frontier of the American West, 1846-1890*. Albuquerque: University of New Mexico Press, 1984.

Summarizes the history of Indian-white relations in the trans-Mississippi West from the mid-nineteenth century to the establishment of Anglo-American political dominance over the western tribes. Presents this history from the perspective of both Indians and whites, emphasizing the complexity of their interactions. Begins with a discussion of the Indian West at mid-century, followed by chapters on the foundations of reservation policy. Indian-white relations during the Civil War; the reform of Indian policy during the late nineteenth century; the reservation, 1880-1890; and the passing of the frontier. Bibliography. Black-and-white reproductions and photographs. Maps.

Viola, Herman J. *Diplomats in Buckskin: A History of the Indian Delegations in Washington City*. Washington, D.C.: Smithsonian Institution Press, 1981.

A history of the authorized and unauthorized visits of tribal delegations to Washington, D.C. The book, focused mainly on the nineteenth century, addresses a number of topics: the reasons that federal officials organized such visits; the varying motives for Indian participation; the hardships delegates encountered on the way to the Capitol; the typical round of appointments, conferences, and excursions to which Indians were exposed; the windfall of such visits for the arts and sciences; and selected examples of meetings between Indian representatives and the "Great Father." Black-and-white reproductions and photographs.

Washburn, Wilcomb E. *The Assault on Indian Tribalism: The General Allotment Law (Dawes Act) of 1887*. Philadelphia: J. B. Lippincott, 1975.

A narrative and documentary history of the motives, goals, and impact of the Dawes or General Allotment Act of 1887. Part 1 describes the volatile relationship between Indian and whites during the post-Civil War period, the challenge that this situation presented to those in charge of Indian policy, the arguments and lobbying efforts by humanitarian reformers for passage of the Dawes Act, and the tragic consequences of that policy on Indian life. Part 2 reproduces nine documents pertaining to the substance and passage of the Dawes Act. Part 3 contains a bibliographical essay.

White, Richard. *The Roots of Dependency: Subsistence, Environment, and Social Change Among the Choctaws, Pawnees, and Navajos*. Lincoln: University of Nebraska Press, 1983.

Attempts to explain why environments that once easily supported Choctaw, Pawnee, and Navajo populations eventually lost their capacity to sustain these groups. Identifies as the common factor of decline white attempts to bring Indian resources, land, and labor into the market. Argues that the collapse of the tribes' subsistence systems and their integration into world markets "brought increasing reliance on the capitalist core, lack of economic choice, and profound political and social changes within their societies." Bibliographical essay. Maps and tables.

Young, Mary E. *Redskins, Ruffleshirts, and Rednecks: Indian Allotments in Alabama and Mississippi, 1830-1860*. Norman: University of Oklahoma Press, 1961.

An account of how Native lands in Alabama and Mississippi were distributed among whites following the forced removal of their former occupants to Indian Territory in the early 1830's. Begins with a summary of removal policy and its application to the Choctaw, Chickasaw, and Creek populations in the two states. Subsequent chapters detail the means which settlers, speculators, and land companies used to acquire both vacated lands as well as those allotted to Indians who had chosen to remain in the Southeast. Bibliography. Black-and-white photographs. Maps, tables, and charts.

Indians in Canada (1776-1990)

Adams, Howard. *Prison of Grass: Canada from the Native Point of View*. Toronto: New Press, 1975.

A powerful indictment of Canada's treatment of its aboriginal populations. Argues that throughout Canadian history, whites have attempted, through a variety of means, to obliterate Native society, culture, and values. Examines the continuation of this policy into the modern era and its disastrous affects on Native lifeways, psychology, and leadership. Concludes with the author's recommendations concerning the means Native Americans must utilize to win freedom and justice.

Babcock, William T. *Who Owns Canada? Aboriginal Title and Canadian Courts*. Ottawa: Canadian Association in Support of the Native Peoples, 1976.

An analysis of the way in which Canadian courts have viewed the land rights of Native peoples. Finds that since the "discovery" of North America, Anglo-European international and common law have "conspired in the Courts to rule against the concept of aboriginal title to land inhabited by Canada's native people." Having no understanding of the Native attitude toward the land, the English unilaterally imposed the common law system on non-Native and Native alike. Since then, Native rights to land have been recognized only when it suited the courts.

Barron, F. Laurie, and James B. Waldram, eds. *1885 and After: Native Society in Transition*. Regina: University of Regina, Canadian Plains Research Center, 1986.

An anthology of twenty papers that examines various aspects of the Northwest "Rebellion" of 1885, a Métis and Indian insurrection against Euro-Canadian domination. The essays are divided into two parts. Those in part 1 concern the events leading up to and including the outbreak of hostilities in 1885. The significance of Louis Riel and other individuals in shaping the nature and goals of the rebellion enter prominently in these discussion. The essays in part 2 describe and analyze transitions in Native society following the Rebellion.

Berry, John W., et al. *Multiculturalism and Ethnic Attitudes in Canada*. Ottawa: Minister of Supply and Services, 1977.

Investigates the attitudes of Canadians toward multiculturalism, definingthe term as the existence of ethnic groups in Canada which derive from cultural traditions other than French or British. The research consists of an examination of four attitude domains: the attitudes held by Canadians toward a variety of ethnic groups in the country; general beliefs regarding cultural diversity; attitudes toward immigration; and the psychological phenomena of ethnic prejudice and discrimination. The study finds that Native peoples "occupy a special position in the attitudes of Canadians; this position may be best characterized by the term 'marginal.' That is, there appears to be some recognition of their special status as indigenous people, but this is insufficient to create a set of positive attitudes toward them." Appendices and tables.

Boldt, Menno, and J. Anthony Long (in association with Leroy Little Bear), eds. *The Quest for Justice: Aboriginal Peoples and Aboriginal Rights*. Toronto: University of Toronto Press, 1985.

Twenty-four essays that examine the relation of Native rights and public policy in Canada. The issues involved in this relation include "the political, legal, and constitutional steps that should be taken to redress historic injustices to Canada's aboriginal peoples and, on a broader scale, how aboriginal people as culturally distinct ethnic groups should relate to the larger society." An introduction by the editors provides a history of Canadian aboriginal policy. The essays that follow examine various political and philosophical perspectives on aboriginal rights, aspects of aboriginal rights in the constitutional and policy-making processes, historical and contemporary legal and judicial philosophies on aboriginal rights, and aboriginal rights and Indian government. Five appendices.

Brown, Jennifer S. H. *Strangers in Blood: Fur Trade Company Families in Indian Country*. Vancouver: University of British Columbia Press, 1980.

A comparative study of the Hudson's Bay and North West fur trade companies "as organizations that differed conspicuously in their origins and characteristics and of the social and domestic relations that developed within them." Topics include variations in the structures and organizations of the two companies before their coalition in 1821; the sexual and marital relations of company officers after 1821; the relations between fur traders and their Métis (mixed blood) children and the social position of these children before 1821; and the socioeconomic factors underlying the tendency of fur trade parents to "place" their children in surroundings where they could receive schooling and technical training. Bibliography. Black-and-white reproductions and photographs. Color plates.

Daniels, Harry W., ed. *The Forgotten People: Métis and Non-Status Indian Land Claims*. Ottawa: Native Council of Canada, 1979.

A selection of articles and essays focusing on the land claims of the 750,000-1,000,000 Métis and Indians not included under Canada's Indian Act. The essays are organized under three mains sections. The first overviews the historical and legal questions surrounding claims research; the second provides a summary of issues involved in claims research in the Maritimes and Central Canada; and the third summarizes the land claims of the Métis in western Canada.

Driben, Paul. *When Freedom Is Lost*. Toronto: University of Toronto Press, 1983.

A study of the political and economic relations that evolved between the Ojibwa Indians of the Fort Hope Band, Ontario, and their government agents before and after the issuance of the Trudeau government's White Paper on Indian affairs in 1969. Documents how the system of agencies and programs spawned by the White Paper has embedded the band in a morass of government dependency rather than generating the economic self-sufficiency it intended. Argues that such dependency need not be the case given that the band villages possess natural resources the development of which can be translated into jobs and opportunities. Bibliography. Black-and-white photographs.

Fisher, Robin. *Contact and Conflict: Indian-European Relations in British Columbia, 1774-1890*. Vancouver: University of British Columbia Press, 1977.
Examines the history of culture contact between the Indians of British Columbia and Europeans from 1774 to the last decade of the nineteenth century. Submits that the passing of the fur trade and the establishment of settlement effected a fundamental change in the nature of Indian-European contact in British Columbia. Whereas the fur trade resulted in only minimal and manageable culture change for Indians, settlement "was disruptive because it introduced major cultural change so rapidly that the Indians began to lose control of their situation." Bibliography. Black-and-white photographs.

Frideres, James S. *Canada's Indians: Contemporary Conflicts*. Scarborough, Ontario: Prentice-Hall, 1974.
An anthology of essays which aims to give the student a new perspective on Canadian Indian-white relations. Argues that the traditional perspective, which views the situation as an Indian problem and approaches it in individualistic terms, is incorrect. Rather, "it can be a white problem . . . [and to] view Indian-white relations from an individualistic perspective will not provide solution . . . to integrating native people into the larger society." Subjects include contemporary Indians, a case study of problems of reserve Indian communities, urban Indians, the alienation Indians experience in white environments, Indian organizations, the Native Brotherhood of British Columbia, and Red Power. Bibliography.

Getty, Ian A. L., and Antoine S. Lussier. *As Long as the Sun Shines and Water Flows: A Reader in Canadian Native Studies*. Vancouver: University of British Columbia Press, 1983.
An anthology of essays and articles which examines the history of Canadian Indian policy from the Royal Proclamation of 1763 to the early 1980's. An introductory essay provides a broad, historical overview of Indian-white relations in Canada. The remaining papers are organized under two headings: "The Evolution of Indian Administration Since the Royal Proclamation of 1763" and "Native Responses to Changing Relations and Circumstances." Includes the texts of "A Declaration of the First Nations, 1981" and the "1983 Constitutional Accord on Aboriginal Rights." Closes with a bibliographical essay entitled "The Indian in Canadian Historical Writing, 1971-1981."

Getty, Ian A. L., and Donald B. Smith, eds. *One Century Later: Western Canadian Reserve Indians Since Treaty 7*. Vancouver: University of British Columbia Press, 1978.
A collection of essays based on papers presented at the Ninth Annual Western Canadian Studies Conference in 1977. The goal of the conference was to evaluate the political, economic, and social status of the western Canadian Indian one hundred years after the signing of Treaty Seven: an agreement by which Blackfoot, Blood, Piegan, Sacree, and Stoney Indians ceded present-day

southern Alberta to the Crown. The book is divided into historical and contemporary sections.

Gough, Barry M. *Gunboat Frontier: British Maritime Authority and Northwest Coast Indians, 1846-90*. Vancouver: University of British Columbia Press, 1984.

Examines the role played by the Royal Navy in imposing the rule of English law over Indians tribes of coastal British Columbia during the second half of the nineteenth century. Describes the institutions, personalities, and events that shaped the evolution of that role as well as the overall practices and goals of Canadian Indian policy. Bibliography. Black-and-white photographs. Maps.

Little Bear, Leroy, and Menno Boldt, eds. *Pathways to Self-Determination*. Toronto: University of Toronto Press, 1984.

An anthology of articles intended to present Indian perspectives on federal relations with the nearly 324,000 "status Indians" of Canada—those individuals whom the Canadian government recognizes as having a distinct constitutional standing as Indians. Among the issues that the authors address are aboriginal rights, treaty rights, the relationship between federal policy and Indian self-government, the nature of Indian government, and a provincial perspective on Indian self-government. Three appendices.

Long, J. Anthony, and Menno Boldt, eds. *Governments in Conflict? Provinces and Indian Nations in Canada*. Toronto: University of Toronto Press, 1988.

A series of papers that examines the role of Canada's provinces in the development of policies and programs affecting Native peoples. The essays in section 1 probe the impact of federal Indian policy on provincial approaches to dealing with Indians. Contained in section 2 are essays exploring the set of interests and perspectives which the provinces' constitutionally mandated participation in negotiations on aboriginal rights have introduced into the negotiating process. Section 3 presents articles that identify the common characteristics of provincial Indian policies and programs. The political and legal issues involved in Indian land claims are the subject of section 4. Section 5 provides information on jurisdictional issues between the provinces and Indians. The concluding set of papers compare federal Indian relations in Canada with those of aboriginal peoples in other countries. Thirteen appendices present selected documents on Indian-provincial relations.

Métis Association of Alberta, et al. *Métis Land Rights in Alberta: A Political History*. Edmonton: Author, 1981.

Outlines and clarifies issues of particular significance to Métis land claims in Alberta. Begins with a historical overview that traces the evolution of Métis sociopolitical identity in the prairie provinces. Subsequent chapters deal with the development of the concept of aboriginal title; the importance in Métis history of "scrip," a government certificate indicating the right of the holder to receive in the form of cash, goods, or land; historically important Métis colonies and settlements; and the bases of Métis land claims in Alberta. Eight appendices. Sepia-toned photographs and maps.

Miller, J. R. *Skyscrapers Hide the Heavens: A History of Indian-White Relations in Canada*. Toronto: University of Toronto Press, 1989.

A study of the evolution of Indian-white relations in Canada organized around two major theses: that the nature of a relationship between two peoples of different background is largely determined by the reasons they have for interacting; and that far from being the passive victims they are often portrayed, Indian peoples were "active, assertive contributors to the unfolding of Canadian history." Views this evolution as displaying four phases. During the first two of these phases, Indians and whites cooperated to their mutual economic and strategic advantage. In the third phase, whites no longer needed Indians and attempted to coerce them into assimilation. In the fourth phase, that of the Indians' recent emergence from irrelevance, no single type of relationship has as yet developed. Selected bibliography. Black-and-white photographs. Maps.

Patterson, E. Palmer, II. *The Canadian Indian: A History Since 1500*. Dons Mills, Ontario: Collier-Macmillan Canada, 1972.

A narrative and analysis of Canada's Indian history. Begins with several chapters that attempt to draw parallels between the experiences of Canadian Native peoples and colonized groups from other parts of the British empire. Establishes a fourfold periodization for the history of Canadian Indians. In phase 1, Indians participated in technological exchange with European while remaining socially, economically, and politically independent of the latter. During phase 2, Europeans used political, economic, and religious means to gain ever-greater control over Native lives. The establishment of Indian reserves and the European dominance of Indian affairs characterize phase 3. The fourth, and present, phase sees a resurgence in Native political independence. Selected bibliography.

Ponting, J. Rick, and Roger Gibbins. *Out of Irrelevance: A Sociopolitical Introduction to Indian Affairs in Canada*. Toronto: Butterworths, 1980.

Describes and analyzes the processes by which the Indians of Canada were reduced to virtual irrelevance in the eyes of mainstream society and recent attempts to rectify this situation. Part 1, "The Context of Indian Affairs," contains chapters on the history of Indian-government relations, a sociodemographic profile of Indians in Canada, and Canadians' perceptions of Indians. Part 2 examines the bureaucratic structure and functioning of Indian administration. Part 3 focuses on the recent politicization of Indian affairs, with particular reference to the history, internal environment, and external relations of the National Indian Brotherhood. Part 4 describes non-Indian support organizations. Bibliography. Appendices.

Ray, Arthur J. *Indians in the Fur Trade: Their Role as Trappers, Hunters, and Middlemen in the Lands Southwest of Hudson Bay, 1660-1870*. Toronto: University of Toronto Press, 1974.

Examines some of the adaptive responses of different Indian groups living in the central and southern portions of Manitoba and Saskatchewan to political and social developments in western Canada between 1660 and 1870. Sees the fur trade as the most pervasive force influencing these developments. Focuses on the perceptions and responses of different Indian groups to the opportunities offered by the fur trade, the different roles that various bands played in the trading of furs, and the importance of this difference for tribal migration, intertribal relations, changes in material culture, and ecological adaptations. Bibliography. Black-and-white photographs and drawings.

Stymeist, David H. *Ethnics and Indians: Social Relations in a Northwestern Ontario Town*. Toronto: Peter Martin Associates, 1975.

Examines the interrelationships between white and Indian ethnics in the small community of Crow Lake, Ontario. Among the study's findings are that relations between Crow Lake whites and Indians take place within a narrow range of social contexts; that Indians are excluded from nearly all sectors of the town's social life; that exclusion from jobs and houses in the town is a principal reason for the return of Indians to reserves; and that programs serving reserve Indians employ many Crow Lake whites and are an important part of the town's economy. Concludes that "[p]rejudice and discrimination are important to the community, for . . . the town as a whole is heavily dependent upon the existence of a separate, unequal, and adjacent Native population." Bibliography.

Trigger, Bruce G. *Natives and Newcomers: Canada's "Heroic Age" Reconsidered*. Montreal: McGill-Queen's University Press, 1985.

A collection of essays on Canada's Native peoples and the first two centuries of their relations with whites. Topics include the image of the Indian in Canadian history, Canada's cultural prehistory, initial Native-European contacts (1497-1600), traders and colonizers (1600-1632), missionaries and epidemics (1632-1663), and a reinterpretation of the founding and internal dynamics of New France. Bibliography. Black-and-white reproductions. Maps.

Weaver, Sally M. *Making Canadian Indian Policy: The Hidden Agenda, 1968-70*. Toronto: University of Toronto Press.

Analyzes the evolution, impact, and implications of the Trudeau government's 1969 White Paper on Indian policy, a document which recommended the termination of all special Indian rights, reserves, and treaties. The author bases her information on fifty-one interviews with thirty-three individuals who were involved in shaping government policy, government documents and reports, and published sources. Seeks to portray the complexity of the policymaking process and to "contribute to a corporate memory in government about Indian policy . . . in the genuine belief that the White Paper experience can provide constructive lessons for both the government and Indians in the future." Bibliography.

Yerbury, John C. *The Subarctic Indians and the Fur Trade, 1680-1860*. Vancouver: University of British Columbia Press, 1986.

An ethnohistorical reconstruction that seeks, first, to contribute a more precise cultural history of the Canadian Athapaskans between 1680 and 1860 with emphasis on their changing ecological and sociocultural traditions; second, to distinguish the economic and ecological adaptations of the precontact, postcontact, and early direct contact organization of the Canadian Athapaskan groups; and third, to demonstrate how certain changes in Athapaskan social structure are attributable to the postcontact fur trade. Finds that the fur trade "acted as a catalyst for successive modifications in Canadian Athapaskan culture history, cultural ecology, and social organization." Maps and tables.

CULTURE AREAS

Northeast

General Studies and References

Duke, James A. *Handbook of Northeastern Indian Medicinal Plants*. Lincoln, Mass.: Quaterman, 1986.

A catalogue of more than seven hundred boreal plants used as medicines by Native Americans. Entries are arranged alphabetically by scientific names of the plants. Annotations include the common name(s) for the plant species as well as summaries of their medicinal uses. Indexes for common names and ailments. Black-and-white diagrams.

Ebbot, Elizabeth. *Indians of Minnesota*, edited by Judith Rosenblatt. 4th ed. Minneapolis: University of Minnesota Press, 1985.

An analysis of issues pertaining to present-day Minnesota Indians. Particular attention is given to tribal and federal relations; state and Indian conflicts over hunting and fishing rights; the problems of Indians living in urban environments; economic development and employment; education; welfare programs and delivery for the state's Native populations; housing, health, and chemical dependency; and Native Americans and the criminal justice system. Four appendices. Selected reading list. Maps and tables. Black-and-white photographs.

Edmunds, R. David. *Kinsmen Through Time: An Annotated Bibliography of Potawatomi History*. Metuchen, N.J.: Scarecrow Press, 1987.

An annotated listing of nearly eleven hundred published materials on the history of the Potawatomi. Designed for the broadest possible audience, including professional scholars, members of the various Potawatomi communities, and the general public. Citations are arranged alphabetically by author according to the following six divisions: general studies; colonial period; the new nation; removal period; Kansas, Oklahoma, and the Midwest: postremoval period, 1847-1900; and twentieth century. The first five pages of the preface provide a brief tribal history.

Feest, Christian F. *Indians of Northeastern North America*. Leiden: E. J. Brill, 1986.

Overviews the ethnohistory and lifeways of Native Americans of the North American Northeast. After briefly describing the culture area and its history, Feest discusses the issue of verbal and visual research sources. Subsequent sections provide information on a number of ethnographic themes, including cosmology and the supernatural, shamans and priests, dreams and visions, medicine societies, seasonal ceremonies and cosmic architecture, economic ritual, war ritual, new religions, Indian Christianity, and death and burial. Bibliography. Includes forty-six black-and-white reproductions and photographs.

Fixico, Donald L., ed. *An Anthology of Western Great Lakes Indian History*. American Indian Studies, College of Letters and Science, University of Wisconsin-Milwaukee. Milwaukee: Board of Regents, University of Wisconsin System, 1987.

An anthology of previously published writings on historical events, personalities, and traditions of indigenous tribes of Michigan, Wisconsin, northern Illinois, northeastern Iowa, and eastern Minnesota. The topics of the papers include differences in pre- and postcontact culture change among Wisconsin-area Indians; the origins of the Métis; the alliance between the French and Potawatomi; the removal of the Stockbridge Indians to Menominee country; Jacksonian Indian policy in the Old Northwest; the Black Hawk War; a character analysis of Pierre Paquette, a Winnebago mixed-blood; the Little Crow War of 1862 in Minnesota; allotment and the White Earth Chippewa Reservation; Menominee termination; and recent decisions on Chippewa hunting and fishing rights. Includes a historical chronology.

Foster, Michael K., et al. *Extending the Rafters: Interdisciplinary Approaches to Iroquoian Studies*. Albany: State University of New York Press, 1984.

A collection of essays by twenty-two authorities on Iroquois history and culture which reflects the influence and contributions of noted ethnohistorian William N. Fenton. Part 1, "Changing Perspectives in the Writing of Iroquoian History," contains ethnological and historical treatments of selected subjects related to the postcontact period. Papers pertaining to the Iroquois worldview are presented in part 2. Archaeological and linguistic perspectives on the problem of Iroquoian origins, movements, and prehistoric culture and society appear in part 3. The anthology closes with papers that explore Fenton's influence on Iroquoian studies and his work as an applied anthropologist. Bibliography of references cited by the contributors and Bibliography of William N. Fenton. Black-and-white diagrams. Maps.

Jennings, Francis, and William N. Fenton, eds. *The History and Culture of Iroquois Diplomacy: An Interdisciplinary Guide to the Treaties of the Six Nations and Their League*. Syracuse, N.Y.: Syracuse University Press for the D'Arcy McNickle Center for the History of the American Indian, Newberry Library, 1985.

An anthology of essays and reference materials which focuses on the political aspects of Iroquois history. Designed especially to help students of this history understand what is being said in the texts of Iroquois treaties. Section 1, "Treaty Diplomacy," contains papers that provide background information about Iroquois political history and culture. Section 2, "Treaty Events," provides a sample treaty with editorial commentary. Section 3 offers lists of reference data, including a calendar of some of the treaty negotiations involving Iroquois Indians, 1613-1913, a gazetteer that identifies place names commonly found in documents and literature dealing with Iroquois treaties and treaty making, and a select roster of persons participating in Iroquois treaties. Bibliography. Five maps.

Kinietz, W. Vernon. *The Indians of the Western Great Lakes, 1615-1760*. Ann Arbor: University of Michigan Press, 1940.
A synthesis of ethnographic materials concerning Great Lakes Indians based on manuscripts and published writings from the early seventeenth to mid-eighteenth century. Chapters are arranged by the following tribal groupings: Huron, Miami, Ottawa, Potawatomi, and Chippewa. Information concerning the history and location, characteristics, dress and ornament, economic life, social life, and religion of each of the groups is presented. Bibliography. One appendix.

Lurie, Nancy Oestrich. *Wisconsin Indians*. Madison: State Historical Society of Wisconsin, 1980.
Briefly describes the effects of federal Indian policy on Wisconsin's Native Americans and their reactions to that policy. Discusses the evolution of Indian policy in the state, including the treaties and compacts entered into by various tribes during the nineteenth century; the land cessions that such agreements entailed; the eventual confinement of the state's Indian population on reservations; the impact of such twentieth century programs as the Indian New Deal, Indian Claims Commission, relocation, and termination; the Menominee struggle against termination; the Lac Court Oreilles Chippewa occupation of Winter Dam in 1971; American Indian Movement activities in Milwaukee during the 1970's; and future prospects for Wisconsin's Indian-white relations. Lists reference materials. Two maps. Black-and-white photographs.

Moeller, Roger W., and John Reid, comps. *Archaeological Bibliography for Eastern North America*, edited by Roger W. Moeller. Attleboro, Mass. and Washington, Conn.: American Indian Archaeological Institute, 1977.
A supplement to *An Anthropological Bibliography of the Eastern Seaboard*, Vol. II, edited by Alfred K. Guthe and Patricia B. Kelly. Cites nearly eight thousand books and articles primarily concerned with prehistoric archaeology in states east of the Mississippi and the eastern provinces of Canada. Entries organized alphabetically under the following subject headings: culture history, artifacts and features, ecology, techniques, reviews (of books and movies on archaeology), theory, mathematics, and physical anthropology.

Nelson, Eunice. *The Wabanaki: An Annotated Bibliography of Selected Books, Articles, Documents About Maliseet, Micmac, Passamaquoddy, Penobscot Indians in Maine Annotated by Native Americans*. Cambridge, Mass.: American Friends Service Committee, 1982.
An annotated listing of nearly three hundred books, articles, and documents related to the history and culture of the Indians of Maine. Materials selected on the basis of their quality, availability, and usefulness to the general reader. Includes a chapter on books for young readers.

Porter, Frank W., III. *In Pursuit of the Past: An Anthropological and Bibliographic Guide to Maryland and Delaware*. Metuchen, N.J.: Scarecrow Press, 1986.
An annotated listing of 760 published and unpublished materials on the archaeology, ethnography, and ethnohistory of Maryland and Delaware's Native populations. Entries are arranged in alphabetical order. Annotations assess the

strengths, weaknesses, and significance of each work. An introductory essay traces the development of archaeological, ethnographical, and ethnohistorical studies from 1840 to the late 1940's, concluding with an evaluation of the past and present commitment of state agencies to such research.

__________. *Indians in Maryland and Delaware: A Critical Bibliography.* Newberry Library Center for the History of the American Indian Bibliographical Series. Bloomington: Indiana University Press, 1979.

A bibliographical essay that reviews 230 books and articles pertaining to the history and cultures of Native peoples in Maryland and Delaware. The essay is divided into the following subheadings: primary sources; bibliographies; county and state histories; archaeology; culture area; tribes, including sections on the Nanticokes, Piscataways, Susquehannocks, Choptanks, and other tribes; subsistence strategies; material culture and technology; language; population and demography; early voyages, explorations, and descriptions; missionaries and their missions; land tenure and reservations; migration; strategies for survival; Indian survivals in the east; and triracial isolates. Lists recommended works for the beginner and for a basic library collection. One map.

Quimby, George I. *Indian Life in the Upper Great Lakes: 11,000 B.C. to A.D. 1800.* Chicago: University of Chicago Press, 1960.

Documents the prehistory and history of Indian peoples of the Upper Great Lakes, an area encompassing most of Michigan, much of Ontario and Wisconsin, and portions of Minnesota, Indiana, and Illinois. The chapters on prehistory examine the relationship between the region's Indians and their changing environment from 11,000 B.C. to the beginning of the seventeenth century A.D. The sections on history deal primarily with transformations in Indian cultures brought about through contacts with whites from 1600 to 1760. The tribes discussed include the Hurons, Chippewas, Ottawas, Potawatomis, Sauks, Fox, Miamis, Winnebagos, and Menominees. A final chapter describes the breakdown of tribal culture between A.D. 1760 and 1820. Glossary. Bibliography. Black-and-white photographs. Maps.

Quinn, David B. *Sources for the Ethnography of Northeastern North America to 1611.* National Museum of Man Mercury Series, Canadian Ethnology Service Paper 76. Ottawa: National Museums of Canada, 1981.

Discusses printed and unpublished materials from the sixteenth and early seventeenth centuries containing information on Indians of northeastern North America. Descriptions include information on location as well as tribal groupings, cultural traits, and contacts mentioned in the texts. Entries arranged in chronological order beginning with the contact episodes reported by John Cabot (1497) to those of Samuel de Champlain (1611). Bibliography.

Ritzenthaler, Robert E., and Pat Ritzenthaler. *The Woodland Indians of the Western Great Lakes.* Garden City, N.Y.: Natural History Press, 1970.

Attempts to communicate the color, drama, and ingenuity of Woodland Indian culture. Begins with an overview of Woodland's environment, peoples, and prehistory. Subsequent chapters describe patterns of subsistence, the life cycle, social organization, material culture, religious and ceremonial life, shamanism and curative techniques, games, music, and folklore. Includes phonetic key and glossary of key Indian terms. Bibliography. Black-and-white photographs. One map.

Salisbury, Neal. *The Indians of New England: A Critical Bibliography*. Newberry Library Center for the History of the American Indian Bibliographical Series. Bloomington: Indiana University Press, 1982.

A bibliographical essay that reviews 257 books and articles pertaining to the history and culture of the New England tribes. The essay is divided by the following subheadings: "Tribal and Regional Histories"; "Before Europeans; Pre-Settlement Contacts, 1500-1620"; "The Decline of Autonomy, including sections for The Colonial Period, The Subjugation of the Southern Bands, and The Northern Frontier"; "Indians and the American Revolution"; "Tribal Enclaves in a Liberal Republic, 1800-1945"; and "A New Politics." Lists recommended works for the beginner and for a basic library collection. Two maps.

Tanner, Helen Hornbeck, et al. *Atlas of Great Lakes Indian History*. Norman: University of Oklahoma Press, 1986.

A detailed textual and cartographic presentation of Indian-white relations in the Great Lakes region from the mid-seventeenth to the late nineteenth century. The chapters and their accompanying maps provide information on: the natural vegetation of the Great Lakes area circa 1600; traditional patterns of Indian subsistence; the distribution of late prehistoric cultures; the Iroquois Wars 1641-1701; French commercial and military presence in the area from 1720 to 1761; Pontiac's war; the shifting boundaries of Spanish, French, British, and American sovereignty within the region; the shifting frontier and its effects on Indian life in the Old Northwest from 1774 to 1794; Indian involvement in the War of 1812; the distribution of Indian villages circa 1830 in upper Canada, Michigan Territory, Indiana, Ohio, Illinois, the Wisconsin region of Michigan territory, and the Minnesota region; Black Hawk War 1832; Indian land cessions 1783-1873; reservation 1783-1889; epidemics among Indians circa 1630-1880; and Indian villages circa 1870. Selected bibliography. Eighty sepia-toned illustrations.

_________. *The Ojibwas: A Critical Bibliography*. Newberry Library Center for the History of the American Indian Bibliographical Series. Bloomington: Indiana University Press, 1982.

A bibliographical essay that reviews 275 books and articles pertaining to the history and culture of the Ojibwa people. The essay is divided by the following subheadings: "Introduction," "The Accounts of Travelers and Explorers," "Missionaries and Their Missions," "Regional Studies," "Anthropological Contributions," "Language and Tradition," "The Portrayal of Ojibwa Life," "Treaties and Claims Cases," and "Sources for Advanced Research." Lists recommended works for the beginner and for a basic library collection.

Tooker, Elisabeth. *The Indians of the Northeast: A Critical Bibliography*. Newberry Library Center for the History of the American Indian Bibliographical Series. Bloomington: Indiana University Press, 1978.

A bibliographical essay that reviews 270 books and articles pertaining to the history and culture of the northeastern tribes. The essay is divided by subheadings for introduction, history, coastal Indians, northern Iroquoians, and Upper Great Lakes Indians. Lists recommended works for the beginner and for a basic library collection.

__________, ed. *Iroquois Culture, History, and Prehistory*. Albany: State Education Department, New York State Museum and Science Service, University of the State of New York, 1967.

Papers from the 1965 Conference on Iroquois Research are arranged by topic and in reverse chronological order. Among the topics addressed are Iroquois acculturation, Seneca factionalism, an etymological analysis of the term "Iroquois," Huron and Iroquois residence patterns, and Iroquois archaeology. One appendix. Bibliographies accompany each paper. Black-and-white photographs and drawings. Maps.

__________, ed. *An Iroquois Source Book*. 3 vols. New York: Garland, 1984-86.

Three readers that anthologize many of the more significant essays on Iroquois society and culture which have appeared since publication of Lewis H. Morgan's *League of the Ho-de-no-sau-ne or Iroquois* in 1851. Preference was given to those articles that contain first-hand ethnographic data and which are most frequently cited. Volume 1 presents works primarily concerned with Iroquois political and social organization. The essays in volume 2 examine the rituals constituting the Iroquois annual ceremonial cycle. The final volume focuses on medicine society rituals. Each contains a list of sources.

Trigger, Bruce G., ed. *Northeast*. Vol. 15 in *Handbook of North American Indians*. Washington, D.C.: Smithsonian Institution, 1978.

A compendium of seventy-three articles that aim to "describe the history, cultural background, and present circumstances of the Indian peoples of the northeastern United States and southeastern Canada." A section on general prehistory contains overviews of northeastern archaeology, post-Pleistocene adaptations, and regional cultural development from 3000 B.C. to A.D. 1000. A tripartite geographical division of Coastal, Saint Lawrence Lowlands, and Great Lakes-Riverine is used to organize essays on the histories and cultures of particular tribes. The volume concludes with a paper on the area's cultural unity and diversity. An eighty-three-page general bibliography lists all references cited in the volume. Black-and-white photographs, reproductions, and drawings. Maps and charts.

Weinman, Paul L. *A Bibliography of the Iroquoian Literature*. New York State Museum and Science Service, Bulletin 411. Albany: University of the State of New York, 1969.

A partially annotated listing of published materials concerned primarily with the Five Nations Iroquois. Entries are arranged alphabetically by author under the following subheadings: archaeology; bibliography; biography; ceremonialism and religion; contemporary movements; folklore and mythology; general ethnology and history; geographical place names; herbalism, foods, medicinal lore, tobacco; history and culture contacts; language; material culture, art, and games; physical anthropology; and social and political. Annotations "are seldom critical and were meant to briefly summarize the material."

Weslager, Clinton A. *The Delaware Indians: A Critical Bibliography*. Newberry Library Center for the History of the American Indian Bibliographical Series. Bloomington: Indiana University Press, 1978.

A bibliographical essay that reviews 224 books and essays that pertain to the history and culture of the Delaware people. The essay is divided by the following subheadings: "Introduction"; "Where Did the Delaware Come From?"; "Seventeenth-century Accounts"; "Early Relations with Whites and with Other Tribes"; "Where Did the Delawares Go? Subdivisions and Clans"; "Delaware Religion, Missions, and Missionaries"; "The Delaware Language"; and "Specialized Studies." List recommended works for the beginner and for a basic library collection.

Wilbur, C. Keith. *The New England Indians*. Chester, Conn.: Globe Pequot Press, 1978.

A profusely illustrated guide to the aboriginal material culture and subsistence patterns of the New England tribes. Chapters are arranged chronologically according to the following archaeological stages: Paleo-Indians (10,500 years ago), Early Archaic Indians (7,000-5,000 years ago), Late Archaic (5,000 years ago to A.D. 300); and Ceramic-Woodland Indians (A.D. 300-1676). The artifacts described in each section are accompanied by highly detailed drawings of their construction and use. Bibliography.

Archaeology

Brose, David S., et al. *Ancient Art of the American Woodlands Indians*. New York: Harry N. Abrams, in association with the Detroit Institute of Arts, 1985.

A historical survey of nearly five thousand years of prehistoric art from the eastern Woodlands. Includes essays on the arts and monuments of the Late Archaic (3000-1000 B.C.), Woodland (1000 B.C.-A.D. 1000), and Mississippian (A.D. 1000-1600) periods. Concludes with an article on continuities of images and symbols in Woodlands arts. According to the editor, the cultural patterns and institutions that resulted in the development of an indigenous Native North American art tradition emerged during the Late Archaic; these patterns and institutions continued to provide the impetus for art making through the Middle Woodland period; and agriculture, which provided the basis of Mississippian subsistence, led to a major reorganization of Woodlands lifeways, and these changes are represented in the art of that period. Lavishly illustrated with black-and-white reproductions, drawings, photographs, and color plates. Charts and maps. Bibliography.

Fitting, James, E. *The Archaeology of Michigan: A Guide to the Prehistory of the Great Lakes Region*. 2d rev. ed. Bloomfield Hills, Mich.: Cranbrook Institute of Science, 1975.

Takes an ecological approach to the description and analysis of nearly twelve thousand years of Michigan/Great Lakes prehistory. The volume's general position is that the "place which man finds within [the] environment is his niche and living within this niche requires adapting to it." Begins with a historical overview of Michigan's natural and cultural areas. Subsequent chapters chronicle changing adaptive patterns for the state's inhabitants during the Paleo-Indian, Archaic, and Woodland phases of its cultural prehistory. Includes references to a number of Michigan's archaeological sites. Bibliography. Black-and-white photographs and drawings. Maps.

Mason, Ronald J. *Great Lakes Archaeology*. New York: Academic Press, 1981.

An introduction to the archaeology of the Great Lakes region which seeks to provide a balanced picture of the prehistoric peoples of that region through a selective examination of representative cultures, assemblages, and sites. Chapter 1 begins with sketches of Indian life in the Great Lakes as it existed on the eve of European contact in the early sixteenth century. The chapters that follow describe the evolution of the area's geology and biological environment; the first infiltrations of Paleo-Indians from 9500 to 8000 B.C.; the late Paleo-Indians/Early Middle Archaic period (8000-3500 B.C.); the cultures of the Late Archaic period (3500-1500 B.C.); the Archaic-Woodland transition (1500-100 B.C.); the Middle Woodland period (200 B.C.-A.D. 500); and the Late Woodland period in the Lower and Upper Lakes (A.D. 500-contact). Lists of references for each chapter. Black-and-white photographs and drawings. Maps.

Potter, Martha A. *Ohio's Prehistoric Peoples*. Columbus: Ohio Historical Society, 1968.

A cultural prehistory for the area currently constituting Ohio and sections of several other states in the Ohio Valley. The chronologically arranged chapters offer brief cultural reconstructions for the following prehistoric groups: Paleo-Indians, Archaic and Glacial Kame, Adena, Hopewell, Intrusive Mound and Cole, and Fort Ancient and Erie. List of additional readings. Multicolored drawings. One table: "Chronology of Ohio's Prehistoric Indians."

Quimby, George I. *Indian Culture and European Trade Goods: The Archaeology of the Historic Period in the Western Great Lakes Region*. Madison: University of Wisconsin Press, 1966.

Uses archaeological data and the first-hand accounts of European missionaries and traders to reconstruct the culture histories of tribes living in the vicinity of Lakes Michigan, Huron, and Superior from the seventeenth through early nineteenth centuries. Following a general introduction, the author briefly reviews the first twelve thousand years of Indian occupation in the upper Great Lakes region. Subsequent chapters combine documentary evidence with the distribution patterns of beads, trade silver, and other European goods to determine the nature and locations of various Native societies during early, middle, and late historic periods. Bibliography. Black-and-white photographs and drawings.

Ritchie, W. A. *The Archaeology of New York State*. Rev. ed. Harrison, N.Y.: Harbor Hills Books, 1980.

A comprehensive summary of New York State's cultural prehistory. The chapters are arranged chronologically according to the following periodization: earliest occupants—Paleo-Indian hunters (8000 B.C.); archaic or hunting, fishing, gathering stage (4500-1300 B.C.); transitional stage—from stone pots to early ceramics (1300-1000 B.C.); and Woodland stage—development of ceramics, agriculture and village life (1000 B.C.-A.D. 1600). The discussion of each period includes, where available, information on geographical and ecological setting, subsistence, tools and other aspects of material culture, settlement and social patterns, and important cultural phases. Bibliography. Black-and-white photographs. Maps and tables.

Ritzenthaler, Robert E. *Prehistoric Indians of Wisconsin*, revised by Lynne G. Goldstein. Milwaukee: Milwaukee Public Museum, 1985.

A concise, highly readable summary of Wisconsin's prehistoric cultures. Chapter 1 presents a brief introduction to archaeological methods and techniques including the finding and dating of sites. Chapters 2, 3, and 4 discuss technology, environment and diet, and human biology, respectively. Chapters 5 through 8 describe various phases of the state's twelve-thousand-year prehistory. A final chapter first identifies issues in need of further research and then notes the various laws protecting archaeological sites. Selected bibliography. Black-and-white photographs.

Snow, Dean R. *The Archaeology of New England*. New York: Academic Press, 1980.

Seeks to outline twelve thousand years of New England cultural prehistory. Chapter 1 summarizes the goals of the book and of archaeology. Chapter 2 presents an ethnohistorical overview of New England tribes for the years around A.D. 1600. Subsequent chapters follow the evolution of the region's prehistoric cultures, from 15,000 B.P. (before present) to the opening of the seventh century A.D. The book's descriptions and analyses are based on a cultural systems approach, which allows one to "follow the evolutions of whole cultures through their successive phases, long developments that are usually called *traditions*." Bibliography. Black-and-white photographs. Maps. Tables and charts.

__________, ed. *Foundations of Northeast Archaeology*. New York: Academic Press, 1981.

A collection of seven papers that examine the special problems and potential that attend the application of archaeology in northeastern North America. Sets as the core of this region New England, New York, and the adjacent portions of Ontario, Quebec, and the Maritime Provinces. Topics include an Iroquoian case study of prehistoric social and political organization, a multidisciplinary research strategy for paleoenvironmental reconstruction in the Northeast, approaches to cultural adaptation in the Northeast, the use of scientific models in northeastern archaeology, demographic archaeology in the Northeast, problems of sampling and the subsequent validity of statistical operations, and the place of osteology in the anthropology of the Northeast.

Struever, Stuart, and Felicia A. Holton. *Koster: Americans in Search of Their Prehistoric Past*. Garden City, N.Y.: Anchor Press/Doubleday, 1979.

A nontechnical report on Koster, a prehistoric site in Illinois occupied from the Early Archaic (7500-6700 B.C.) to the Mississippian period (A.D. 1000-1200). Chapters describe the archaeological methods used at the dig; selected materials belonging to the site's thirteen (or possibly fourteen) horizons; interpretations concerning climate, social organization, housing, modes of subsistence, and mortuary customs; and the significance of Koster for redefining extant concepts of prehistoric peoples. One appendix. Black-and-white photographs and color plates. One map. Tables.

Tuck, James A. *Onondaga Iroquois Prehistory: A Study in Settlement Archaeology*. Syracuse, N.Y.: Syracuse University Press, 1971.

A study of the prehistory of the Onondaga Iroquois based on excavations carried out in central New York State during 1965 through 1967 and examinations of collections by other archaeologists made before and after that time. Analysis is founded on a settlement approach to archaeology, which considers "not the artifact but the settlement where artifacts and other evidence of human habitation are found." The investigations delineated three distinct communities in the research area, two that contributed directly to the evolution of the Onondaga people. Two appendices. Bibliography. Black-and-white photographs and drawings. Tables.

Webb, William S., and Charles E. Snow. *The Adena People*. Knoxville: University of Tennessee Press, 1974.

A study of the prehistory of the Ohio River valley, centered on the analysis of material culture and skeletal remains extracted from the Kentucky earth mounds belonging to the Adena Complex. Among the authors' conclusions are that there is close similarity of the total Adena cultural complex with that of the Hopewell; the Adena were the earliest people of their region to build wooden houses, to smoke, make pottery, and use corn, sunflower seed, and squash as food; and Ohio Hopewell developed its highest manifestation at the center of the Adena occupancy. Black-and-white photographs. Tables.

Webb, William S., and Raymond S. Baby. *The Adena People, No. 2*. Columbus: Ohio Historical Society, 1957.

A supplement to *The Adena People* by Webb and Snow. Seeks to augment the original publication with data drawn from an additional forty-nine Adena sites found in Ohio, Kentucky, Indiana, West Virginia, and Pennsylvania and, to analyze, interpret, and synthesize these data with those previously known. Discussion includes Adena use of animal masks, evidence of medicine bags, Adena tablets, the possible relation of the Southern Cult to Adena-Hopewell, and radiocarbon dates for Adena. There are also chapters on the food of Adena people and Adena portraiture contributed by Robert M. Goslin and Charles E. Snow, respectively. Bibliography. Black-and-white photographs and drawings. Tables.

Folklore, Sacred Narrative, Religious Belief and Practice

Barnouw, Victor. *Wisconsin Chippewa Myths and Tales and Their Relation to Chippewa Life*. Madison: University of Wisconsin Press, 1977.

A collection and interpretation of Chippewa oral narratives which aims to "elucidate the attitudes and values implicit in the stories as well as clues to the nature of Chippewa social organization and personality patterns as expressed in the narratives." An introductory chapter provides a summary discussion of the tribe's social organization, culture, religious institutions, and folklore. Chapter 2 provides an analysis of a Wenebojo (trickster-culture hero) origin myth from Lac du Flambeau reservation. Subsequent chapters compare the themes found in this myth with those occurring in other kinds of Chippewa narratives and in the oral traditions of different Native American groups. Bibliography. Maps.

Cornplanter, Jesse J. *Legends of the Longhouse*. Philadelphia: J. B. Lippincott, 1938.

An anthology of seventeen traditional Seneca narratives recounted by a member of that tribe. Among the most important of these is the story of Sky-Woman, whose fall from the celestial world led to the origin of the earth and all its creatures. Also included is an account of the origin of the False Face Society, an association empowered with doctoring the sick. The book contains ten illustrations by the author.

Dewdney, Selwyn. *The Sacred Scrolls of the Southern Ojibway*. Toronto: University of Toronto Press for the Glenbow-Alberta Institute, Calgary, Alberta, 1975.

A detailed discussion of the sacred, birch bark scrolls of the southern Ojibwa Mdewiwin, or Grand Medicine Society, based mainly on interviews with Mide shaman James Red Sky, Sr. Engraved on these scrolls are tribal traditions concerning the origins of the world and man, death, the Mdewiwin, and the Ojibwa people; migration charts for the Mdewiwin and the Ojibwa; and depictions of rituals, their personnel, and spiritual (manito) helpers that were used to instruct the society's candidates. Appendix: inventory to birchbark scrolls and charts. Bibliography. Black-and-white photographs and drawings.

Fenton, William N. *The False Faces of the Iroquois*. Norman: University of Oklahoma Press, 1987.

Examines the place of the Society of Faces, its ceremonies, and its masks within the context of Iroquois social and religious life. Sees the Society of Faces as "one of the climax features of Iroquois culture. . . . [Its masks] are the external manifestation of cultural beliefs and represent a long tradition of relationships between humans and supernaturals." Discusses the fundamental classes of beings and masks, traditional accounts of their origins, styles and tradition of mask carving, and associated ceremonial belief, practice, and paraphernalia.

Bibliography. Illustrated with black-and-white drawings, photographs, and color plates. Charts.

Hale, Horatio E., ed. *The Iroquois Book of Rites*. Brinton's Library of Aboriginal American Literature 11. Philadelphia: D. G. Brinton, 1883.

A faithful reproduction, with English translation, of the Iroquois "Book of Rites" or "Book of the Condoling Council." Contained among the texts are "the speeches, songs, and other ceremonies, which, from the earliest period of the [Iroquois] confederacy, have composed the proceedings of their council when a deceased chief is lamented and his successor is installed in office. The fundamental laws of the league, a list of ancient towns, and the names of the chiefs who constituted their first council, chanted in a kind of litany, are comprised in the collection." An editor's introduction discusses the nature of the Huron-Iroquois Nations, the Iroquois League and its founders, the composition of the Book of Rites, the condoling council, the ceremony of condolence and installation, the laws of the Iroquois League, and Iroquois character, policy, and language. Appendix. Glossary.

Harrington, M. R. *Religion and Ceremonies of the Lenape*. Indian Notes and Monographs 19. New York: Museum of the American Indian, Heye Foundation, 1921.

An examination of the religious beliefs and practices of the Lenape (Delaware) based mainly on information gathered from the tribe's Oklahoma bands. The first several chapters discuss the various beings constituting the Lenape pantheon and the centrality of the recital of visions and thanksgiving to the Great Spirit in the religious system. Subsequent chapters describe in detail major and minor Lenape rites, including the Annual Ceremony, Big House Ceremony, Otter Ceremony, Peyote Rite, and Ghost Dance. Black-and-white drawings and color paintings by Shawnee artist Ernest Spybuck.

__________. *Sacred Bundles of the Sac and Fox Indians*. University of Pennsylvania, University Museum Anthropological Publications, vol. 4, no. 2. Philadelphia: University Museum, 1914.

Describes the nature and function of Sac and Fox sacred bundles: packages containing objects of religious power and ceremonial significance. An introduction sets forth the general characteristics of such bundles and their contents. Following is a brief overview of Sac and Fox culture. Subsequent sections discuss tribal beliefs concerning the origin of sacred bundles, a classification of bundle types as well as customs applying to their storage and use, and descriptions and analyses of selected bundles housed in the University of Pennsylvania's museum. Black-and-white reproductions of paintings by Indians, photographs, and drawings.

Landes, Ruth. *Ojibwa Religion and the Mdewiwin*. Madison: University of Wisconsin Press, 1968.

A detailed study of the beliefs, rituals, and social organization of the Ojibwa Mdewiwin, a curing society whose procedures simultaneously treat the sick and instruct novices and veterans about the origins and powers of mide rites. An introduction provides an ethnographic background for the chapters to follow. Part 1 discusses the fundamental categories of Ojibwa religion, religious practitioners, and curing. Part 2 presents the society's activities in Ojibwa villages of western Ontario and northern Minnesota during the 1930's.

Simmons, William S. *Spirit of the New England Tribes: Indian History and Folklore, 1620-1984*. Hanover, N.H.: University Press of New England, 1986.
Documents and explains the persistence and transformations of key symbols found in New England Indian folklore from prehistoric times to the present. Particularly interested in the relation between this folklore and the historical events that affected New England Indian communities—"which symbols persist, which ones change, where innovations come from, and what can be said about the pattern and timing of change." The material for the study is derived from 240 texts, a variety of manuscript sources, and field research with living people. Bibliography.

Skinner, Alanson. *Associations and Ceremonies of the Menomini Indians*. American Museum of Natural History, Anthropological Papers, vol. 13, pt. 2. New York: The Trustees, 1915.
Describes the history, nature, and functions of selected Menominee societies and ceremonies. The associations described include the Society of Dreamers, whose primary importance rests in doctoring, and the Witches Society, composed with eight *kin'ubik-inaniwuk*, or serpent men. Among the dances and ceremonies discussed are Harvest or Crop Dance, Rain Dance, Braves Dance, and Bear Ceremony. A concluding section briefly comments on the (then) recent introduction of peyote among the Menominee. Black-and-white drawings.

__________. *Folklore of the Menomini Indians*. American Museum of Natural History, Anthropological Papers, vol. 13, pt. 3. New York: The Trustees, 1915.
Provides a collection and analysis of Menominee narratives. An introduction begins by distinguishing five classes of Menominee folklore: sacred myths pertaining primarily to cosmogony, the birth of Ma nabus as culture hero, and the origin of the medicine lodge; minor myths of Ma nabus as trickster; fairy tales; stories of war, the chase, dreams, and conjurings considered true; and fairy tales of European origin. The remaining sections of the introduction discuss characteristic features of the narratives, the relation of folklore and religion, the historical value of such oral traditions, and other subjects of analytic importance.

__________. *Social Life and Ceremonial Bundles of the Menomini Indians*. American Museum of Natural History, Anthropological Papers, vol. 13, pt. 1. New York: The Trustees, 1913.
An ethnological discussion of selected aspects of Menominee society and religion. Section 1 contains brief descriptions of tribal life and customs, including patterns of domesticity; social organization; marriage customs; terms of relationship; children, birth, and naming; vision questing; menstrual rites; games; and burial practices. Section 2 first examines central elements of Menominee cosmology, then probes the nature, types, and uses of collections

of medicines known as "medicine bundles." Bibliography. Black-and-white photographs and drawings.

Speck, Frank G. *Midwinter Rites of the Cayuga Long House*. Philadelphia: University of Pennsylvania Press, 1949.

An account of the religious beliefs and rites of the Canadian Cayuga Indians of the Sour Spring Long House. Part 1 first contextualizes Cayuga ceremonies within the history and sociology of the community. It then discusses essential elements of the Cayuga religious system, including the succession of spirit forces, the annual ceremonial cycle, and ceremonial officiaries, foods, instruments, and costumes. Part 2 presents a description and analysis of the Midwinter Ceremony, or New Year's Festival, which integrates "practically all the separate elements of ritual (medicine society rites, sacred and social dances, symbolical and sacrificial acts) which are known to the religious leaders of the group, and which appear either as independent performances or as grouped elements in other periodic ceremonies of the Cayuga annual cycle." Two appendices. Bibliography. Black-and-white photographs and drawings.

__________. *Oklahoma Delaware Ceremonies, Feasts and Dances*. Memoirs of the American Philosophical Society 7. Philadelphia: American Philosophical Society, 1937.

Describes twenty ceremonies and rites that were still being practiced by the Delaware Indians of Oklahoma as of 1932, two centuries after their removal from Pennsylvania and New Jersey. Begins by sketching the dominant traits of the Delaware ritual system in the Oklahoma division of that nation. Subsequent chapters examine specific ceremonies, including family feasts, the Bear and Otter Rites of the Grease Drinking Ceremony, the Mask Dance ritual, the Opossum Dance, the Doll Dance, the Buffalo Dance, and the Corn Harvest Ceremony. There are also discussions of social or "stomp" dances and various ceremonial games. Several Delaware narratives associated with the ceremonies are presented with interlinear and free translations. Bibliography of authorities quoted. Black-and-white reproductions and photographs.

__________. *Penobscot Shamanism*. Memoirs of the American Anthropological Association, vol. VI, no. 4. Lancaster, Pa.: American Anthropological Association, 1919.

A study of the nature, history, and functions of shamanism among the Penobscot and other northeastern tribes. Describes the chief activities of Penobscot shamans, the means of acquiring shamanic power, spiritual helpers, continuity and change in beliefs and practices associated with shamans and shamanism; and oral traditions portraying the exploits of shamans. Concludes with several shamanistic tales in the Wabnaki dialects accompanied by free translations.

Tantaquidgeon, Gladys. *Folk Medicine of the Delaware and Related Algonkian Indians*. Harrisburg: Pennsylvania Historical and Museum Commission, 1972.

Presents the curing practices and plant lore of Wi-tapanoxwe (Walks With Daylight), a Delaware Indian of Dewey, Oklahoma. Augments the theories, practices, and beliefs of Wi-tapanoxwe with data on Native medical practices and folk beliefs that represent the common property of the tribe. An introduction provides information on Delaware theories concerning the causes of disease, the nature and functions of curers, love charms, food taboos, the sweat lodge ritual, the medicine bundle complex, and medicinal stones obtained from the digestive organs of the blacktail deer. Subsequent chapters record plants used in cures and their preparation, theories concerning witches and witchcraft, and Delaware food resources and their importance to health. Supplementing the materials on the Oklahoma Delaware are data on Mohegan, Nanticoke, and Canadian Delaware medicine practice and folk beliefs. Bibliography of references cited. Charts list information of plants and plant uses of the Oklahoma Delaware, Canadian Delaware, and Nanticoke, including botanical names, common names, Native application, part of the plant used, and type of medicine. Photographs.

Tooker, Elisabeth. *The Iroquois Ceremonial of Midwinter*. Syracuse, N.Y.: Syracuse University Press, 1970.

A description and analysis of the Iroquois midwinter ceremonial, "the longest and most complex of Iroquois rituals." Part 1 examines the central principles of Iroquois ritualism. Part 2 demonstrates how these principles operate in the midwinter celebrations of various contemporary Iroquois longhouses. A concluding section provides an ethnohistorical treatment of the ritual complex, documenting its continuity and change from the seventeenth century to the present day. One appendix. Bibliography. Black-and-white photographs. One map and one table.

__________, ed. *Native North American Spirituality of the Eastern Woodlands: Sacred Myths, Dreams, Visions, Speeches, Healing Formulas, Rituals, and Ceremonies*. Mahwah, N.J.: Paulist Press, 1979.

Seeks to explain and illustrate themes characteristic of the spiritual beliefs and practices of North America's eastern Woodlands Indians. An introduction stresses the need for a culturally sensitive reading of the anthologized texts. These texts are arranged according to the following chapter headings: "Cosmology," "Dreams and Visions," "Delaware Big House Ceremonial," "Winnebago Night Spirits Society Ceremonial," Menominee Bundle Ceremonials," "Fox Clan Ceremonials," "Winnebago Clan Ceremonials," "Iroquois Ceremonials," and "Southeastern Indian Formulas." Each text is preceded by an explanatory note. Bibliography.

Vecsey, Christopher. *Traditional Ojibwa Religion and Its Historical Changes*. Philadelphia: American Philosophical Society, 1983.

Explores the continuity and change in the religious traditions of the Ojibwa. The first three chapters summarize Ojibwa culture and history, the missionary work of various Christian denominations among the tribe, and native responses to missionization. Subsequent chapters discuss Ojibwa conceptions of, and relations with, the ultimate sources of existence. Such conceptions include the Ojibwa understanding of themselves as the human subjects of their religion; the essential role of extremely powerful beings, known as *manitos*, for the continuation of human life; modes of individual and group communication with the manitos; the centrality of medicine in Ojibwa religion; and religious leadership. Each chapter concludes with a description of how the religious element in question "has deteriorated, changed, or persisted through the historical period since first contact with whites." Bibliography. Five maps.

Wallace, Anthony F. C. *The Death and Rebirth of the Seneca*. New York: Alfred A. Knopf, 1969.

Documents the destruction and demoralization of the Seneca people during the second half of the eighteenth century and their subsequent regeneration through the prophecies and doctrines of Indian visionary, Handsome Lake. Part 1 portrays the cultural and religious patterns of the Seneca, the most populous and powerful member of the Iroquois confederacy, at their peak in the seventeenth and early eighteenth centuries. Part 2 describes the events that led to the collapse of the confederacy and the general decline of Iroquois lifeways. Part 3 discusses the visions and preaching of Handsome Lake, a reformed alcoholic whose gospels of spiritual and social revitalization represent a powerful combination of traditional Iroquois religion and Quaker Christianity. Bibliography. Black-and-white reproductions. Maps.

Witthoft, John. *Green Corn Ceremonialism in the Eastern Woodlands*. Occasional Contributions from the Museum of Anthropology of the University of Michigan, no. 13. Ann Arbor: University of Michigan Press, 1949.

Examines the widely distributed Eastern Woodlands ritual associated with the ripening of corn and, in many areas, marking a major division of the year. Describes the ceremony as practiced by the Algonquian peoples of New England and New York, the Delaware and southeastern Algonquians, the Iroquois, the Cherokee, the southeastern Siouan tribes, the Creek Indians and their neighbors, and the Natchez and tribes outside the eastern Woodlands area. Includes a section on the corn origin myths of the area. Bibliography of references cited. One table.

Subsistence and Land Use

Bishop, Charles A. *The Northern Ojibwa and the Fur Trade: An Historical and Ecological Study*. Toronto: Holt, Rinehart and Winston, 1974.

Examines the successive eras of social and economic change and adaptation among the Northern Ojibwa from their first contact with Europeans in the seventeenth century to the late 1960's. Argues that institutional changes were the result, on the one hand, of transformations in Northern Ojibwa relations with fur traders, missionaries, government agents, and other Indian peoples, and, on the other, ecological pressures that called for adaptive responses. Bibliography. Black-and-white photographs. Maps, tables, and charts.

Densmore, Frances. *Uses of Plants by the Chippewa Indians*. Bureau of American Ethnology, Annual Report 44 (1926-1927). Washington, D.C.: U.S. Government Printing Office, 1928.

A study of the various uses to which the Chippewa Indians of Minnesota, Wisconsin, and Ontario put the wild plants of their environment. A section on plants as food provides discussion of the making of maple sugar, beverages, seasonings, cereals, vegetables, and fruits and berries, and the gathering of wild rice. Section 2, describes treatment by means of plants and presents a list of medicinal plants and their uses. It also contains information on non-plant remedies, medicinal appliances, surgical treatment and appliances, dental surgery, and a classification of diseases and injuries. Section 3 lists plants used as dye, and describes the process of dyeing and formulas for dyes. The next two sections discuss plants used as charms and in useful and decorative arts, respectively. The monograph closes with legends concerning birch and cedar trees, a report on the gathering of birch and cedar bark, and an enumeration of articles made from birch bark. Includes a table listing plants by botanical, common, and native names. Black-and-white photographs.

Krech, Shepard, III, ed. *Indians, Animals, and the Fur Trade: A Critique of Keepers of the Game*. Athens: University of Georgia Press, 1981.

Seven critiques of Calvin Martin's thesis that Northeastern and Subarctic Indians blamed animal spirits for the diseases introduced by Europeans and vented their anger by zealous participation in the fur trade. Some of the essays find fault with the basic theoretical and methodological assumptions of Martin's study. Others suggest that his explanation is limited in its ethnohistorical application. The critiques are accompanied by an introductory essay in which Martin summarizes his position and a closing comment in which he responds to the contributors. A bibliography accompanies each paper.

Martin, Calvin. *Keepers of the Game: Indian-Animal Relationships and the Fur Trade*. Berkeley: University of California Press, 1978.

Examines the effects of European contact on the relationship between Northeastern and Eastern Subarctic Indians and their habitat. Argues that Indians blamed offended wildlife spirits for the epidemics introduced by Europeans. Bewildered and angered by this breach in traditional spiritual rapport, the Indians retaliated by declaring war on fur bearers.

Parker, Arthur C. *Iroquois Uses of Maize and Other Food Plants*. New York State Museum Bulletin 144. Albany: University of the State of New York, 1910.

Notes on the Iroquois preparation and use of maize and other food plants, based on ten years of fieldwork among members of that nation. Part 1 is concerned exclusively with maize and includes discussion of the history of Indian corn, early records of corn cultivation, the importance of corn in ceremony and narratives, the varieties of maize, the terminology associated with the cultivation of corn, utensils used to prepare corn for food, and cooking and eating customs. Part 2 contains information on other food plants. Described here are beans and bean foods, squashes and other vine vegetables, leaf and stalk foods, fungi and lichens, fruits and berrylike foods, nuts, sap and bark foods, and root foods. Bibliography of references cited. Black-and-white photographs and drawings.

Vennum, Thomas, Jr. *Wild Rice and the Ojibway People*. St. Paul: Minnesota Historical Society, 1988.

A synthesis of research on wild rice intended for those interested in Ojibwa culture, ethnobotanists, ethnohistorians, students of Indian-white relations, "and for those who have tasted wild rice and are curious to know more about it." Chapter 1 provides botanical data on wild rice, including its classification, germination and growth, enemies, and habitat. Chapter 2 describes the place of the plant in the traditional Ojibwa diet, how it was cooked, and the reactions of European explorers to this food item. Chapter 3 documents the special status wild rice holds in Ojibwa legends, customs, and ceremonies. Subsequent chapters concern the technical and social aspects of harvesting the rice, its changing place in the tribe's economy, the legal history of Ojibwa ricing, and the role of wild rice in that people's future. Bibliography. Black-and-white photographs. Maps and charts.

Waugh, F. W. *Iroquois Foods and Food Preparation.* Canada Department of Mines, Geological Survey, Memoir 86. Ottawa: Government Printing Office, 1916.

Offers a comprehensive treatment of Iroquois foods and food customs based on the author's fieldwork in Ontario, Quebec, and New York State from 1912 to 1915. Includes discussion of agricultural methods, ceremonials, and lore; cookery and eating traditions; utensils used in gathering, preparing, and eating foods; and food materials, including varieties of corn, beans, roots, leaves, fungi, nuts, fruits, animals, fish, maple syrup and sugar, and honey. Recipes for each food type are provided. Bibliography. Black-and-white photographs and drawings.

Yarnell, Richard A. *Aboriginal Relationships Between Culture and Plant Life in the Upper Great Lakes Region.* Anthropological Paper 23, Museum of Anthropology, University of Michigan. Ann Arbor: University of Michigan, 1964.

Examines the interrelationships between aboriginal culture and plant life in the upper Great Lakes. Particular attention is given, first, to the native use of plants and plant products as disclosed by ethnographic and archaeological research; second, aboriginal agriculture in relation to its history and to the distribution of length of frostless season; and third, the effects of aboriginal activities on the natural vegetation of the study region. One of the conclusions of the study is that plant foods have been used by inhabitants of the upper Great Lakes at least since the beginning of the Archaic period. Eight appendices. Tables.

Family and Society

Axtell, James, ed. *The Indian Peoples of Eastern America: A Documentary History of the Sexes.* New York: Oxford University Press, 1981.

A collection of sixty-seven primary sources pertaining to the life cycle of Indian men and women of eastern North America. Argues that by "viewing the lives of native men and women in tandem as they moved from birth to death, we can distinguish the workings of culture from those of biology in the formation of their distinctive personalities and social roles." Chapter subheadings include birth, coming of age, love and marriage, peace and war, heaven and earth (that is, differences of gender and their relation to religious belief and practice), and death. A brief discussion of relevant background and themes introduces each chapter and essay. Concludes with an annotated list of suggested readings.

Callender, Charles. *Social Organization of Central Algonkian Indians*. Milwaukee Public Museum Publications in Anthropology 7. Milwaukee: Milwaukee Public Museum, 1962.

A compilation and analysis of available materials on the social organization of Algonquian-speaking peoples of the upper Great Lakes and Ohio Valley areas. Begins with a brief history of the tribes involved, including the Sauk, Fox, Kickapoo, Prairie Potawatomi, Shawnee, Miami, Illinois, and Menominee. Next reconstructs central Algonquian social systems as they existed about 1800. Following is a chapter which considers the evolution of these systems and their relation to those of the northern Algonquian and central Siouan. Concludes with a discussion of how recent acculturative forces have resulted in changes in traditional patterns of social organization. Three appendices. Bibliography. Black-and-white diagrams. Maps.

Gearing, Frederick O. *The Face of the Fox*. Chicago: Aldine, 1970.

A selective portrayal of life in a community of six hundred Fox Indians located on the outskirts of Tama, Iowa. The highly personal narrative focuses on the nature and sources of the community's social paralysis; the inability of local whites to comprehend and relate to their Indian neighbors; and the painful process by which the author came, first, to recognize his own estrangement from the Fox and then gain an increased sense of their humanity. Black-and-white photographs.

Hilger, M. Inez, Sr. *Chippewa Child Life and Its Cultural Background*. Bureau of American Ethnology, Bulletin 146. Washington, D.C.: U.S. Government Printing Office, 1951.

Documents Chippewa concepts and practices related to the development and socialization of children. Argues that childhood among the Chippewa was divided into two periods: the first lasting from birth to the event of walking; the second, from walking to puberty. The first eight sections are primarily concerned with phases in the development of children, including the prenatal period, birth, postnatal customs, nursing and weaning, naming the child, puberty fasts, and puberty rites for boys and girls. The last nine sections discuss the cultural milieu in which the child was reared. Among its topics are religious beliefs and ceremonies, health measures, moral training, mental training, diversions, vocational training and domestic economy, and courtship and marriage. An appendix lists some plants used by the Chippewa. Bibliography. Black-and-white photographs. One map.

Landes, Ruth. *Ojibwa Sociology*. Columbia University Contributions to Anthropology 29. New York: Columbia University Press, 1937.

A detailed description of the various institutions, statuses, and roles of Ojibwa social life. Part 1 deals with the political structure of the tribe's villages. Part 2 examines kinship organization, describing categories of relations, the domestic family, and the functions of relatives. Part 3 discusses the characteristic features and operations of social divisions known as *gentes*. Ojibwa ideas and customs surrounding marriage are the subjects of part 4. The monograph concludes with a discussion of Ojibwa classifications and notions regarding property. Bibliography. Charts.

_________. *The Ojibwa Woman*. New York: Columbia University Press, 1938.
An ethnological field study that shows how Ojibwa social institutions determine the behavior of that tribe's men and women. Chapters on youth, marriage, occupations, abnormalities, and life histories. Finds that among the Ojibwa, "only the male half of the population and its activities fall under the traditional regulations, while the female half is left to spontaneous and confused behavior."

Spittal, W. G., ed. *Iroquois Women: An Anthology*. Ohsweken, Ontario: Iroqrafts, 1990.
An anthology of reprinted articles written between 1884 and 1989 on various aspects of Iroquois womanhood. The essays are presented in chronological order "so the reader may follow the evolution of the analysis and judge the worth of the presentations." Among the topics discussed are the social and political position of Iroquois women, the functions of women in Iroquois society, and the differential rate of acculturation between Onondaga men and women during the 1950's and the 1960's. Black-and-white photographs.

Material Culture and the Arts

Densmore, Frances. *Chippewa Music*. 2 vols. Bureau of American Ethnology, Bulletins 45 and 53. Washington, D.C.: U.S. Government Printing Office, 1910-1913.
A study of songs collected on four of Minnesota's Chippewa reservations during the first decade of the twentieth century. Begins with a general description of the songs, which includes information on intonation, rhythm, tone material, and musical structure; a tabulated analysis of 180 songs; musical instruments; and the origin, beliefs, songs, and practices of the Mide, or Grand Medicine Society. Next presents transcriptions and ethnological and musicological analyses for examples of the following categories of Mide and social songs. Bibliography. Black-and-white photographs and drawings.

_________. *Menominee Music*. Bureau of American Ethnology, Bulletin 102. Washington, D.C.: U.S. Government Printing Office, 1932.
Seeks to determine the similarities and differences between Menominee songs and those of other tribes. Begins with a brief tribal history; description of musical instruments and their uses; and a tabular comparison of Menominee songs with Chippewa, Sioux, Ute, Mandan, Hidatsa, Papago, and Pawnee songs. It next presents transcriptions and ethnological and musicological analyses for selected Menominee songs of the following types: songs of games played in a ceremonial manner, songs connected with the gift of medicine to the Indians, songs connected with war and hunting bundles, dream songs, songs connected with the treatment of the sick, songs connected with legends of Manabus (a culture hero and trickster), songs of the drum religion, tobacco dance songs,

miscellaneous dance songs, war songs, moccasin game songs, love songs, and songs for children. Bibliography. Black-and-white photographs and diagrams.

Kurath, Gertrude P. *Dance and Song Rituals of Six Nations Reserve, Ontario*. National Museum of Canada, Bulletin 220, Folklore Series 4. Ottawa: Queen's Printer, 1968.

A survey of the music and choreography associated with the four ceremonial centers, or longhouses, of Ontario's Six Nation Reserve. Part 1 first describes the eight seasonal ceremonies observed by these longhouses, then presents elements of the social and ritual structure typical of the ceremonies. Part 2 details the ground plans, steps, postures, and gestures of the dances. Part 3 recreates the songs and dances of the ceremonies through choreographic and musical symbols. Part 4 relates traditional style and variation in Iroquois dances. Costume types and uses are the subjects of part 5. Part 6 addresses the issue of continuity and change in longhouse song and dance. Bibliography. Black-and-white photographs.

__________. *Iroquois Music and Dance: Ceremonial Arts of Two Seneca Longhouses*. Bureau of American Ethnology, Bulletin 187. Washington, D.C.: U.S. Government Printing Office, 1964.

Examines the music and dance of ceremonials performed by members of the Seneca longhouses of Coldsprings and Tonawanda. Part 1 begins with a description of the dance cycles associated with various categories of longhouse rituals, providing information on the function, occasions, songs, and dance of each performance. It then presents musical and choreographic analyses of these ceremonials, focusing on their formal or artistic aspects. Parts 2 and 3 provide transcriptions of the songs and texts of the two longhouses. Bibliography. Black-and-white photographs.

Lyford, Carrie A. *Iroquois Crafts*. Lawrence, Kans.: Haskell Institute Press, 1945.

Describes the arts and material culture of the Iroquois Nation. Sections 1 through 6 briefly summarize the tribe's history and lifeways. Section 7 contains information on traditional Iroquois crafts organized by materials used: antlers, stones, bones, shells, clay, bark, wood, corn husks and cobs, silver, and hides. The eighth and final section discusses Iroquois decorative arts, including moose hair embroidery, quill work, bead work, ribbon work, table cloths, bedspreads, and blankets. Attention is given to designs, symbolism, colors used, and dyes and their preparation. Bibliography. An appendix provides drawings of typical Iroquois designs. Black-and-white photographs and drawings.

__________. *Ojibway Crafts*. Lawrence, Kans.: Haskell Institute Press, 1943.

A detailed presentation of the methods and manufactures of Ojibwa (Chippewa) crafts. The first nine sections overview selected aspects of Chippewa history, traditional culture, and contemporary reservation life. Sections 10 through 25 are specifically concerned with crafts and craftsmanship. Topics include wood and bark in craft work, preparation of cord and twine, birch bark work, basket making, woven yarn bands and sashes, woven bags, woven mats, preparation and use of hides, costume decorations and accessories, quill work, bead work, ribbon work or appliqué, designs, use of colors, and native dyes. Bibliography. Black-and-white photographs and drawings.

Morgan, William N. *Prehistoric Architecture in the Eastern United States.* Cambridge, Mass.: MIT Press, 1980.

Presents a comprehensive overview of prehistoric architecture in the Eastern United States from about 2200 B.C. until the beginning of the sixteenth century A.D. Provides interpretive reconstructions of eighty-two sites, placing primary focus on the relationship of the architectural elements of the large earth structures found at these sites and to the natural environment. Groups these reconstructions chronologically into three parts: period 1, circa 2200-1000 B.C.; period 2, 500 B.C.-A.D. 200; and period 3, A.D. 800-1500. Each part begins with a brief discussion of its period's chief architectural characteristics. The description of each site includes concise architectural information, one or more diagrams, and references. Bibliography.

Vennum, Thomas, Jr. *The Ojibwa Dance Drum: Its History and Construction.* Smithsonian Folklore Studies 2. Washington, D.C.: Smithsonian Institution Press, 1982.

Seeks to investigate the significance of the dance drum in Ojibwa culture and to document its construction. Part 1 begins with a brief history of the Ojibwa until 1900, then reviews the inventory of Ojibwa musical instruments. Subsequent chapters discuss the origin and early history of the dance drum, the Drum Dance and its functions, the decline of the Drum Dance during the twentieth century, and the implications of the recent resurgence of Indian pride in their heritage for the future of the Ojibwa dance drum and drum dancing. Part 2 describes steps in the building and decoration of the traditional Ojibwa dance drum as well as beliefs associated with these processes. Four appendices. Glossary. Bibliography. Black-and-white photographs and drawings. One map. Tables.

Tribal life

Anson, Bert. *The Miami Indians.* Norman: University of Oklahoma Press, 1970.

A comprehensive history of Miami Indians, part of the Illinois division of Algonquian speaking peoples. Begins with a summary of early Miami settlements and life based on seventeenth century documentary sources. Subsequent chapters discuss the tribe's relations with the French and British from 1700 to 1783; its responses to white expansionism during the late eighteenth century; the disastrous repercussions of the War of 1812 for Miami power and influence on the frontier; events culminating in the partial emigration of the Miami from Indiana to Oklahoma during 1846-1847; overviews of the tribe's Oklahoma and Indiana divisions, 1846-1968; and the social and political status of modern Miamis. Bibliography. Black-and-white reproductions and photographs. Maps.

Brasser, Ted J. *Riding on the Frontier's Crest: Mahican Indian Culture and Culture Change.* National Museum of Man Mercury Series, Canadian Ethnology Service Papers 13. Ottawa: National Museums of Canada, 1975.

A culture history of the Mahican Indians, an Algonquian-speaking group whose original homeland lay in New York State's Hudson Valley. Begins with a description of Mahican culture and social organization before the arrival of whites. Subsequent chapters focus on the dramatic changes in tribal lifeways that resulted from participation in the fur trade, contact with missionaries, emigrations west, and confinement on various reservations. One appendix: "Chronological List of Mahican Locations." Bibliography. Black-and-white reproductions.

Campisi, Jack, and Laurence M. Hauptman, eds. *The Oneida Indian Experience: Two Perspectives*. Syracuse, N.Y.: Syracuse University Press, 1988.

A collection of essays presenting two separate perspectives—the views of the academic world and those of the Oneida community—on the resiliency of Oneida identity. The papers in part 1 examine Oneida responses to crises stemming from their involvements with Europeans and Americans during the seventeenth and eighteenth centuries. Contained in part 2 are articles dealing with the removal of the Oneida from their New York homeland to Wisconsin, the Wisconsin Oneida during the preallotment years, and the legal ramifications of the allotment of the Oneida Reservation. Part 3 provides essays by tribal members and anthropologists concerning the strategies which twentieth century Oneidas have devised to maintain their peoplehood. Selected bibliography. Maps.

Clifton, James A. *The Prairie People: Continuity and Change in Potawatomi Indian Culture, 1665-1965*. Lawrence, Kans.: Regents Press of Kansas, 1977.

A detailed history of the Potawatomi Indians focusing on the events and processes that led to the evolution of the Prairie Potawatomi, now located in Kansas. Includes discussion of tribal pre- and protohistory; colonial relations with the French, British, and Americans; responses to American expansionism in the Old Northwest from 1796 to 1837; the continuities and changes in Potawatomi worldview, religion, and social organization during the late eighteenth and early nineteenth centuries; tribal migrations and resettlements between 1835 and 1847, leading to the emergence of the Prairie Potawatomi; the reservation adaptations of the Prairie people, 1848 to 1905; and present-day (circa 1965) Potawatomi community life. Three appendices. Bibliography. Black-and-white reproductions, photographs, and drawings. Maps.

Danzinger, Edmund Jefferson, Jr. *The Chippewas of Lake Superior*. Norman: University of Oklahoma Press, 1979.

A history of the Chippewas based on documentary evidence as well as fieldwork carried out on the tribe's Minnesota reservations. Part 1 sketches the tribe's circumstances and lifeways prior to the coming of whites, their relations with the French and British during the colonial period, and confinement to reserves under the Americans. The second part is primarily concerned with the effects of federal policy on the quality of Chippewa cultural and economic life during the twentieth century.

Densmore, Frances. *Chippewa Customs*. Bureau of American Ethnology, Bulletin 86. Washington, D.C.: U.S. Government Printing Office, 1929.

A brief ethnography touching on many aspects of Chippewa society and culture.

A series of short introductory sections provide information on the derivation of the name "Chippewa," the character of the people, tribal history, the group's totemic system, and Chippewa phonetics. Subsequent sections contain more extended discussions on dwellings and domestic life, foodstuffs, health and medical treatment, the life cycle, religious beliefs and practices, games, modes of subsistence and economics, social and political organization, and material culture and the arts. Bibliography. Black-and-white photographs and diagrams.

Edmunds, R. David. *The Potawatomis: Keepers of the Fire*. Norman: University of Oklahoma Press, 1978.

A history of Potawatomi people centering on the period between their initial contact with the French in the mid-seventeenth century and their removal to Kansas in the 1840's. Discussion includes the tribe's relations with the French and British and with other Indian groups during the colonial period; their participation in the Pontiac Rebellion of 1763, the Revolutionary War, and the War of 1812; coerced land cessions in the face of white intrusions and settlements; and events leading to Potawatomi removal beyond the Mississippi. Bibliography. Black-and-white reproductions. Maps.

Gibson, Arrell M. *The Kickapoos: Lords of the Middle Border*. Norman: University of Oklahoma Press, 1963.

Provides a history of the Kickapoos, an Algonquian-speaking people living in what is now southern Wisconsin at the time of European contact in the seventeenth century. Includes discussion of the tribe's relations with the French, Spanish, and British during the colonial era; their campaigns against American expansion into the Old Northwest in the late eighteenth and early nineteenth centuries; the division of the tribe into northern and southern divisions; their various land cessions and removals through the opening years of the twentieth century; the rise and decline of Kickapoo dominance over the middle border, a corridor about one hundred miles wide and extending from the Missouri River southward into the upper reaches of Coahuila, Mexico; and Senate investigations of Oklahoma Kickapoo land frauds. Bibliography. Black-and-white reproductions and photographs. One map.

Hagan, William T. *The Sac and the Fox Indians*. Norman: University of Oklahoma Press, 1958.

An ethnohistory of the Sac and Fox Indians focusing on the period between the Treaty of 1804 and the conclusion of the Black Hawk War in 1832. Discussion includes an overview of Sac and Fox cultural patterns; the discord and distrust characterizing relations between the Sacs and Foxes and the United States both before and following the Treaty of 1804; Sac and Fox responses to the increasing white settlement in their territories; their participation in the War of 1812; tribal land cessions between 1804 and 1842; the causes, outbreak, and consequences of the Black Hawk War; removal to reservations in Kansas (1845) and Oklahoma (1867); and adjustment to reservation life up to 1954. Bibliography. Black-and-white reproductions and photographs. Maps.

Hickerson, Harold. *The Chippewa and Their Neighbors: A Study in Ethnohistory*. Prospect Heights, Ill.: Waveland Press, 1988.

Explains the nature and importance of ethnohistorical research and utilizes this methodology to explore various facets of Chippewa culture history. Examines the continuity and change in Chippewa clans; the origins of the Mdewiwin, or Grand Medicine Society; and the historical and ecological background of Chippewa expansion from southern Lake Superior into Minnesota and their consequent warfare with the Dakota. Concludes with a review essay of the strengths and weaknesses of Hickerson's findings and a bibliographical supplement (1988) by Jennifer S. H. Brown and Laura L. Peers. Recommended readings for each chapter. Sparsely illustrated with black-and-white maps, photographs of Chippewa material culture, and reproductions of paintings by Rindisbacher and Eastman.

Keesing, Felix M. *The Menomini Indians of Wisconsin: A Study of Three Centuries of Cultural Contact and Change*. Philadelphia: American Philosophical Society, 1939.

Focuses on the changes in traditional Menominee lifeways that have resulted from three hundred years of contact with non-Indians. Begins with an overview of the tribe's prehistoric migrations and its relationship with other Indian peoples. A summary of Menominee culture of the "pre-white days" is next provided. The body of the work concerns the Menominees' historical relationships with the French, British, and Americans and the transformations in their culture brought about through these relations. The author identifies three main threads in the three centuries of Menominee-white relations: "the progressive modification and in most recent times the disintegration of the old Menomini culture; second, the building up of a reservation life based on the dependence relation of wardship; and third, the manifestation of not a little social and personal disorganization, also of opposition to white control and penetration." Black-and-white reproductions, photographs, and diagrams. Five maps.

Kraft, Herbert C. *The Lenape: Archaeology, History, and Ethnography*. Newark: New Jersey Historical Society, 1986.

Provides a cultural history of the Lenape, or Delaware Indians. Chapter 1 discusses the various sources available for reconstructing the patterns of aboriginal Delaware life. Chapters 2 through 5 trace the evolution of Lenape culture from the Paleo-Indian through Late Woodland periods (11,000 B.C.-A.D. 1650). Chapter 6 describes the tribe's religious beliefs and ceremonies. Chapter 7 reports on Lenape contact with Europeans, giving special attention to the spread of trade goods, alcohol, and diseases. Chapter 8 recounts the conflicts between Delaware and whites which eventually led to the latter's dispossession from their homelands. Black-and-white reproductions, photographs, and drawings. Maps.

Morgan, Lewis Henry. *League of the Ho-de-no-sau-nee or Iroquois*. Rochester, N.Y.: Sage and Brothers, 1851.

A classic account of Iroquois social and political organization from the early days of American anthropology. Describes the motives that gave rise to the formation of the league; relations among its five member nations; the structure and functioning of various league and tribal councils; the centrality of matrilineal kinship (descent traced through the mother's line) in Iroquois sociology; religious beliefs, ceremonies, and dances; customary forms of marriage, warfare, inheritance, and subsistence; selected elements of material culture and arts; and the characteristic features of the Iroquois language. Black-and-white and color plates. Two appendices. Maps.

Newcomb, William W., Jr. *The Culture and Acculturation of the Delaware Indians*. Anthropological Papers, Museum of Anthropology, University of Michigan, No. 10. Ann Arbor: University of Michigan, 1956.

Seeks to reconstruct the early historic lifeways of the Delawares and to describe and explain the changes they experienced under the impact of European and American cultures. Part 1 begins with a discussion of Delaware origins and affiliations. Following this are portrayals of aboriginal Delaware culture, sociology, and ideology. The various sections of part 2 examine the changes in Delaware lifeways that resulted from the tribe's ever-increasing contact with whites from 1524 to the 1950's. Bibliography.

Ourada, Patricia K. *The Menominee Indians: A History*. Norman: University of Oklahoma Press, 1979.

A tribal history of the Menominee Indians of northern Wisconsin. Chapter 1 briefly describes selected elements of Menominee aboriginal culture. Chapters 2 and 3 treat the tribe's economic and political involvements with the French and English up through the War of 1812. Subsequent chapters focus on Menominee relations with Anglo-America, from the early nineteenth century to the 1970's. Discussion includes treaties and land cessions, the establishment of a Menominee reservation in 1854, reservation life, participation in the Civil and Spanish-American wars, Menominee termination in 1954, and the restoration of their tribal status in 1973. Bibliography. Black-and-white reproductions and photographs. Maps.

Radin, Paul. *The Winnebago Tribe*. Bureau of American Ethnology, Annual Report 37 (1915-1916). Washington, D.C.: U.S. Government Printing Office, 1923.

A detailed discussion of Winnebago history and culture based on fieldwork from 1908 to 1913. Part 1 begins with a historical summary utilizing oral tradition and documentary sources and focusing on the tribe's contacts with the French and the influence of the Shawnee prophet. It then considers Winnebago archaeology, material culture, general social customs, burial and funeral observances, the practice of warfare and the meeting of councils, and traditional systems of education. Part 2 details the units and processes of Winnebago social organization, curing practices, and religious concepts. Part 3 contains descriptions of the tribe's ceremonial organization, religious societies, medicine and other dances, the Peyote Cult, and clan war bundle feasts. Black-and-white reproductions, photographs, and drawings. Maps.

Ritzenthaler, Robert E. *The Oneida Indians of Wisconsin*. Bulletin of the Public Museum of the City of Milwaukee, vol, 19, no. 1. Milwaukee, Wis.: Board of Trustees, 1950.

Provides a brief culture history of the Wisconsin Oneida. Part 1 presents a short tribal history from pre-Columbian times to the present day. Part 2 describes some of the shifts in the tribe's economic, social, and religious life that have resulted from three centuries of contact with whites. Concludes with the observation that "it is a tribute to the toughness of culture that any of the old culture has survived in the face of the long period of white contact and pressures and the complete lack of refertilizing Indian influence." An appendix on Oneida orthography. Bibliography. Sepia-toned photographs.

__________. *The Potawatomi Indians of Wisconsin*. Bulletin of the Public Museum of the City of Milwaukee, vol. 19, no. 3. Milwaukee, Wis.: Board of Trustees, 1953.

An ethnography of northeastern Wisconsin's Potawatomi people which focuses on the structure and function of the contemporary Potawatomi community (circa 1953), its relation with local white communities, and continuity and change in the band's traditional lifeways. An introductory chapter furnishes a brief tribal history and a phonetic key for the Potawatomi terms that appear in the text. Part 1 begins with an examination of various aspects of modern Potawatomi society, including economic, political, and social institutions. It next describes anti-Indian feelings among local whites and their relationship to the social problems existing in the Potawatomi community. Part 2 is concerned with the surviving elements of traditional society, including the life cycle, ceremonial pattern, games, and material culture. Bibliography. Black-and-white photographs.

Speck, Frank G. *The Iroquois: A Study in Cultural Evolution*. Cranbrook Institute of Science Bulletin 23. Bloomfield Hills, Mich.: Cranbrook Institute of Science, 1945.

A short presentation of the Iroquois people and their cultural development. Begins by examining the Iroquoian linguistic family and population. Subsequent chapters provide descriptive and historical information on the social and civil aspects of Iroquois culture; economic and ecological aspects of Iroquois culture; arts and crafts; decorative design and symbolism; and religious belief and practice, including ceremonial properties, societies, and modern worship. Bibliography. Black-and-white photographs.

__________. *Penobscot Man: The Life History of a Forest Tribe in Maine*. Philadelphia: University of Pennsylvania Press, 1940.

An ethnography of aboriginal Penobscot culture based on the author's long-term association with that tribe. The first chapter provides a brief tribal history, information on Penobscot relations with neighboring Indian peoples, and the names and locations of extant villages. Chapter 2 contains a highly detailed description of Penobscot subsistence and material life, including housing, hunting, traps, the use of dogs, modes of transportation, fishing, cultivation and gathering, food preparation, tools, and dress. Described in Chapter 3 are

Penobscot arts and crafts. Chapter 4 discusses social groupings, family relations, political organization, the life cycle, and religious belief, ceremony, and dance. Bibliography. Black-and-white photographs and drawings. Maps.

Spindler, George, and Louise Spindler. *Dreamers Without Power: The Menomini Indians*. New York: Holt, Rinehart and Winston, 1971.

Examines the results of the prolonged confrontation between the incongruent cultural systems of Menominee and Euro-Americans. Focuses on the various adaptive strategies the Menominee have employed in order to survive this confrontation. Identifies these strategies as Native oriented, peyote, transitional, and acculturated. Discusses the primary social and psychological characteristics of each. A concluding chapter probes the question of whether a Menominee culture will continue to exist. Bibliography of references. Annotated list of recommended readings. Black-and-white photographs and drawings.

Tooker, Elisabeth. *An Ethnography of the Huron Indians, 1615-1649*. Bureau of American Ethnology, Bulletin 190. Washington, D.C.: U.S. Government Printing Office, 1964.

An introduction to Huron culture and culture change based primarily on ethnographic data contained in seventeenth century descriptions. Begins with a discussion of the Huron League, or Wendat, an association of four nations sharing a common language but each retaining its own customs. Next identifies the Huron's neighbors, including the Tobacco League, Neutral League, Iroquois League, and various Algonquian peoples. The chapters that follow provide information on dress, travel, intertribal relations, the village, government, crime, suicide, etiquette, subsistence, the seasonal cycle, religious beliefs and practices, the life cycle, and mythology. Four appendices. Bibliography of references.

Trigger, Bruce G. *The Huron: Farmers of the North*. New York: Holt, Rinehart and Winston, 1969.

An ethnohistory of the Huron, an Iroquoian people that was virtually decimated by warfare and disease in the mid-seventeenth century. Views Huron culture as a working system concentrating on the interrelationship among its various parts. These parts include the economy, warfare, kinship and family life, government and law, concepts and structures of social privilege and power, and institutions which promoted solidarity among tribal members, and beliefs and practices concerning sickness, curing, and death. Bibliography. List of recommended readings. Black-and-white reproductions.

Weslager, Clinton A. *The Nanticoke Indians—Past and Present*. Newark: University of Delaware Press, 1983.

Traces the history of the Nanticoke Indians, from their "discovery" by John Smith on the eastern shore of Maryland in the seventeenth century to their present-day life in Delaware and New Jersey. Among the critical junctures in this history were the tribe's near-dissemination through warfare with Maryland colonists and disease; the decision of many Nanticoke families in the mid-eighteenth century to resettle on Iroquois lands in Pennsylvania and New York;

the alliance of these emigrants with Iroquois and English forces during the American Revolution; the tribe's dispersal to various regions following the war; and the formation of an Indian Association in 1921 by descendants of those Nanticoke who had remained in Maryland. Concludes with a discussion of the recent revitalization of Nanticoke identity. Appendices. Bibliography. Black-and-white photographs and maps.

Biography and Autobiography

Black Hawk (Ma-ka-tai-me-she-kia-kiak). *An Autobiography*, edited by Donald Jackson. Urbana: University of Illinois Press, 1955.

Black Hawk (d. 1838), the great Sauk leader, tells of his people's efforts to protect their homelands from invasion by whites; the engagements and consequences of the Black Hawk War (1832); his surrender and imprisonment as a prisoner of that war; and his subsequent travels through the United States. Black-and-white reproductions. Maps.

Mountain Wolf Woman. *Mountain Wolf Woman, Sister of Crashing Thunder: The Autobiography of a Winnebago Indian*, edited by Nancy O. Lurie. Ann Arbor: University of Michigan Press, 1961.

A Winnebago Indian woman born in 1884 recalls the major events in her life amid the changing culture of her tribe. Discussion includes her earliest recollections, traditional modes of livelihood, youth, marriage, conversion to peyote religion, medicines, dances and feasts, and children and grandchildren.

Radin, Paul, ed. *The Autobiography of a Winnebago Indian*. University of California Publications in American Archaeology and Ethnology, vol. 16, no. 7. Berkeley: University of California Press, 1920.

The reminiscences and reflections of S. B., a Winnebago Indian. The author, born in the mid-nineteenth century, tells of his childhood, vision quests, travels with an Indian show, bouts with drinking, involvement in and arrest for the murder of Potawatomi, and conversion to the peyote religion. The autobiography is accompanied by a system of social and religious precepts the author learned as a boy.

Rogers, John (Chief Snow Cloud). *Red World and White: Memories of a Chippewa Boyhood*. Norman: University of Oklahoma Press, 1974.

Vignettes from Rogers' youth on the White Earth Reservation in Minnesota which serve to underscore the nurturing character of traditional Chippewa culture and document the acculturative forces operating on tribal members during the late nineteenth and early twentieth centuries.

Williams, Ted C. *The Reservation*. Syracuse, N.Y.: Syracuse University Press, 1976.

The recollections of a Tuscarora man who grew up on that tribe's reservation in Lewiston, New York. Communicates the ambiguous nature of reservation life: its economic hardships, high rate of alcoholism, and factionalism coupled with the survival of kinship and religous values.

Southeast

General Studies and References

Blumer, Thomas J. *Bibliography of the Catawba*. Metuchen, N.J.: Scarecrow Press, 1987.

Seeks to create a comprehensive guide to all secondary sources on Catawba history and culture, including monographs, periodical articles, newspaper articles, and manuscript materials. Contains more than four thousand annotated entries, arranged in chronological order "so that events may be seen in proper historical perspective." Covers the period between 1680 and 1985.

Burt, Jesse, and Robert B. Ferguson. *Indians of the Southeast: Then and Now*. Nashville: Abingdon Press, 1973.

Provides a historical and cultural survey of Indian peoples living in the area now encompassing the states of Tennessee, North and South Carolina, Florida, Georgia, Alabama, Mississippi, and Louisiana. The first half of the book contains information on traditional patterns of subsistence, religion, games, dance and music, and the rearing of children. The second half traces the history of Indian-white relations in the area from the sixteenth century to the present day. Included in this overview are biographical sketches of Indian people of particular historical note. Glossary. Bibliography. Black-and-white reproductions, photographs, and drawings. Color plates. Maps.

DePratter, Chester B., ed. *The Late Prehistoric Southeast: A Source Book*. New York: Garland, 1986.

An anthology of twenty-three reprinted articles on southeastern archaeology that "reflect methodological and interpretive developments beginning in the late eighteenth century and continuing up to the present." The essays are arranged according to the five periods in the evolution of archaeological science discussed in Gordon Willey and Jeremy Sabloff, *A History of American Archaeology* (see the "Culture" section): Speculative period (early explorations to 1840); Classificatory-Descriptive period (1840-1914); Classificatory-Historical period (1914-1940)—Chronology; Classificatory-Historical period (1940-1960)—Context and Function; and Explanatory period (Beginning 1960). An extended introduction discusses the character of each of these periods and its importance for Southeastern prehistory. A bibliography of sources precedes the introduction.

Dobyns, Henry F. *Their Number Become Thinned: Native American Population Dynamics in Eastern North America*. Knoxville: University of Tennessee Press, 1983.

An anthology of seven essays which seeks to identify the underlying causes for the steady decline in Indian population from historic times until the late nineteenth century. Topics include the major European diseases that sharply reduced North America's aboriginal population, estimates of precolonial populations, the food resource potential of Florida under aboriginal Native American management, the number and distribution of Timucua-speaking populations in 1560, the nature of Timucuan sedentarism, an analysis of the devastating effects of Old World diseases on Florida's Native Americans, and depopultion as a dynamic of culture change. Bibliography. Maps, tables, and charts.

Fogelson, Raymond D. *The Cherokees: A Critical Bibliography*. Newberry Library Center for the History of the American Indian Bibliographical Series. Bloomington: Indiana University Press, 1978.

A bibliographical essay that reviews 347 books and articles pertaining to the history and culture of the Cherokee people. The essay is divided by the following subheadings: introduction; basic reference works; general sources on the Cherokees; prehistory and archaeology; the colonial period; the revolution and its aftermath; regeneration; removal; Cherokees in the West; the Eastern Cherokees; language; ecology, natural history, and material culture; social organization; worldview, religion, and medicine; and personality and biography.

Green, Michael D. *The Creeks: A Critical Bibliography*. Newberry Library Center for the History of the American Indian Bibliographical Series. Bloomington: Indiana University Press, 1979.

A bibliographical essay that reviews 216 books and articles pertaining to the history and culture of the Creek people. The essay is divided by the following subheadings: southeastern archaeology, Creek ethnography, and Creek historiography, including sections for general studies; sixteenth and seventeenth centuries; eighteenth century—Creeks and Europeans; peace, prosperity, and peril—1783-1813; the Creek War; removal; resettlement in Indian Territory; the United States Civil War; the late nineteenth century; the allotment crisis; and the Creeks in the twentieth century. Lists recommended works for the beginner and for a basic library collection.

Hoyt, Anne K. *Bibliography of the Chickasaw*. Metuchen, N.J.: Scarecrow Press, 1987.

A partially annotated listing of more than sixteen hundred materials pertaining to Chickasaw history and culture. Entries are arranged alphabetically and include books, periodical articles, dissertations, theses, and government documents. Annotations are primarily descriptive in nature. Subject index and index of joint authors and editors.

Hudson, Charles M., ed. *Ethnology of the Southeastern Indians*. New York: Garland, 1985.

An anthology of anthropological studies dating from 1888 to 1971 on various aspects of Indian cultures of the southeastern United States. Topics includes the classification of southeastern cultures, systems of belief, subsistence, social organization, ritual, and recreation. An introduction by the editor provides a historical overview of nineteenth and twentieth century ethnology among the southeastern tribes. Black-and-white photographs. Maps. Charts.

__________, ed. *Four Centuries of Southern Indians*. Athens: University of Georgia Press, 1975.

A collection of essays which seeks to counter the social biases, stereotypes, and prejudices that have led to ignorance concerning the extent of aboriginal cultural diversity that existed among southern Indians and the importance of their role in American history. The essays were written by both historians and anthropologists. Subjects include relations between the eastern Timucuan Indians and the French and Spanish from 1564 to 1567; southern Indian participation in the War of American Independence; Spanish policy toward the southern Indians in the 1790's; the myths and realities of Indian westward removal; Louisiana Choctaw life at the end of the nineteenth century; an analysis of Cherokee sorcery and witchcraft; institution building among Oklahoma's traditional Cherokee; and Indians and Blacks in white America. A bibliography accompanies each essay. One black-and-white reproduction. Two maps.

__________, ed. *Red, White, and, Black: Symposium on Indians in the Old South.* Southern Anthropological Society Proceedings 5. Athens: University of Georgia Press, 1971.

A collection of papers originally presented at a symposium on Indians of the Old South at the 1970 meeting of the Southern Anthropological Society. Among the topics discussed are the use of early maps in reconstructing southern Indian landscapes, the physical anthropology of Indians of the Old South, southeastern Indian linguistics, the archaeology of European-Indian contact in the Southeast, and the hostility that whites strategically engendered between Indians and Blacks. A bibliography accompanies each essay. Black-and-white reproductions. Five maps.

Hudson, Charles M. *The Southeastern Indians.* Knoxville: University of Tennessee Press, 1976.

An introduction to the Indian peoples of the southeastern United States which traces the main outlines of their prehistory, history, and social institutions. An introductory chapter provides broad overviews of the area's regions, languages, native groups. Chapter 2 recounts the prehistory and early history of the Southeast, from its earliest inhabitants, through the Paleo-Indian, Archaic, Woodland, and Mississippian traditions, to its first European explorers. The remaining chapters discuss the area's various forms of belief system, social organization, subsistence, ceremony, art, music, and recreation. A concluding chapter focuses on white colonization, the federal policy of removal, and those Indians who managed to escape deportation. Bibliography. Black-and-white reproductions, photographs, and diagrams. Maps.

Kersey, Harry A., Jr. *The Seminole and Miccosukee Tribes: A Critical Bibliography.* Newberry Library Center for the History of the American Indian Bibliographical Series. Bloomington: Indiana University Press, 1987.

A bibliographical essay that reviews 249 publications pertaining to the Seminole and Miccosukee tribes of Florida. The essay is divided by the following subheadings: Southeastern Indian sources, general sources on the Seminoles, history and ethnohistory, and Seminole cultural epochs (including Creek origins and migration, 1716-1763; becoming Seminole, 1763-1817; the wars of removal, 1818-1858; withdrawal, stabilization, and reemergence, 1858-1925; reservations; the New Deal through World War II, 1926-1956; from near termination to self-determination, 1957-1982). Lists recommended works and books for a basic library.

Kidwell, Clara Sue, and Charles Roberts. *The Choctaws: A Critical Bibliography.* Newberry Library Center for the History of the American Indian Bibliographical Series. Bloomington: Indiana University Press, 1980.

A bibliographical essay that reviews 234 books and articles pertaining to the history and culture of the Choctaw people. The essay is divided by the following subheadings: archaeology and ethnography; Choctaw relations with European colonies; critical years of transition, 1783-1820; Choctaw removal; Choctaws in Indian Territory, 1830-1907; Choctaws of Oklahoma, 1907 to the present; and Choctaws in Mississippi and Louisiana. Lists recommended works for the beginner and for a basic library collection. Two maps.

Kniffen, Fred B., et al. *The Historic Indian Tribes of Louisiana, from 1542 to the Present.* Baton Rouge: Louisiana State University Press, 1987.

A history of Louisiana's Indian peoples from the mid-sixteenth century to present day, a period "marked by such catastrophic events as the disappearance of tribes, the extinction of languages and other ancient culture traits, large scale migration, and traumatic changes in economic and political status and custom." Begins with synopses of Louisiana's natural setting and prehistory. The next four chapters describe the status of Louisiana's tribes in 1700, initial contacts with Europeans, native Louisiana tribes after 1700, and immigration tribes from 1764 to 1900. Subsequent chapters report on various aspects of Indian society and culture, including tribal settlements, languages, arts and crafts, dress and adornment, subsistence, tribal law, kinship and political organization, life crises, religion and medicine, amusements, and warfare. A conclusion discusses the contemporary situation of the state's Indians. Black-and-white reproductions and photographs, Maps.

Lewis, Thomas M. N., and Madeline Kneberg. *Tribes that Slumber: Indians of the Tennessee Region.* Knoxville: University of Tennessee Press, 1958.

A cultural prehistory of the region comprising present-day Tennessee written for students, amateur archaeologists, and all others interested in Native American life. Includes chapters on the Archaic era, the Early Woodland period; the Burial Mound builders; Mississippian Culture; and precontact Muskogean, Yuchi, and Cherokee peoples. Bibliography. Black-and-white drawings.

Milanich, Jerald T., ed. *The Early Prehistoric Southeast: A Source Book.* New York: Garland, 1985.

An anthology of nineteen previously published essays primarily on the formative period of Southeastern prehistory: a period beginning about 2000 B.C. with the invention of pottery and characterized by nascent village life, more extensive trade, and larger populations than preceding periods. Some of the topics discussed are the beginnings of cultivation, Adena and the eastern Burial Cult, interaction spheres of prehistory, cultural traditions in Florida prehistory, and settlement patterns in the lower Mississippi Valley. An introductory essay briefly reviews the history of southeastern archaeology. A bibliography of sources precedes the introduction.

Milanich, Jerald T., and Samuel Proctor, eds. *Tacachali: Essays on the Indians of Florida and Southeastern Georgia during the Historic Period*. Gainesville: University Presses of Florida, 1978.

A collection of nine papers organized around the project of describing and interpreting the changes that occurred in the aboriginal cultures of Florida and southeastern Georgia during the historic period. Topics include Spanish-Indian relations, 1500-1763; Tocobago Indians and the Safety Harbor Culture; acculturation and change among the western Timucua; fusion and assimilation among the eastern Timucua; the impact of Spanish missions on the Guale Indians of the Georgia coast; the last of the South Florida aborigines; the ethnoarchaeology of the Florida Seminole; and the University of Florida's oral history project. A bibliography accompanies each essay.

O'Donnell, James Howlett, III. *Southeastern Frontiers: Europeans, Africans, and American Indians, 1513-1840*. Newberry Library Center for the History of the American Indian Bibliographical Series. Bloomington: Indiana University Press, 1982.

A bibliographical essay that reviews 337 books and articles pertaining to the ways Africans, Europeans, and Indians met and mingled in the American Southeast. The essay is divided by the following subheadings: "The First Wave—Spain and the Sixteenth-Century Frontier"; "A Double Wave—Englishmen and Africans"; "Mounting Tides—Anglo-French Expansionism and Conflict"; "Angry Seas—The American Revolution and the Early National Period"; and "Removal." Lists recommended works for the beginner and for a basic library collection.

Perdue, Theda. *Nations Remembered: An Oral History of the Five Civilized Tribes, 1865-1907*. Westport, Conn.: Greenwood Press, 1980.

A collective autobiography of Southeastern Indians from the Civil War to Oklahoma statehood. Based on excerpts from interviews with Oklahoma Indians whose ancestors lived in the southeastern United States, conducted in the 1930's by the Writer's Project of the Works Progress Administration. Specific narratives were chosen to present a broad spectrum of perspectives, experiences, attitudes, and life styles.

Peterson, John H., Jr., ed. *A Choctaw Source Book*. New York: Garland, 1985.

Assembles twenty-six essays, written between 1828 and 1968, on Choctaw history and culture. An editor's introduction places these articles in context and assesses their relationship to current research. Among the topics discussed are Choctaw religion, archaeological and anthropometrical work in Mississippi, patterns of courtship and marriage, funeral customs, the western removal of the Mississippi Choctaw, subsistence and diet, sacred narratives, and concepts of the afterworld. A bibliography follows the introduction.

Sturtevant, William C., ed. *A Creek Sourcebook*. New York: Garland, 1987.

A collection of twenty-two anthropological articles, published between 1853 and

1980, which focuses on the core peoples of the multitribal, multilingual Creek Confederacy: the Muskogee-speaking Creek proper and the Hitichi speaking towns. Among the topics discussed are laws of the Creek nation, towns and villages of the Creek Confederacy in the eighteenth and nineteenth centuries, dialects of the Muskogee language, ceremonial songs of the Creek and Yuchi, Creek intertown relations, Creek social organization and government, the emergence of contemporary Creek identity, and kinship and descent in the ethnic reassertion of the eastern Creek Indians. A list of sources precedes a brief introduction.

__________, ed. *A Seminole Sourcebook*. New York: Garland, 1987.

An anthology of nineteen essays, written between 1911 and 1978, "that includes most of the published work on the Seminole Indians of Florida and Oklahoma that meets anthropological standards." Among the topics are the formation of the Seminole people, the ethnoarchaeology of the Florida Seminole, Seminole pottery, medicine bundles of the Florida Seminole and the Green Corn Dance, the social organization of the Cow Creek Seminole of Florida, Seminole men's clothing, the socioeconomic status of the Oklahoma Seminoles, and the effect of federal legislation and administrative treatment on the government of the Seminole nation of Oklahoma. A list of sources precedes a brief introduction.

Swanton, John R. *The Indians of the Southeastern United States*. Bureau of American Ethnology, Bulletin 137. Washington, D.C.: U.S. Government Printing Office, 1946.

A highly detailed treatment of the history and culture of the Southeastern tribes. The first eight chapters survey the geography of the Southeast; estimates for its aboriginal population; the relation of the aboriginal population to the natural areas; prehistoric movements; and the history of Southeastern Indians from the period of first white contact to post-De Soto. Next are descriptions of 178 Southeastern tribes and their populations. Subsequent sections provide information on the interpretations of tribal names; physical and mental characteristics; various modes of subsistence; housing; clothing and ornamentation; tools and manufactures; arts and music; societal and ceremonial life, including social organization, games, war, courtship and marriage, crime and punishment, means of communication, trade, religious beliefs and usages, and medical practices. A conclusion identifies common cultural characters, cultural differences, and cultural subareas. Also compares the Southeast with corresponding areas in other parts of the world. Black-and-white reproductions, photographs, and drawings. Maps and tables.

__________. *Source Material for the Social and Ceremonial Life of the Choctaw Indians*. Bureau of American Ethnology, Bulletin 103. Washington, D.C.: U.S. Government Printing Office, 1931.

A compilation of passages from primary sources on various aspects of Choctaw social and religious life. Topics include the Choctaw origin legend, material culture, social organization, government, property, crime and punishment, regulations for women and childbirth, personal names, education, marriage, the sexual division of labor, games, travels and greetings, war customs, burial customs, and religion and medicine. One appendix. Bibliography. Black-and-white reproductions and one drawing.

Williams, Walter L., ed. *Southeastern Indians Since the Removal Era*. Athens: University of Georgia Press, 1979.

A collection of essays by historians and anthropologists which seeks to provide a total picture of the lifeways of Native American groups that remained in the Southeast despite federal attempts in the early nineteenth century to expel them. An introductory essay briefly summarizes the prehistory and history of Southeastern Indians through the period of removal. The first of two sections contains papers on native groups that avoided removal, including various Indian tribes of Virginia, the North Carolina Lumbee, the Houma and Tunica of Louisiana, and the Catawba of South Carolina. Papers on southeastern remnants of removed nations are presented in section 2. Numbered here are Alabama Creeks, the Choctaws of Mississippi, the Eastern Band of Cherokee, and the Seminoles of Florida. A concluding essay identifies patterns in the history of the remaining Southeastern Indians for the period 1840 to 1975. Bibliographical essay. Black-and-white photographs. Maps and tables.

Wright, J. Leitch, Jr. *The Only Land They Knew: The Tragic Story of the American Indians in the Old South*. New York: Free Press, 1981.

A historical overview of Southeastern Native peoples focusing on their relations with Europeans and Blacks from the sixteenth through the eighteenth centuries. Among the author's primary themes are the devastating effects of European-introduced diseases on the South's aboriginal populations and cultures, the use of Indians as slaves, and the significant role played by Indian culture and genetics in the evolution the "American Negro" race. Bibliography. Black-and-white reproductions and photographs.

Archaeology

Chapman, Jefferson. *Tellico Archaeology: 12,000 Years of Native American History*. Knoxville: Tennessee Valley Authority, 1985.

An introduction to fourteen years of archaeological surveys and excavations in the lower Little Tennessee River valley which sought to recover data on the prehistoric and historic occupation of the area before its inundation by the Tennessee Valley Association's Tellico Reservoir project. The main section of the monograph identifies and describes the five culture periods that constitute the more than 12,000 years of Indian occupation in the valley. Concludes with a cultural description of the Overhill Cherokee and their forced removal from the Little Tennessee River valley in 1838. Black-and-white photographs and drawings. Maps.

Davis, Dave D., ed. *Perspectives on Gulf Coast Prehistory*. Gainesville: University Presses of Florida, 1984.

A collection of essays which focuses on the Woodland and Mississippian periods of Gulf Coast prehistory. The papers are unified by the assumption that prehistoric events and processes on the Gulf Coast were sufficiently different from those of the interior valleys to demand independent research. A number of the essays present archaeological overviews on specific subregions of the study area. Others concentrate on selected topics, including geoarchaeology (an integration of geological and archaeological methodologies), the location of historic Indian villages in the Mississippi Delta, and the prehistoric development of Calusa society in southwest Florida. Bibliography. Black-and-white photographs and drawings. Maps, tables, and charts.

Dickens, Roy S., Jr. *Cherokee Prehistory: The Pisgah Phase in the Appalachian Summit Region*. Knoxville: University of Tennessee Press, 1976.

An introductory description and synthesis of a late prehistoric phase in the Appalachian Summit, the interior region of the southern Appalachian Mountains inhabited by the Cherokee tribe during historic times. The period under study lasted from the beginnings of South Appalachian Mississippian culture to the emergence of an identifiable Cherokee presence. The discussion is organized by the following topics: sites, structures, and features; burials; artifacts; ceramics; and food remains. Two appendices. Bibliography. Black-and-white photographs and drawings.

Gilliland, Marion Spjut. *The Material Culture of Key Marco, Florida*. Gainesville: University Presses of Florida, 1975.

Discusses Frank H. Cushing's archaeological expedition to Key Marco, Florida, in 1895 and the rich variety of artifacts it unearthed. Part 1 begins with a historical reconstruction of the Cushing dig, then provides information on the materials found at the Cushing site and their significance for southeastern archaeology. Part 2 presents a generous photographic sampling of Key Marco remains, organized according to the following materials of manufacture: wood, shell, bone, antler, stone, pottery, netting and cordage, and cucurbits and gourds. Also included is a section on human remains. Commentaries accompany each specimen. Bibliography. Black-and-white photographs. One map.

Howard, James H. *The Southeastern Ceremonial Complex and Its Interpretation*. Missouri Archaeological Memoir 6. Columbia: Missouri Archaeological Society, 1968.

Provides an outline of the late prehistoric developments known as the Mississippian culture and describes the complex of Mississippian ritual objects and motifs designated as the Southeastern Ceremonial Complex or Southern Cult. Among its conclusions are that the Southeastern Ceremonial Complex represents the trappings of the Mississippian state religion and that the complex is clearly related to the Busk or Green Corn Ceremony, still practiced among many Southeastern tribes; that surviving ceremonial practices of Southeastern groups seem to indicate a strong fire-sun-deity concept that explains certain motifs of the Southern Cult; and that there exists a continuity from the prehistoric Mississippian past to the present for many ritual objects and motifs of the Southern Cult. One appendix: "The 1965 Yuchi Green Corn Dance at

Kellyville, Oklahoma" by Norman Feder. Bibliography. Black-and-white photographs and drawings. One map.

Milanich, Jerald T., and Charles H. Fairbanks. *Florida Archaeology*. New York: Academic Press, 1980.

An overview of Florida prehistory written for students as well as those with a lay interest in the subject. The first chapter summarizes the history of archaeological work in the state, beginning in 1834 and continuing to the present. Remaining sections identify and describe the various periods of Florida's more than 13,000 years of prehistoric cultural development. The organization is both chronological and regional, stressing the importance of such ecological factors as cultural traditions, contact or lack of contact with other peoples, and varying plant and animal resources. Bibliography. Black-and-white photographs and drawings. Maps and tables.

Morse, Dan F., and Phyllis A. Morse. *Archaeology of the Central Mississippi Valley*. New York: Academic Press, 1983.

Describes cultural development in the Mississippi valley lowlands during the 11,000 years preceding the De Soto expedition of 1539-1543. Chapters are arranged chronologically by period, from Paleo-Indian through Archaic, Woodland, Mississippian, and early historic. Uses selected artifacts and sites to document the increasing cultural complexity of the region. Bibliographies accompany each chapter. Black-and-white photographs and drawings. Maps and tables.

Neuman, Robert W. *An Introduction to Louisiana Archaeology*. Baton Rouge: Louisiana State University Press, 1984.

A study of prehistoric and early historic native populations in Louisiana which attempts to collate the available material, present it clearly and objectively, and provide appropriate interpretations. Begins with the Paleo-Indian era (10,000 B.C. to 6000 B.C.) and moves through the Meso-Indian era (6000 B.C. to 2000 B.C.) and Neo-Indian era (2000 B.C. to A.D. 1600). Provides extensive discussion on the important Neo-Indian era cultures of Poverty Point, Tchefuncte, Marksville, Troyville-Coles Creek, Caddo, Plaquemine, and the Mississippian. A final chapter discusses archaeological research at historic Indian sites inhabited during the early eighteenth century and exhibiting signs of European contact. Bibliography. Black-and-white photographs. Maps.

Powell, Mary Lucas. *Status and Health in Prehistory: A Case Study of the Moundville Chiefdom*. Washington, D.C.: Smithsonian Institution Press, 1988.

Examines the effects of selected environmental and cultural factors on human health and disease patterns at Moundville, the major community of a Mississippian chiefdom in west central Alabama. Argues that the analysis of a large sample of skeletal material does not support the hypothesis that the health of the Moundville elite greatly differed from the nonelite segments of the society. One appendix. Maps, tables, and graphs.

Smith, Marvin T. *Archaeology of Aboriginal Culture Change in the Interior Southeast: Depopulation During the Early Historic Period*. Gainesville:

University Presses of Florida, 1987.

Examines the types of culture changes that European contact brought to various aboriginal chiefdoms of the interior southeastern United States. Among the study's goals are: to increase knowledge concerning the critical timing of culture and population collapse caused by European and African contacts in the New World and to explore the application of archaeological methods in demonstrating the disintegration of chiefdoms in relation to general population decline. Two appendices. Bibliography of references cited. Black-and-white photographs. Maps and tables.

Walthall, John A. *Prehistoric Indians of the Southeast: Archaeology of Alabama and the Middle South*. Tuscaloosa: University of Alabama Press, 1980.

A cultural prehistory for the region that is present-day Alabama, spanning the 11,000 years between "the earliest documented appearance of human beings in the area to A.D. 1750, when the early European settlements were well established." Divides this period into five developmental stages: Paleo-Indian, Archaic, Gulf Formational, Woodland, and Mississippian. Chapters of the book detail current knowledge regarding these stages based on the research of professional and amateur archaeologists and laboratory analysis. Glossary of archaeological terms. Bibliography. Black-and-white photographs and drawings. Maps.

Folklore, Sacred Narrative, Religious Belief and Practice

Howard, James H. *Shawnee!: The Ceremonialism of a Native American Tribe and Its Cultural Background*. Athens: Ohio University Press, 1981.

A detailed ethnography of the Shawnee with particular emphasis on their religious beliefs and practices. Chapter 1 discusses the origins and early history of the tribe. Subsequent chapters treat the derivation of the name "Shawnee"; the tribe's five great divisions; traditional history; subsistence and diet; costume and decorative art; housing, settlement, and travel; kinship and social organization; government, war, and peace; the life cycle; religion and cosmology; magicians, prophets, and sacred bundles; present-day Shawnee ceremonialism; spring and early summer ceremonials; late summer and autumn ceremonial; the nighttime dances; and obsolete dances and dance customs. One appendix. Bibliography. Black-and-white reproductions and photographs.

Howard, James H., and Willie Lena. *Oklahoma Seminoles: Medicines, Magic, and Religion*. Norman: University of Oklahoma Press, 1984.

A traditionalist interpretation of Oklahoma Seminole religion and culture based largely on the testimony of informant Willie Lena. Begins with a synopsis of Seminole history. Subsequent chapters discuss herbal remedies, nonherbal remedies, magic and witchcraft, ceremonialism, the Green Corn Ceremony, the Nighttime Dances, sports and games, supernaturals, distinctively Indian aspects of the Seminole world, and mortuary practices. The author comments on the surprising amount of traditional culture still remaining among today's Oklahoma Seminole "in spite of more than four hundred years of exposure to European and American culture on the part of the Seminoles and their Creek forbears, and many conflicts and forced migrations of a most disruptive nature." Bibliography. Black-and-white photographs and drawings (by Lena).

Hudson, Charles M., ed. *Black Drink: A Native American Tea*. Athens: University of Georgia Press, 1979.

An anthology of papers on "black drink," a tea made from the parched leaves and twigs of the Yaupon holly (*Ilex vomitoria*) and used as a ceremonial purgative by certain groups of Southeastern Indians. The essays include a botanical analysis of the plant, archaeological and ethnohistorical studies on its use in the Southeast, the various functions of the drink among the Creek, and a history of the beverage's use by non-Indians. Bibliography. Black-and-white reproductions, photographs, and drawings. Two maps.

Mooney, James. *Myths of the Cherokee*. Bureau of American Ethnology, Annual Report 19 (1897-1898). Washington, D.C.: U.S. Government Printing Office, 1900.

A collection and analysis of Cherokee oral narratives based on materials collected between 1887 and 1890 in western North Carolina. Begins with a summary of Cherokee-white relations from 1540 to the end of the nineteenth century. The discussion of Cherokee stories and storytellers which follows includes the following fourfold typology of Cherokee myths: sacred myths, animal stories, local legends, and historical traditions. The author next provides biographical information on his major informants. Remaining sections provide English translations of numerous Cherokee narratives. Black-and-white photographs and drawings.

__________. *The Sacred Formulas of the Cherokees*. Bureau of American Ethnology, Annual Report 7 (1885-1886). Washington, D.C.: U.S. Government Printing Office, 1891.

A summary of Cherokee medico-religious knowledge that includes a sample of ritual formulas transcribed in the Cherokee language by healers living on the tribe's reservation in North Carolina. Among the topics treated by the summary are the character of Cherokee formulas, the myth concerning the origin of disease and medicine, the theory of disease, selected plants used in curing, medical practices (sweat bath, medicine dances, and so on), the payment of shamans, ceremonies for gathering plants and preparing medicine, color symbolism, and the language of the formulas. The formulas contained in the monograph are organized according to the categories of medicine, hunting, love, and miscellaneous. Black-and-white reproductions.

Speck, Frank G. *Ceremonial Songs of the Creek and Yuchi Indians*. University of Pennsylvania, Museum Anthropological Publications, vol. 1, no. 2. Philadelphia: University Museum, 1911.

A collection and description of forty-two Creek dance and medicine songs and seven Yuchi dance songs. A transcription is provided for each song, accompanied by ethnographic information on its meaning and performance. Provides a table of twenty Creek medicines, including their Native names, translations,

English names, botanic names, diseases for which they are used, and the reputed causes of these diseases. Ends with a traditional narrative that relates the origin of disease and medicine and two Shawnee love songs. Black-and-white drawings.

Swanton, John R. *Myths and Tales of the Southeastern Indians*. Bureau of American Ethnology, Bulletin 88. Washington, D.C.: U.S. Government Printing Office, 1929.

A collection of traditional narratives belonging to the Creek, Hitchiti, Alabama, Koasati, and Natchez Indians. Narratives are organized by tribe. The texts of each people are then arranged in the following order: stories that concern natural phenomena or the doings of ancient native heroes; stories that deal with visits to the world of the dead; stories describing encounters between humans and supernatural beings in animal form; accounts of interactions among animals, including the Southeastern trickster Rabbit; and stories known to have been borrowed from Euro- and Afro-Americans. Concludes with a discussion of the relative resemblances in the narratives. One table.

__________. *Religious Beliefs and Medical Practices of the Creek Indians*. Bureau of American Ethnology, Annual Report 42 (1924-1925). Washington, D.C.: U.S. Government Printing Office, 1928.

A description of Creek religious beliefs and medical practices based primarily on the early reports of trader John Adair, the author's own fieldwork, and Native myth and legend. Section 1 begins with Creek speculations on the nature of the cosmos. It is followed by discussions of tribal deities and spiritual beings; objects used to procure supernatural help; the afterlife; sacrifices; taboos; music and ceremonials, including *asi* (the ceremony of the black drink) and "busk" (the Creek New Year). Section 2 concerns shamanism and medicine and describes various statuses of religious specialists, witchcraft, and diseases and remedies. Bibliography. Black-and-white photographs.

Subsistence and Land Use

Goodwin, Gary C. *Cherokees in Transition: A Study of Changing Culture and Environment Prior to 1775*. University of Chicago Department of Geography Research Paper 181. Chicago: Department of Geography, University of Chicago, 1977.

Provides a comparative eco-historical analysis of Cherokee society and culture. Chapter 1 presents a summary of the study's theoretical and methodological assumptions. Chapter 2 details the geography, climate, and natural resources of the precontact Cherokee habitat. Chapters 3 and 4 examine precontact Cherokee ecology: settlement patterns, use of native plants and animals, and so on. Chapters 5 and 6 describe and compare those factors responsible for Cherokee culture-ecological change in the postcontact period. Bibliography. Maps and tables.

Larson, Lewis H. *Aboriginal Subsistence Technology on the Southeastern Coastal Plain During the Late Prehistoric Period*. Gainesville: University Presses of

Florida, 1980.
A study intended to further understanding of the ecology of prehistoric cultures of the Southeastern Coastal Plain. Examines aboriginal cultural adaptations within three broad environmental areas: the Coastal Sector, characterized by hunting, gathering, and two types of shifting maize agriculture; the South Florida Sector, dominated by cultures lacking in agriculture and totally dependent on the native flora and fauna; and the Pine Barrens Sector, devoid of population because of a lack of technological ability to exploit its resources. Bibliography. One map.

Family and Society

Strickland, Rennard. *Fire and the Spirits: Cherokee Law from Clan to Courts*. Norman: University of Oklahoma Press, 1975.
Challenges the widely held presumption that "Cherokees dramatically broke with their ancient law ways and passed from a state of complete 'savage' lawlessness to a highly sophisticated, efficiently operating 'civilized' system of tribal laws and courts." Demonstrates that the Cherokee court system evolved through a gradual process of acculturation that intermingled aboriginal legal customs with those of Euro-Americans. Characterizing this system was a unique fusion of newly written laws and traditional Cherokee spiritual culture. Bibliography. Black-and-white drawings and one color illustration. Maps.

Swanton, John R. *Social and Religious Beliefs and Usages of the Chickasaw Indians*. Bureau of American Ethnology, Annual Report 44 (1926-1927). Washington, D.C.: U.S. Government Printing Office, 1928.
A detailed discussion of Chickasaw society, culture, and religion. Begins with several variants of tribal origin legends. Next treats terms of relationship, including those for birth and marriage relations. Subsequent discussions concern names and naming, primary groupings of social organization, government, property rights, crime and punishment, regulations regarding women, childbirth and education of children, marriage customs, the sexual division of labor, burial customs, hunting, games, time consciousness and modes of communication between tribes, general religious beliefs, concepts of afterlife, dances, the central curing ceremony known as *Pishofa*, and traditional doctors and medicines. Bibliography.

__________. *Social Organization and Social Usages of the Indians of the Creek Confederacy*. Bureau of American Ethnology, Annual Report 42 (1924-1925). Washington, D.C.: U.S. Government Printing Office, 1928.
A detailed presentation of Creek society and social customs. Section 1 contains Native narratives dealing with Creek history, including tribal origins; the first meeting between Creeks and white people; and prophecies concerning the fate of the Indians. Section 2 begins by identifying and describing the primary components of Creek social organization: the household; family; clans, phratries, and moieties; and towns. Next discusses the evolution of the Creek confederacy, government, rules pertaining to property, and crime and

punishment. Section 3, "General Customs," provides information on the life cycle, divisions of the day and year, war, agriculture, hunting, spoken and sign language, traveling and hospitality, trade, counting, and games. Bibliography. Black-and-white photographs and drawings. Tables.

Material Culture and the Arts

Densmore, Frances. *Choctaw Music*. Bureau of American Ethnology, Bulletin 136. Washington, D.C.: U.S. Government Printing Office, 1943.

Identifies and analyzes various types of Choctaw songs. Song categories include war songs, songs with games, Tick Dance songs, Drunken-Man Dance songs, Duck Dance songs, Snake Dance songs, Steal-Partner Dance songs, Bear Dance songs, Stomp Dance songs, miscellaneous dance songs, hunting songs, and songs connected with pastimes. A summary of the general features of each category is presented, followed by transcriptions and ethnological and musicological analyses of selected songs. Bibliography. Black-and-white photographs.

__________. *Seminole Music*. Bureau of American Ethnology, Bulletin 161. Washington, D.C.: U.S. Government Printing Office, 1956.

A study of Seminole songs based on fieldwork with many of the tribe's Florida bands during the 1930's. The introductory section first presents information on the author's singers and informants, then provides a brief tribal history and ethnography. The body of the monograph contains transcriptions and ethnological and musicological analyses of selected ceremonial and social songs. Included in the sample are Corn Dance and Hunting Dance songs, songs connected with treatment of the sick, songs for success in ball games, and children's dance songs. Concludes with a summary of the analyses of the songs and comparisons between Seminole songs and other tribes. Bibliography of authorities cited. Black-and-white photographs and one diagram.

Fundaburk, Emma Lila, and Mary Douglas Fundaburk Foreman, eds. *Sun Circles and Human Hands: The Southeastern Indians, Art, and Industries*. Luverne, Ala.: Emma Lila Fundaburk, 1957.

A profusely illustrated prehistory of the arts and technology of the Southeastern Indians. Divides this prehistory into four culture periods: Paleo (? 8000-4000 B.C.); Archaic (4000 B.C.-1000 B.C.); Woodland (1000 B.C.-A.D. 900); and Mississippi (A.D. 900-1600). Chapter 1 discusses the chief characteristics of each period. Subsequent chapters offer extended quotations by noted archaeologists concerning various aspects of southeastern material culture. Among the topics discussed are native trade; motifs, symbols, and artifacts associated with the Southeastern Ceremonial Complex; Key Marco, an important archecological site in Florida; and materials made from stone, copper, pottery, wood, and animal products. Bibliography. Black-and-white reproductions and photographs accompanied by extended commentaries.

Howard, James H., and Victoria L. Levine. *Choctaw Music and Dance*. Lincoln: University of Oklahoma Press, 1990.

A short, though detailed study of the surviving dance forms of the Mississippi and Oklahoma Choctaws, especially as they were practiced in the period 1965 to 1972. Chapter 1 provides background on Choctaw history and culture. Chapter 2 discusses the public performance of dances, musical instruments, and costumes. Chapter 3 provides descriptions of each of the surviving Choctaw dances. Transcriptions and analyses of several Choctaw dance songs are provided in the final sections of the book. Bibliography of sources cited. Black-and-white photographs.

Leftwich, Rodney L. *Arts and Crafts of the Cherokee*. Cullowhee, N.C.: Land-of-the-Sky Press, 1970.

A discussion of the traditional arts and crafts still practiced by the Eastern Band of Cherokee. An editor's introduction briefly describes recent attempts to promote the production and marketing of these works. Following a brief tribal history, discussion turns to specific art/craft forms, including basketry, pottery, woodcrafts, weaving, stonecrafts, bead and shell work, metalcrafts, weapon making, featherwork, and leathercrafts. Bibliography. Black-and-white photographs.

Tribal Life

Baird, W. David. *The Chickasaw People*. Phoenix: Indian Tribal Series, 1974.

Traces the history of the Chickasaw people from earliest times to the 1970's. Begins by summarizing tribal legends that describe the Chickasaws' migration from their original homeland somewhere in the distant West to the area encompassed by present-day Mississippi. Subsequent sections treat traditional patterns of subsistence, government, society, and religion; relations during the colonial era with Spain, Britain, and France; events leading to their removal to Indian Territory in the 1830's; the disasters of the Civil War, white inundation of tribal lands, reservation allotment, and the demise of the Chickasaw nation. A conclusion offers some predictions concerning the tribe's future. List of suggested readings. Black-and-white photographs and color plates. Maps.

_________. *The Choctaw People*. Phoenix: Indian Tribal Series, 1973.

Provides a concise history of the Choctaw, a Muskogean-speaking group whose traditional homelands lay in what is now central and southern Mississippi. Begins with a sketch of the tribe's pre-Columbian social and cultural patterns. Section 2 overviews Choctaw relations with the Spanish, British, and French from 1540 to 1783, noting how the European presence altered the people's traditional lifeways and inter- and intratribal relationships. Subsequent sections examine Choctaw-American relations for the periods before and after the tribe's forced removals to Indian Territory in the 1830's. The conclusion offers a few speculations concerning the Choctaws' future. List of suggested readings. Black-and-white reproductions, photographs, and color plates. Maps.

Blu, Karen I. *The Lumbee Problem: The Making of an American Indian People*. Cambridge, England: Cambridge University Press, 1980.

Examines how the Lumbee Indians of Robeson County, North Carolina, have achieved social and legal recognition as Native Americans despite having no records of treaties, reservations, Indian language, or distinctly Indian customs. Argues that the key to Lumbee success in these and other realms in based on continuities and transformations in how they have conceived themselves as a group. Beginning with their own traditional conviction that they were descended from Indians, they "proceeded gradually to persuade others to recognize them, legally and socially, as Indians. In the process of convincing others of their Indianness, Robeson County Indians have altered some aspects of their ideas about who they are (their origins from particular Indian groups), changed the emphasis of other aspects (from 'not Black' to, increasingly, 'non-White'), and apparently maintained still others . . . though with different emphases at different periods." One appendix. Bibliography. Maps and tables.

Finger, John R. *The Eastern Band of Cherokees, 1819-1900*. Knoxville: University of Tennessee Press, 1984.

An ethnohistory of those Cherokees who managed to avoid removal to the West during the 1830's. Argues that from the early to late nineteenth century, the eastern band of Cherokee participated in a legally precarious and ambiguous relationship with the state of North Carolina and the federal government which posed a continuous threat to their homeland and psychological health; and despite this situation, they managed to maintain their Indian identity. Bibliography. Black-and-white photographs. Maps.

Garbarino, Merwyn S. *Big Cypress: A Changing Seminole Community*. New York: Holt, Rinehart and Winston, 1972.

A description of contemporary life on Big Cypress, one of four federal reservations for the Seminole Indians of Florida. Particular attention is given the decision-making processes that underlay the tribe's change to a cattle economy in the 1950's and the effect of this change on traditional patterns of Seminole leadership and political relations. Also contains a brief tribal history and overview of present-day culture and social organization. Bibliography of references. List of recommended readings. Black-and-white photographs.

Gibson, Arrell M. *The Chickasaws*. Norman: University of Oklahoma Press, 1971.

Documents the major events affecting the Chickasaw Indians from the mid-sixteenth to early twentieth century. Chapter 1 briefly portrays selected features of the tribe's aboriginal society and culture. Chapters 2 through 5 describe how the Chickasaws' involvement in the colonial policies and ambitions of the Spanish, British, French, and Americans led to an erosion of their independence, fragmentation of their social order, and corruption of their traditional ways. Chapters 6 through 9 discuss the events leading up to the tribe's removal from Mississippi and Alabama; the liquidation of the Chickasaw estate; and their relocation in Indian Territory during the late 1830's. Subsequent chapters detail the tribe's troubled yet successful attempt to establish a new nation in the West; their alliance with the Confederacy during the Civil War and harsh Reconstruction Treaty of 1866; and the legal demise of the Chickasaw republic in 1907, the date of Oklahoma's admission as the country's forty-sixth state. Bibliography. Black-and-white reproductions and photographs. Maps.

Hudson, Charles. *The Catawba Nation*. Athens: University of Georgia Press, 1970.
A historical reconstruction of the Catawba Indian society which employs the perspectives of ethnohistory and folkhistory. Chapters 2 through 5 provide an ethnohistorical account of the Catawba's transition from an aboriginal, sovereign people to one of the many groups that terminated their status as Indians with the Bureau of Indian Affairs. Chapter 6 examines how the Catawbas and their white neighbors think of themselves in terms of their past. Finds that the white and Catawba histories "are in essential agreement in accounting for the remote past, but when they account for events and conditions nearer to the present, they begin to diverge." They are most at odds in characterizing the principle governing Catawba history from the colonial era to the present. Bibliography. Black-and-white photographs.

King, Duane H., ed. *The Cherokee Indian Nation: A Troubled History*. Knoxville: University of Tennessee Press, 1979.
An anthology of twelve essays exploring selective topics in Cherokee Indian history. Among the subjects treated are the origins and development of Cherokee culture; Cherokee legal notions concerning homicide; the distribution of Cherokee settlements in the eighteenth century; the diplomatic exploits of pseudo-Cherokee charlatan William A. Bowles; nineteenth century Cherokee political organization; the development of plantation slavery among the Cherokee before removal; upheavals within the Cherokee Nation between 1828 and 1835; factionalism among the postremoval Cherokee; the origins of the Eastern Cherokee as a social and political entity; the efforts of William Holland Thomas, trader and tribal adoptee, to secure financial claims for the Eastern Cherokee; social change among the Eastern Cherokee; and the Five County Northeastern Oklahoma Cherokee Organization, a political revival based on traditional social processes which flourished between 1965 and 1972. Black-and-white reproductions and photographs. Maps and tables.

McKee, Jesse O., and Jon A. Schlenker. *The Choctaws: Cultural Evolution of a Native American Tribe*. Jackson: University Press of Mississippi, 1980.
Provides an ethnohistory of the Choctaw Indians from the indigenous period to 1979. The discussion is framed by the following periodization: Indigenous (?-1698); European-American contact (1699-1800); Choctaw land cessions and acquisitions (1801-1830); removal to Indian Territory and a new nation (1831-1906) and Mississippi Choctaws (1831-1917); and Mississippi Choctaws (1918-1979) and Oklahoma Choctaws (1907-1979). Each chapter first presents the significant historical events occurring during each period and then summarizes the changes in culture which resulted from these events. Bibliography. Black-and-white reproductions and photographs. Maps, tables, and charts.

McReynolds, Edwin C. *The Seminoles*. Norman: University of Oklahoma Press, 1957.
A history of the Florida and Oklahoma Seminole Indians, Muskogean- speaking groups descended from the Lower Creek. Chapter 1 provides a selective discussion of the tribe's aboriginal lifeways and relations with European

explorers and colonials up to the late eighteenth century. Chapters 2 through 8 describe the Seminole alliance with the British during the War of 1812; their war with settlers of Georgia and Alabama (the First Seminole War, 1817-1818); their involvement in Spanish, British, and American contests over Florida; and their confinement to a reservation, by terms of the Treaty of Camp Moultrie, in 1824. Subsequent chapters treat white agitation for Indian removal, 1826-1834; Seminole resistance to expulsion from the Southeast; the forced emigration of many of the tribe to Indian Territory (the Seminole Trail of Tears); the struggle of these exiles to build a new nation in the West; the involvement of the western Seminole in the American Civil War; Reconstruction and recovery; and the legal abolishment of the Seminole tribe in 1906. Bibliography. Black-and-white reproductions and photographs. Maps.

Merrell, James H. *The Indians' New World: Catawbas and Their Neighbors from European Contact Through the Era of Removal*. Chapel Hill: University of North Carolina Press, for the Institute of Early American History and Culture, Williamsburg, Virginia, 1989.

Examines how the Catawba and neighboring Indian groups coped with changes brought about by European and Anglo-American contact. Focuses on Indian responses to the effects of diseases, trade, colonial and U.S. Indian policy, Christian missionization, and white encroachment on tribal lands. The discussion, which is organized topically within a chronological framework, demonstrates how "Indians had to blend old and new ways that would permit them to survive in the present and prepare for the future without utterly forsaking their past."

Perdue, Theda. *The Cherokee*. New York: Chelsea House, 1989.

A brief, highly readable introduction to Cherokee history and culture. Chapter 1 begins with the traditional Cherokee account of world and tribal origins. It next summarizes what is known about aboriginal Cherokee culture. The remaining chapters focus on the disruptions to Cherokee lifeways caused by colonial and U.S. Indian policies. Discussion includes the tribe's attempts at self-directed "civilization" during the eighteenth and early nineteenth centuries; the intratribal factionalism that resulted from differing responses to removal and the Civil War; Cherokees in the West and those who remained in the East after removal; and Cherokees in the twentieth century. Bibliography. Black-and-white reproductions, photographs, and drawings. Color plates. Maps.

Pierce, Earl Boyd, and Rennard Strickland. *The Cherokee People*. Phoenix: Indian Tribal Series, 1973.

A historical overview of the Cherokee Nation of Oklahoma. Early sections deal with the failure of the young American government to keep its treaty obligations with the Cherokees and the events leading to their forced removal to Indian Territory in 1837-1838. Also described are the rivalries that developed between the traditionalist and proassimilationist factions of the tribe.

Rountree, Helen C. *The Powhatan Indians of Virginia: Their Traditional Culture*. Norman: University of Oklahoma Press, 1989.

A historical ethnography of the seventeenth century Powhatan, the collective designation for Algonquian-speaking groups of Virginia's coastal plain. Uses information from archaeology and from the writings of Englishmen in some fashion knowledgeable of these Indians to reconstruct their patterns of subsistence; town life; sex roles and family; social distinctions; law, politics, and war; medicine, and religion. An epilogue analyzes Powhatan culture as a whole and compares it with the lifeways of other Indian groups. Bibliography. Black-and-white reproductions and photographs. Maps.

Speck, Frank G. *Ethnology of the Yuchi Indians*. University of Pennsylvania, University Museum, Anthropological Publications, vol. 1, no. 1. Philadelphia: University Museum, 1909.

A cultural survey of the Yuchi Indians, whose traditional homeland lay within the present-day borders of Georgia and South Carolina. Begins with a brief description of the tribe's ethnic and linguistic relations with other Southeastern peoples followed by sketches of their history, population, environment, and language. Subsequent sections examine Yuchi material culture, decorative art and symbolism, music, division of time, social and political organization, warfare, games, the life cycle, religion, and mythology. Black-and-white photographs and color plates.

Wardell, Morris L. *A Political History of the Cherokee Nation, 1838-1907*. Norman: University of Oklahoma Press, 1938.

Examines the history of the Western Band of Cherokee, from their forced removal to Indian Territory in the 1830's to their passing as a political unit in 1907 with the emergence of the state of Oklahoma. Contains considerable discussion of the new nation forged by the removed group and of the effects of the Civil War and Reconstruction on Cherokee institutions and intratribal relations. Appendices. Bibliography.

Wells, Samuel J., and Roseanna Tubby, eds. *After Removal: The Choctaw in Mississippi*. Jackson: University of Mississippi Press, 1986.

Eight historical studies concerning those Mississippi Choctaw who escaped removal to Indian Territory in the early nineteenth century. An introductory paper overviews the history of the Mississippi Choctaw from the Removal Treaty to their federal recognition in 1918. Subsequent essays treat the settlement patterns and life styles circa 1830, the roles of mixed bloods in Mississippi Choctaw history, the public career of Greenwood LaFlore, a prominent Choctaw mixed-blood, the socioeconomic status of Choctaw fullbloods during post-removal Mississippi, efforts of the Catholic church on behalf of the band, an additional effort at removal during the early twentieth century, and the band's economic development since 1945. Selected bibliography. Black-and-white photographs.

Biography and Autobiography

Baird, W. David. *Peter Pitchlynn: Chief of the Choctaws*. Norman: University of Oklahoma Press, 1972.

Examines the life and career of Peter Pitchlynn, a mixed-blood Choctaw who exercised great influence over the political and economic affairs of his people prior to, during, and following their removal to Indian Territory. Discussion includes a description of the various strands of Pitchlynn's white and Indian heritage, his struggle for power within the Choctaw leadership hierarchy, his role in rebuilding the postremoval Choctaw republic, his public and private speculative interests, his election as chief in 1864, and his position as Choctaw representative in Washington following the Civil War. Bibliography. Black-and-white photographs and drawings. Maps.

Edmunds, R. David. *The Shawnee Prophet*. Lincoln: University of Nebraska Press, 1983.

A biography of Tenskwatawa, Shawnee visionary of the early nineteenth century and younger brother of Tecumseh. Documents how the prophet's movement of religious and cultural revitalization acted to consolidate opposition to white expansion into the Old Northwest. Bibliography. Black-and-white reproductions. Maps.

Grayson, G. W. *A Creek Warrior for the Confederacy: The Autobiography of Chief G. W. Grayson*, edited by W. David Baird. Norman: University of Oklahoma Press, 1988.

The reminiscences of George Washington Grayson, a Creek mixed blood, focusing on his experiences during the Civil War as a captain in Company K of the Confederacy's Second Creek Regiment. The author also discusses his role in the postwar politics of the Creek Nation, including his numerous trips to Washington, D.C., as a tribal delegate.

Perdue, Theda, ed. *Cherokee Editor: The Writings of Elias Boudinot*. Knoxville: University of Tennessee Press, 1983.

Presents a biography and selected writings of Elias Boudinot, Cherokee statesman and journalist of the early nineteenth century. The selections include several of Boudinot's contributions to various periodicals, an address to the whites, and letters and other papers relating to Cherokee affairs. Also presented are numerous pieces that originally appeared in the *Cherokee Phoenix*, a newspaper published by Boudinot in Sequoian syllabary and English. Black-and-white photographs.

Southwest

General Studies and References

Anderson, Frank G. *Southwestern Archaeology: A Bibliography*. New York: Garland, 1982.

Lists all important published and selected unpublished writings on the archaeology of America's Southwest appearing before the end of 1977. Coverage includes the states of Utah, Arizona, New Mexico, Chihuahua, Sonora, western and southern Colorado, trans-Pecos Texas, and the southeastern extremities of

California and Nevada. Entries are alphabetically arranged by author. A subject index classifies the titles by subarea and topic.

Bahti, Tom. *Southwestern Indian Tribes*. Las Vegas: KC Publications, 1968.

A brief, profusely illustrated introduction to the history and cultures of southwestern Native Americans. Begins with introductory discussions of early man in the Southwest and white intrusions and settlement in the region. Subsequent sections focus on the history and lifeways of particular groups, including the Pueblo tribes, Paiute, Chemehuevi, Apaches, Tohono O'otam (formerly Papago), Yaqui, Pima, Cocopa, Mojave, Maricopa, Yuma, Hualapai, Yavapai, Havasupai, and Ute. A short bibliography follows each section. Black-and-white and color reproductions, photographs, and drawings. Two maps.

Barnett, Franklin. *Dictionary of Prehistoric Indian Artifacts of the American Southwest*. Flagstaff, Ariz.: Northland Press, 1973.

Concerned with Native American artifacts from the period prior to recorded history in southeastern Utah, southwestern Colorado, and the area falling within the boundaries of Arizona and New Mexico. Includes entries for more than 250 different major types of artifacts listed in alphabetical order. Entries provide information on culture of origin, dates, use, and measurements. The dictionary is preceded by an introductory essay that discusses southwestern prehistoric periods, the basic materials from which artifacts were typically made, and modes of shaping and decoration. Photographs accompany entries. Includes a glossary of archaeological terms. Black-and-white and color photographs.

Dobyns, Henry F., and Robert C. Euler. *Indians of the Southwest*. Newberry Library Center for the History of the American Indian Bibliographical Series. Bloomington: Indiana University Press, 1980.

A bibliographical essay that reviews 434 books and articles on the history and culture of Indians in America's Southwest (excluding the Apache and Navajo). The essay is divided by the following major subheadings: the region; the Puebloan peoples, including sections for chroniclers, colonial records, the Tiwa, Towa, Tano, Tewa, Keresan, Zunis, Hopis, and remnant Southern Pueblos; the Rancherian peoples, including sections for the Cahitans, northern Piman speakers, Opatas, Tarahumaras, Riverine Yuman speakers, Arizona Upland Yumans, Numic speakers, and Seris; and urbanization. Lists recommended works for the beginner and for a basic library collection. Two maps.

Dozier, Edward P. *The Pueblo Indians of North America*. New York: Holt, Rinehart and Winston, 1970.

A summary of Pueblo history and culture which focuses on Pueblo adaptations to changing physical, socioeconomic, and political conditions. Part 1 provides an overview of the Pueblos today, touching on such subjects as their economy; changes in Pueblo life; education; health; community life; and relations with the Bureau of Indian Affairs, non-Pueblo neighbors, and other Indians. Part 2 synthesizes 10,000 years of Pueblo prehistory. Part 3 overviews traditional social and political organization for the Western, Eastern or Rio Grande, and Tanoan Pueblos. Concludes with a discussion of general Pueblo cultural characteristics, including language, ceremonies, government organization, and worldview, concepts, and symbols. Glossary. Lists for references cited and recommended readings. Black-and-white photographs and diagrams. Maps and charts.

Dutton, Bertha P. *Indians of the American Southwest*. Englewood Cliffs, N.J.: Prentice-Hall, 1975.

Intended as a source of authoritative information on the Southwestern Indians for students, teachers, and travelers. An introductory chapter briefly discusses the physical aspects of the American Indians, the Southwest and its original inhabitants, and the development of the area's aboriginal socioreligious patterns. The next five chapters provide histories and cultural surveys for the Pueblo peoples, the Athapascans (Navajo and Apache), the Ute Indians, Southern Paiute, and Rancheria peoples. A final chapter describes Southwestern Indian arts and crafts. Includes a calendar of annual Indian events and population figures. Bibliography. Black-and-white photographs and drawings. Maps.

Ferguson, T. J., and Richard E. Hart. *A Zuni Atlas*. Norman: University of Oklahoma Press, 1985.

Summarizes the history, ethnography, and current conditions of the Zuni people in relation to their natural environment by use of maps, photographs, and text. Topics include location, topography, and climatic conditions of the Zuni area; the general direction of Zuni origin and migration; major Zuni archaeological sites and culture areas; sixteenth century Zuni villages and Spanish entradas; traditional areas of Zuni agriculture, grazing, hunting, plant collection, mineral collection, and religious use; Zuni trade relationships; Zuni reservation changes, 1877-1982; grazing units on the Zuni reservation; and mineral and energy resources and extractions on the Zuni reservation. Two appendices: Zuni land use sites; and summary of land use by site. Bibliography.

Ford, Richard I., ed. *The Prehistoric American Southwest, a Source Book: History, Chronology, Ecology, and Technology*. New York: Garland, 1987.

An anthology of twenty seminal essays, published between 1886 and 1945, on the prehistory of the American Southwest. Represented in the collection are pieces by Frank Cushing, Charles Avery Amsden, Emil Haury, Alfred Kidder, Alfred L. Kroeber, and Julian Steward. An editor's introduction provides a culture history for the Southwest, a review of archaeological work in that region, and discussions of issues related to chronology, the interaction of southwestern prehistoric peoples to their environment, and technology. A list of sources precedes the introduction.

Frisbie, Charlotte J. *Music and Dance Research of Southwestern United States Indians*. Detroit Studies in Music Bibliography 36. Detroit: Information Coordinators, 1977.

States as its goals to critically review the orientations, methodologies, and interests of past research; identify present-day research interests and methods; and suggest problems and areas of future research. Appendices. Black-and-white drawings.

Goddard, Pliny E. *Indians of the Southwest*. New York: American Museum of Natural History, 1913.

A classic survey of the modern and prehistoric cultures of the American Southwest. An introduction defines the area of study and discusses how physical environment in combination with habits of life have molded the varying cultural patterns exhibited by southwestern Indians. Chapter 1 reconstructs the lifeways of the area's ancient peoples. Chapter 2 is primarily concerned with the distribution and customs of contemporary (circa 1913) Pueblo groups. Chapter 3 describes the material cultures, social customs, political organizations, games, religions, and ceremonies of the Southwest's non-Pueblo peoples.

Goodman, James M. *The Navajo Atlas: Environments, Resources, People, and History of the Dine Bikeyah*. Norman: University of Oklahoma Press, 1982.

Contains forty-eight maps profiling selected aspects of Navajo history, demography, and subsistence. The maps in part 1 place Navajo country within the American Southwest, identify its various regions, and locate key administrative and political subdivisions. Parts 2 through 6 provide maps on the physical environment, Navajo history, population, livelihood, resources and services, and the disputed Navajo-Hopi lands. Each part begins with a summary of its topic and translation of the data displayed by its maps.

Hedrick, Basil C., et al., eds. *The Classic Southwest: Readings in Archaeology, Ethnohistory, and Ethnology*. Carbondale: Southern Illinois University Press, 1973.

Brings together for ready access twelve significant papers on southwestern archaeology, ethnohistory, and ethnology written between 1880 and 1940. Argues that "many of the basic inferences and the comprehensive syntheses upon which modern investigators in the American Southwest must depend were developed during this period." Among the most notable of the essays are J. Walter Fewke's "The Feather Symbol in Ancient Hopi Designs"; A. V. Kidder's "Speculations on New World Prehistory"; "Aboriginal Turquoise Mining in Arizona and New Mexico" by William P. Blake; and William Duncan Strong's "An Analysis of Southwestern Society." Bibliography. Black-and-white diagrams. Maps and charts.

Iverson, Peter. *The Navajos: A Critical Bibliography*. Newberry Library Center for the History of the American Indian Bibliographical Series. Bloomington: Indiana University Press, 1976.

A bibliographical essay that reviews 189 books and articles pertaining to the history and culture of the Navajo people. The essay is divided by the following subheadings: introduction, bibliographies, Navajo accounts and documents, newspapers and newsletters, origins and early history, the long walk era, the stock reduction era and contemporary history, social organization and language, government and law, education, economy, and health and religion. Lists recommended works for the beginner and for a basic library collection.

Laird, W. David. *Hopi Bibliography, Comprehensive and Annotated*. Tucson: University of Arizona Press, 1977.

Contains more than 2900 annotated entries for materials concerned with the Hopi Indians. Citations are arranged alphabetically by author. Length of annotations ranges from a few words to one-third of a page. Annotations are both descriptive and evaluative in nature. Indexes for titles and subjects.

Melody, Michael Edward. *The Apache: A Critical Bibliography*. Newberry Library Center for the History of the American Indian Bibliographical Series. Bloomington: Indiana University Press, 1977.

A bibliographical essay that reviews 223 books and articles pertaining to the history and culture of the Apache peoples. The essay is divided by the following subheadings: general reference works; basic ethnographic works, including sections for primary sources, secondary sources, western Apachean ethnography, and eastern Apachean ethnography; basic historical materials, including sections for general works, the Spanish-Mexican period, and the American period; the way of the Apaches, including sections for mythology, religion, and ritual; ethnographic notes, including sections for art and basketry, costume, government, language and linguistics, photographs; conclusion. Lists recommended works for the beginner and for a basic library collection.

Oppelt, Norman T. *Southwestern Pottery: An Annotated Bibliography and List of Types and Wares*. 2d rev. ed. Metuchen, N.J.: Scarecrow Press, 1988.

A reference for those researching prehistoric and historic southwestern pottery and related subjects. Part 1 provides an annotated listing, arranged alphabetically by author, of 965 resources on southwestern ceramics. Part 2 identifies approximately 1240 pottery types, wares, and variety names.

Ortiz, Alfonso, ed. *New Perspectives on the Pueblos*. Albuquerque: University of New Mexico Press, 1972.

A collection of twelve essays which attempts to present novel lines of inquiry concerning Pueblo history and culture. Topics include an ecological analysis of Eastern Pueblo societies; Puebloan prehistory; the nature of dual social organization (moiety) in the pueblos; Pueblo linguistics; ritual drama and Pueblo worldview; a new interpretation of the Pueblo ritual clown; an overview of Pueblo religion; Pueblo literature; eastern Pueblo ethnomusicology; and acculturation and population dynamics. Concludes with a summary of key points discussed in the essays. Bibliography. Maps and tables.

__________, ed. *Southwest*. Vol. 9 in *Handbook of North American Indians*. Washington: Smithsonian Institution, 1979.

The first of two volumes on the Southwest, presenting fifty-nine essays by noted scholars of the Pueblo tribes of that region. Essays examine southwestern regional archaeology, linguistic study, Pueblo-white relations from the sixteenth century to the present, the histories and cultures of particular Pueblo groups, and Pueblo fine arts. Provides most extensive coverage for the Zuni and Hopi with separate essays on the prehistory, history, social and political organization, economy, semantics, and religion and worldview of each group. A fifty-five-page general bibliography lists references cited by the authors. Black-and-white reproductions, drawings, and photographs. Maps and charts.

__________, ed. *Southwest*. Vol. 10 in *Handbook of North American Indians*. Washington, D.C.: Smithsonian Institution, 1983.
The second of two volumes on the Southwest, presenting fifty-six essays by noted scholars of the Circum-Pueblo, or non-Pueblo, peoples of that region. Includes papers on the prehistory, history, languages, and cultures of selected groups, including Yumans, Havasupai, Walapai, Yavapai, Mojave, Maricopa, Quechen, and Cocopa. Provides coverage of Pima, Papago, Apache, and Navajo. A fifty-nine-page general bibliography lists references. Black-and-white photographs, reproductions, drawings, maps, and charts.

Spicer, Edward H. *Cycles of Conquest: The Impact of Spain, Mexico, and the United States on the Indians of the Southwest, 1533-1960*. Tucson: University of Arizona Press, 1976.
Describes and interprets the important events affecting Indian-white relations from the entrance of the Spaniards in the Southwest during the early sixteenth century to 1960. An introduction focuses on the characteristics of the Indians of northwestern New Spain in 1600. Part 1 traces the history of Anglo contacts with the Tarahumaras, Mayos and Yaquis, Lower Pimas and Opatas, Seris, upper Pimas, Eastern and Western Pueblos, Navajos, Western Apaches, and Yumans. Part 2 examines Spanish, Mexican, and Anglo-American programs for "civilizing" Indians. Part 3 discusses the political, linguistic, communal, religious, and economic consequences of Indian contact with whites. Part 4 describes the processes of acculturation. The author identifies as a major finding of his study that the "objectives of military and political domination over Indians were eventually achieved, after about 350 years, but even given the control that this made possible, most of the Indians simply did not respond as the conquerors thought they would or should." Bibliography. Black-and-white drawings by Hazel Fontana. Maps.

Weaver, Thomas, ed. *Indians of Arizona: A Contemporary Perspective*. Tucson: University of Arizona Press, 1974.
A collection of articles intended to dispel the many false notions and misunderstandings concerning the Indians of Arizona. An introductory essay briefly describes some of the major issues and dilemmas facing the state's Native Americans. The remaining papers provide information on Arizona's prehistoric peoples; Indian-white relations from 1539 to 1854; twentieth century legislation; the living conditions of contemporary Indians; Arizona's urban Indians; the legal basis of tribal government; employment, economic development, and assistance programs; and Indian education. List of suggested readings. Black-and-white photographs. Tables and maps.

Zuni People. *The Zunis: Self-Portrayals*, translated by Alvina Quam. Albuquerque: University of New Mexico Press, 1972.
Contains forty-six stories from the oral traditions, literature, and history of the Zuni. Texts are organized under the following categories: society, history, fables, fables of moral instruction, religion, and war and defense. Black-and-white photographs and drawings. Maps.

Archaeology

Cordell, Linda S. *Prehistory of the Southwest*. Orlando, Fla.: Academic Press, 1984.

An up-to-date synthesis of southwestern prehistory intended for use by students, scholars, and lay readers. The first three chapters provide essential theoretical and substantive background for the chronologically arranged chapters that follow. Chapters 4 and 5 review southwestern prehistory from its oldest archaeological complexes to the period immediately following the acceptance of domestic crops from Mesoamerica (circa 9000 B.C. to A.D. 1). Chapters 6 and 7 examine the progressive spread of agriculture and sedentism in the area. Chapter 8 discusses Chaco Canyon and other early, large-scale cultural centers of the Southwest. Chapter 9 recounts the systematic collapse of these centers during the period A.D. 1150 to 1300. The concluding chapter is concerned with the archaeological evidence and interpretation for the years 1300 to 1540. Bibliography. Black-and-white photographs and drawings. Maps and charts.

Haury, Emil W. *The Hohokam: Desert Farmers and Craftsmen, Excavations at Snaketown, 1964-1965*. Tucson: University of Arizona Press, 1976.

A description and analysis of the excavations at Snaketown, a prehistoric village in southwestern Arizona inhabited by Hohokam peoples from 300 B.C. through the late fifteenth century. Sets as its goals to reexamine the basis for the Hohokam chronology; to develop a clearer picture regarding Hohokam origins; to evaluate the kind, extent, and time of Mesoamerican influences; and to focus on the history of irrigated agriculture. Contains extended discussions of Snaketown's architecture, stratigraphic record, subsistence activities, and material culture. Bibliography. Black-and-white photographs and drawings. Maps and tables.

Kent, Kate P. *Prehistoric Textiles of the Southwest*. Santa Fe: School of American Research; and Albuquerque: University of New Mexico Press, 1983.

Retraces the long and complex development of weaving in the prehistoric Southwest. Sets as its primary concern "to describe and to ascertain the origin of the kinds of fabrics made by Indians of the prehistoric Southwest, in order to understand the history and evolution of the textile crafts and their importance in the lives of the people." Includes discussion of the preparation of fibers and dyes used in textile manufacture; nonloom techniques of weaving; loom-woven fabrics; classes of woven design; and the various forms and functions of textiles, including wearing apparel, utilitarian articles, and ceremonial paraphernalia. Final chapter considers regional and temporal styles and suggests the interplay between them. Black-and-white drawings, photographs, color plates, and tables.

Kidder, Alfred V. *An Introduction to the Study of Southwestern Archaeology*. New Haven, Conn.: Yale University Press, 1962.

A revised edition of the author's 1924 classic on Pueblo prehistory. Begins with an overview of modern Pueblo society and culture. Follows with a description of the prehistoric Pueblos organized around a scheme of nine culture areas based on river drainages. Claims that such an approach is "not only a convenient method for arranging material but . . . the river drainages form in most cases definite areas of specialization." Each chapter surveys the significant sites of each culture area. Concludes with a summary that combines the data presented into a coherent whole. An introduction by Irving Rouse updates Kidder's work. A bibliography accompanies each section. Also included is an account of Kidder's fieldwork at the site of Pecos. Black-and-white photographs and drawings.

Lister, Robert H., and Florence C. Lister. *Chaco Canyon: Archaeology and Archaeologists*. Albuquerque: University of New Mexico Press, 1981.

Documents the history of archaeological research in Chaco Canyon, a rich zone of prehistoric Pueblo sites located in northwestern New Mexico. Chapters 1 through 6 provide a chronological description of the work of various teams of investigators, beginning in the mid-nineteenth century to the present day. Chapter 7 synthesizes what is currently known about the canyon's human prehistory. Black-and-white photographs and diagrams. Maps and charts. Appendix: "Inventory of Investigated Chaco Canyon Archaeological Sites."

McGuire, Randall H., and Michael B. Schiffer, eds. *Hohokam and Patayan: Prehistory of Southwestern Arizona*. New York: Academic Press, 1982.

Eleven essays on the archaeological resources and prehistory of southwestern Arizona intended for both professional archaeologists and lay readers. The book is organized in three parts. The papers in part 1 provide introductions to the area's environment, aboriginal societies, and history of archaeological research. Part 2 begins with evaluative summaries of previous scholarship on southwestern Arizona culture history and adaptations, then provides detailed discussions of Patayan and Hohokam chronologies. Part 3 contains a critical assessment of past archaeological surveys in the region, a review of existing data and known sites, and recommendations for increasing knowledge concerning the area's archaeological resources. Ten appendices. Bibliography. Black-and-white photographs. Maps, tables, and charts.

Minnis, Paul E. *Social Adaptations to Food Stress: A Prehistoric Southwestern Example*. Chicago: University of Chicago Press, 1985.

Provides a case study from the prehistoric American Southwest of organizational and economic responses of nonstratified societies to food stress. Defines "food stress" as "any shortage of food or perception of vulnerability to food acquisition problems that requires some action on the part of human groups." Develops a predictive model of responses to periods of food stress; estimates the severity and frequency of food stress experienced by prehistoric peoples of the Rio Mimbres drainage, New Mexico; and considers how these groups might have responded to food stress by recourse to the model. Appendix: plant names. Bibliography. Black-and-white photographs. Tables and graphs.

Noble, David G., ed. *New Light on Chaco Canyon*. Santa Fe, N.M.: School of American Research Press, 1983.

A collection of nontechnical reports on Chaco Canyon, the center of a complex prehistoric culture in northwestern New Mexico which reached its zenith from

A.D. 1100 to 1130. An editor's introduction briefly overviews the prehistory of the Canyon. Among the topics of the essay that follow are Chacoan archaeoastronomy, rock art, architecture, as well as the Anasazis and Navajos who once occupied the thirty-two-square-mile area. Bibliography. Black-and-white photographs, drawings and color plates.

Schaafsma, Polly. *Indian Rock Art of the Southwest*. Albuquerque: University of New Mexico Press, 1980.

Describes the many styles of southwestern rock art from the first millennium B.C. to the historic period. Defines "rock art" as "drawings produced by the application of paint (rock painting) or the cutting away of the rock surface." An introductory chapter distinguishes two categories of rock art: representational and abstract; overviews the history of rock art studies; and provides a theoretical framework for the investigation that follows. Subsequent chapters examine rock art sites associated with such major prehistoric traditions as the Hohokam, Anasazi, Fremont, and Mogollon; Pueblo rock art after A.D. 1300; and Navajo and Apache rock art. Black-and-white photographs, drawings, and color plates. Maps and charts.

Tanner, Clara Lee. *Prehistoric Southwestern Craft Arts*. Tucson: University of Arizona Press, 1976.

Surveys the major arts of the prehistoric Southwest, including baskets, textiles, pottery, and jewelry. An introductory chapter provides a brief cultural prehistory for the area. Each of the subsequent chapters focuses on a particular art, describing the materials, technologies, and equipment used in its manufacture; its characteristic forms; design styles; and artistic development. Bibliography. Black-and-white drawings, photographs, and color plates. Charts and maps.

Folklore, Sacred Narrative, Religious Belief and Practice

Aberle, D. F. *The Peyote Religion Among the Navaho*. New York: Wenner-Gren Foundation for Anthropological Research, 1966.

A historical and social-psychological analysis of the Navajo peyote cult. Part 1 provides a general description of the evolution, doctrines, and rituals of the peyote religion. Part 2 presents a tribal history of the Navajo, focusing on the calamities caused by federally enforced livestock reductions from 1933 to 1951. Parts 3 and 4 treat the history and nature of peyote religion among the Navajo, emphasizing the rejection of the cult by the majority of the tribe as well as factors underlying its differential appeal among individuals and communities. Part 5 argues the controversial thesis that it is a religion of the oppressed "providing an ethic adjustive for people in the condition of American Indians." Bibliography. Black-and-white photographs and drawings. Tables.

Bahr, Donald M. *Pima and Papago Ritual Oratory: A Study of Three Texts*. San Francisco: Indian Historian Press, 1975.

An analysis of the style and content of three Pima and Papago shamanic oral texts. An introduction discusses the place of oratory in Piman culture and the way to approach its study. Chapter 2 describes the relation of oratory to other forms of Piman literature, its structure and cultural functions, and the history of collecting orations. The third chapter contains the three orations. Chapter 4 provides a stylistic analysis of the texts and compares the development of the story they relate. By viewing the three stories as alternative expressions of common underlying ideas, the analysis aims to go "into the world view expressed in ritual oratory." Bibliography of references cited. Black-and-white photographs and drawings.

_________, et al. *Piman Shamanism and Staying Sickness*. Tucson: University of Arizona Press, 1973.

A introduction to the Piman theory of sickness, based on the collaboration of a Papago shaman, a Papago Indian translator, a Papago Indian linguist, and a non-Indian anthropologist. Materials analyzed were the transcribed texts of interviews held with shaman Juan Gregorio concerning the nature and causes of disease. The interviews were first translated from Piman to English and then examined for the interrelated categories and assumptions they contained. One appendix. Bibliography. Black-and-white reproductions and photographs.

Bahti, Tom. *Southwestern Indian Ceremonials*. Las Vegas: KC Publications, 1982.

A brief, profusely illustrated introduction to the religious life of the Southwestern Indians. Begins with a historical summary of white attempts to suppress the traditional religions of the Native Southwest. Subsequent sections discuss key elements in the belief and worship of the Navajo, Rio Grande Pueblos, Zuni, Hopi Pueblos, Apache, and Yaqui. A concluding section describes the history, distribution, and character of peyote religion among Southwestern Indians. Provides a calendar of Southwestern Indian ceremonials. Bibliography of suggested readings. Black-and-white and color reproductions, photographs, and drawings.

Benedict, Ruth. *Zuni Mythology*. 2 vols. New York: Columbia University Press, 1935.

Presents English translations for more than one hundred traditional Zuni narratives. An introductory essay identifies the prominent themes in Zuni folklore, the relation of these themes to Zuni behavior and values, and the roles of tradition and creativity in the process of narration. The narratives are arranged under the following categories: the emergence and other kachina tales, Ahaiyute (twin war gods) adventures, tales of courtship, tales of despised and unacknowledged children, tales of husbands and wives, tales of war and famine, animal tales, and miscellaneous tales. Each volume concludes with abstracts of narratives that are discussed in relation to previously recorded Zuni tales and discussions that relate the themes of the narratives to the beliefs and practices of Zuni culture.

Dockstader, Frederick J. *The Kachina and the White Man: The Influences of White Culture on the Hopi Kachina Cult*. Rev., enlarged ed. New York: Atheneum. 1985.

An analysis of the evolution of the Hopi kachina cult which focuses on changes that have resulted from contact with Euro-American culture. The first chapter briefly discusses aboriginal Hopi lifeways; the tribe's contacts with other Indian groups before the incursion of the Spanish; and the growth of Hopi religion. Chapter 2 summarizes the nature and functions of Hopi kachinas and kachina ceremonies. Evidence for the prehistoric origin of the kachina cult is presented in chapter 3. Chapters 4 through 7 document Hopi contact with the non-Indian world from the sixteenth through the twentieth century. Subsequent chapters seek to identify the effects these contacts have had on the kachina cult. Contains a summary of Hopi-white contacts from 1540 to 1850 and a glossary of Hopi words used in the text. Black-and-white photographs and drawings; black-and-white and color plates. Bibliography.

Farella, John R. *The Main Stalk: A Synthesis of Navajo Philosophy*. Tucson: University of Arizona Press, 1984.

Attempts to elucidate selected concepts in Navajo philosophy and to demonstrate their relationship to *sa'a naghai bik'e hozho*, the conceptual center of that philosophical system. Draws on and critiques the works of Haile, Reichard, and other students of Navajo culture and religion. Argues that *sa'a naghai bik'e hozho* denotes a "continuous generational animation" that is the source of all animation on the earth's surface. Bibliography.

Frisbie, Charlotte J. *Navajo Medicine Bundles or Jish: Acquisition, Transmission, and Disposition in the Past and Present*. Albuquerque: University of New Mexico Press, 1987.

Examines, first, the past and present place of medicine bundles (*Jish*) within the religious system of the Navajo Indians and, second, "the larger issues that now encompass them and will continue to do so in the future." Part 1, "Traditional Navajo Religion and Its Ceremonial Equipment," begins with an introduction to the religious world of the Navajo people. It then discusses linguistic, mythological, archaeological, and ethnohistorical perspectives on the origin and meaning of Jish; attempts by previous researchers to classify the types of medicine bundles used by Navajo; factors affecting variations in Jish contents; differences in status accorded medicine bundles as well as rules for their acquisition, transmission, and disposition. Parts 2 through 4 provide in-depth considerations of the acquisition and use of Jish; the mechanisms and options associated with Navajo-to-Navajo Jish transmissions; and the mechanisms and options pertaining to Jish disposition before 1977, respectively. Part 5 describes how increased Indian activism, court decisions, and other developments have led to demands for repatriation of Jish housed in museums and art collections. Part 6 presents reflections on future research needs and a summary. Eight appendices. Bibliography. Black-and-white reproductions and photographs. Tables.

__________, ed. *Southwestern Indian Ritual Drama*. Albuquerque: University of New Mexico Press, 1980.

A collection of essays on traditional ritual dramas of the Native American Southwest. An operational definition of "ritual drama" is presented in the prologue. Most of the papers that follow focus on selected elements of specific Indian rites, including performances by the Zuni Kachina Society, Hopi Ogres drama, the Picuris Pueblo Deer Dance, Mescalero Apache Girl's Puberty Ceremony, Navajo House Blessing Ceremony, Navajo Shootingway, and Papago Skipping Dance. Three other papers discuss filming a Tewa ritual dance, eastern Pueblo ritual dramas, and Havasupai song *vocables*—"meaningless" syllables forming part or all of a song text. Bibliography of references. Black-and-white photographs and drawings. Song transcriptions. Tables.

Gill, Sam D. *Sacred Words: A Study of Navajo Religion and Prayer*. Westport, Conn.: Greenwood Press, 1981.

A study of Navajo prayer based on a sample of three hundred prayer texts analyzed in isolation from their ritual contexts. States as its hypothesis that a description of the structuring principles informing the performance of Navajo prayer acts will disclose the basic premises and categories of Navajo religious processes. Chapters present the constituents from which Navajo prayers are constructed, a classification of prayers on the basis of their structures, and a typology of prayer acts. Three appendices. Bibliography. Black-and-white drawings. Tables.

Haile, O. F. M., Fr. Berard, comp. and trans. *Navajo Coyote Tales: The Curly To Aheeddliinii Version*, edited by Karl Luckert. Lincoln: University of Nebraska Press, 1984.

Presents seventeen Navajo narratives whose central character is Coyote, a complex figure appearing as excrement, corpse, fool, gambler, imitator, trickster, witch, hero, savior, and god. An introductory essay by Karl Luckert discusses the varying statuses of Coyote in terms of the categories less-than-human, equal-to-human, and greater-than-human. He demonstrates how Coyote shifts among these statuses in different stories and within single narratives. The texts are presented both in Navajo and in free English translations.

Hinton, Leanne, and Lucille J. Watahomigie, eds. *Spirit Mountain: An Anthology of Yuman Story and Song*. Tucson: University of Arizona Press. 1984.

A bilingual presentation of stories and songs from the Yuman Indian whose original tribal territories included portions of present-day Arizona, Nevada, and southern California. Contains sections on Hualapai, Yavapai, Paipai, Diegueno, Maricopa, Mojave, and Quechan literatures. Brief overviews of each people and its oral traditions accompanies the selections. Bibliography. Black-and-white photographs and drawings.

Kluckhohn, Clyde. *Navaho Witchcraft*. Boston: Beacon Press, 1962.

An account of Navajo beliefs and practices concerning witchcraft. Part 1 presents ethnographic data on categories of Navajo witches and witchcraft, including witchery way and were-animals, sorcery, wizardry, and prostitution way. It also reports on the measures Navajos take to protect themselves against and cure themselves of witchcraft. Part 2 attempts historical and cultural analyses of the data. It seeks first to discover the origins of the cultural forms that characterize Navajo witchcraft beliefs and practices, then investigates why the Navajo selected particular cultural forms and rejected others. Nine appendices. Bibliography.

McNeley, James K. *Holy Wind in Navajo Philosophy*. Tucson: University of Arizona Press, 1981.

Documents the importance of the concept of air, or Holy Wind, in the Navajo theory of life and behavior. Chapters discuss the Navajo structure of the world, the relationships of various holy powers to each other and to the Navajo people, and the role played by the Holy Wind in human conception, life processes, morality, and well-being. Offers a critique of previous analyses of Holy Wind and suggestions for further research. Appendix: Navajo texts. Bibliography.

Malotki, Ekkehart. *Hopitutuwutsi: Hopi Tales*. Flagstaff: Museum of Northern Arizona Press, 1978.

A bilingual collection of ten Hopi folktales. An editor's preface briefly discusses some essential characteristics of Hopi stories and storytelling. Portions of the Hopi texts and their English translations have been placed opposite each other to facilitate cross referencing. The pen-and-ink drawing accompanying the narratives (by Anne-Marie Malotki) were derived from kiva mural drawings and ceramics. Bibliography.

Newcomb, Franc J., and Gladys A. Reichard. *Sandpaintings of the Navajo Shooting Chant*. New York: J. J. Augustin, 1937.

A description and analysis of the Navajo healing ceremony known as the Shooting Chant. An introduction discusses the authors' long-standing association with the Navajo and the assumptions underlying their study of that tribe's culture and religion. Chapter 2 details some of the essential characteristics of Navajo chants, chanters, and chanting. Chapter 3 presents an extended account of the role of painters and painting in the Shooting Chant. In chapter 4, the myth associated with the Shooting Chant ritual is recounted. Chapters 5 through 9 provide symbolic analyses of selected elements of the myth and its sandpaintings, including the Holy People, the Sacred Twins, bow and arrow, lightning arrows, snakes, earth and sky, clouds, rainbow, mirage, thunders and water monsters, plants and animals, and locality. The final two chapters examine the principles of artistic composition and devices. Color plates and black-and-white drawings of the sandpaintings accompany the text.

Parsons, Elsie C. *Hopi and Zuni Ceremonialism*. Memoirs of the American Anthropological Association 39. Menasha, Wis.: American Anthropological Association, 1933.

Compares and contrasts selected aspects of Hopi and Zuni ceremony. Among the topics discussed are the relation of the groups' clan systems to ceremonial leadership, kachina conceptualism and ritual, the use of kivas, the organization of dance groups, ceremonial calendars, and pantheons. Bibliography.

__________. *Pueblo Indian Religion*. 2 vols. Chicago: University of Chicago Press, 1939.

Attempts to provide an integrated depiction and comparison of Pueblo religious life. An introductory chapter surveys elements of society and culture important to an understanding of Pueblo religion. Beginning the discussion of religion *per se* are descriptions of ceremonial organization and sacred beliefs. Subsequent chapters treat the ceremonial calendar for various Pueblo communities, the character and functions of particular ceremonies, a town-by-town summary of ceremonial life, variations in ceremonies and loan elements, and processes of change affecting Pueblo religion. One appendix. Bibliography. Black-and-white photographs and drawings.

__________. *The Social and Ceremonial Organization of the Tewa of New Mexico*. Memoirs of the American Anthropological Association 36. Menasha, Wis.: American Anthropological Association, 1929.

A general survey of the social and religious life of the Tewa Pueblos. The first seven chapters describe the character and customs of the Tewa family, kinship, descent groups, kivas, and political institutions. The next four chapters discuss Tewa ceremonial organization, the ceremonial round, rituals, and sacred beings. Concluding discussion delineates elements of Tewa society and religion the author believes were borrowed from other groups. Bibliography. Genealogies. Black-and-white photographs, drawings and color plates.

Reichard, Gladys A. *Navaho Indian Religion: A Study of Symbolism*. 2 vols. New York: Pantheon Books, 1950.

Examines the complex ritual life of the Navajos and the considerable differences that exist between the essential principles of this religious system and those of Euro-Americans. The first part of volume 1 identifies and analyzes the essential areas of Navajo dogma. It sees this dogma as based on a cosmogony that "tries to account for everything in the universe by relating it to man and his activities." Topics include worldview, the nature of man, pantheons, the theory of disease, the theory of curing, and ethics. Part 2 examines the interrelated series of symbols that integrate all aspects of Navajo dogma and ritual. Part 3 sets forth the primary features of ritual, including song, the nature and use of prayersticks, the classification of ceremonies, and ritual organization. Volume 2 contains a series of concordances that list and characterize supernatural beings, ritualistic ideas, and rites. Bibliography. Black-and-white drawings. Tables.

Spencer, Katherine. *Mythology and Values: An Analysis of Navaho Chantway Myths*. Memoirs of the American Folklore Society 48. Philadelphia: American Folklore Society, 1957.

Documents how the sacred narratives associated with Navajo ceremonials, or chantways, reflect the tribe's life views and values. Identifies four value themes central to the plot construction of these narratives: the maintenance of health, the acquisition of supernatural power, the maintenance of harmony in family relationships, and the process of a young man's attainment of adult status. A concluding section contains abstracts of numerous chantways. Bibliography. One chart details the value elements in the chantway texts.

Stevenson, Matilda C. *The Zuni Indians: Their Mythology, Esoteric Fraternities, and Ceremonies*. Bureau of American Ethnology, Annual Report 23 (1901-1902). Washington, D.C.: U.S. Government Printing Office, 1904.

A detailed treatise on the religion and sociology of the Zunis based on field research performed in the late nineteenth century. Among the many topics discussed are the tribe's cosmology and mythology; calendar and calendric ceremonials; the annual festival of the *Shalako* (giant couriers of the rainmakers); tribal history, arts, and customs; medical practices and practitioners; witchcraft; and the origins, compositions, and functions of selected socioreligious organizations. Black-and-white reproductions and photographs.

Tyler, Hamilton A. *Pueblo Animals and Myths*. Norman: University of Oklahoma Press, 1975.

Examines the place of selected animals in the pantheon, mythology, and ceremony of the Pueblo Indians. Included among these "beast gods" are the badger, pronghorn antelope, deer, bison, American elk, mountain sheep, rabbit, coyote, bear, and mountain lion. A concluding chapter speculates on the tribal experiences that gave rise to animal deities. Bibliography.

Underhill, Ruth M. *Papago Indian Religion*. New York: Columbia University Press, 1946.

Examines traditional Papago ceremonies as practiced and remembered by residents of the Sell Reservation between the years 1931 and 1935. An introduction provides general information on Papago culture and ceremonial practices. Part 2 describes communal rituals, including the rainmaking ceremony, the Prayer Stick Festival, ceremonies to promote growth, and for hunting, and intervillage games. Part 3 presents ceremonies associated with individual power: the Salt Pilgrimage, Eagle Killing, Girls' Puberty Dance, and rituals of warfare. The ceremonial use of power by shamans and other healers is the subject of part 4. The book concludes with a discussion of the affects of acculturation on modern ceremonial life. Bibliography.

_________. *Singing for Power: The Song Magic of the Papago Indians of Southern Arizona*. Berkeley: University of California Press, 1938.

A collection of Papago ceremonial songs. An introductory chapter describes how the ability of Papago songs to call upon the powers of nature and constrain them to human will not only made them "the practical basis of Papago life, but also the most precious possession of the people." The chapters that follow present a representative sample of such songs in their ritual contexts. A concluding chapter overviews Papago songs and singing in the late 1930's. Black-and-white drawings.

Washburn, Dorothy K., ed. *Hopi Kachina: Spirit of Life*. Seattle: University of Washington Press, 1980.

A collection of essays focusing on Hopi kachinas, "supernatural messengers who mediate between the harsh realities of Arizona's environmental limitations and the daily needs of the Hopi people." An introductory essay discusses the prehistoric and historic occupation of the Hopi mesas. Next is a paper on mural decorations from ancient Hopi kivas. Subsequent presentations highlight the symbolic and ritual aspects of the kachina in Hopi culture, the central place of the kachina cult within Hopi social organization, and kachina representations in contemporary Hopi crafts. Bibliography. Glossary of Hopi alphabet. Black-and-white photographs and color plates.

Wyman, Leland C., ed. *Beautyway: A Navaho Ceremonial.* Princeton, N.J.: Princeton University Press, 1957.
Presents the literary and graphic arts associated with the Navajo curing ceremony of Beautyway. Part 1 discusses the uses, mythology, songs, and geographical setting of the ceremonial. Part 2 contains variants of the myth of Beautyway, one told by Singer Man and recorded and translated by Fr. Bernard Haile; the other, recited by Wilito Wilson and recorded by Maud Oakes. Also featured is a text of the Jicarilla Apache Holiness Rite, a ritual that presents striking parallels with Beautyway. Part 3 offers color reproductions of Beautyway sandpaintings with commentary on their symbolism. Bibliography. One map. Charts.

__________. *Blessingway.* Tucson: University of Arizona Press, 1970.
Presents three versions of the myth of Blessingway, a Navajo rite "concerned with peace, harmony, and good things." An introductory chapter discusses the derivation of the ceremony's name, its uses, primary spiritual powers, symbols, and implements. The next three sections provide extended descriptions of the major mythic motifs, dry paintings, and ceremonial procedures associated with the rite. The myth's versions, told by Slim Curly, Frank Mitchell, and River Junction Curly, respectively, were recorded and translated from the Navajo by Father Berard Haile, O. F. M. Black-and-white reproductions.

Subsistence and Land Use

Beaglehole, Ernest. *Hopi Hunting and Hunting Ritual.* Yale University Publications in Anthropology 4. New Haven, Conn.: Yale University Press, 1936.
Describes the contributions of hunting to Hopi economy and ritual. Finds that all the animals hunted "were used either for ceremonial purposes alone, or for food, materials for clothing and blankets, and for the manufacture of items of material culture as well." Discussions include the hunting of antelope, deer, mountain sheep, rabbit, other small game and birds, eagles, and turtles. There is also a description of the hunting initiation for Hopi youths. Bibliography.

__________. *Notes on Hopi Economic Life.* Yale University Publications in Anthropology 15. New Haven, Conn.: Yale University Press, 1937.
A study of Hopi economic processes and values based on fieldwork at the two Second Mesa villages of Mishongnovi and Shipaulovi in 1932 and 1934. Begins with a summary of the organization of Hopi household, kin and clan units, stressing the economics of these institutions. The chapters that follow concern the ownership and control of property; economic organization, the division of labor, education, specialization, seasonal calendar of work, the economic cycle, the organization of work, and work psychology; agriculture; seconding productive activities, hunting and herding, the gathering of natural products, craft activities, and house building; foods and their preparation; and the distribution of Native wealth through ceremonies and exchange. Bibliography.

Buskirk, Winfred. *The Western Apache: Living with the Land Before 1950.* Norman: University of Oklahoma Press, 1986.

A historical description and analysis of Western Apache economics and associated material culture. Includes discussion of the continuity and change in the tribe's traditionally mixed subsistence pattern of agriculture, hunting, and gathering wild plant foods; methods of procuring, processing, storing, and preparing food resources; and social and religious beliefs, values, and activities associated with economic life. Assesses Western Apache subsistence economy in terms of environmental factors, percentage of total natural resource use, and nonecological conditions. One of the study's conclusions is that "[c]onsidering the cultural possibilities and limitations of both pre-American and post-American periods, the Western Apache made more complete use of their natural environment before the whites came than afterward." Bibliography.

Castetter, Edward F., and Willis H. Bell. *Pima and Papago Indian Agriculture.* Albuquerque: University of New Mexico Press, 1942.

A comprehensive study of traditional Piman (Pima-Papago) agriculture. Chapter 1 summarizes what is known of aboriginal Piman lifeways and populations. The topography, climate, and vegetation of Piman territory are the subjects of chapter 2. Chapter 3 presents archaeological, historical, and ethnographic evidence for early Piman subsistence, including the utilization of native wild plants and animals. Chapter 4 identifies and describes the wide variety of crops cultivated by the Pima and Papago. Chapter 5 discusses the selection, clearing, and development of cultivated land; landownership; the fencing and size of cultivated plots; and the division of agricultural labor. Agricultural implements are described in chapter 6. Chapter 7 concerns modes of planting, irrigation, and cultivation. The harvest, storage, and seed selection of crops are the subjects of chapter 8. Chapters 9 reports on the practical and ritualistic aspects of tobacco cultivation. The book concludes with a discussion of the general ceremonial aspects of Piman agriculture. Bibliography. Black-and-white drawings and one photograph. One map.

__________. *Yuman Indian Agriculture.* Albuquerque: University of New Mexico Press, 1951.

Concerned chiefly with the traditional agriculture of Yuman tribes, including the Mojave, Yuma, and Cocopa Indians on the lower Colorado River and the Maricopa on the Gila River. Chapter 1 discusses the topography, climate, and vegetation of Yuman territory . Chapter 2 presents an overview of the prehistory and history of the Yuman tribes. Subsequent chapters provide information on agricultural implements; cultivated crops; modes of clearing land, water utilization, planting, and harvesting, and storage; the use of wild plants and animals; and Yuman rituals and group activities. Bibliography. Black-and-white photographs. Maps.

Cushing, Frank H. *Zuni Breadstuff.* New York: Museum of the American Indian, Heye Foundation, 1920.

A detailed account of Zuni subsistence in relation to the tribe's history, sacred lore, and lifeways. Pays particular attention to the centrality of corn, as reflected in Zuni economy, diet, traditional narratives, and religious practices. Provides information on the social aspects of Zuni meals and eating, customary foods, rules of land inheritance, and the agricultural cycle. Black-and-white photographs and drawings.

Hill, W. W. *The Agricultural and Hunting Methods of the Navaho Indians*. Yale University Publications in Anthropology 18. New Haven, Conn.: Yale University Press, 1938.

Examines the economic and technological aspects of traditional Navajo life. Among the materials presented are: a description of Navajo agricultural and hunting methods, with special attention to the types of ritual associated with each; historical data concerning these aspects of Navajo life; and local adaptations of more general subsistence patterns. Among its conclusions are that Navajo hunting resembles that of the Great Basin and Plains and that the closest Pueblo resemblances are in agricultural and pottery techniques. Bibliography. Black-and-white photographs and drawings. One map.

Kelley, Klara B. *Navajo Land Use: An Ethnoarchaeological Study*. Orlando, Fla.: Academic Press, 1986.

Employs documentary analysis, interviews with tribal members, participant observation, and the archaeological record to describe and explain the changes in land use patterns of Navajo families living around McKinley Mine, a coal strip operation in New Mexico. First relates changes in land use to two major causes: the conquest, colonization, and oppression of the Navajo people instrumented by U.S. mercantile and industrial capitalism; and atomistic, family-based production decisions traditional to Navajo society. Then describes and analyzes changes in family land use during a series of historic periods. Two appendices: methodology and genealogy. One map, tables, and figures.

Reno, Philip. *Mother Earth, Father Sky, and Economic Development: Navajo Resources and Their Use*. Albuquerque: University of New Mexico Press, 1981.

Examines Navajo resources in relation to issues concerning that tribe's potential economic growth. Focus is directed primarily on water and its availability for future agricultural development; Navajo forest lands; and mineral/energy resources such as coal, oil, and uranium. Suggests that a "model is needed to keep development on the rocky road to self-determination, rather than the easy road of selling resources for others to develop." This model should "incorporate new technology in the Navajo institutional framework, and adapt that institutional framework to take advantage of the new technology." Black-and-white photographs. Tables and maps.

Wills, W. H. *Early Prehistoric Agriculture in the American Southwest*. Santa Fe, N.M.: School of American Research Press, 1988.

Examines the transformation of certain Southwestern Indian subsistence modes from hunting and gathering to agriculture. Views the study of the decision-making processes underlying this transformation as important for understanding the development of different socioeconomic forms. Argues that "the decision to adopt fully domesticated plants can be understood as a product of selective advantage for enhanced resource predictability."

Family and Society

Basso, Keith H., ed. *Western Apache Raiding and Warfare, from the Notes of Grenville Goodwin*. Tucson: University of Arizona Press, 1971.

A discussion of Western Apache raiding and warfare based on ethnographic data and personal narratives gathered over several years by anthropologist Grenville Goodwin. Part 1 contains six chronologically arranged narratives by six Apache men and women who either participated in raids and war parties or were well informed of these through relatives who did so. Comprising part 2 are briefer narratives arranged under the following headings: weapons, war dance, leadership, preparations and conduct, taboos and warpath language, taboos for women, the use of 'power', scalping, the victory celebration, captives, and the novice complex. Preceding the study is a biographical note on Goodwin by Edward H. Spicer. Black-and-white photographs. Maps.

__________. *Western Apache Witchcraft*. Anthropological Papers of the University of Arizona 15. Tucson: University of Arizona Press, 1969.

Seeks to document and analyze Western Apache beliefs associated with witchcraft. Defines witchcraft beliefs as a set of ideas "which imply that certain individuals purposely kill and injure others by means involving neither face-to-face interaction nor the use of any item of material culture." Part 1 describes Apaches' shared interpretations concerning witchcraft. Part 2 examines the sociology of witchcraft accusations, focusing on patterns of witch-accuser relationships. Part 3 provides a functional analysis of Apache witchcraft. Two appendices. Maps, diagrams, and tables.

Boyer, L. Bryce. *Childhood and Folklore: A Psychoanalytic Study of Apache Personality*. New York: Library of Psychological Anthropology, 1979.

A Freudian interpretation of the folklore of Chiricahua and Mescalero Apaches living on the Mescalero Indian Reservation in south central New Mexico. Argues that folklore is one means Apaches use in expressing and temporarily resolving unresolved, repressed infantile conflicts; traditional lore projectively reflects Apache personality configurations and socialization experiences; and an understanding of a group's oral literature can aid in an interpretation of its members verbal and nonverbal communication. Bibliography.

Buchanan, Kimberly M. *Apache Women Warriors*. El Paso: University of Texas Press, 1986.

Uses anthropological and historical sources to document the participation of Apache and other Native American women in martial activities. Focuses on the Warm Spring Apache woman known as Lozen whose abilities as a warrior earned her legendary status among her people. Argues that Indian women warriors "gained respect and status because their respective societies gave them the opportunities to strive for pursuits traditionally considered to be reserved for males." Bibliography. Black-and-white photographs. Maps.

Bunzel, Ruth L. *Zuni Texts*. Publications of the American Ethnological Society 15. New York: G. E. Strechert, 1933.

A collection of forty narratives on various aspects of Zuni society and religion.

Part 1, "Ethnological Texts," includes discussions of planting, house building, making an oven, weaving, women's work, witchcraft, selected ceremonies, priesthood, and war. Assembled in part 2, "Tales," are a number of sacred narratives. The texts are presented in Zuni and accompanied by an English translation.

Courlander, Harold, ed. and trans. *Hopi Voices: Recollections, Traditions, and Narratives of the Hopi Indians*. Albuquerque: University of New Mexico Press, 1982.

An anthology of seventy-four narratives by Hopi Indians. The contents of the texts include sacred narratives; legends; clan origins and distributions; the beginning and demise of selected villages; traditional customs and arts; the Pueblo Revolt of 1680; relations with the U.S. government, missionaries, and hippies; individual exploits and adventures; the pranks and games of Pokanghoya and Palengahoya, the Warrior Brothers of Hopi sacred oral literature; and tales about the trickster, Coyote, and other animals. Contains a glossary and pronunciation guide for the Hopi terms that appear in the narratives. Selective bibliography.

Dobyns, Henry, and Robert C. Euler. *Wauba Yuma's People: The Comparative Socio-Political Structure of the Pai Indians of Arizona*. Prescott, Ariz.: Prescott College Press, 1970.

Presents evidence on the social and political structures of the aboriginal Pai, ancestors of the present-day Walapai and Havasupai. Chapter 1 briefly examines Pai language, self-definition, patterns of marriage, and tribal boundaries. Chapter 2 identifies the various units of Pai sociopolitical organization. Subsequent chapters examine the position of the Pai in the Greater Southwest and the process of federal Indian administration that split the Pai into the two legally recognized tribes of Hualapai and Havasupai. Bibliography. Chart.

Eggan, Fred. *Social Organization of the Western Pueblos*. Chicago: University of Chicago Press, 1950.

Seeks to examine the social organizations of the Hopi, Hano, Zuni, Acoma, and Laguna Indians from both a comparative and a historical standpoint. The data are organized according to a common framework so that similarities and differences among these groups are readily apparent. The divisions of this framework include the kinship system, the clan system, ceremonial organization, and (for the Hopi) political organization. A concluding section both identifies the common features and variations of Western Pueblo social organization and presents some hypotheses regarding the nature of Western Pueblo social and cultural change. Bibliography. Maps and tables.

Goodwin, Grenville. *The Social Organization of the Western Apache*. Chicago: University of Chicago Press, 1942.

A detailed examination of the principles, divisions, and processes of Western Apache society. The first chapter discusses the territories formerly occupied by various Western Apache groups and bands as well as their attitudes and relations to each other. Chapter 2 reviews Western Apache prehistory and their contacts with other Indian peoples. The chapters that follow report on clans; the family and local group; kinship; marriage; social adjustments, including sanctions for assorted forms of socially disapproved of behavior; the life cycle; and various social concepts and practices. Twelve appendices. Black-and-white photographs and drawings. Maps and charts.

Kaut, Charles R. *The Western Apache Clan System: Its Origins and Development*. Albuquerque: University of New Mexico Press, 1957.

Concerned primarily with the history and development of the matrilineal clan system of the Western Apache. Argues that this clan system, in which membership was determined by descent through one's mother, served as the basis of the tribe's social organization. The study's first section examines the systems of kinship terminology and behavior in the Southwest to which that of the Western Apache is historically related. Section 2 probes the history, structure, and function of the Western Apache clan system. The study concludes with a discussion of changes the clan system has undergone in one contemporary Western Apache community. Four appendices. Bibliography. Maps and charts.

Kluckhohn, Clyde. *Culture and Behavior*, edited by Richard Kluckhohn. New York: Free Press, 1962.

A collection of essays by one of the foremost students of Native American lifeways. Several of the papers examine selected elements of Navajo society and culture. Among these are an analysis of Navajo women's knowledge of their song ceremonials, social and personal aspects of Navajo ceremonial patterns, a longitudinal study of the development of two Navajo children, Navajo morals, and personality formation among members of the tribe. There is also a description of conceptions of death among Southwestern Indians. Bibliography of references. Bibliography of Clyde Kluckhohn compiled by Lucy Wales.

Kroeber, Alfred L. *Zuni Kin and Clan*. American Museum of Natural History Anthropological Papers, vol. 18, pt. 2. New York: The Trustees, 1917.

A detailed discussion of Zuni kinship terms, behavior, and organization. Identifies kinship as the foundation of Zuni society, observing that "[w]ithout a realization of this fact, it is possible to know what a Zuni may do, but impossible to understand the emotions that dictate his actions." Part 1 first presents the meaning and use of the several kinship terms. It is followed by an analysis of the general features and principles inherent in the Zuni system. Subsequent chapters describe the house and marriage, the clan and its social and religious function, and the town. Black-and-white drawings. Maps, charts, and tables.

Lamphere, Louise. *To Run After Them: Cultural and Social Bases of Cooperation in a Navajo Community*. Tucson: University of Arizona Press, 1977.

An analysis of the economic and ritual activities that are the behavioral consequences of Navajo concepts of help, aid, and cooperation. Includes discussion of the criteria operating in strategies for recruiting aid as well as the etiquette of request making. Uses the data and analytical methods utilized in the study to critique previous investigations of Navajo society and culture. Includes case reports. Four appendices. Bibliography. Tables and maps.

Roessel, Ruth. *Women in Navajo Society*. Rough Rock (Navajo Nation), Ariz.: Navajo Resource Center, Rough Rock Demonstration School, 1981.

An examination of the role of women in a changing Navajo society that reflects the personal experiences and attitudes of the author, a Navajo woman, on this subject. Chapter 1 briefly reviews and comments on the literature pertaining to Navajo women. The author's commentary is particularly concerned with differentiating between those writings that are of some value to the Navajo and those composed merely for the benefit of academics. Part 2 begins with a summary of Navajo socialization patterns as reflected in the tribe's oral traditions, including stories of Changing Woman and her two sons. It then presents the sacred story of the first birth and the growth of Changing Woman. Subsequent chapters concern Navajo marriage, including the wedding ceremony, abortions and birth control, and divorce; women as the center of the home; the contemporary world of Navajo mother and child; the seasonal roles of Navajo women; Navajo medicine women; and Navajo women and leadership. Part 3 first narrates the story of Raggedy Lady, the author's great-grandmother, who typifies all that a good Navajo woman should be, then presents the author's own childhood and education. The book concludes with the author's philosophy, which is that her Navajo culture makes her who she is and what she is. Bibliography. Black-and-white photographs and drawings.

Underhill, Ruth M. *Social Organization of the Papago Indians*. Columbia University Contributions to Anthropology 30. New York: Columbia University Press, 1939.

An examination of Papago social groups and customs, based mainly on information gathered from inhabitants of the Sells reservation in southern Arizona. Chapter 1 pinpoints the present locations of American and Mexican Papago groups and presents a brief tribal history. Subsequent chapters provide information on the nature and formation of kin groupings, behavior between kin, village groupings, village government, modes of subsistence, social behavior and law, knowledge and teaching, war, games and betting, youth, marriage and sexual behavior, death, social mores, and culture change. Two appendices. Bibliography.

Material Culture and the Arts

Adair, John. *The Navaho and Pueblo Silversmiths*. Norman: University of Oklahoma Press, 1944.

Attempts to portray the importance of silversmiths and their art in Navajo and Pueblo cultures. Part 1 focuses on Navajo silver. It begins with a history of silverwork from its origins in the mid-nineteenth century to the 1940's. Following this history are accounts of the development of designs, characterizations of modern craftsmen, the place of silver in Navajo culture, and the economics of the craft. Part 2 is primarily concerned with the history, present status, and aesthetics of Zuni silverwork. A final section briefly overviews the silver of other pueblos. Five appendices. Bibliography. Black-and-white photographs and drawings.

Amsden, Charles, A. *Navajo Weaving*. Santa Ana, Calif.: Fine Arts Press in cooperation with the Southwestern Museum, 1934.

A classic analysis of Navajo weaving which focuses on the history and technology of that art. Part 1 contains descriptions of finger weaving, loom development in America, the Navajo loom, Navajo weaves, the development and formulas of Navajo dyes, and the types and uses of Navajo textiles. Part 2 identifies and characterizes different periods in the evolution of Navajo weaving. Black-and-white photographs and drawings. Color plates. Bibliography of cited works.

Bahti, Mark. *Southwestern Indian Arts and Crafts*. Las Vegas: KC Publications, 1983.

A concise, richly illustrated introduction to the arts and crafts of southwestern Native Americans. Section 1 addresses the relation between economics and artistic production. Subsequent discussions focus on the history and character of particular arts. These include silverwork, beadwork, turquoise jewelry making, rug weaving, basketry, pottery, and sand painting. Additional sections concern the practice of pawning jewelry, Zuni fetishes, the individual in Indian art, and the buying and care of Indian crafts. Short bibliographies accompany each section. Black-and-white and color reproductions and photographs. One map.

Bunzel, Ruth L. *The Pueblo Potter: A Study of Creative Imagination in Primitive Art*. New York: Columbia University Press, 1929.

Treats the dynamics of decorative style in pottery making at Zuni and other pueblos. Defines "decorative style" as "the mode of plastic expression characteristic of any group at any given time." Focuses on the way in which an individual potter operates within the contours of an established style, "or finding that impossible, creates new values and wins for them social recognition." The opening chapter describes the technology and forms of pueblo ceramics. Next, the fundamental principles of design characterizing Zuni, Acoma, Hopi, and San Ildefonso pottery are identified. Chapter 4 analyzes the way in which the individual artist works within the limits of the style or transcends it. Subsequent chapters consider the problem of symbolism and continuity verses change in technique and style. Three appendices provide illustrations of Zuni, Hopi, and San Ildefonso designs. Bibliography.

Chapman, Kenneth M. *The Pottery of San Ildefonso Pueblo*. Albuquerque: University of New Mexico Press for the School of American Research, 1970.

A discussion of pottery making at San Ildefonso, a Tewa pueblo located twenty miles northeast of Santa Fe, New Mexico, on the east bank of the Rio Grande. Chapter 1 presents a historical overview of the village. Chapter 2 discusses the general features of San Ildefonso ceramics, with sections on previous descriptions, terminology of pueblo pottery forms, the process of manufacture, modes of decoration, a census of San Ildefonso decorated pottery in museums and private collections as of 1937, the availability of data on San Ildefonso pottery makers, and the condition of old pottery. The chapters that follow deal with the culinary ware produced at the pueblo; San Ildefonso black-on-cream ceramics; San Ildefonso black-on-red ceramics; the forms and development of San Ildefonso polychrome ceramics (wares in which more than two colors appear); polished black and red wares; and a history of painted Tewa pottery. Bibliography. Color plates.

_________. *The Pottery of Santo Domingo Pueblo: A Detailed Study of its Decoration*. Memoirs of the Laboratory of Anthropology, Santa Fe, New Mexico, vol. 1. Washington, D.C.: W. F. Roberts Co., 1938.

An analysis of pottery forms and manufacture at Santo Domingo, a pueblo of Keresan lingusitic stock situated about thirty miles southwest of Sante Fe, New Mexico, on the east bank of the Rio Grande. Section 1 provides a brief description of the village. Section 2 discusses the continuity and change in pottery made before and following Spanish contact. Section 3 concerns pottery for use in cooking over an open fire. Section 4 treats the forms, uses, technology, decoration, and motifs of black-on-cream ware, which for centuries was the typical decorated pottery of Santo Domingo. Sections 5, 6, and 7 deal with black-on-red ware (made from comparatively early times in small quantity), black-and-red-on-cream ware (introduced in relatively recent times and manufactured chiefly for tourists), and forms of polished ware (lately introduced in imitation of those produced by the Tewa pueblos of Santa Clara and San Ildefonso). Bibliography. Black-and-white photographs and drawings. Color plates. One map.

Densmore, Frances. *Music of Acoma, Isleta, Cochiti, and Zuni Pueblos*. Bureau of American Ethnology, Bulletin 165. Washington, D.C.: U.S. Government Printing Office, 1957.

A study of music collected from the Pueblo tribes of Acoma, Isleta, Cochiti, and Zuni during the second and third decades of the twentieth century. An introduction provides brief tribal histories and information on Pueblo musical instruments. The body of the book contains transcriptions and ethnological and musicological analyses of eighty-two ceremonial and social songs. Bibliography of references. Black-and-white photographs.

_________. *Music of Santo Domingo Pueblo, New Mexico*. Southwest Museum Papers 12. Los Angeles: Southwest Museum, 1938.

A collection and analysis of songs of Santo Domingo pueblo based on interviews with members of the Turquoise division of that community. Begins with a historical sketch and summary of the social, cultural, and religious patterns of the pueblo. Following are notes on various dances and descriptions of traditional musical instruments, including flutes, whistles, drums, stone gongs, and rattles. The bulk of the remaining sections contain transcriptions and ethnological and musicological analyses of selected ceremonial and social songs. Concludes with a summary of the melodic analyses. Bibliography of literature cited. Black-and-white photographs and drawings.

__________. *Papago Music*. Bureau of American Ethnology, Bulletin 90. Washington, D.C.: U.S. Government Printing Office, 1929.

A study of songs collected on the Papago Reservation in southern Arizona. Begins with an ethnographic sketch of the tribe and a discussion of their four musical instruments, the gourd rattle, scraping sticks, basket-drum, and flute. Next presents a tabulated, melodic comparison of Papago songs with those of the Chippewa, Sioux, Ute, Mandan, and Hidatsa. The book contains transcriptions and ethnological and musicological analyses of selected ceremonial and social songs. Black-and-white photographs.

__________. *Yuman and Yaqui Music*. Bureau of American Ethnology, Bulletin 110. Washington, D.C.: U.S. Government Printing Office, 1932.

A study of the songs of the Yuman and Yaqui tribes living along the Colorado River and in northwestern Mexico. Begins with brief histories and ethnographic summaries for the Yaqui and the three Yuman groups—the Cocopa, Yuma, and Mojave—under consideration. Special consideration is given to the general characteristics of their music and musical instruments. The book presents transcriptions and ethnological and musicological analyses of selected Yuman and Yaqui songs. Bibliography. Black-and-white photographs and diagrams.

Jett, Stephen C., and Virginia E. Spencer. *Navajo Architecture: Forms, History, Distributions*. Tucson: University of Arizona Press, 1981.

Surveys the evolution, form, and function of various Navajo structures. An introduction briefly describes the physical geography of Navajo country, Navajo culture history, and Navajo settlement patterns. Subsequent chapters discuss the general characteristics of Navajo dwellings; the classification of Navajo dwellings; origins, evolution, and forms of temporary and summer dwellings; hogan origins, evolution, and forms; the Navajo adoption of houses; the origins, evolution, and forms of the Navajo house; roof forms; subsistence-activity structures; food-processing and storage structures; ceremonial and recreational structures; structures relating to travel, defense, and death; areal and temporal distributions of dwelling types; and Navajo architecture and acculturation. One appendix: frequencies of common hogan and house forms. Photographs and drawing. Maps and charts.

Kent, Kate Peck. *Navajo Weaving: Three Centuries of Change*. Santa Fe, N.M.: School of American Research Press, 1985.

Traces the evolution of Navajo weaving from the mid-seventeenth century to modern day. An introductory chapter first identifies three major stylistic periods of Navajo weaving: the Classic, 1650 to 1865; the Transition, 1865 to 1895; and the Rug, 1895 to the present. It then briefly reviews the significant studies of this art. Chapter 1 considers the tribe's textile production within the wider contexts of its economic and social history. Chapter 2 describes the techniques and materials of Navajo weaving. Chapters 3 through 5 document the continuity and change in design and manufacture during the Classic, Transition, and Rug periods. The final chapter addresses the problem of Navajo aesthetics. One appendix: "The School of American Research Collection of Navajo Textiles." Black-and-white photographs, drawings, and color plates.

__________. *Pueblo Indian Textiles: A Living Tradition*. Santa Fe, N.M.: School of American Research Press, 1983.

An introduction to the history and manufacture of Pueblo Indian textiles focusing on the period 1848-1880. Chapter 1 provides a periodization for Pueblo textiles in historic times. The periods identified are that of Spanish domination, 1540-1848; the "classic" period of historic Pueblo weaving, 1848-1880; the period of growing Anglo-American influence and the decline of weaving, 1880-1920; and the revival of certain forms of Pueblo textiles leading to present-day scene, 1920-1950. Chapter 2 describes the tools and materials used in Pueblo weaving. In chapter 3 ten categories of textiles are identified and grouped according to use and style. One appendix: "The School of American Research Collection of Pueblo Textiles." Black-and-white photographs, drawings, and color plates.

Moulard, Barbara L. *Within the Underworld Sky: Mimbres Ceramic Art in Context*. Pasadena, Calif.: Twelvetrees Press, 1981.

An analysis and album of Classic Mimbres painted pottery from North America's prehistoric Southwest. Part 1 of the analysis discusses the evolution of Mimbres ceramics within the context of the region's cultural prehistory. Particular attention is paid to the contribution of other prehistoric people to this ceramic tradition. Part 2 presents an interpretation of Mimbres pottery iconography. An attempt is made to understand the characteristic forms and decorations employed by Mimbres potters through recourse to key elements in Pueblo culture, values, and worldview. Contained in part 3 are commentaries on the images found on the one hundred vessels reproduced in the book. The author states that most of these "were formulated with the hypothesis that the ceramic art was made for a ritual purpose and embodies information concerning an ideology centered around an ancestor cult and the division of the universe into four cardinal directions, as well as the above, center and below, where the supernatural beings reside." Map and graphs.

Nabokov, Peter. *Architecture of Acoma Pueblo: The 1934 Historic American Buildings Survey Project*. Sante Fe, N.M.: Ancient City Press, 1986.

Reproduces the drawings and photographs of the Historic American Building Survey's 1934 study of Acoma Pueblo, one of the oldest continuously inhabited settlements in North America. Accompanying the illustrations is a history of the origins and organization of the project and a brief discussion of changes that have occurred in the village's architecture fifty years after completion of the project. Notes on sources.

Tanner, Clara Lee. *Indian Baskets of the Southwest*. Tucson: University of Arizona Press, 1983.

Examines the art of basketry for all Native southwestern historic groups from a little before 1880 to the 1980's. Chapter 1 presents some general observations on the aesthetics of Southwestern Indian basketry including the role of the individual weaver, factors influencing change and development, the influence of religion on basketry design and symbolism, the use of color, and variations in weave, forms, decoration, and design. Chapter 2 provides an overview of the Southwest environment and peoples. The technology of basket weaving and design analysis are the subjects of chapter 3. Chapters 4 through 7 examine Pueblo, Apache, Piman, and Yuman basketry. The book closes with a description and analysis of Navajo, Ute, Paiute, and Chemehuevi baskets. Bibliography. Black-and-white drawings, photographs, and color plates.

__________. *Southwest Indian Painting: A Changing Art*. 2d ed. Tucson: University of Arizona Press, 1973.

Traces the history of easel painting among Native Americans of the Southwest from its introduction in the early 1900's to 1971. Argues that Indian easel artists quickly "developed distinctive, traditional styles which were deeply rooted in their rich past and which became and continued to be dominant in all such paintings into the 1960s." The first several chapters briefly characterize the styles and techniques of southwestern prehistoric and historic decorative arts. Subsequent chapters discuss the events, institutions, and painters important to the transition from decorative arts to easel arts among the eastern and western Pueblos, Navajos, Apaches, and other tribes. Bibliography. Black-and-white reproductions and photographs. Color plates.

Underhill, Ruth M. *Pueblo Crafts*. Lawrence, Kans.: Haskell Institute Press, 1944.

A description of modern Pueblo crafts that takes into account the various factors influencing these works. Chapter 1 briefly traces the history of pueblo crafts from the Basketmaker Period (A.D. 300-700) to the Modern Era (1880-). The remaining chapters focus on the techniques associated with basketry, weaving, pottery, music, and painting. A concluding chapter describes the ongoing changes affecting contemporary (circa 1944) pueblo crafts. Bibliography. Sepia-toned photographs and drawings.

Wright, Barton. *Hopi Material Culture: Artifacts Gathered by H. R. Voth in the Fred Harvey Collection*. Flagstaff, Ariz.: Northland Press and the Heard Museum, 1979.

A sample and discussion of the Hopi manufactures collected by Reverend H. R. Voth, a Mennonite missionary who worked among that tribe during the late nineteenth and early twentieth century. An introductory essay by Fred Eggan focuses on the ethnological contributions of Voth. The body of the monograph presents detailed descriptions of items of dress, tools and devices, and ritual objects. Each entry provides the Hopi designations for a given item, its method of fabrication, and customary use. Bibliography. Black-and-white photographs and drawings.

Tribal Life

Basso, Keith H. *The Cibecue Apache*. New York: Holt, Rinehart and Winston, 1970.

A cultural description of the western Apache living in Cibecue, a community on the Fort Apache Reservation in east-central Arizona. Primary emphasis is given to the group's religious beliefs and rituals. Sees at the center of the Cibecue religious system the concept of *diyi?*, a set of abstract and invisible powers that may select an individual to be its owner or be sought after by humans. Once acquired, such power may be used for the benefit of the community or, in the case of witchcraft, for evil. Glossary. Bibliography of references. Black-and-white photographs. Maps, tables, and graphs.

Crampton, C. Gregory. *The Zunis of Cibola*. Salt Lake City: University of Utah Press, 1977.

An outline of Zuni history, from late prehistoric to present times, that attempts to portray the Zuni perspective on their past. Pays particular attention to the continuities in Zuni personality and culture despite more than five hundred years of environmental change, contact with other Indian peoples, and aggressions by whites. Bibliography. Black-and-white photographs and drawings.

Dobyns, Henry F. *The Mescalero Apache People*. Phoenix: Indian Tribal Series, 1971.

An introductory survey of Mescalero Apache history and culture. Begins by describing the social and subsistence patterns of the tribe's Southern Athapascan-speaking ancestors. The next several sections relate the dramatic social and cultural changes that occurred after Apaches acquired horses. Subsequent sections detail the different phases of Mescalero-white relations, including the Spanish, Mexican, and Anglo-American periods. Particular attention is given to the conquest of the tribe by U.S. forces, the creation of the Mescalero Indian Reservation in 1873, and the consequences of various eras of federal Indian relations on Mecalero life. List of suggested readings. Black-and-white photographs and color plates. Maps.

Dobyns, Henry F., and Robert C. Euler. *The Havasupai People*. Phoenix: Indian Tribal Series, 1971.

Overviews the history and culture of Havasupai Indians, a Yuman-speaking group that currently live at the bottom of Cataract Canyon on the western fringe of Grand Canyon National Park or in nearby settlements. The first few sections briefly discuss the tribe's language, prehistoric culture, clothing, and shelter. Next discussed are the successive periods of Havasupai subjugation by the Spanish, Mexican, and Anglo-American governments. Primary attention is given to the consequences of various phases of federal Indian policy on the tribe. A continuous feature of this policy has been a "disregard for the Havasupai as a people with human rights." The book concludes with several predictions concerning the tribe's future. List of suggested readings. Black-and-white photographs and color plates. Maps.

__________. *The Navajo People*. Phoenix: Indian Tribal Series, 1971.

A historical sketch of the Navajo, the most populous of all Native North American peoples. Begins with the tribe's migration from what is now north-central Canada to the American Southwest during the fourteenth or fifteenth century. Next briefly discusses changes in their aboriginal social, economic, and religious patterns that resulted from this move. Subsequent chapters trace the history of Navajo relations with a succession of white governments, including those of Spain, Mexico, and the United States. Particular attention is given the effects of various periods of federal Indian policy on the tribe. A concluding section examines long-term prospects for Navajo population, Indianness, and religion. Annotated list of suggested readings. Black-and-white and color photographs. Maps.

Downs, James F. *The Navajo*. New York: Holt, Rinehart and Winston, 1972.
A case study of contemporary community life on the Navajo reservation. Focus is given to the centrality of livestock and herding in Navajo society and culture, treating various other elements "within the framework of the ongoing and unending work required to keep sheep and cattle herds and maintain a social and cultural system based on this activity." Among the topics discussed are the evolution of the Navajo people, the reservation and its physical environment, social and political organization, religion, wealth and traders, and change and continuity. Bibliographies for references and supplementary reading. Black-and-white photographs. One map.

Dozier, Edward P. *Hano: A Tewa Indian Community in Arizona*. New York: Holt, Rinehart and Winston, 1966.
A history and ethnography of Hano, a Tewa village located on the first (easternmost) of the three Hopi mesas in Arizona. Chapter 1 summarizes the nature and consequences of Spanish-Tewa relations during the sixteenth and seventeenth centuries. Chapter 2 describes how the Hopi harbored the Tewa and other Rio Grande Pueblo refugees after their abortive revolts against Spanish rule in 1696. In chapter 3, the Hanos' relations with the Hopi, Navajo, missionaries, traders, tourists, and the federal government are analyzed. There is also discussion of the persistence of Tewa ceremonies and customs at the village. Subsequent chapters detail the community's social and political organization; religious beliefs, practices, and values; and modes of subsistence. Bibliography. List of recommended readings. Black-and-white photographs. One map.

Euler, Robert C., and Henry F. Dobyns. *The Hopi People*. Phoenix: Indian Tribal Series, 1971.
A brief introduction to the history and culture of northern Arizona's Hopi Indians. The first several sections discuss the tribe's prehistory and aboriginal social, economic, and ceremonial life. Next described are Hopi-Spanish relations, including the coming of the Spaniards in 1540, Franciscan attempts to win Hopi converts, Hopi participation in the Pueblo Revolt of 1680, and the effects of the revolt. Following a short consideration of Mexican rule over the Hopi, the nature and consequences of American policy toward the tribe are reviewed. Among the topics covered are the establishment of the Hopi Indian Reservation in 1882; contemporary patterns of social, religious, and political structure; the development of Hopi crafts; and the transformations in Hopi clothing, housing, and education. Concludes with predictions regarding the

tribe's future. List of suggested readings. Black-and-white photographs and color plates. Maps.

Forbes, Jack D. *Warriors of the Colorado: The Yumas of the Quechan Nation and Their Neighbors*. Norman: University of Oklahoma Press, 1965.

A history of the Indians of southwestern Arizona which focuses on the Quechan, a Yuman-speaking group that lived at the junction of the Colorado and Gila rivers. Begins with a reconstruction of the group's origins and precontact lifeways (circa 1000-1540) based on archaeological data, linguistic analysis, and tribal narratives. Next draws on documentary sources to describe Quechan culture as it existed from the sixteenth through early nineteenth century. Subsequent chapters narrate the Quechans' 312-year struggle with Spanish, Mexican, and American invaders, ending in their reduction to a conquered people during the second half of the nineteenth century. Despite this status, however, "they have preserved to this day their tribal identity, much of their religion and folklore, and their numbers are on the increase." Appendix. Bibliography. Black-and-white reproductions and photographs.

Gunnerson, Dolores A. *The Jicarilla Apache: A Study in Survival*. De Kalb: Northern Illinois University Press, 1974.

An ethnohistory that utilizes archaeological, ethnological, linguistic, and historical data to trace the development of the Jicarilla Apache of New Mexico. Part 1 examines Apache relations with other southwestern tribes and with Spanish conquistardores and colonists from 1525 to 1700. Part 2 documents Jicarilla history for the period 1700 to 1801. Of the tribe the author comments, "[t]he Jicarilla Apaches survived the impact of enemy tribes and alien cultures because of their flexibility in dealing with other peoples." Bibliography. Black-and-white drawings. Maps.

Iverson, Peter. *The Navajo Nation*. Westport, Conn.: Greenwood Press, 1981.

A history of the Navajo people, concentrating on the period between 1934 and 1979, which documents "their strength, resilience, and persistence." Chapter 1 briefly describes the continuities and changes in Navajo lifeways from the late 1400's or early 1500's (the time of their migration to the American Southwest) through the opening decades of the twentieth century. Chapter 2 discusses the application of the 1934 Indian Reorganization Act to the Navajo, focusing on tribal resistance to its policy of livestock reduction. Chapter 3 deals with tribal growth and change during the 1940's and 1950's. Chapter 4 examines the new era in Navajo politics and life introduced by the 1963 election of Raymond Nakai. Chapters 5 and 6 treat the advances achieved under Chairman Peter McDonald as well as the controversies arising during his administrations. Selected bibliography. Black-and-white drawings. Maps, tables, and charts.

Joseph, Alice, et al. *The Desert People: A Study of the Papago Indians*. Chicago: University of Chicago Press, 1949.

Part of the Indian Education Research Project, a series of studies that sought to describe, analyze, and compare the development of personality in five American Indian tribes "in the context of the total environmental setting—social, cultural, geographical, and historical—for implications in regard to Indian administration." Part 1 describes contemporary life (circa 1949) on the Papago reservation in southwestern Arizona. It also includes sections on geography, prehistory, and history. Part 2 discusses the development typical for Papago children. Part 3 presents the results of psychological tests given to children in two research areas of the reservation. One appendix. Bibliography. Black-and-white photographs. Maps and tables.

Kluckhohn, Clyde, and Dorothea Leighton. *The Navaho*. Cambridge, Mass.: Harvard University Press, 1946.

Describes the lifeways of the Navajo, the problems they face as an ethnic minority, and the possibilities of applying technical knowledge to their situation without disrupting the fabric of human life. Holds as its central hypothesis that federal attempts to improve Navajo life have met with incomplete success because of the ethnocentrism of administrators and their lack of understanding of Navajo human relations. Sets as its primary aim "to supply the background needed by the administrator or teacher who is to deal effectively with The People in human terms." Chapters on Navajo history, subsistence, society and culture, relations with and attitudes toward whites, religious beliefs and practices, language, and worldview. Bibliography. Black-and-white photographs.

Kroeber, Alfred L., ed. *Walapai Ethnography*. Memoirs of the American Anthropological Association 42. Menasha, Wis.: American Anthropological Association, 1935.

An ethnographic anthology on the Walapai, a Yuman-speaking people of northwestern Arizona. Begins with a version of the Walapai origin narrative. The chapters that follow describe the tribe's natural environment; modes of subsistence; houses; manufactures and industries; dress and ornament; knowledge and arts; social institutions and the life cycle; religious belief, ceremony, and specialists; autobiographies; dreams; and myths and tales. One appendix. Black-and-white photographs. Maps.

Lange, Charles H. *Cochiti: A New Mexico Pueblo, Past and Present*. Austin: University of Texas Press, 1959.

Provides, first, a contemporary portrait (circa 1946-1953) of Cochiti; and, second, a prehistory and history of that New Mexican pueblo. Chapter 1 briefly considers the pueblo's geographical setting. Chapter 2 begins by reviewing what is known concerning Cochiti's prehistory. Next presented are the major periods in its history, from the beginning of the Spanish contact in 1540 through the American period, 1846-1959. Finally, considers long-term non-Indian cultural impacts. Subsequent chapters discuss aspects of present-day life at Cochiti, *including resources, property, and ownership; subsistence and diet; political organization; ceremonial organization; ceremonies; calendar and paraphernalia; social organization; and the life cycle. Forty-four appendices. Bibliography. Black-and-white photographs and drawings.

Leighton, Dorothea, and John Adair. *People of the Middle Place: A Study of the Zuni Indians*. New Haven, Conn.: Human Relations Area Files Press, 1966.

One in a series of studies from the 1940's comprising the Indian Education Personality and Administration Project. The goal of this project was to investigate and compare the development of personality in five Indian tribes "in the context of their total environment—sociocultural, geographical, and historical—for implications related to Indian Service Administration." Part 1 provides a portrait of Zuni culture based on ethnographic observation and the available literature. Part 2 presents information on Zuni personality gathered from the results of standardized tests. One of the study's conclusions is that the Zuni individual learns his behavioral code as a result of strong social pressure exerted by members of his extended family and others in the community. Bibliography. Black-and-white photographs. Maps, tables, and charts.

Minge, Ward Alan. *Acoma: Pueblo in the Sky*. Albuquerque: University of New Mexico Press, 1976.

A culture history of the Acomas, a Keres-speaking people located in western New Mexico. Chapter 1 pieces together the little archaeological and documentary evidence available on Acoma prehistory. Chapter 2 describes the nature and consequences of Spanish rule over the tribe from 1598 to 1821. Included in this description are the Spanish reorganization of Acoma civil life, the tribe's participation in the Pueblo Revolt of 1680, and its reconquest in 1696. Chapter 3 summarizes the brief period of Mexican rule, 1821-1846. Chapter 4 focuses on the tribe's struggles in the years following the transfer from Mexican to Anglo-American governance. Key among these were white encroachments on Indian farmlands, the territorial disputes between Acoma and Laguna, and the largely disastrous economic and social policies of the Indian Bureau. Concludes with an overview of modern Acoma life. Seven appendices. Black-and-white photographs and color plates. Bibliographical essay.

Ortiz, Alfonso. *The Tewa World: Space, Time, Being, and Becoming in a Pueblo Society*. Chicago: University of Chicago Press, 1969.

An ethnographic description and analysis of the Tewa pueblo of San Juan that focuses on "the more intellectual aspects of Tewa culture—on the ideas, rules, and principles, as these are reflected in mythology, world view, and ritual, by means of which the Tewa organize their thought and conduct." Demonstrates the importance of several forms of dualistic thought in Tewa culture and the various ways in which that culture achieves social continuity and integration. Bibliography. Black-and-white drawings and tables.

Russell, Frank. *The Pima Indians*. Bureau of American Ethnology, Annual Report 26 (1904-1905). Washington, D.C.: U.S. Government Printing Office, 1908.

A detailed ethnography of southern Arizona's Pima Indians. Section 1, "History," discusses Piman prehistoric ruins, contact with the Spaniards, relations with Americans, and calendar sticks. Subsequent sections describe modes of subsistence, trade, tools, pottery, basketry, textiles, architecture, clothing, personal adornment, music, dancing, festivals, sports and entertainments, social organization, alliances and warfare with neighboring peoples, sacred narratives and folktales, religious beliefs and practices, classes of medicine men, theories of disease, linguistics, song types, and oratory. Black-and-white photographs. One map.

Spicer, Edward H. *Pascua: A Yaqui Village in Arizona*. Chicago: University of Chicago Press, 1940.

An ethnography of Pascua Village, a Yaqui settlement in the northwest corner of Tucson, Arizona. Places primary focus on the relationship between the acculturated economic life of the community and its social and religious organization. Finds that though there is little or no relation between the supernatural beliefs of the village and its economic institutions, a close tie exists between these beliefs and the social structure. "The ceremonial and the social systems are all of one piece, and the former provides the ultimate sanctions for the latter." Bibliography. Black-and-white photographs and drawings. Maps and tables.

Spier, Leslie. *Havasupai Ethnography*. American Museum of Natural History Anthropological Papers, vol. 29, pt. 3. New York: The Trustees, 1928.

Details the culture of the Havasupai, a Yuman-speaking people living in north-central Arizona. Begins with brief overviews of the tribe's natural environment, linguistic and sociocultural relations with neighboring groups, and yearly round of life. Subsequent sections describe modes of subsistence; manufactures; measurements, time reckoning, directions, and colors; houses, dress, and adornment; social groups and relations; dances; religious beliefs, curing, prayers, taboos, and magic; death observances; the life cycle; and historical narratives. Bibliography. Black-and-white photographs and drawings. Maps, tables, and charts.

__________. *The Yuman Tribes of the Gila River*. Chicago: University of Chicago Press, 1933.

A detailed ethnographic description concerned mainly with the Maricopa and Kaveltcadom peoples of southwestern Arizona. Chapter 1 discusses the tribal distribution and intertribal relations of these two groups. Subsequent chapters provide information on patterns of subsistence; houses; dress and adornment; manufactures; time reckoning, directions, colors, and numbers; social and kinship relations; dances; religious beliefs and practices; customs surrounding death; the life cycle; and traditional narratives. Bibliography. Black-and-white photographs. Maps and tables.

Thompson, Laura, and Alice Joseph. *The Hopi Way*. Chicago: University of Chicago Press, 1945.

An ethnography of the Hopi Indians, the westernmost representatives of Pueblo peoples. Focuses on the development of Hopi personality in relation to the tribe's natural, social, and cultural environments viewed in historical perspective. Topics include Hopi social and political organization, the life cycle, eleven portraits of young tribal members, and patterns of socialization. A concluding chapter summarizes the findings on Hopi character development and highlights implications the authors find particularly significant. Four appendices. Black-and-white photographs and drawings. Charts.

Titiev, Mischa. *Old Oraibi: A Study of the Hopi Indians of the Third Mesa*. Papers of the Peabody Museum of American Archaeology and Ethnology, Harvard University, vol. 22, no. 1. Cambridge, Mass.: Peabody Museum, 1944.

An ethnography of the Hopi pueblo of old Oraibi, Arizona, the only village on the Third Mesa until 1906, when a series of successive splits resulted in a number of new towns. Part 1 contains discussions of kinship terminology, behavior, and groups; political organization; the processes underlying the pueblo's breakup; and the distribution of its population after 1906. Part 2 describes and analyzes Hopi ceremonialism, including sections on its basic pattern and underlying concepts; the kachina cult; tribal initiation; solstitial and solar ceremonies; customs and rituals relating to war; women's ceremonies; and the meaning of Hopi religion. Part 3, "Miscellany," provides information on selected aspects of Hopi culture. Nine appendices. Bibliography. Glossary of native terms. Black-and-white drawings. Tables and charts.

Underhill, Ruth M. *The Navajos*. Norman: University of Oklahoma Press. 1956.

Traces the experiences of the Navajo Indians "as they changed from food-collecting nomads to gardeners and pastoralists to, finally, modern wage earners." Chapters 1 through 3 discuss the circumstances surrounding the migrations of the Navajo's hunter-gatherer ancestors from northwestern North America to the Southwest during the thirteenth or fourteenth centuries. Chapters 4 and 5 describe their acquisition of sheep and horses from the Spanish and adaptations of selected elements of Pueblo culture and religion. The chapters that follow treat Navajo territorial expansion after 1690; raids on Spanish and Mexican settlements; the arrival of white Americans; wars and treaties with the United States; adjustment to reservation life; relations with traders, agents, missionaries, and teachers; Navajo responses to the Indian Reorganization Act of 1934; changes in reservation life following World War II; and the Navajo today (circa 1954) and prospects for the future. Black-and-white photographs.

Biography and Autobiography

Iverson, Peter. *Carlos Montezuma and the Changing World of American Indians*. Albuquerque: University of New Mexico Press, 1982.

Traces the career of Southern Yavapai spokesman Carlos Montezuma in relation to the dominant currents in late nineteenth and early twentieth century federal Indian policy. Focuses on the circumstances that transformed Montezuma from an advocate of Indian assimilationism to an impassioned supporter of traditionalism. Bibliography.

Kelly, Jane H. *Yaqui Women: Contemporary Life Histories*. Lincoln: University of Nebraska Press, 1978.

Presents the autobiographies of four present-day Yaqui women: Dominga Tava, Chepa Moreno, Domingo Ramirez, and Antonia Valenza. The author contributes interpretive treatments of each life history, focusing on "the structuring of interpersonal relationships and adaptive strategies exercised by each woman." Black-and-white photographs.

Newcomb, Franc Johnson. *Hosteen Klah: Navaho Medicine Man and Sand Painter*. Norman: University of Oklahoma Press, 1964.

A biography of a respected Navajo medicine man, stockman, and weaver based primarily on interviews with the subject and members of his family. Begins with a series of chapters that weave together two hundred years of Navajo history with biographical sketches of the Hosteen's great- grandfather, Chief Narbona, and mother, Slim Woman. The remaining chapters present Hosteen Klah's life, focusing on his boyhood at Nee-yai-tsay in the Tunicha Mountains, his sojourn with an Apache uncle, his education as a medicine man and a weaver, and his growing reputation as a medicine man. Bibliography. Black-and-white photographs.

Opler, Morris E. *Apache Odyssey: A Journey Between Two Worlds*. New York: Holt, Rinehart and Winston, 1969.

The autobiography of "In the Middle" (Chris), an Apache Indian from the Mescalero reservation in southeastern New Mexico. Begins with a cultural and historical portrait of the Mescalero people. The autobiography is divided into four parts, denoting the four major periods of the subject's life. The text is punctuated with numerous ethnographic annotations by the editor.

Underhill, Ruth M. *Papago Woman*. New York: Holt, Rinehart and Winston, 1979.

A verbatim presentation of Underhill's interviews with Chona, a member of the Papago tribe, recorded between 1931 and 1933. In describing the major events of her life, the subject (who was approximately ninety years old at the time) provides a wealth of information on traditional Papago customs and values, particularly those relating to the status and roles of women. Selected bibliography. Black-and-white photographs.

Webb, George. *A Pima Remembers*. Tucson: University of Arizona Press, 1959.

George Webb, born about 1893 on the Gila River Reservation, discusses selected aspects of traditional Pima culture and the influences of Western society on his own life and that of his people. His narrative includes several Pima legends as well as descriptions of the old ways, the tribe's first contacts with whites, rabbit hunting, Pima games, the Apache wars, and the Pima language.

Whitewolf, Jim. *The Life of a Kiowa Apache Indian*, edited by Charles S. Brant. New York: Dover, 1969.

The reminiscences of Jim Whitewolf, a Kiowa Apache born in the latter part of the nineteenth century. Whitewolf recounts his infancy and childhood, experiences at a white school, marriage and divorce, and participation in traditional tribal ceremonies and the peyote religion. The subject also discusses episodes from the recent history of the Kiowa Apache. The editor states that he has "tried to present a life history which will convey some feeling for the reality of a man's experiences under conditions of stressful culture contact and social disorganization. . . . Mirrored in Jim's story are tribal and individual reactions to the assorted virtues and vices brought to the Kiowa Apache by Euro-Americans."

California

General Studies and References

Anderson, Eugene N., Jr., comp. *A Revised, Annotated Bibliography of the Chumash and Their Predecessors*. Socorro, N. Mex.: Ballena Press, 1976.

An update of the compiler's 1964 bibliography on the Chumash Indians of southern California. The annotated entries are listed alphabetically by author according to the following categories: archaeology (with separate sections for general works and publications on petroglyphs and pictographs), ethnology, history and historical sources, linguistics, and physical anthropology. One map.

Bean, Lowell J., and Thomas C. Blackburn, eds. *Native Californians: A Theoretical Retrospective*. Socorro, N. Mex.: Ballena Press, 1976.

An anthology of papers highlighting the variety of approaches anthropologists have employed to describe and analyze selected aspects of Native Californian societies and cultures. Among the topics discussed are the evolution of cultural complexity in aboriginal California, social organization among Native Californians, ceremonial integration and social interaction in California tribes, Mojave concepts of the soul, the role of religion among the Luiseno, Yokuts-Mono chiefs and shamans, the economic exchanges of Chumash villages, Yokuts patterns of culture-environment integration, the adaptive responses of the Towola Indians to their environment, Pomo kinship and politics; sib affiliation among the Diegueno, and principles of Nomlaki social organization and status differentiation. Bibliography. A few black-and-white illustrations. One map.

Bean, Lowell J., and Harry W. Lawton, comps. *A Bibliography of the Cahuilla Indians of California*. Banning, Calif.: Malki Museum Press, 1967.

A listing of research materials on the Cahuilla Indians of southern California. The surveyed sources include scholarly publications in anthropology and history; unpublished scholarly works; general reference works, popular treatments, and periodicals; government documents; fiction; and local newspapers.

Bean, Lowell J., and Sylvia B. Vane. *California Indians: Primary Resources—A Guide to Manuscripts, Artifacts, Documents, Serials, Music, and Illustrations*. Ramona, Calif.: Ballena Press, 1977.

Locates and describes known primary sources on Native Californians. Stress is given to ethnographic and ethnohistorical materials, with secondary emphasis on archaeological, linguistic, and historical resources. Part 1 discusses the location and use of government documents and government archives. Part 2 contains a listing of institutions whose holdings include manuscripts, archival materials, photographs, and other research materials on California Indians. These institutions are arranged alphabetically by geopolitical area. Part 3 presents descriptions of serials, audiovisual materials, and commercially available materials.

Cook, Sherburne F. *The Population of the California Indians, 1769-1970*. Berkeley: University of California Press, 1976.

Six essays on themes and issues pertaining to Indian population and demography in California. Among the topics addressed are estimates of the state's aboriginal population, the Indian population of California from 1860 to 1970, age distribution among the California tribes, vital statistics, degrees of blood, and the distribution of California Indians. A conclusion summarizes the factors that led to the drastic diminution in Indian population following white contact. Bibliography.

Heizer, Robert F., ed. *California*. Vol. 8 in *Handbook of North American Indians*. Washington, D.C.: Smithsonian Institution, 1978.

A compendium of seventy-one essays by noted scholars which seeks to summarize what is known concerning the prehistory, history, and cultures of about sixty California tribes. The volume begins with overviews of the history of research on California Indians; the area's natural history; prehistoric, protohistoric, and historic archaeology; Native languages; historical demography; and the impact of Euro-American exploration and settlement on aboriginal populations. Section 2 contains brief treatments of the histories and cultures of selected tribes. The concluding section provides articles on assorted themes, including arts, worldview, mythology, comparative literature, cults, social organization, sex status and roles, trade, intergroup conflict, treaties, litigation, and twentieth century secular movements. A sixty-seven-item bibliography lists all the references cited in the volume. Black-and-white photographs, reproductions, and drawings. Maps and charts.

Heizer, Robert F., et al. *California Indian History: A Classified and Annotated Guide to Source Material*. Ramona, Calif.: Ballena Press, 1975.

Cites nearly seven hundred readily available works on California Indian history. Materials have been selected and organized on the basis of topic, process, and chronology rather than tribal coverage. Part 1, "Period of Native History (? B.C.-A.D. 1542)," contains entries for resources on prehistoric and historic archaeology, linguistics, physical anthropology and demography, ethnography, and folklore (origin myths) and music. Part 2, "Period of Spanish and Mexican Contact (1542-1846)," lists materials on exploration, settlement (missions, forts, secularization), and the Indian response. The third part, "Period of Anglo Conquest (1846-1873)," includes writings on the legal status of Indians, the gold rush (relations of Indians and miners), treaty making and land titles, reservation (relations of military and Indians, federal Indian policy), and social conditions. Materials on "The Aftermath of Conquest (1873-1974)" are found in part 4. Its subheadings are reservation affairs, condition of Indians, and acculturation; condition of mission Indians of southern California; education; religious movements; legal status of Indians; and claims cases. Part 5, "Period of Indian Nationalism (1920-1974)," lists publications on Indian welfare organizations, political organizations of Indians, and recent Indian nationalism. Parts 6 and 7 include entries for "Works Written by Indians" and "Source Materials," respectively. Indexes for tribes referred to and authors.

__________, ed. *A Collection of Ethnographical Articles on the California Indians*. Ramona, Calif.: Ballena Press, 1976.

A collection of twenty-one previously published essays, written between 1851 and 1920, on California Indians and their cultures. The articles are organized by the regional subdivision of northeastern, central, and southern California. Topics include material culture, religion, medicine, patterns of subsistence, dances, and artifacts. Among the scholars represented are Alfred L. Kroeber, Pliny E. Godard, Stephen Powers, and J. G. Bourke.

_________. *The Indians of California: A Critical Bibliography*. Newberry Library Center for the History of the American Indian Bibliographical Series. Bloomington: Indiana University Press, 1976.

A bibliographical essay that reviews 193 books and articles pertaining to the history and culture of California Indians. The essay is divided by the following subheadings: introduction, the study of Indian civilization, Native worldview, demography, Indian-white relations to 1870, the reservation period and urbanization, and Indians and the law. Lists recommended works.

Heizer, Robert F., and Albert B. Elsasser. *The Natural World of the California Indians*. Berkeley: University of California Press, 1980.

An ethnographic overview of California's original inhabitants. Provides coverage for tribes, languages, and territories; regional lifeways; ecological types of California Indian cultures; modes of subsistence; material culture; the procurement and use of nonfood resources; archaeology; art objects produced by ancient Californians; worldview; and the impact of whites on aboriginal populations and lifeways. Three appendices. Listing of selected references. Black-and-white reproductions and drawings. Color plates. Maps and tables.

_________, comps. *A Bibliography of California Archaeology*. Contributions of the University of California Archaeological Research Facility 6. Berkeley: Department of Anthropology, University of California, 1970.

A 78-page listing of publications on California prehistory. Entries are arranged alphabetically by author under 29 topical and regional headings.

_________, comps. *A Bibliography of California Indians: Archaeology, Ethnography, and Indian History*. New York: Garland, 1977.

A two-part bibliography on the Indian peoples of California. Part 1 contains nearly 2300 citations for published and unpublished materials concerning Californian prehistory. Part 2 features more than 1000 entries on Indian history, organized by the following periodization and topics: period of Native history (? B.C.-A.D. 1542); period of Spanish and Mexican contact (A.D. 1542-1846); period of Anglo conquest (A.D. 1846-1873); the aftermath of conquest (1873-1977); period of Indian nationalism (1920-1973); works written by Indians; source materials; and obituaries of anthropologists (who interviewed California Indians as part of their professional work). Indexed by author and tribe. Maps.

Heizer, Robert F., and Mary A. Whipple, comps. and eds. *The California Indians: A Source Book*. 2d rev., enlarged ed. Berkeley: University of California Press, 1971.

An anthology of fifty articles and extracts on California Indians intended for the nontechnical reader. The selections are grouped under the following categories:

general surveys; archaeology; historical accounts of Native Californians; ethnology: material culture and economy; and ethnology: social culture. Bibliography. Black-and-white photographs. Maps, tables, and charts.

Kroeber, Alfred L. *Handbook of the Indians of California*. Bureau of American Ethnology, Bulletin 78. Washington, D.C.: U.S. Government Printing Office, 1925.

Provides ethnographic portraits for fifty of California's aboriginal peoples. Among the groups discussed are the Yurok, Karok, Pomo, Modoc, Maidu, Miwok, Yokuts, Chumash, Washo, Luiseno, and Kawaiisu. Topics vary from group to group. Includes a few chapters that are wholly summary and comparative. Black-and-white drawings. Maps and tables.

Kroeber, Theodora, and Robert F. Heizer. *Almost Ancestors: The First Californians*, edited by F. David Hales. San Francisco: Sierra Club Books, 1968.

An album of portraits representing California tribes exterminated by whites. The photographs in part 1 are arranged by cultural subarea. Those in part 2 are organized around the following topics: children, men and their world, women and their roles, elders, the aftermaths of conquest, and carriers of cultural traditions. Accompanying commentaries provide information on tribal histories and cultures.

Margolin, Malcolm, ed. *The Way We Lived: California Indian Reminiscences, Stories, and Songs*. Berkeley: Heyday Books, 1981.

A collection of texts and songs intended to portray the enormous diversity that existed among California's aboriginal cultures. The pieces are ordered under the following subject headings: "Growing Up"; "The Conflict of Love" (relations between the sexes); "An Ordered World" (social life and customs); "Old Age and Death"; "The Aliveness of All Things" (cosmology, sacred belief, and ceremony); "Getting Power" (the quest and use of religious power); "Dream Time" (the significance of dreams); "Mythic Time"; "Coyote Tales"; and "After the Coming of Whites." Black-and-white photographs. One map.

Powers, Steven. *Tribes of California*. Washington, D.C.: U.S. Government Printing Office. 1877.

An early summary of Native Californian peoples and cultures based on the author's travels during the summers of 1871 and 1872. Among the groups covered are the Karok, Yurok, Tolowa, Hupa, Patwin, Mattole, Wailaki, Yuki, Pomo, Wintu, Shasta, Modoc, Maidu, Yosemite, and Yokuts. Concludes with some generalizations concerning California Indians and a brief survey of aboriginal botany. Black-and-white drawings.

Strong, William D. *Aboriginal Society in Southern California*. University of California Publications in American Archaeology and Ethnology, vol. 26. Berkeley: University of California Press, 1929.

Examines the social and ceremonial organizations of the Serrano; Desert, Pass, and Mountain Cahuilla; Cupeno; and Luiseno Indians of southern California. Information on the primary social divisions, political leadership, and religious practices are presented for each group. A concluding chapter offers generalizations concerning aboriginal society in southern California. Maps and tables.

Weber, Francis J. *A Select Bibliography: The California Missions, 1765-1972*. Los Angeles: Dawson's Book Shop, 1972.

Lists and briefly describes five hundred books, articles, and pamphlets pertaining to the twenty-one California missions established by the Catholic church during the latter half of the eighteenth century and which stretched from San Diego to San Francisco Bay. Entries are alphabetically arranged by author.

Archaeology

Chartkoff, Joseph L., and Kerry K. Chartkoff. *The Archaeology of California*. Stanford, Calif.: Stanford University Press, 1984.

Seeks to provide a unified perspective on California's archaeological record which is understandable to the nonspecialist. Utilizes a framework that covers more than 13,000 years of the state's cultural development and includes societies ranging from small bands of Paleo-Indians to twentieth century urban dwellers. Divides this framework into four time periods: Paleo-Indian, Archaic, Pacific, and Historical. Introduces each of these divisions with a brief reconstruction of group life in that time. Follows these reconstructions with discussions of themes, archaeological phases, and ways of life for the four periods. Limits the presentation of data, especially artifacts, to what is required to describe a past lifeway adequately. Seven appendices. Bibliography. Black-and-white photographs and drawings. Maps.

Moratto, Michael J. *California Archaeology*. New York: Academic Press, 1984.

A synopsis of California prehistory which traces the development of that state's peoples and cultures from the Ice Age to the eve of Indian contact with whites. Designed as both an introduction for students and general readers as well as an up-to-date resource for archaeologists who are not Californianists. Chapters 1 through 3 provide an areal focus for California's historic and ancient environments, evidence of Pleistocene (Ice Age) lifeways; and assemblages dating from 8,000 to 12,000 years ago. Chapter summarize cultural developments in eight archaeological regions for the period 6000 B.C. to A.D. 1750-1850. Concludes with a synthesis stressing linguistic prehistory. Bibliography. Black-and-white photographs and diagrams. Maps and tables.

Folklore, Sacred Narrative, Religious Belief and Practice

Applegate, Richard B. *Atishwin: The Dream Helper in South-Central California*. Socorro, N. Mex.: Ballena Press, 1978.

A discussion of the beliefs and practices associated with the dream helper, an elaboration of the guardian spirit complex found among Indian peoples of south-central California. Described are modes of seeking a dream helper, elements typical of dream helper vision, varying responses to such visions, talismans associated with the complex, the stylistics and practice of dream songs, the relationship between dream helper and dreamer, the shaman and his helpers, and the dream helper in wider ethnographic perspective. Two appendices. Bibliography.

Barrett, S. A. *Ceremonies of the Pomo Indians*. University of California Publications in American Archaeology and Ethnology, vol. 12, no. 10. Berkeley: University of California Press, 1917.

A brief discussion of ceremonies and dances held by the Pomo Indians of western California. Section 1 identifies the statues, roles, and general features of the tribe's ceremonial organization. Sections 2 and 3 describe the motives and rituals associated with the Ghost and Guksu ceremonies, respectively. Section 4 treats dances that are either performed in connection with the aforementioned ceremonies or unrelated to them. Section 5 deals with the "Messiah" cult which was introduced among the Pomo by the Wintun of the Sacramento valley during the late nineteenth century. Among the author's conclusions are that Pomo ceremonies were generally quite simple, characterized by an absence of any fixed ceremonial season or sequence of ceremonies and any extensive priesthood or specialized group controlling ceremonial matters. Black-and-white photographs.

__________. *Pomo Myths*. Bulletin of the Public Museum of the City of Milwaukee 15. Milwaukee: The Trustees, 1933.

A collection and analysis of sacred narratives belonging to Pomo Indians of California's central coast. Part 1, which provides an ethnological treatment of the texts, includes sections on territory and environment, methods used in recording the texts, the characteristics and subject matter of Pomo myths, the position of Pomo mythology in the California area, Pomo concepts of the universe, supernatural beings, magic places, methods of storytelling, and the nature of the Pomo mythological system. Part 2 contains more than one hundred Pomo myths arranged under the following headings: myths of creation and transformation of human beings, myths of miscellaneous creations and regulations, myths of destruction (the burning of the world), myths of destruction (deluge), myths of the sun, myths of supernatural beings, trickster stories, myths of magic devices, myths of deer and bear children, miscellaneous animal tales, and miscellaneous tales. Following the narratives are discussions of the use of numbers in Pomo myths, catch phrases in Pomo mythology, and the relation of Pomo mythology to that of other tribes in central California. Includes abstracts and notes for the texts and a Pomo-English/English-Pomo glossary. Bibliography.

Blackburn, Thomas C., ed. *December's Child*. Berkeley: University of California Press, 1975.

A collection and analysis of narratives belonging to the Chumash Indians of southern California. Part 1 begins with a descriptive summary of the general characteristics and content of the narratives. It next identifies the elements of Chumash material culture, social organization, interpersonal relationships, and worldview and philosophy the narratives mention or reflect. Also considered is the significance of the distortions and fantastic elements occurring in the stories.

Part 2 contains 111 narratives in free translation. One appendix and a glossary of Chumash words and phrases. Bibliography. Black-and-white photographs and drawings.

________, ed. *Flowers of the Wind: Papers on Ritual, Myth, and Symbolism in California and the Southwest*. Socorro, N. Mex.: Ballena Press, 1977.

A collection of seven papers presented at a symposium entitled "Mythology, Ritual, and World View in Native California and the Southwest" organized for the 1976 meeting of the Southwestern Anthropological Association. Four of the essays concern forms of religious belief, symbols, and ceremony found among California tribes. These include discussions of the supernatural world of the Kawaiisu; selected behavioral patterns found in Chemehuevi myths; Native California concepts of the afterlife; and the sacred significance and psychoanalytic symbolism of wealth and work in northwestern California. Bibliography.

Gifford, E. W. *Miwok Cults*. University of California Publications in American Archaeology and Ethnology, vol. 18, no. 3. Berkeley: University of California Press, 1926.

Discusses two cults found among the Central and Northern Miwok of the Sierra Nevada region of central California. Section 1 describes the beliefs, attitudes, and observances associated with the bird cult, in which birds of prey in particular are venerated. Section 2 considers the historical stratum and features of the god-impersonating cult. A conclusion speculates on the sources of these two religious traditions and the manner in which they have blended among the Miwok.

Goldschmidt, Walter, and Harold Driver. *The Hupa White Deerskin Dance*. University of California Publications in American Archaeology and Ethnology, vol. 35, no. 8. Berkeley: University of California Press, 1940.

A study of the ceremonial, religious, social, and socioeconomic aspects of the White Deerskin Dance, a protracted festival celebrated by several tribes of northwestern California. An opening section offers a summary of Hupa culture. The main portion of the monograph describes the organization, ceremonies, music, chronology, regalia, religious manifestations, shamanistic activities, and informal attitudes associated with the dance. A conclusion presents speculations concerning the festival's history and function. Tables and figures. Black-and-white photographs.

Hudson, Travis, et al., eds. *Eye of the Flute: Chumash Traditional History and Ritual as Told by Fernando Librado Kitsepawit to John P. Harrington*. Santa Barbara, Calif.: Santa Barbara Museum of Natural History, 1977.

Descriptions of Ventureno Chumash ritual organization and activities, based on the collaboration between ethnographer John P. Harrington and native informant Fernando Librado Kitsepawit. An introduction provides biographical background on Harrington and Kitsepawit and their working relationship. Part 1 contains information on Chumash political and ritual life prior to Spanish domination and missionary work. Part 2 presents accounts of tribal ceremonies, rituals, and beliefs. Part 3 consists of appendices meant to aid in interpreting the data contained in the preceding sections. Black-and-white drawings.

Kroeber, Alfred L. *Indian Myths of South Central California*. University of California Publications in American Archaeology and Ethnology, vol. 4, no. 4. Berkeley: University of California Press, 1906-1907.

An analysis and sample of sacred narratives belonging to tribes of south-central California. Includes texts from the Costanoans, Miwoks, Yokuts, and Shoshoneans. An introduction compares the mythology of these groups with that of tribes in the state's north central region. Provides abstracts of the narratives.

Kroeber, Alfred L., and E. W. Gifford. *Karok Myths*, edited by Grace Buzaljko. Berkeley: University of California Press, 1980.

Contains two major collections of Karok folklore: the first amassed by Alfred L. Kroeber during the early twentieth century; the second, by Edward Gifford in the 1940's. A "folkloristic commentary" by the editor briefly discusses selected themes found in the texts and the significance of the collections for students of Native American narratives. Provides an index of parallel plot elements (by the editor) and a Karok linguistic index (contributed by William Bright). Bibliography. Black-and-white photographs. One map.

__________. *World Renewal: A Cult System of Native Northwest California*. University of California Publications, Anthropological Records, vol. 13, no. 1. Berkeley: University of California Press, 1949.

Details the motives, principles, and ceremonies of the world renewal religion of northwestern California's Yurok, Hupa, Karok, and Wiyot Indians. Identifies as the central purpose of this cult system to provide an abundance of food and universal good health and to renew or repair the earth. Argues that the linguistic diversity of the tribes practicing the religion "is in striking contrast to the uniformity of the principal observances of the cult, a uniformity which is not obscured by the numerous local elaborations of the fundamental pattern." Six appendices. Bibliography. Black-and-white photographs and drawings. Maps and tables.

Kroeber, Theodora. *The Inland Whale*. Bloomington: Indiana University Press, 1959.

An anthology of nine stories selected from the narrative traditions of the Yuroks, Wintus, Yanas, Maidus, Karoks, Mojaves, and other California peoples. The latter part of the book includes a general discussion of the importance of oral traditions for comparative literature and observations on "the literary and the human aspects of the stories, comparing them one with another and with the categories of modern Western literature." Black-and-white drawings by Joseph Crivy.

Meighan, Clement W., and Francis A. Riddell. *The Maru Cult of the Pomo Indians: A California Ghost Dance Survival*. Los Angeles: Southwest Museum, 1972.

A description and analysis of the Maru religion of the Pomo Indians, a direct descendant of the Ghost Dance movement of the late nineteenth century. An introductory chapter discusses the Maru cult in relation to the Ghost Dance and other nativistic movements. The chapters that follow provide information on the setting of Maru activities; the Bighead Dance, the major ceremony of the religion; popular dances accompanying the Bighead Dance; and audience composition, placement, and participation. A conclusion discusses the historical development of the Maru cult and the status of Maru ceremonies in the late 1940's and 1950's when fieldwork for the study was performed. Four appendices. Bibliography. Black-and-white drawings and photographs. One map and tables.

Spott, Robert, and Alfred L. Kroeber. *Yurok Narratives*. University of California Publications in American Archaeology and Ethnology, vol. 35, no. 9. Berkeley: University of California Press, 1942.

An anthology of thirty-seven narratives belonging to the Yurok Indians of northwestern California. The narratives are organized into three groups: case histories of specific individuals and their doings, primarily from the period 1820 to 1890; stories of a legendary character; and accounts of the institutors of the world and their exploits. Bibliography of principal works referred to.

Zigmond, Maurice L. *Kawaiisu Mythology: An Oral Tradition of South-Central California*. Socorro, N. Mex.: Ballena Press, 1980.

A collection of sixty-five myths belonging to the Kawaiisu Indians, a Shoshonean-speaking tribe living in the Tehachapi Mountains north of Los Angeles. An editor's introduction first analyzes correspondences between Kawaiisu myths and those of the Chemehuevi people of the southern Great Basin. It then considers the complex and enigmatic personality of Coyote, the central character of most of the narratives. Accompanying the Kawaiisu texts are two Kitamemuk and five Panamint myths. Bibliography. Black-and-white photographs. One map.

Subsistence and Land Use

Barrows, David P. *The Ethno-Botany of the Coahuilla Indians of Southern California*. Banning, Calif.: Malki Museum Press, 1977.

Studies plant knowledge and use of southern California's Cahuilla Indians. Chapter 1 discusses the group's linguistic and tribal affinities. Subsequent chapters describe the tribe's habitat; houses and house-building; baskets and basket-making; plant products used in arts and crafts; the gathering, preparation, and storing of foods; the variety of wild and cultivated plants used as foods; and plants used in the production of drinks, narcotics, and medicines. An introduction by Harry Lawton presents a biographical sketch of Barrows. Also included in the volume are an overview of Barrow's ethnographic contributions by Lowell Bean and an essay by William Bright on the Cahuilla language.

Bean, Lowell J. *Mukat's People: The Cahuilla Indians of Southern California*. Berkeley: University of California Press, 1973.

Uses Cahuilla society to test two conflicting assumptions concerning the role of ritual and religion in the ecological adaptations of human groups. One assumption holds that ritual and worldview are more ecologically nonadaptive than adaptive; the other, conversely, suggests that ritual and worldview are more ecologically adaptive than nonadaptive. The Cahuilla materials overwhelmingly support the view that ritual and worldview are more ecologically adaptive than nonadaptive. According to the author, religious and other institutions in Cahuilla society "meshed together very neatly and were closely related to the needs imposed upon the culture by their environmental conditions." Bibliography.

Bean, Lowell J., and Katherine S. Saubel. *Temalpakh: Cahuilla Indian Knowledge and Usage of Plants*. Banning, Calif.: Malki Museum Press, 1972.

Documents how the Cahuilla, a Shoshonean-speaking people of southern California, adapted to their natural environment. Focuses on the influence of local flora on Cahuilla culture. Section 1 describes the various life zones of the tribe's habitat. Section 2 discusses plants in relation to Cahuilla lifeways and includes information on the seasonal subsistence round, the trading of plant products, the use of plants in basketry, the division of labor governing plant gathering, plant remedies, and Cahuilla plant use today. It also provides a botanical folk taxonomy. Section 3 contains an annotated list of Cahuilla plants, listed alphabetically by genera, followed by the species in alphabetical order within each genus. Citations supply the common names of the plants, Cahuilla designations for them, their uses, and sources of information. Bibliography. Black-and-white photographs.

Felger, Richard S., and Mary B. Moser. *People of the Desert and Sea: Ethnobotany of the Seri Indians*. Tucson: University of Arizona Press, 1985.

Concerned primarily with the botany of the Comcaac, or Seri, Indians: a traditionally hunting, gathering, and seafaring people who live along the Gulf of California in Sonora, Mexico. Part 1, "The People and the Setting," provides an overview of Seri history, culture, and environment. Part 2, "Biological Ethnography: The Desert and the Sea in Seri Culture," focuses on Seri conceptions of and relations to the natural world. Among the topics discussed are the Seri calendar, their classification of the biological world, water and food quest, medicinal uses of plants and animals, shelter and fuel, dress and adornment, and basketry. Part 3, "Plants in Seri Culture," describes the place of nonflowering and flowering plants in Seri culture. Each entry includes a plant's scientific name, Seri name and gloss, free translation, Spanish and English common names, and use. Two appendices. Bibliography. Black-and-white photographs and drawings. Maps and tables.

Kroeber, Alfred L., and S. A. Barrett. *Fishing Among the Indians of Northwestern California*. University of California Publications, Anthropological Records, vol. 21, no. 1. Berkeley: University of California Press, 1960.

A detailed study of the technological, social, and cultural dimensions of fishing among selected tribes of extreme northwestern California. Chapter 1 discusses fishing rights, varieties of fish utilized, and fishing methods. Chapter 2 describes the use of fixed and movable weirs. Chapters 3 and 4 provide information on net types and net making and netting implements, respectively. Chapter 5 deals with basketry traps. Chapters 6 and 7 portray the wide variety of aboriginal fishing devices and methods. Chapter 7 treats the transport, preservation, storage, and cooking of fish. Chapter 9 concerns the beliefs, restrictions, and ceremonies surrounding fishing. Chapters 10 and 11 focus on the harvest and use of shellfish and sea mammals. One appendix. Glossary. Bibliography. Black-and-white photographs and drawings. Maps.

Lewis, Henry T. *Patterns of Indian Burning in California: Ecology and Ethnohistory*. Ramona, Calif.: Ballena Press, 1973.

Applies modes of analysis developed by contemporary studies in fire ecology and wildlife management to ethnographic and historical reports on the use of fire by California Indians to drive game, enhance seed production, and limit the amount of brush. Concludes that Indian burning of woodland-grass, chaparral, and coniferous forest zones represented a "significant form of environmental management which resulted in a dynamic balance of natural forces." Preceding the monograph is an article by Lowell Bean and Harry Lawton entitled "Some Explanations for the Rise of Cultural Complexity in Native California with Comments on Proto-Agriculture and Agriculture." Bibliography.

Shipek, Florence C. *Pushed into the Rocks: Southern California Indian Land Tenure, 1769-1986*. Lincoln: University of Nebraska Press, 1987.

A description and analysis of changing patterns of land tenure and land use among the Indians of southern California from the mid-eighteenth century to the mid-1980's. The opening chapters describe land tenure and use as traditionally practiced by the Indians of the area. Chapter 3 examines the federal allotment of Indian lands in the late nineteenth century and its consequences for tribal structures and landholdings. The remaining chapters identify modern forms of tenure, their interaction with traditional legal tenure, and the problems and future implications of this interaction. Seven appendices. Bibliography of references cited. Maps.

Family and Society

Bean, Lowell J., and Thomas F. King, eds. *?ANTAP: California Indian Political and Economic Organization*. Ramona, Calif.: Ballena Press, 1974.

Seven papers that explore various aspects of California's aboriginal societies "as complex, hierarchal, interacting systems." Topics include social organization in Native California, the evolution of complex political systems among San Francisco Bay hunter-gatherers, social change in prehistoric central California, an examination of bead use in prehistoric and early historic California, ceremonial integration and social interaction in aboriginal California, warfare and alliance dynamics in the lower Colorado River area, and an ecological perspective on Chumash baptism. Bibliography. Maps, tables, and charts.

Devereux, George. *Mohave Ethnopsychiatry and Suicide: The Psychiatric Knowledge and the Psychic Disturbances of an Indian Tribe*. Bureau of American Ethnology, Bulletin 175. Washington, D.C.: U.S. Government Printing Office, 1961.

A systematic study of the psychiatric theories and practices of the Mojave people. Seeks to explore Mojave ideas, beliefs, and behaviors regarding mental derangements; to record all obtainable information on psychiatric illnesses in the tribe; and to analyze them in their social and cultural settings. Part 1 deals with the fundamentals of Mojave psychiatry, including etiology (theories of causation), nosology (the classification of various mental disorders), modes of diagnosis and treatment, and the position of the insane in Mojave society. Subsequent sections provide extended discussions of specific mental pathologies and suicide. One appendix and an addendum. Bibliography. Black-and-white reproductions and photographs. Tables.

Material Culture and the Arts

Barrett, Samuel A. *Material Aspects of Pomo Culture*. Bulletin of the Public Museum of the City of Milwaukee, vol. 20, pts. 1 and 2. Milwaukee, Wis.: Board of Trustees, 1952.

Details the modes of subsistence, diet, tools, technologies, and manufactures of the Pomo Indians of northwestern California. Part 1 is primarily concerned with tribal patterns associated with food acquisition and preparation, modes of transportation, shelter, implements and utensils, and warfare. Part 2 provides information on Pomo arts, clothing, personal adornment, musical instruments, games, mnemonic records, medicines, and charms. Six appendices. Bibliography. Black-and-white photographs.

Densmore, Frances. *Music of the Maidu Indians of California*. Publications of the Frederick Webb Hodge Anniversary Publication Fund, vol. 7. Los Angeles: Southwest Museum, 1958.

A study of Maidu music based on interviews held in 1937 with the only two tribal members who remembered the old songs. Begins with a brief characterization of the singers and a description of traditional musical instruments, including drums, rattles, musical bow, flutes, and whistles. The body of the monograph contains transcriptions and ethnological and musicological analyses of selected social and ceremonial songs. Concludes with notes on the structure of Maidu songs and a summary of the melodic analyses. Bibliography of authorities cited. Black-and-white photographs and diagrams.

Grant, Campbell. *The Rock Painting of the Chumash: A Study of a California Indian Culture*. Berkeley: University of California Press, 1965.

Provides a description and analysis of the rock and cave painting of the Chumash Indians, a tribe whose homelands encompassed about 6,500 square miles of southern California. Chapters 1 through 3 provide brief discussions of Chumash lands, history, and culture. Chapter 4 focuses on the pictographs, including discussions of their locations; subject matter; pigments, techniques, and styles; meaning; age; the problems of erosion and vandalism; methods of recording; and comparison with rock paintings of other areas. Five appendices. Bibliography. Glossary. Black-and-white reproductions, photographs, and drawings. Color plates. Maps.

Tribal Life

Conrotto, Eugene L. *Miwok Means People: The Life and Fate of the Native Inhabitants of Goldrush Country.* Fresno, Calif.: Valley Publishers, 1973.

A cultural and historical survey of the Miwok people of southern California. Begins with a tribal history covering the periods both before and following white contact. The chapters that follow briefly describe traditional Miwok worldview and lifeways, overview their contemporary situation, provide a Miwok vocabulary, and identify Miwok village sites. Bibliography. Black-and-white reproductions, photographs, and drawings.

Drucker, Philip. *The Tolowa and Their Southwest Oregon Kin.* University of California Publications in American Archaeology and Ethnology, vol. 36, no. 4. Berkeley: University of California Press, 1937.

An ethnographic summary focusing on the Tolowa, with additional information on other Athapascan-speaking peoples of northwestern California and southwestern Oregon. Chapters discuss various aspects of Tolowa geography, modes of subsistence, material culture, money and property, social life, life cycle, and religion and ritual. Following the discussion of the Tolowa are chapters on neighboring peoples of the Chetco, lower Rogue, and upper Coquille rivers, and Galice creek. Bibliography. One map.

Du Bois, Cora. *Wintu Ethnography.* University of California Publications in American Archaeology and Ethnology, vol. 36, no. 1. Berkeley: University of California Press, 1935.

A cultural description of the Northern Wintu, one of three groups of Wintun-speaking peoples inhabiting California's Sacramento valley. Topics addressed include the tribe's modes of subsistence, social life, life cycle, manners of time reckoning and counting, religious beliefs and practices, clothing and ornaments, housing, musical instruments, weapons, tools, and band basketry. A conclusion discusses the Wintu's cultural status and history in relation to the rest of northern California. Black-and-white photographs and drawings. Tables, charts, and one map.

Foster, George. *A Summary of Yuki Culture.* University of California Publications Anthropological Records, vol. 5, no. 3. Berkeley: University of California Press, 1947.

Seeks to reconstruct the life and manners of the aboriginal Yuki of northern California. Includes discussion of ethnogeography, subsistence, material culture, division of labor, ownership and property, trade and transportation, medicine, social organization and institutions, time reckoning, colors, counting, and religious belief and ceremony. A concluding chapter assesses the Yukis' general adjustment to life. Two appendices. Bibliography. Black-and-white drawings. One map.

Goddard, Pliny E. *Life and Culture of the Hupa.* University of California Publications in American Archaeology and Ethnology, vol. 1, no. 1. Berkeley: University of California Press, 1903-1904.

An summary of ancestral Hupa lifeways derived from data collected on the

Hoopa Valley Reservation in northern California during the last decade of the nineteenth century. Sections on natural and intertribal environments, history, villages, houses, dress and ornamentation, subsistence and diet, sexual division of labor, measuring and money, social life and organization, entertainments, warfare, curers and curing, burial observances, and religion. Black-and-white drawings. One map.

Heizer, Robert F., ed. *The Costanoan Indians*. Local History Studies 18. Cupertino, Calif.: California History Center, De Anza College, 1974.

A collection of texts depicting the aboriginal language and lifeways of southern California's Costanoan Indians. Chapters contain an ethnohistory of the Costanoans of San Francisco Bay (by Linda Stevens Switzer); Costanoan words for plants, animals, certain natural phenomena, and numbers; responses by Franciscan missionaries to an early nineteenth century Spanish government questionnaire concerning the California Indians; miscellaneous pieces on Costanoan songs, place names, language, mythology, traditions, autobiography, and missionization; and images of Costanoan Indians by nineteenth century visitors to California. Black-and-white reproductions.

James, Harry C. *The Cahuilla Indians*. Los Angeles: Westernlore Press, 1960.

An introductory survey of southern California's Cahuilla Indians. The author includes information on aboriginal social organization; patterns of subsistence; legends; religious belief and ceremony; Cahuilla notables, including Ramona Lubo (the titled heroine of Helen Hunt Jackson's novel), Fig Tree John, and Juan Antonio; and contemporary (circa 1960) conditions on the Cahuilla Indian Reservation. One appendix. A brief annotated bibliography. Black-and-white photographs and drawings. One map.

Jewell, Donald P. *Indians of the Feather River: Tales and Legends of the Concow Maidu*. Menlo Park, Calif.: Ballena Press, 1987.

An anthology of narratives, collected from tribal elders, concerning the history and culture of northeastern California's Concow Maidu Indians. Among the contents are selected myths and legends; accounts of traditional beliefs and lifeways, including ceremonies, patterns of socialization, courtship and marriage, methods of social control and corporate punishment, doctoring, and gods and supernaturals; and the virtual annihilation of Concow Maidu villages by white settlers. Bibliography. Black-and-white photographs and drawings.

Johnston, Bernice E. *California's Gabrielino Indians*. Los Angeles: Southwest Museum, 1962.

An ethnographic and historical survey of the Gabrielino Indians, a culturally extinct people who once occupied the coastal region of Los Angeles County, the northwest portion of Orange County, and several offshore islands. Based primarily on archaeological research and the documents of Spanish explorers and missionaries, the monograph reconstructs the tribe's modes of subsistence, social organization, religious beliefs and practices, and colonization by whites. Bibliography. Black-and-white reproductions, photographs, and drawings. One map.

Kroeber, Alfred L. *The Patwin and Their Neighbors*. University of California Publications in Archaeology and Ethnology, vol. 29, no. 4. Berkeley: University of California Press, 1932.

An ethnographic survey primarily concerned with the Patwin, Wintun, and Wintu peoples of California's lower Sacramento River. Provides information on the political divisions within each group, their modes of warfare, social organization, and subsistence. Also includes extensive discussion of the region's kuksu cults: "system[s] of rituals performed by initiated members of societies impersonating supernatural beings." Black-and-white drawings. One map and one table.

__________. *The Seri*. Southwest Museum Papers 6. Los Angeles: Southwest Museum, 1931.

A brief cultural description of the Seri Indians living on Tiburon island, Sonora, in the Gulf of California. Part 1 furnishes data on various aspects of Seri life collected by the author. Among the topics discussed are kinship, calendar and astronomy, myth fragments, shamanism, taboos, dances, songs, games, and material culture. Part 2 reviews and critiques the information contained in W. J. McGee's 1898 ethnography of the Seri. Subsequent sections examine Serian territory and tribes, language, and physical type, and compare Seri culture with other tribes. Black-and-white photographs.

Landberg, Leif C. W. *The Chumash Indians of Southern California*. Los Angeles: Southwest Museum, 1965.

Reconstructs the history and culture of the Chumash Indians, original occupants of the area now making up part of Los Angeles, Ventura, Santa Barbara, and San Luis Obispo counties. The study begins with a historical overview of Chumash-white relations divided into the following periods: Spanish exploration period (1542-1769), mission period (1769-1834), rancho period (1834-1849), and American period (1849-present). It next describes various aspects of Chumash society and culture including the plan and population of their villages, magic and religion, craft specialization, the division of labor, social organization, technology, and tools. Subsequent sections treat the tribe's subsistence base, the relation of seasonal variations in food supply to Chumash demography and settlement patterns, their subsistence round or calendar, and an ecological interpretation of sociocultural evolution on California's southern coast. Two appendices. Bibliography. Black-and-white photographs and drawings. Maps, tables, and charts.

Margolin, Malcolm. *The Ohlone Way: Indian Life in the San Francisco-Monterey Area*. Berkeley: Heyday Books, 1978.

Provides a historical and cultural overview of the Ohlone, or Costanoan, Indians, a population of forty loosely and nonaffiliated Indian tribelets whose traditional homelands comprised the coastal area between Point Sur and the San Francisco Bay. Part 1 describes the subsistence modes of these groups. Part 2 details elements of their social life, including birth and childhood, marriage, intratribal relations, trade, political organization, and warfare. Part 3 treats religious belief and practice. Part 4 discusses the affects of two centuries of contact with whites on Ohlone lifeways. Bibliography. Black-and-white drawings (illustrations by Michael Harney).

Miller, Bruce W. *Chumash: A Picture of Their World.* Los Osos, Calif.: Sand River Press, 1988.

Examines the lifeways of the Chumash, a tribe of the Hokan language family which once occupied California's southern coast. Chapter 1 provides a tribal ethnohistory based primarily on Spanish documents. Chapter 2 deals with material culture, including sections on basketry, wooden bowls and jars, stone tools, equipment for hunting and fishing, food, clothing, and shelter. Chapter 3 treats village life and social organization, trade, religion, language, entertainment, and rock art. Bibliography. Black-and-white photographs and drawings. Maps.

Miller, Virginia. *Ukomno'm: The Yuki Indians of Northern California.* Socorro, N. Mex.: Ballena Press, 1979.

Documents the factors that resulted in the dissemination of northern California's Yuki population and white confiscation of their lands. Identifies starvation and the introduction of Euro-American diseases as two important causes. The author argues, however, that these two causes "were far outweighed by intentional, calculated genocide on the part of the Europeans in their greed for the Indians' land." By 1865, whites had succeeded in killing most of the Yuki.

Nelson, Byron, Jr. *Our Home Forever: A Hupa Tribal History*, edited by Laura Bayer. Salt Lake City: University of Utah Printing Service, for the Hupa Tribe, 1978.

An ethnohistory of northern California's Hupa Indians focusing on their responses and adjustments to white contact. Begins with an extended discussion of the tribe's traditional lifeways and customs. Subsequent chapters outline the strategies Hupas adopted to counter white attempts to expel them from their homelands, the formation of the Hupa reservation in 1864, the effects of late nineteenth century assimilationist policy on the tribe, and tribal developments under the Indian Reorganization Act of 1934. Five appendices. Bibliographical essay on sources of Hupa history.

Ray, Verne F. *Primitive Pragmatists: The Modoc Indians of Northern California.* Seattle: University of Washington Press, 1963.

An ethnographic account of north-central California's Modoc Indians. Provides information on tribal organization, legal processes, concepts of wealth, worldview, modes of acquiring supernatural power, initiation of shamans and shamanism, selected rituals, the life cycle, entertainments, warfare and slavery, houses, sweat houses and sweating, dress, body care and adornment, and modes of subsistence. Three appendices. Bibliography. Black-and-white drawings. Maps.

Spier, Leslie. *Southern Diegueno Customs.* University of California Publications in American Archaeology and Ethnology, vol. 20, no. 16. Berkeley: University of California Press, 1923.

Provides ethnographic data on the Southern Diegueno of San Diego County. Topics include the structure and functioning of aboriginal social organization, religious beliefs and ceremonies, song cycles, sacred narratives, modes of subsistence, houses, dress and adornment, manufactures, musical instruments, weapons, games, calendar, and star lore. Black-and-white drawings. One map.

Biography and Autobiography

Heizer, Robert F., and Theodora Kroeber, eds. *Ishi, the Last Yahi: A Documentary History*. Berkeley: University of California Press, 1979.

An anthology of thirty-seven documents concerning Ishi, the last of northeastern California's Yahi Indians. The texts, organized around four chronologically devised topics, provide information on the attitudes and knowledge of whites concerning local Indians before the appearance of Ishi, Ishi's entrance into western civilization in 1911, his five- year residence at the University of California anthropological museum, and his death from tuberculosis on March 26, 1916. Black-and-white photographs. Maps.

Shipek, Florence C., ed. *The Autobiography of Delfina Cuero: A Diegueno Indian*. Los Angeles: Dawson's Book Shop, 1968.

The reminiscences of Delfina Cuero, a Diegueno Indian of southern California. Provides information on the subject's childhood, marriage, and traditional Diegueno beliefs, knowledge, and practices transmitted to her by her grandmother. According to the editor, we see in Delfina's story "the way in which some families managed to survive the disintegration of their economy and social structure under the pressures of a stronger, more aggressive civilization." One black-and-white photograph. One map.

Great Basin

General Studies and References

D'Azevedo, Warren L. *Great Basin*. Vol. 11 in *Handbook of North American Indians*. Washington, D.C.: Smithsonian Institution, 1986.

A collection of forty-five summary essays on the environment, culture history, and lifeways of the indigenous peoples of North America's Great Basin. Part 1 begins with a historical overview of the area's Indian-white relations and a discussion of the volume's organization. Following are articles on the history of Great Basin research, prehistoric and historical environments, subsistence, and the Numic and Washoe languages. Part 2 contains essays on Great Basin regional prehistory, prehistoric arts and material culture, early trade, and contract anthropology. Part 3 presents ethnological portraits of the Western Shoshone, Northern Shoshone and Bannock, Eastern Shoshone, Ute, Southern Paiute, Kawaiisu, Owens Valley Paiute, and Washo. Historical treatments of Indian-white relations; the introduction of the horse; treaties, reservations, and land claims; tribal politics; Indian economics, 1950-1980; and Indian perspectives on jurisdictional and economic issues are provided in part 4. It also includes a discussion of tribal historical projects. Concludes with articles on population; kinship; mythology and religious concepts; oral tradition; the Ghost Dance, Bear Dance, and Sun Dance; peyote religion; music; and ethnographic basketry. Seventy-seven-page bibliography. Hundreds of black-and-white photographs, reproductions, and maps.

__________, et al. eds. *The Current Status of Anthropological Research in the Great Basin: 1964*. Desert Research Institute, Social Sciences and Humanities Publications 1. Reno, Nev.: Publications Office of the Desert Research Institute, 1966.

An anthology of papers and comments drawn from the Great Basin Anthropological Conference, 1964. Seeks "both to summarize and interpret our present knowledge of the Great Basin and to ask new questions based on that knowledge." Topics include Great Basin ethnohistory, the manipulation of the environment as a factor in the area's cultural evolution, the work of anthropologists on Great Basin languages, linguistic studies among the Washo, the geographic underpinnings of desert culture, theoretical issues in Western prehistory, and tribal distributions and boundaries in the Great Basin. Comments by discussants address general issues as well as those of history, ecology and culture change, linguistics, prehistory, and tribal distribution. Bibliography. One figure, thirty-four maps.

Forbes, Jack D. *Nevada Indians Speak*. Reno: University of Nevada Press, 1967.

An anthology providing Native sources on the history of Indian-white relations in Nevada. The selections in part 1 deal with the first intensive contacts between Native Nevadans and whites during the early nineteenth century. Part 2 is concerned with the Anglo-Indian wars of the 1860's and 1870's and the immediate aftermath of white conquest. Parts 3 and 4 cover Native responses to the deteriorating conditions of reservation life during the late nineteenth and early twentieth centuries, respectively. The collection closes with texts portraying the contemporary status of Indian affairs in Nevada. Black-and-white photographs.

Fowler, Catherine S. *Great Basin Anthropology: A Bibliography*. Desert Research Institute, Social Science and Humanities Publications 5. Reno, Nev.: Publications Office of the Desert Research Institute, 1969.

A listing of more than 6,500 materials pertaining to the history and culture of Great Basin Indians. The entries are divided among the following categories: introduction to the Great Basin, archaeology, ethnohistory, anthropology, and federal and state documents. Numerous subheadings are used to further organize the items falling within each major category. An appendix of federal and state documents concludes the book. Five maps.

Stewart, Omer C. *Indians of the Great Basin: A Critical Bibliography*. Newberry Library Center for the History of the American Indian Bibliographical Series. Bloomington: Indiana University Press, 1982.

A bibliographical essay that reviews 364 articles and books pertaining to the

Indian peoples of the Great Basin. The essay is divided into the following subheadings: prehistory; ethnology, with separate sections for the Utes, Southern Paiutes, Shoshonis, Northern Paiutes, and Washos; linguistics; petroglyphs and pictographs; historical sources; and miscellaneous publications. Lists of recommended works for the beginner and for a basic library collection. Three maps.

Thomas, David H., ed. *A Great Basin Shoshonean Source Book.* New York: Garland, 1986.

An anthology of eighteen papers and monographs written between 1869 and 1974 on the Shoshonean peoples of the Great Basin. An introduction summarizes the essential themes of each essay. The papers are organized according to the following subheadings: ethnohistory, primary ethnography, Shoshonean origins, and aboriginal Great Basin social organization. Among the scholars represented are Stephen Powers, Robert H. Lowie, Julian H. Steward, Elman Service, Don Fowler, Catherine Fowler, and David Hurst Thomas. A bibliography of sources precedes the introduction.

Archaeology

Bedwell, Stephen F. *Fort Rock Basin: Prehistory and Environment.* Eugene: University of Oregon Press, 1973.

Examines changes in prehistoric environment and material culture found at Fort Rock Basin, an ancient Pleistocene lake, now extinct, in the extreme northern part of the northern Great Basin. Among the study's conclusions are that the basin has been the site of human occupation for more than 13,000 years; the basin was subject to increasing aridity between 13,000 and 3,000 years ago, which greatly affected the human habitat; and the primary change in the cultural inventory occurred between 8,000 and 7,000 B.P. with the introduction of new projectile points and flaking techniques. Bibliography. Black-and-white photographs and drawings. Maps.

Jennings, Jesse D. *Danger Cave.* University of Utah, Department of Anthropology, Anthropological Papers 27. Salt Lake City: University of Utah Press, 1957.

Records the findings from a series of excavations at Danger Cave and other sites in western Utah. Begins with a summary of regional and local environmental conditions, then provides a narrative of Great Basin cultural prehistory. Following are site reports for Raven, Juke Box, and Danger Caves; a consideration of geological and climatic events important for evaluating the data recovered at the sites; and a discussion of material culture. Argues that the findings support the use of "Desert culture" as a "convenient label for a long stable lifeway and as a means of calling attention to the age, stability and similarity of the Basin pattern." Bibliography. Black-and-white photographs and drawings. One map, tables, and charts.

Madsen, David B., and James F. O'Connell, eds. *Man and Environment in the Great Basin.* Society for American Archaeology Papers 2. Washington, D.C.: Society for American Archaeology, 1982.

A collection of thirteen papers that treat various topics in the archaeology of Great Basin environment and human ecology. The papers are organized under four broad subject areas: environmental prehistory, the span and nature of human occupation of the Great Basin, patterns of subsistence and settlement, and the identification of the region's archaeological cultures. Black-and-white photographs and drawings. Bibliographies accompany the essays.

O'Connell, James F. *The Prehistory of Surprise Valley*. Ramona, Calif.: Ballena Press, 1975.

Presents evidence pertinent to the primary controversy surrounding the prehistoric ecology of the Great Basin: whether the human-environment relationships throughout this region have remained essentially unchanged for nearly 10,000 years, or whether these relationships have varied greatly in different subregions and through time due to climatic and environmental factors. Begins with a brief introduction to the monograph's research problem and the methodology. Summarizes Great Basin biotic communities, subsistence resources, and prehistoric environmental change. Following are discussions of principal archaeological investigations, prehistoric subsistence and settlement patterns, and spatial diversity in Great Basin human ecology. Bibliography.

Folklore, Sacred Narrative, Religious Belief and Practice

Downs, James F. *Washo Religion*. University of California Publications, Anthropological Records, vol. 16, no 9. Berkeley: University of California Press, 1961.

A description of the religious beliefs and practices of Washo Indians living in selected communities in California and Nevada. The first section is concerned with figures appearing in Washo mythology, including water babies, giants, coyotes, and other figures. Section 2 examines curing and shamanism. Related topics touched on in this section include the spectacular though noncurative displays of Indian doctors to impress their patients, divining and rainmaking, sorcery and witchcraft, and war power. In section 3 the place of dreams and dreamers is discussed. Section 4 describes the ritual aspects of conception and contraception, birth, puberty for girls and boys, marriage, and death. Ritual in subsistence is the subject of section 5. Concludes with comments on miscellaneous ritual and the influence of Christianity on Washo life. Bibliography.

Jorgensen, Joseph G. *The Sun Dance Religion: Power for the Powerless*. Chicago: University of Chicago Press. 1972.

A discussion of the Sun Dance religion of the Shoshones and Utes of the central Rocky Mountains and Great Basin areas. Provides comparative analyses of the political and economic factors that possibly gave rise to the Sun Dance among the Wind River Shoshones in 1890 and its subsequent diffusion to other Shoshone groups and Utes; the modern Sun Dance religion; and the Sun Dance community as an interreservation phenomenon. The author argues that four factors help to explain the origins and persistence of Shoshone and Ute Sun Dance: "1) the *deprivation* (not relative) these people have suffered since the beginning of reservation times; 2) . . . the political-economic machinery that has been a major cause of this deprivation; 3) . . . the sheer beauty of the Sun dance religion itself; and 4) . . . the religious experiences the Sun Dance provides for adherents." (The last two are causal effects.) Appendix. Bibliography. Black-and-white photographs. Maps.

Kelly, Isabel T. *Southern Paiute Shamanism.* University of California Publications, Anthropological Records, vol. 2, no. 4. Berkeley: University of California Press, 1938-1940.

An investigation of shamanistic beliefs and practices in seven Southern Paiute bands. The shamanistic features common to these groups are: the presence of both male and female shamans; the derivation of powers from unsolicited dreams in which a spirit (usually an animal) communicates songs and instructions for curing; that shamans alone have guardian spirits; that powers, songs, and shamanistic office tend not to be inherited; that sickness is usually attributed to the intrusion of material objects and ghosts which the shaman cures by song sucking (on rarer occasions when disease is explained by soul loss, the shaman pursues and restores the wandering soul); the distinction drawn between the rattlesnake shaman and the general practitioner; and that weather control and the location of lost objects, while shamanistic functions, appear sporadically and are not stressed.

Laird, Carobeth. *Mirror and Pattern: George Laird's World of Chemehuevi Mythology.* Banning, Calif.: Malki Museum Press, 1984.

A collection and analysis of Chemehuevi myths that, according to the author, "were the pattern and are for us the mirror of a culture which has perished from the earth." Part 1 presents a candid portrait of the author's scientific and personal relationship with Chemehuevi informant George Laird. Part 2 discusses selected themes, styles, and personages of Chemehuevi myths and their relationship to the tribe's culture. Part 3 contains thirty-eight myths, many of which are coyote tales. Part 4 presents seven interpretive essays on central elements of Chemehuevi narratives. Two appendices. Pen-and-ink drawings.

Siskin, Edgar E. *Washo Shamans and Peyotists: Religious Conflict in an American Indian Tribe.* Salt Lake City: University of Utah Press, 1983.

Focuses on the emergence of Washo peyotism in 1936 and the subsequent conflicts that arose between the adherents of that religion and the followers of traditional shamanism. Begins with a sketch of Washo culture. Chapter 2 reviews the nature of Washo shamanism, describing in turn the Washo worldview and the shaman, spirits, the acquisition of power, ceremonial paraphernalia, dance house ceremonies, the nature of disease, the curing ceremony, feats of supernatural process by shamans, specializations among shamans, and the social status of the Washo shaman. Chapter 3 examines the relation of Washo shamanism with the religious beliefs and practices of Indian peoples in other areas. Chapters open with brief discussions of the history of the peyote cult, the Washo peyote ritual, and a comparison of Washo peyotism and the Plains rite. It then recounts the introduction of peyote to the Washo, the divisive influence of that introduction, and the reasons some people accepted while others rejected peyotism. In chapter 5 the conditions underlying peyotism's rapid and widespread acceptance among the Washo and its equally swift decline are set forth. An epilogue reviews Washo shamanism and peyotism since 1939. Argues that peyote "precipitated a crisis from which the old Washo religion never recovered. It was the critical factor contributing to the dissolution of shamanism." Bibliography. Black-and-white photographs and drawings.

Stewart, Omer C. *Washo-Northern Paiute Peyotism: A Study in Acculturation.* University of California Publications in American Archaeology and Ethnology, vol. 40, no. 3. Berkeley: University of California Press, 1944.

Examines the history and status of the peyote religion among the Northern Paiute and Washo peoples of the Great Basin. An introductory section provides information on the peyote plant, the ideology of peyotism, and the Peyote Ceremony. The location of the Washo and Northern Paiute tribes and the author's research methods are next discussed. The body of the work concerns the introduction and spread of peyotism among the two groups, a comparison of Washo-Northern Paiute peyotism with that of other tribes, the social relations among fellow religionists and between adherents and opponents of the religion, and a theoretical analysis of the diffusion of Washo-Northern Paiute peyotism. Four appendices: a description of the Washo-Northern Paiute peyote ritual, peyote element distribution list, statistical data, and peyotists and their relatives. Bibliography. Black-and-white plates. Two maps.

Whiting, Beatrice B. *Paiute Sorcery.* Viking Fund Publications in Anthropology 15. New York: Viking Fund, 1950.

Seeks to describe and analyze the manner in which social control operates among the Harney Valley Paiutes; develop hypotheses regarding correlations between certain conditions and types of social control; and test these hypotheses cross-culturally. Finds that within Paiute society retaliation, in the form of direct physical violence or sorcery, is the essential mechanism for maintaining social control. Sees a functional relationship in Paiute society between sorcery and so-called coordinate social control, "the essential characteristics of which are the absence of an individual or group of individuals with delegated authority to settle disputes and punish offenses and the presence of retaliation administered by peers as the major mechanism for social control." Cross-cultural analysis finds a high correlation between the importance of sorcery and coordinate control. Bibliography. One map and four tables.

Subsistence and Land Use

Fowler, Don D., ed. *Great Basin Cultural Ecology: A Symposium.* Desert Research Institute Publications in the Social Sciences 8. Reno, Nev.: Publications Office of the Desert Research Institute, 1972.

An anthology of papers and comments exploring theoretical, methodological, and substantive aspects of Great Basin cultural ecology drawn from the Great Basin Anthropological Conference, 1972. The essays are organized around the three procedures of cultural ecology as outlined by Julian Steward. First, the interrelationship of exploitative or productive technology must be analyzed; second, the behavior patterns involved in exploitation of an area by a particular technology must be examined; and finally, the extent to which behavior patterns entailed in exploiting the environment affect other aspects of the culture must be determined.

Sutton, Mark Q. *Insects as Food: Aboriginal Entomophagy in the Great Basin.* Menlo Park, Calif.: Ballena Press, 1988.

Examines the use of insects for food (entomophagy) by Indians of the Great Basin. Chapters present the description and ecology of various insects as well as ethnographic and archaeological data on their consumption. Concludes that "insects probably constituted a major rather than a minor resource in the Great Basin . . . [and] were fully integrated into the various economies of the aboriginal Great Basin." Bibliography. Black-and-white diagrams. Maps.

Turner, Allen C. *The Kaibab Paiute: An Ecological History.* New Haven, Conn.: Human Relations Area Files Press, 1985.

Examines the strategies Kaibab Paiute have employed to adapt to the radical changes in their natural and social environments brought on by white occupation of the Great Basin. Part 1 provides a brief ethnographic overview of the tribe. Part 2 discusses various aspects of Kaibab ecology and economy as they existed before white contact. Part 3 traces the changes in the group's society and culture which resulted from white colonization. Part 4 summarizes the key features of Kaibab responses to reservation life. Contends that the Kaibab have "changed within a Southern Paiute pattern and despite superficial appearances to the contrary, [they] maintain continuity with a tradition based on a millennium of successful use of material, social, and symbolic resources." Bibliography. Tables.

Wheat, Margaret. *Survival Arts of the Primitive Paiutes.* Reno: University of Nevada Press, 1967.

A brief discussion of traditional modes of Paiute subsistence. Part 1 provides an overview of the annual round of subsistence activities. Part 2 discusses the effects of white contact on the Paiute and their lifeways. Part 3 presents in photographs and text the survival arts of the tribe, including the harvesting of pine nuts; fishing and making harpoons; the use of arrows and deadfalls; building houses; the fabrication of articles from rabbit pelts, buckskin, bark, soft fibers, and willow; making a duck decoy, cradle boards, and cordage. Black-and-white photographs. Glossary.

Family and Society

Houghton, Ruth M., ed. *Native American Politics: Power Relationships in the Western Great Basin Today.* Reno: Bureau of Government Research, University of Nevada, 1973.

Papers and comments by political scientists and anthropologists from a symposium on contemporary Great Basin political life held at the Great Basin Anthropological Conference, 1972. Topics include the development of political power in the Southern Paiute communities of Kaibab and Cedar City; channels of political expression among the Western Shoshone-Goshute; the factionalism in a Northern Paiute tribe caused by the Indian Reorganization Act; the relationship of reservation politics and the Office of Economic Opportunity community development, 1965-1971; the nature of Bureau of Indian Affairs presence on Indian reservations; a case study of political resources made available through the Wheeler-Howard Act; and Nevada law and the Indians. Four panelists offer comments on the papers.

Knack, Martha. *Life Is with People*. Socorro, N. Mex.: Ballena Press, 1980.

A social analysis of the contemporary Paiute community of Utah focusing on the extended family household and interhousehold networks between particular sets of kinsmen. Argues that such extended family structures are not merely a cultural survival, but "continue to exist precisely because they aid, rather than interfere with, Paiute survival in their difficult contemporary social and economic environment." Bibliography. Tables.

Steward, Julian H. *Basin-Plateau Aboriginal Sociopolitical Groups*. Bureau of American Ethnology, Bulletin 120. Washington, D.C.: U.S. Government Printing Office, 1938.

Seeks to identify Shoshonean sociopolitical groups and their ecological and social determinants. Finds that the subsistence habits required for each region of the Basin-Plateau area largely determined the size, nature, and permanency of population units. "Among the Western Shoshoni, and many of their Northern and Southern Paiute neighbors it was physically impossible for families either to remain in one place for any considerable time or for more than a few families to remain in permanent association . . . [while other] ecological factors permitted the growth of more complex sociopolitical forms in certain parts of the Basin-Plateau area." Seven appendices. Bibliography. Maps and tables.

Stewart, Omer C. *The Northern Paiute Bands*. University of California Publications, Anthropological Records, vol. 2, no. 3. Berkeley: University of California Press, 1938-1940.

Attempts to locate accurately the boundaries of the Northern Paiute tribe; discern the subdivisions of that people at the time of white contact, circa 1850; and demonstrate the number, size, and political organization of these subdivisions. Provides information on twenty-one Northern Paiute bands. Argues that the Northern Paiute pictured exact boundaries between themselves and surrounding tribes while interband divisions were often vague and indefinite and that the fact that the bands occupied a single physiographic province, spoke similar dialects of one linguistic family, and possessed cultures and traditions in common signifies their tribal unity.

Material Culture and the Arts

Densmore, Frances. *Northern Ute Music*. Bureau of American Ethnology, Bulletin 75. Washington, D.C.: U.S. Government Printing Office, 1922.

A study of songs recorded among the White River, Uinta, and Uncompahgre bands of Ute during the second decade of the twentieth century. The introductory section first identifies and briefly characterizes the author's singer-informants. Subsequent sections include a glossary of Ute words; an ethnographic overview of the tribe, including some general comments on Ute songs and musical instruments; and a tabulated, melodic comparison of Ute, Chippewa, and Sioux songs. The body of the book contains transcriptions and ethnological and musicological analyses of selected Ute ceremonial and social songs, including Sun Dance songs, songs connected with doctoring, parade songs, and Hand Game songs. One appendix. Black-and-white photographs and diagrams.

Heizer, Robert F., and Martin A. Baumhoff. *Prehistoric Rock Art of Nevada and Eastern California*. Berkeley: University of California Press, 1962.

Provides a description and analysis of Great Basin petroglyphs. The study was undertaken in two phases. The initial, historiographic phase, sought first to record and collate data from as many Nevada petroglyph sites as possible in order to isolate significant stylistic distinctions; next, to place these styles in a relative time sequence; then, to record the distribution of petroglyph elements and styles; and finally to extract historical inferences from this distribution. Phase 2 tested the thesis "that most Nevada petroglyphs have 'meaning' in terms of one of the hunting patterns of the prehistoric inhabitants of the state." Seven appendices. Bibliography. Black-and-white photographs and drawings. Maps and tables.

Tribal Life

Barrett, S. A. *The Washo Indians*. Public Museum of the City of Milwaukee, vol. 2, no. 1. Milwaukee: Milwaukee Public Museum, 1917.

A brief study of the Washo Indians which stresses their strong cultural affinities with neighboring peoples of the California and Great Basin areas. Sections on the environment; social organization; social customs; material culture including houses, various foods and their preparation, and implements of stone and wood; and the materials, techniques, and decorations used by Washo basket makers. Black-and-white photographs and drawings. One map.

Bunte, Pamela A., and Robert J. Franklin. *From the Sands to the Mountain: Change and Persistence in a Southern Paiute Community*. Lincoln: University of Nebraska Press, 1987.

Provides a sociopolitical history and ethnography of the San Juan Southern Paiute tribe. Focus is on "the connection between the political and social processes at work in a modern Southern Paiute community and this community's social, economic, and political history." Chapter 1 first places the historic experiences and sociocultural background of the San Juan tribe within the wider arena of Southern Paiute history and lifeways. It then reexamines theories of political organization that have been applied to Great Basin peoples and presents a new perspective that the authors believe better interprets the available data. Chapters 2, 3, and 4 examine persistence and change in the social, economic, and political institutions of the San Juans, concentrating on both the internal and external forces underlying these processes. Chapters 5, 6, and 7 describe the present situation of the San Juans and the strategies and forces shaping community planning. Three appendices: "Guide to Southern Paiute Orthography and Pronunciation"; "Southern Paiute/Ute Kinship Terminologies"; and "Residential Groupings and Resource Use by Household Among the Ethnographic Study Group, Summer 1983." Four maps.

Conetah, Fred A. *A History of the Northern Ute People*, edited by Kathryn L. MacKay and Floyd A. O'Neil. Fort Duchesne, Utah: Uintah-Ouray Ute Tribe, 1982.

Traces Northern Ute history from prehistoric times to 1960. Begins with an overview of Ute religion and society. Next describes the traditional distribution of Ute bands and their modes of subsistence. The succession of white intruders, from the sixteenth through the nineteenth centuries, is the subject of the following chapter. Subsequent discussions describe the shameful history of the federal government's negotiations and unfulfilled agreements with the Ute people; the travels of Ute delegations to Washington to protest the steady alienation of their lands; the effects of interactions with Euro-Americans on the Uintah, White River, and Uncompahgre Ute peoples; the trials and adjustments of the Ute from 1882 to 1933; and the changes in tribal life since the Indian Reorganization Act of 1934. Twenty-six black-and-white photographs. Ten maps.

D'Azevedo, Warren L., ed. and comp. *The Washo Indians of California and Nevada*. University of Utah Anthropological Papers 67. Salt Lake City: University of Utah Press, 1963.

An anthology of ten papers and an annotated bibliography on the Washo Indians of the western Great Basin. An editor's introduction provides a brief overview of the history of Washo studies. The topics of the remaining articles include a reconstruction of aboriginal Washo social organization, the persistence of the tribe's traditional ceremonies, Washo beliefs concerning supernatural power and ghosts, Washo witchcraft, social factors contributing to hypertension among tribal members, Washo prehistory, selected aspects of the Washo life cycle, the different responses of Paiutes and Washo to white contact, and the Washos' lack of enthusiasm for animal husbandry. One map. Tables and charts.

Downs, James F. *The Two Worlds of the Washo*. New York: Holt, Rinehart and Winston, 1966.

Combines fieldwork, the testimony of tribal elders, and materials found in historical and ethnographic documents to describe how the Washo Indians of western Nevada have managed to adjust to a century of radical changes without losing their cultural identity. First presents a description of the Washo's traditional local, physical appearance, and language. The next three chapters examine traditional modes of Washo subsistence, social structure, and basic concepts and figures of religious life. The remaining chapters describe how acculturative forces operating between the early nineteenth and twentieth centuries all but erased the outward signs of Washo culture. The author insists, however, that while the "physical, economic, and social changes have been almost complete [the] mental and ideological changes have been less extreme and constitute the core of Washo existence today." Thus, the Washo live in two worlds. Bibliographies of references used and recommended reading. Black-and-white photographs. One map.

Euler, Robert C. *The Paiute People*. Phoenix: Indian Tribal Series, 1972.

An introduction to the history and contemporary life of the Southern Paiute. Begins with a reconstruction of the tribe's prehistory based on archaeological and linguistic evidence. The sections that follow are largely devoted to tracing the history of Southern Paiute-white contacts, including the incursions of Spanish and Anglo explorers, Mormon missionaries, and Mormon and non-Mormon settlers. Focus is placed on the deculturation of the Southern Paiute which resulted from these contacts. The book concludes with sections on the tribe's recent history, present situation, and prospects for the future. Bibliography. Sixteen black-and-white and color photographs. Four maps.

__________. *Southern Paiute Ethnohistory*. Salt Lake City: University of Utah Press, 1966.

Uses eighteenth and nineteenth century reports by travelers, explorers, trappers, and settlers on the Southern Paiute to discern something of the nature of the tribe's contact with whites and its subsequent acculturation. Argues that through 1830, there is "but little documentation indicative of acculturation," and between 1831 and 1848, the annual caravans moving through Southern Paiute territory and slaving expeditions from New Mexico and California probably had considerable effect on the tribe's culture. Increased cross-cultural stress led to periodic hostilities and a new plant domesticate, beans, was probably introduced during this period. Mormon missionization and colonization beginning in 1852 initiated a second period of marked cultural and material change. By the first decade of the twentieth century, the transculturation/deculturation of Southern Paiute culture was virtually complete. Includes a section, "Environmental Setting and Natural Resources," by Catherine Sweeny Fowler. Two appendices: Frederick S. Dellenbaugh's notes on Hiller's Southern Paiute photographs; "The Pai Ute," and extract from Frederick S. Dellenbaugh's, "The Past and Present of the Basin of the Colorado." Bibliography. Black-and-white photographs, maps, tables.

Harnar, Nellie Shaw. *Indians of Coo-yu-ee-Pah (Pyramid Lake)*. Sparks, Nev.: Davis Printing and Publishing, 1974.

A culture history of the Kuyui Dokado, a Northern Paiute band living in the Pyramid Lake vicinity of western Nevada. The first two chapters briefly discuss the location of various groups of Northern Paiute and the cultural background of Kuyui Dokado. Chapters 3 through 7 overview the history of the band's relations with whites, from the early nineteenth century to 1959. The final three chapters track the drastic changes in traditional lifeways that have resulted during the course of this history. Included in the discussion are biographical sketches of seven Pyramid Lake leaders and how they helped their people meet the challenges of the times. Bibliography. Black-and-white photographs. Maps.

Intertribal Council of Nevada. *NEWE: A Western Shoshone History*. Reno: Intertribal Council of Nevada, 1976.

A history of the Western Shoshone (Newe) based on the testimony of tribal elders as well as documentary and secondary sources. Chapter 1 sets forth the patterns of traditional Newe society and culture. The next two chapters tell of the successive invasions of trappers, "Forty-Niners," Mormons, and government agents during the first half of the nineteenth century and the struggle of the Newe to maintain their traditions in the face of increasing white settlement, military confrontations, and federal pressures to relocate them on reservations. The remaining narrative describes Newe life during the reservation era. A conclusion argues that despite a century and a half of massive changes at the hands of a foreign culture, "the Shoshone have preserved much of their culture, and they look to its wisdom to provide direction for their future." Two appendices: "The Treaty of 1855" and "The Treaty of 1863." Bibliography. Black-and-white photographs and drawing. Seven maps.

___________. *NUMA: A Northern Paiute History*. Reno: Intertribal Council of Nevada, 1976.

A brief history of the Numa or Northern Paiute. The first chapter describes aspects of Northern Paiute society and culture before the coming of whites. The second and third chapters recount how the ever- increasing settlement of Euro-Americans on Numa lands during the nineteenth century eventually resulted in the Pyramid Lake War of 1860. The final chapters describe the relocation of Northern Paiute on reservations and the establishment of colonies for tribal members forced to leave the reservations to provide for their families. Focus is given to the problems that resulted from these nontraditional forms of life and to the attempts of modern Numa to address such issues as land and water rights. Bibliography. Black-and-white drawings and photographs. Eight maps.

___________. *NUWUVI: A Southern Paiute History*. Reno: Intertribal Council of Nevada, 1976.

A history of the Southern Paiute (Nuwuvi) told from that people's point of view. The first chapter is primarily concerned with traditional modes of Southern Paiute subsistence. The following four chapters briefly describe the tribe's encounter with successive waves of white invaders during the eighteenth and nineteenth centuries. The establishment of and life on the reservations of Moapa, Shivwits, Las Vegas, and Cedar City is the subject of the final chapter. Each chapter begins with a selection from Southern Paiute oral tradition, including accounts of how corn came to earth, the tribe's acquisition of pine nuts, the origin of the echo, and the great flood. Two appendices: chronology and land claims. Bibliography. Black-and-white photographs. Four maps.

___________. *WA SHE SHU: A Washo Tribal History*. Reno: Intertribal Council of Nevada, 1976.

Uses interviews with knowledgeable tribal members, primary documents, and secondary materials to reconstruct the history of the Washo (Wa she shu) people. Begins with a description of precontact Washo life, including their traditional modes of subsistence, kinship, ceremonial life, and oral traditions. The two chapters that follow document the devastating effects of white intrusions and domination during the nineteenth century on Washo lands and culture. The concluding chapter briefly overviews the history of the Washo from the beginning of the twentieth century to the mid-1970's. Bibliography. Black-and-white photographs. Four maps.

Johnson, Edward C. *Walker River Paiutes: A Tribal History*. Schurz, Nev.: Walker River Paiute Tribe, 1975.

An ethnohistory of the Paiute (Numa) peoples who lived around Walker Lake (Agai Pah), based on interviews with older members of the tribe and on letters and reports written by early white settlers, Indian agents, and newspaper journalists. Chapter 1 first describes precontact modes of Paiute subsistence, then presents one of the tribe's traditional accounts of its origins. The tensions arising in the early nineteenth century between the Northern Paiutes and an ever-increasing number of white immigrants is the subject of chapter 2. Chapter 3 describes the causes behind the Pyramid Lake War of 1860, the formation of the Walker River Indian Reservation in 1859, and the depletion of the area's scarce resources by miners, farmers, and ranchers. Subsequent chapters on Wovoka and the Ghost Dance (1860-1895); farming, water rights, and irrigation (1859-1902); the relation between officials of the Carson and Colorado Railroad Company and the Southern Paiute (1880-1900); changes in Southern Paiute life style (1870-1900); allotment of the Walker River Reservation and its opening for white settlement (1902-1909); life on the Walker River Agency (1909-1935); the ratification of the Indian Reorganization Act in 1937 and its effects on reservation life to 1974; sports and recreation (1889-1974); and reports on the Walker Lake Sea Serpent. Two appendices: "Walker River Tribal Leaders (1850-1974)" and "A Chronology of Events Affecting the Walker River People (1776-1974)." Black-and-white photographs.

Kelly, Isabel T. *Ethnography of the Surprise Valley Paiute*. University Publications in American Archaeology and Ethnology, vol. 31, no. 3. Berkeley: University of California Press, 1932.

A detailed discussion of the society and culture of the Paviotso, or Northern Paiute, whose traditional homelands encompassed the northeastern corner of California and adjacent sections of Oregon and Nevada along the western borders of the Great Basin. A brief description of the nature and scope of the tribe's territory is followed by sections on Paviotso place names, houses, dress and adornment, manufactures and industries, the use of dogs, transportation, trade, measurement systems for time and space, kinship, the life cycle, entertainments, political organization, diplomacy and warfare, and religious beliefs and practices. Bibliography. Black-and-white photographs and drawings. One map.

Knack, Martha, and Omer C. Stewart. *As Long as the River Shall Run: An Ethnohistory of Pyramid Lake Indian Reservation*. Berkeley: University of California Press. 1984.

Examines the tactics used by white miners, ranchers, and farmers to expropriate lands and resources belonging to the Northern Paiute of Pyramid Lake Reservation in northwestern Nevada. Chapter 1 describes the tribe's aboriginal adaptations to Great Basin climate and environment. Chapters 2 and 3 discuss the Paiute's first contacts with Anglos in the early nineteenth century, the sources of contention between the two populations, and the outbreak of conflict. Chapter 4 deals with the opening of Pyramid Lake Reservation in 1859 and government attempts to assimilate the Paiute. Subsequent chapters recount white encroachments on Paiute territory, waters, and wildlife to the present. Bibliography. Black-and-white photographs. Maps.

Laird, Carobeth. *The Chemehuevis*. Banning, Calif.: Malki Museum Press, 1976.

An ethnography of the Chemehuevi Indians of the southwestern Great Basin based primarily on the recollections of tribal member George Laird, the author's informant and husband. Presents information on the tribe's ancestry, aboriginal distribution, and organization; shamanism, religious beliefs, and ceremonies; kinship and personal relationships; concepts concerning the natural world; names for places, trails, and other tribes; and mythology. Two appendices. Glossary of Chemehuevi terms. Two maps.

Madsen, Brigham D. *The Bannock of Idaho*. Caldwell, Idaho: Caxton Printers, 1958.

Traces the history of the Bannock Indians, a branch of the Northern Paiute whose aboriginal homelands encompassed a large portion of the upper Great Basin. Chapter 1 provides a brief discussion of the tribe's aboriginal lifeways. Subsequent sections detail their participation in the early nineteenth century fur trade; responses to an ever-increasing white immigration during the 1840's and 1850's; relations with the Mormons of the Lehmi River valley; wars and treaties with the U.S. government; their removal to the Fort Hall Reservation in southeastern Idaho; and the additional land cessions and allotments demanded of them in the late nineteenth century. Bibliography. Black-and-white drawings and one color painting by M. D. Stewart.

Park, Willard Z. *Willard Z. Park's Ethnographic Notes on the Northern Paiute of Western Nevada, 1933-1944*. Vol. 1, compiled and edited by Catherine S. Fowler. University of Utah Anthropological Papers 114. Salt Lake City: University of Utah Press, 1989.

A collection of previously unpublished materials on the Northern Paiute by ethnographer Willard Z. Park. An introduction reviews Park's ethnographic career. The bulk of the collection deals with Northern Paiute subsistence modes and material culture. Contains additional data on territory and intergroup relationships, houses, clothing and adornment, transportation, dogs and horses, medicines, and political organization. One appendix. Bibliography of references cited. Black-and-white photographs and drawings. Maps.

Smith, Anne M. *Ethnography of the Northern Utes*. Museum of New Mexico, Papers in Anthropology 17. Sante Fe: Museum of New Mexico Press, 1974.
Describes the pre-reservation life of the Northern Ute "as pictured by informants who had participated in that life, or who remembered their parents' accounts." Topics covered included Ute origins, shelters, modes of subsistence, fire making, clothing and adornment, crafts and manufactures, the life cycle, shamanism and curing, peyote, the Sun Dance and other dances, games, war, trade, and mythology. Glossary of Northern Ute terms. Bibliography. Black-and-white photographs and drawings.

Steward, Julian H. *Ethnography of the Owens Valley Paiute*. University of California Publications in American Archaeology and Ethnology, vol. 33, no. 3. Berkeley: University of California Press, 1932.
A detailed study of the society and culture of the Owens Valley Paiute, the southernmost of Nevada's Northern Paiute peoples. Topics discussed are the distribution of Paiute bands; population; subsistence, including seed gathering, fishing, hunting, domesticated animals, and trade and transportation; material culture, including weapons, houses, pottery, the weaving of blankets and baskets, and clothing; musical instruments, songs, and dances; the life cycle of birth, childhood, puberty, marriage, death; names; kinship terms and usages; political organization; religious belief and practice, including shamanism and medicines; and mythology. Six appendices: place names and key to maps, passes and trails, vocabulary, botanical lore, archaeology, and genealogies. Black-and-white drawings, photographs, and maps.

Underhill, Ruth M. *The Northern Paiute Indians of California and Nevada*. Washington, D.C.: U.S. Department of the Interior, Bureau of Indian Affairs, 1940.
A brief ethnography and history of the Northern Paiute living in California and Nevada. An introductory chapter rapidly defines the tribe's geographical setting and ethnolinguistic affiliations. Subsequent chapters furnish information on patterns of subsistence, clothing, housing, social and political organization, systems of kinship and family life, religious belief and practice, and history of relationship with Euro-Americans. Black-and-white drawings.

Biography and Autobiography

Hopkins, Sarah Winnemucca. *Life Among the Piutes: Their Wrongs and Claims*. New York: G. P. Putnam's Sons, 1883.
Hopkins, daughter of the Paiute leader Winnemucca, presents an account of her life that is rich in details concerning the history and traditions of her people. In chapters 1 and 2 the author describes the first meeting between Paiutes and whites, occurring shortly after her birth in 1844, her childhood, family, and selected Paiute customs. Subsequent chapters treat U.S. relations with the Paiute, Yakima, and Bannock.

Intertribal Council of Nevada. *Life Stories of Our Native People: Shoshone, Paiute, Washo*. University of Utah Printing Service for the Intertribal Council of

Nevada, 1974.

A collection of thirty-seven biographical sketches of Shoshoni, Paiute, and Washo people who contributed to the development of the Great Basin. Among the subjects are Gumalanga, a Washo leader of the late nineteenth century; Wovoka, the Northern Paiute holy man from whose vision stemmed the Ghost Dance Movement; and the Winnemuccas, a family of Northern Paiutes of many accomplishments. Blue-toned photographs.

Scott, Lalla. *Karnee: A Paiute Narrative*. Reno: University of Nevada Press, 1966.

The autobiography of Annie Lowry (1867-1943), a mixed-blood Paiute. In addition to recounting the major events in her life, the subject provides information on Paiute history and culture. A major theme of the narrative is the marginal position occupied by mixed bloods. According to Lowry: "I am a half-breed. That means I live on the fringe of two races. My white friends think I am just a plain old Paiute, while the Indians say I think I am better than they because my father was a white man. When the time came to make a choice between the Indian and the white race, I made up my mind to be an Indian. ... I know I was right to choose the Indians for my people because I loved them more. Anything Indian I learned quickly, but to the white teaching my mind was closed."

Steward, Julian H. *Two Paiute Autobiographies*. University of California Publications in American Archaeology and Ethnology, vol. 33, no. 5. Berkeley: University of California Press, 1934.

Presents two autobiographical narratives which the author recorded as part of his ethnographic study of the Owens Valley Paiute of eastern California during 1927 and 1928. The goal was to supply "subjective data indicating psychological attitudes and social values implicit in the culture." The two subjects, Sam Newland and Jack Stewart, reached maturity before the coming of the white man into Owens Valley in 1861. Their stories reveal extraordinary differences of personality and cultural achievement.

Plains

General Studies and References

Albers, Patricia, and Beatrice Medicine. *The Hidden Half: Studies in Plains Indian Women*. Lanham, Md.: University Press of America, 1983.

A collection of ten papers concerned with research and analyses on Plains Indian women. Aims to review and assess received tradition concerning the status and role of Plains Indian women and to reconsider the position of these women in light of recent strides in anthropology and women's studies. The papers are organized under the following four topics: images of women, women's work, the status of women, and female identity. A bibliography accompanies each essay.

Bataille, Gretchen M., et al., eds. *The Worlds Between Two Rivers: Perspectives on American Indians in Iowa.* Ames: Iowa State University Press, 1978.

An anthology of essays, primarily concerned with Native Americans in Iowa, which seeks to "provide some insights into an area where current and accurate materials are generally lacking." The first three chapters examine the distorted image of American Indians in literature, movies, and history texts. Chapters 4, 5, and 7 present aspects of Indian history and culture from the perspectives of an archaeologist and two members of the Mesquakie tribe. Chapter 6 reproduces some of Durran J. H. Ward's early twentieth century photographs of a Mesquakie Indian settlement. The next three chapters examine issues related to Indian urbanization and education. The final three essays are concerned with the past, present, and future status of Indian ethnicity in Iowa. Concludes with a selected bibliography of works on the American Indian in Iowa.

Blaine, Martha R. *The Pawnees: A Critical Bibliography.* Newberry Library Center for the History of the American Indian Bibliographical Series. Bloomington: Indiana University Press, 1980.

A bibliographical essay that reviews 274 books and articles pertaining to the history and culture of the Pawnees. The essay is subdivided by the following headings: the Spanish and French colonial period; after the Louisiana Purchase: explorers, U.S. military expeditions, treaty commissioners, and others; Pawnee military affairs: depredations and hostilities; traders and trappers; the promotion of civilization: missionaries, teachers, agents, and others; Pawnee and United States relationships; Pawnee history and ethnohistory: recollections; Pawnee archaeology; Pawnee culture studies, with separate sections for general works, sacred ceremonies and rituals, Skidi Band social organization, marriage and kinship, traditions, myths, and legends, subsistence activities, the Pawnee language, Pawnee music, Pawnee crafts and construction, paintings of Pawnees, and paintings by Pawnees. Lists recommended works for the beginner and for a basic library. Two maps.

Cash, Joseph, and Herbert Hoover, eds. *To Be an Indian: An Oral History.* New York: Holt, Rinehart and Winston, 1971.

Presents transcriptions of interviews with Native Americans from Minnesota, North and South Dakota, Nebraska, Montana, Wyoming, and Idaho on Plains Indian history and culture. The testimonies contained in section 1 concern spiritual life and folklore. Those in section 2 deal with the years immediately following the forced confinement of Plains Indians on reservations during the late nineteenth century. Section 3 provides perspectives on John Collier's Indian Reorganization Act of 1934 and its consequences. In section 4, informants discuss termination, relocation, and other federal policies of the 1950's and 1960's.

Dempsey, Hugh A., and Lindsay Moir. *Bibliography of the Blackfoot.* Metuchen, N.J.: Scarecrow Press, 1989.

A partially annotated listing of nearly two thousand published materials on the three tribes that constitute the Blackfoot nation: the Blood, Blackfoot, and

Peigan. Entries are arranged alphabetically by author under the following subheadings: general, bibliographies, journals and newspapers, archaeology and anthropology, arts and artists, biography, education, fiction and poetry, fur trade, government relations, health, history, language, legends and folklore, literature—collections and stories, material culture, military police, missionaries, reservation affairs, rites and religion, social life and customs, travellers and explorers, treaties, and warfare. Author and general indexes.

Gilmore, Melvin R. *Prairie Smoke*. New York: Columbia University Press, 1929.
Seeks to introduce the non-Native American reader to the traditional life and lore of Plains and Prairie Indians. Among its subjects are Indian concepts of nature, life, and health, the socialization of children, the characteristics of village life, the sacred concepts of the circle and number four, Indian painting, modes of subsistence, trade, ideas concerning property, the importance of the pipe, personal names and naming, and traditional narratives concerned with four-footed tribes (animals) and tribes of the air (birds). Illustrated with black-and-white drawings by Louis Schellbach.

Herring, Joseph. *The Enduring Indians of Kansas: A Century and a Half of Acculturation*. Lawrence: University of Kansas Press, 1989.
Examines the various ways in which the Indian groups of Kansas experienced and responded to processes of acculturation and assimilation. Begins with a discussion of the Jacksonian policy of Indian removal and the resulting resettlement of many tribes from the east in Kansas. Subsequent chapters focus on the strategies of the Vermillion Kickapoo, Chippewas, Munsee Delawares, Prairie Potawatomis, and other peoples in resisting cession of their lands or becoming imitation white farmers. A concluding chapter brings up to the present "the Indians' enduring struggle to retain their Kansas lands and to hold on to their distinct and cherished tribal cultures."

Gregory, H. F., ed. *The Southern Caddo: An Anthology*. New York: Garland, 1986.
A collection of twenty-four essays written between 1806 and 1980 on the Caddo Indians. An introduction briefly overviews the history and present status of Caddoan studies. The papers are organized according to the following subheadings: ethnohistory, socioculture, linguistics, physical anthropology, archaeology, material culture and the arts, and overview. Among the outstanding scholars represented are George Dorsey, Alice Fletcher, Herbert Bolton, Alexander Lesser, Leslie Spier, Mildred Mott Wedel, and Helen Hornbeck Tanner. A bibliography of sources precedes the introduction.

Hoebel, E. Adamson. *The Plains Indians: A Critical Bibliography*. Newberry Library Center for the History of the American Indian Bibliographical Series. Bloomington: Indiana University Press, 1979.
A bibliographical essay that reviews 205 books and articles pertaining to Plains Indian history and culture. The essay is subdivided by the following headings: general introduction to the Plains Indians; the Plains area; prehistory; early historical contacts; and tribal cultures, with separate sections for village tribes

of the Missouri Basin: Mandan, Hidatsa, Arikara, Omaha, Osage, Ponca, Iowa, and Oto, Pawnee; and nomadic tribes: Arapaho, Cheyenne, Gros Ventre (Atsina), Crow, Teton Dakota (Lakota Sioux), Blackfoot (also Blackfeet, including Piegan), Assiniboin, Plains Cree, Kiowa, Kiowa-Apache, and Comanche. Lists recommended works for the beginner and for a basic library.

Hoover, Hebert T. *The Sioux: A Critical Bibliography*. Newberry Library Center for the History of the American Indian Bibliographical Series. Bloomington: Indiana University Press, 1979.

A bibliographical essay that reviews 213 books and articles pertaining to the history and culture of the Sioux. The essay is subdivided by the following headings: general histories, with sections for the tribes and special monographs; autobiographies and biographies, with subheadings for Sitting Bull, Crazy Horse, Red Cloud, and others; battles and wars, with categories for general accounts, Ash Hollow, and Spirit Lake (1862-65), the Great Sioux War of 1876, Wounded Knee 1973, and the Sioux and the United States government; observations and influences of non-Indian groups, including works on explorers and traders, Catholic missionaries, Congregational and Presbyterian missionaries, Episcopal missionaries, and captives; special Sioux groups; and culture, with sections on general studies, language, religion, legends, and other cultural material. Lists recommended books for the beginner and a basic library.

Iverson, Peter, ed. *The Plains Indians of the Twentieth Century*. Norman: University of Oklahoma Press, 1985.

An anthology of new and previously published essays that focuses on Plains Indian history of the present century. An introduction overviews the continuity and change in the lifeways of Indian peoples of the Plains. The editor observes that "one of the most remarkable features of the history of the modern Plains is that Indians have remained a part of it." In the chapters that follow, issues, events, and themes of central importance to the recent history of selected Plains peoples are discussed. Included are the adjustment made by the Kiowa and Apache to the opening of their reservations for homesteading in the early twentieth century; the significant reduction in the land base of Indians living on Oklahoma's Cheyenne-Arapaho Agencies; the relative success of Cheyenne River Sioux in maintaining their land base and adjusting to contemporary reservation life; the importance of the Winter's Doctrine for Indian water rights; Indian reactions to Collier's Indian New Deal; the effects of participation in World War II on Indian self-esteem and culture; the impact of the Pick-Sloan Plan on North and South Dakota Sioux; the operation of tribal government on the Wind River Reservation; tribal control over energy resources in Indian country; the distinctive status of Indian rights; and the central importance of tradition to the continuation of Cheyenne life. Sixteen black-and-white photographs. Two maps.

Johnson, Bryan R. *The Blackfeet: An Annotated Bibliography*. New York: Garland, 1988.

Annotated entries for nearly twelve hundred works on the Blackfeet Indians. A broad range of publication types is covered, including scientific monographs, popular novels, "coffee table" books, films, sound recordings, government documents, religious tracts, and manuscript collections. Entries are arranged alphabetically by author. Concludes with a list of significant manuscript collections.

Lowie, Robert H. *Indians of the Plains*. New York: McGraw-Hill, 1954.

The standard text on Plains Indian culture. Begins with brief observations on tribal sociology, politics, and precontact demographics. The chapters that follow treat characteristic features of the region's material culture, social organization, forms of recreation, and religious belief and ceremony. Concludes with discussions of Plains Indian prehistory, history, and acculturation. Illustrated with forty-four black-and-white drawings and thirty-six photographs. Includes suggestions for further reading.

Mails, Thomas. *Mystic Warriors of the Plains*. Garden City, N.Y.: Doubleday, 1972.

An overview of the Plains Indian peoples and cultures as they existed from the mid-eighteenth to mid-nineteenth century. Begins with a discussion of the origin, distribution, and nature of the people of the Plains. Subsequent chapters describe the daily life of the region's tribes, social customs, personal qualities and values, form of government, the beliefs and practices of Plains religious life, the paramount importance of the buffalo and the horse, artwork, clothing and modes of personal adornment, hunting and hunting gear, the birth and socialization of the boy, warfare, and the relocation of Indian tribes on reservations. Includes hundreds of sepia-toned and color illustrations by the author.

Marken, Jack W., and Herbert T. Hoover, comps. *Bibliography of the Sioux*. Metuchen, N.J.: Scarecrow Press, 1980.

A partially annotated listing of nearly 3500 important books and articles on the Sioux published through 1978. Subheadings include bibliographies; journals, newspapers, and special reports; appraisals and cessions; archaeology; arts and culture; autobiographies; Canadian Sioux; captivity literature; contemporary Sioux; education; fiction and other works; forts and military posts; fur traders and scouts; George A. Custer; history; illnesses and health care; Indian authors; judicial claims, laws, and treaties; language; leaders and heroes; literature—collections and stories; the Minnesota Sioux War; missionaries; religion; reservation affairs; settlers and agents; travelers and explorers; types of literature; warfare among tribes; wars of the East; wars of the West; Wounded Knee I and II; and theses and dissertations. Name and subject indexes.

Newcomb, W. W., Jr. *The Indians of Texas: From Prehistoric to Modern Times*. Austin: University of Texas Press, 1961.

A comprehensive, nontechnical overview of the Native American tribes that once inhabited the coasts and interior of the present state of Texas. Part 1 presents a somewhat dated summary of the state's prehistoric peoples. Parts 2, 3, and 4 reconstruct the aboriginal patterns of historic Indian cultures. They are arranged in an ascending order of technological productivity, concerning, respectively, gatherers of the western Gulf culture area, the nomadic tribes of the plains, and gardeners of Southwest, North, and East. A final chapter describes the decimation of these groups by European and American invaders. Bibliography. Black-and-white drawings. Maps.

Powell, Peter J. *The Cheyennes, Ma'heo'o's People: A Critical Bibliography*. Newberry Library Center for the History of the American Indian Bibliographical Series. Bloomington: Indiana University Press, 1980.

A bibliographical essay that reviews 241 books and essays pertaining to the history and culture of the Cheyenne people. The essay is subdivided by the following headings: primary sources; the holy traditions and holy ceremonies; the struggle to preserve the Cheyenne way; government: the Council of the Forty-four and the warrior societies; early villages and archaeology; language; art; major Christian mission work among the people; United States government and tribal relations; theses and dissertations; and epilogue. Lists recommended works for the beginner and for a basic library. Two maps.

Salzmann, Zdenek. *The Arapaho Indians: A Research Guide and Bibliography*. Westport, Conn.: Greenwood Press, 1988.

Lists more than 1350 publications, archival sources, and museum collections containing materials relevant to Arapaho history and culture. Part 1 provides a historical and ethnographic overview of the Arapaho people. Part 2 contains the bibliography itself, preceded by a guide to sources concerning the Arapaho Indians and an introduction and followed by a topical index. Part 3 cites information from reference guides to federal documents containing information on the Arapaho. Part 4 identifies archives and museums possessing significant collections pertaining to the Arapaho Indians.

Schneider, Mary Jane. *North Dakota Indians: An Introduction*. Dubuque, Iowa: Kendall/Hunt, 1986.

Seeks to present organized and reliable information on the history and cultures of Indians living in North Dakota. Includes discussions of Indian identity; tribal histories from both Indian and white perspectives; traditional Indian cultures of North Dakota; federal Indian policy and North Dakota Indians; North Dakota reservations; trends in Indian population and demography; reservation economies, resources, and economic development; reservation government and law; education; Indian health; and prospects for the future. Appendix: important dates in Indian-White relations. Bibliography. Black-and-white photographs. Maps and tables.

Svoboda, Joseph G., comp. *Guide to American Indian Resource Materials in Great Plains Repositories*. Lincoln: Center for Great Plains Studies, University of Nebraska, 1983.

Lists source materials on American Indians available in archives and other institutions of the Great Plains. Emphasis is placed on unpublished sources, including manuscript collections, diaries, correspondences and other records of various government agencies, photographs, mission records, taped interviews, newspapers, and magazines. The guide is first divided by state and province, with further divisions by city and then individual repository. Holdings for repositories are arranged under the following types: manuscript collection, photographs, government records, oral history, and newspaper.

Swanton, John R. *Source Material on the History and Ethnology of the Caddo Indians*. Bureau of American Ethnology, Bulletin 132. Washington, D.C.: U.S. Government Printing Office, 1942.

A collection of primary materials on the history and culture of the Caddo, a tribe whose traditional homeland lay within the boundaries of Arkansas, Louisiana, Texas, and Oklahoma. The bulk of the materials presented pertain to Caddo material culture; social institutions, organization, and behaviors; and religious beliefs and practices. Bibliography.

Tate, Michael L. *The Indians of Texas: An Annotated Research Bibliography*. Metuchen, N.J.: Scarecrow Press, 1986.

A listing of nearly 3800 entries, many of which are annotated, for materials on the history and culture of tribes either native to or associated with Texas. Subdivided into two books. The entries of book 1 concern the lifeways of various Indian peoples and are organized by tribe. Those in book 2 pertain to the history of Indian-white relations and are arranged by period. Name and subject indexes.

Unrau, William E. *The Emigrant Indians of Kansas: A Critical Bibliography*. Newberry Library Center for the History of the American Indian Bibliographical Series. Bloomington: Indiana University Press, 1979.

A bibliographical essay that reviews 187 books and articles pertaining to "the more than ten thousand native American who were forced to emigrate from the Old Northwest to the future Kansas in the decade and a half after 1830." The essay is divided by the following subheadings: historical setting and cultural identification; changing federal Indian policy; removal to the Kansas "desert"; conflict between federal land and Indian policies; tribal leadership and factional response; role of the missionaries; impact of malnutrition, disease, and alcohol; and expulsion from Kansas. Lists recommended works for the beginner and for a basic library collection.

Wedel, Waldo R., ed. *A Plains Archaeology Source Book: Selected Papers of the Nebraska Historical Society*. New York: Garland, 1985.

An anthology of five papers, written between 1935 and 1940, for the Nebraska Historical Society. An introduction briefly reviews the importance of this period for Plains archaeology. Concludes with the statement that the archaeology of the Plains "is substantially rooted in these five papers, no less than in later contributions by these and other workers and writers." Among the scholars represented are A. T. Hill, Paul Cooper, Marvin Kivett, George Metcalf, and Waldo Wedel.

Weist, Katherine M., and Susan R. Sharrock. *An Annotated Bibliography of Northern Plains Ethnohistory*. Missoula: Department of Anthropology, University of Montana, 1985.

A listing of more than seven hundred annotated entries intended to aid anthropologists, historians, Native Americans, and others researching the history of Indians living on the Northern Plains during the pre-reservation period (1690-1880) Seeks to include all primary documents essential for the beginning researcher. Entries contain three parts: the bibliographic citation, the annotation, and a description of other subjects mentioned in the document. Alphabetical arrangement of entries by author.

Wilson, Terry P. *Bibliography of the Osage*. Metuchen, N.J.: Scarecrow Press, 1985.

An annotated listing of more than seven hundred books, articles, theses, and dissertations on Osage history and culture. Items arranged alphabetically by author under the following subheadings: archaeology, anthropology, and culture; history before 1871; and history after 1871. An introductory essay overviews the major events and developments in Osage history. Author and subject indexes.

Wood, W. Raymond, and Margot Liberty, eds. *Anthropology on the Great Plains*. Lincoln: University of Nebraska Press, 1980.

An anthology of twenty-two essays by experts on the physical anthropology, archaeology, ethnology, and languages of Plains Indians. Among the topics treated are the influence of Plains ethnography on the development of anthropological theory, prehistoric studies on the Plains, a summary of Great Plains physical anthropology, a review of studies in Plains linguistics, ethnohistory and Plains area scholarship, the Sun Dance, the Ghost Dance, the Native American church, Plains Indian arts, music and dance of the Plains tribes, Plains Indian women, and research in Plains health and healing. Black-and-white photographs and drawings. Maps.

Wright, Muriel H. *A Guide to the Indian Tribes of Oklahoma*. Norman: University of Oklahoma Press, 1951.

A comprehensive guide containing compact and authentic accounts of all the Indian tribes and parts of tribes living in Oklahoma. The sixty-five tribes included are listed in alphabetical order. Discussion of each contains the following topics: names, present location, numbers, history, government and organization, contemporary life and culture, ceremonials and public dances, and suggested readings. Concludes with a complete list of suggested readings and bibliography. Black-and-white photographs.

Archaeology

Bell, Robert E., ed. *Prehistory of Oklahoma*. New York: Academic Press, 1984.

A collection of seventeen essays by experts on Oklahoma prehistory meant to serve as "a joint summary report on our current knowledge of the region." Begins with an overview of the state's environmental history, developments in Oklahoman archaeology, and important lithic resources and quarries. Most of the subsequent chapters present descriptive summaries of particular archaeological periods, phases, and cultural complexes within specified regions. These essays are arranged chronologically, from early Archaic (circa 19,000 B.P.) to Protohistoric (A.D. 1500-1750). Bibliography. Black-and-white photographs and diagrams. Tables and maps.

Frison, George. *Prehistoric Hunters of the High Plains*. New York: Academic Press, 1978.

A detailed cultural prehistory for that section of the northwestern Plains encompassing all of Wyoming, the drainage of the Yellowstone and Madison rivers in northern Wyoming and southern Montana, western South Dakota and Nebraska, the southwestern corner of North Dakota, and the northern border of Colorado. Introductory chapters describe the area's ecology and establish its cultural chronology. The topics of succeeding chapters include various archaeological sites, the prehistoric hunting of bison and lesser game, studies of animal populations in archaeological sites and their use in biological and cultural interpretation, prehistoric methods of butchering and processing kills, an analysis of prehistoric hunting equipment, and hunting and gathering subsistence strategies. Four appendices: "Archeology of the Northwestern Plains" (by John P. Albanese); "Mammoths (Mammuthus) from the Colby Site" (by Cary T. Madden); "Petroglyphs and Pictographs of the Northwestern Plains" (by George Frison); and "Human Skeletal Remains on the Northwestern Plains" (by George Frison). Bibliography. Black-and-white photographs and drawings; maps and tables.

McKusick, Marshall. *Men of Ancient Iowa*. Ames: Iowa State University Press, 1964.

Traces the prehistory of Iowa from 10,000 B.C. to the late sixteenth century. Chapter 1 identifies some general developments and turning points in North America's archaeological record. Chapter 2 discusses the various types of prehistoric sites found in Iowa. In chapter 3 the earliest evidence of the state's human occupation is presented. Subsequent chapters document the continuity and change in the lifeways of Iowa's prehistoric societies, from the Archaic period through various phases of the Woodland and Mississippian traditions. Concludes with a section on the displacement of Iowa Indians by Euro-American settlers. An appendix discusses radiocarbon dates from Iowa. Bibliography. Sepia-toned photographs and drawings. Maps.

Phillips, Philip, and James A. Brown. *Pre-Columbian Shell Engravings from the Craig Mound at Spiro, Oklahoma*. 6 vols. Cambridge, Mass.: Peabody Museum of Archaeology and Ethnology, Harvard University, 1978-1983.

A discussion of engraved shell specimens attributed to the so-called Southern Cult, a prehistoric ceremonial complex that developed during the late Mississippian period (circa A.D. 1200) and whose major sites are found from Georgia to Florida and central Illinois to Oklahoma. The first volume provides highly detailed discussions of the history of archaeological research at Spiro (Oklahoma) and patterns of style and symbol of artifacts unearthed at Craig Mound. The remaining volumes contain hundreds of black-and-white photographs with accompanying commentaries. Bibliography.

Wedel, Waldo R. *Central Plains Prehistory: Holocene Environments and Culture Change in the Republican River Basin.* Lincoln: University of Nebraska Press, 1986.

A summary of research and findings on the prehistoric peoples of the Republican Basin in the central Great Plains. Coverage extends from the waning of the Pleistocene (circa 15,000 B.C.) to the mid-nineteenth century. Focuses on the major cultural transformations that occurred during this period: "the slow progression from heavy dependence by early man on the specialized hunting of large game of species now mostly extinct, through a hunting-gathering or forager stage, to semisedentary maize-growing communities." Two appendices: "Republican Valley Indian Populations" and "Mammal, Bird, and Molluscan Remains Identified from Upper Republican Sites." Bibliography. Black-and-white photographs and drawings. Maps and tables.

__________. *An Introduction to Kansas Archeology.* Bureau of American Ethnology, Bulletin 174. Washington, D.C.: U.S. Government Printing Office, 1959.

Reports the findings of three archaeological surveys of Kansas sponsored by the National Museum in 1937, 1939, and 1940. Among the primary tasks of these field projects were to sample the archaeological materials in various sections of the state, identify the remains of historic tribal groups, assess the similarities and differences of artifacts and complexes with those of adjacent states, gather information on the manner in which inhabitants of different times and areas adjusted their lifeways to the natural environment, and to integrate the findings into a larger picture of Great Plains prehistory. Bibliography. Maps, tables, and diagrams.

__________. *Prehistoric Man on the Great Plains.* Norman: University of Oklahoma Press, 1961.

Sets two primary objectives: to review 10,000 years of human prehistory on the North American Great Plains and to present this prehistory in a manner that neither repels the nonspecialist nor sacrifices clarity and accuracy. An introductory chapter briefly describes the objectives and methods of archaeologists. Chapter 2 presents the primary environmental features of the Great Plains as they exist today and as they existed in the recent historic past. Chapters 3 through 8 discuss the first human groups to inhabit the area and the careers of prehistoric peoples in the Central Plains, Southern Plains, middle Missouri, the region's northeastern periphery, and the northwestern Plains. In the final chapter, the author disputes the thesis "that the Western Plains were largely an uninhabited tract before the introduction of the horse." Bibliography. Black-and-white photographs, drawings, and maps.

Zimmerman, Larry J. *Peoples of Prehistoric South Dakota.* Lincoln: University of Nebraska Press, 1985.

A brief summary of South Dakota prehistory. The first three chapters describe the aims and methods of archaeology and the history of archaeological research in the state. Chapters 3 through 6 sketch South Dakota's geography and people.

The body of the book provides an overview of the South Dakotan archaeological record, from the Archaic period to 1700. A conclusion discusses the prospects of future archaeological research in South Dakota.

Folklore, Sacred Narrative, Religious Belief and Practice

Beckwith, Martha W., comp. *Mandan-Hidatsa Myths and Ceremonies*. Memoirs of the American Folklore Society 32. New York: J. J. Augustin, 1938.

Contains nearly fifty traditional narratives collected between 1929 and 1932 from Hidatsa and Mandan informants living on the Fort Berthold reservation. An introductory essay briefly reviews the predominant themes of the texts. It then identifies the two forms of stories recognized by members of the tribes: holy stories and secular tales, including comic and hunting narratives. Many of the sacred stories explain the origins of ceremonies. Others concern Coyote, a trickster who holds an important and honorable place in the ceremonial lodge. Bibliography of references. Black-and-white photographs and diagrams.

Brown, Joseph E. *The Sacred Pipe: Black Elk's Account of the Seven Rites of the Oglala Sioux*. Norman: University of Oklahoma Press, 1953.

Black Elk, an Oglala holy man, discusses the origins, ceremonies, and meanings of the seven rituals of the Sioux. He begins by describing how long ago the White Buffalo Calf Woman brought the tribe its Sacred Pipe. Each of the subsequent chapters focuses on a particular rite: the keeping and releasing of the soul of a departed loved one; the Sweat Bath, a ritual of purification; the Vision Quest; the Sun Dance; the making of relatives; preparing a girl for womanhood after her first menstrual period; and Throwing-the-Ball, a ritual of blessing. Black-and-white photographs and drawings.

Catlin, George. *O-Kee-Pa: A Religious Ceremony; and Other Customs of the Mandans*. Philadelphia: J. B. Lippincott, 1867.

A first-hand account of Mandan religious life by artist-explorer George Catlin. Focuses on the ritual of O-Kee-Pa, celebrated annually to commemorate the "subsiding of the waters" of the Deluge; the Bull Dance, on whose correct performance depended the coming of the buffalos; and initiating boys who had come into adulthood. The author reports the beliefs and practices associated with each of these divisions. Accompanying this description are paintings of key personages or moments in the ceremony. Appendix.

DeMallie, Raymond, ed. *The Sixth Grandfather: Black Elk's Teachings Given to John G. Neihardt*. Lincoln: University of Nebraska Press, 1984.

Reproduces the transcripts of John Neihardt's 1931 and 1944 interviews with Sioux spiritual leader Black Elk which served as the bases of his two famous interpretations of Lakota religion, culture and history, *Black Elk Speaks* (1932) and *When the Tree Flowered* (1951). The present work seeks to aid those curious about Neihardt's role as Black Elk's amanuensis. Part 1 contains a biographical sketch of Black Elk. Parts 2 and 3 present the texts of the 1931 and 1944 interviews, respectively. Appendix A provides a concordance of material in the interviews and pages in *Black Elk Speaks* and *When the Tree Flowered*.

Appendix B is an orthography used for rewriting Lakota throughout the interviews. "With access to the source material, readers can now compare for themselves Neihardt's literary treatment with the full recording of the notes." Bibliography.

DeMallie, Raymond, and Douglas R. Parks, eds. *Sioux Indian Religion*. Norman: University of Oklahoma Press, 1987.

A collection of essays taken from talks given by Indian and white participants in a conference on Sioux religious life and history held at Bismarck, North Dakota, in 1982. Part 1, "Foundations of Traditional Sioux Religion," contains papers about Lakota (Teton Sioux) belief and ritual in the nineteenth century, an analysis of Lakota traditions of cosmogenesis, the importance of the Sacred Pipe in contemporary Sioux life, and historical and modern interpretations of the Lakota Sun Dance. Part 2 concerns Christianity and the Sioux, including essays on the impact of Episcopal and Catholic missionary work, the views of a Catholic priest on contemporary Indian mission, and a statement by a Lakota member of the Christian Life Fellowship church. Part 3, "Traditional Religion in the Contemporary Context," offers perspectives on the place of Indian women in the renaissance of traditional religion, contemporary *Yuwipi* ceremony, the Naive American Church of Jesus Christ, and tractional Lakota religion in modern life. Bibliography. Thirteen illustrations by Sioux artist Arthur Amiotte.

Dorsey, George A. *The Cheyenne*. Field Columbian Museum Anthropological Series, vol. 9, nos. 1 and 2. Chicago: The Museum, 1905.

An anthropological description of Southern Cheyenne religion based on data collected in the early twentieth century. Volume 1 discusses selected personnel, beliefs, and rituals associated with the tribe's ceremonial organization. Most prominent among these are the role of the Sacred Arrow Keeper and the ceremony of Renewing the Sacred Arrows. Volume 2 contains a highly detailed presentation of the Southern Cheyenne Sun Dance.

__________. *Traditions of the Skidi Pawnee*. Boston: Houghton, Mifflin, 1904.

A collection of oral narratives belonging to the Skidi subdivision of the Pawnee people. An introduction first presents an ethnographic overview of the tribe, including some discussion of Pawnee origins, earth lodges, warfare and hunting, dress, arts, social organization, and religious beliefs and practices. It then describes the system that the author has devised to organize the narratives. The headings of this system include cosmogenic (tales relating to origins, rituals, special ceremonies, and afterlife), boy heroes, medicine, animal tales, people marry animals or become animals, and miscellaneous. Black-and-white photographs.

Fletcher, Alice C. *The Hako: A Pawnee Ceremony*. Bureau of American Ethnology, Annual Report 22. (1900-1901). Washington, D.C.: U.S. Government Printing Office, 1904.

A highly detailed description and analysis of the Pawnee *Hako*, a ceremonial complex held to insure tribal strength, plenty, and peace. A series of introductory sections discuss the derivation of the term *Hako*, its key personnel, requisite instruments, timing, and structure. Subsequent chapters describe the numerous rituals that constitute the preparation and celebration of the ceremony. Included in these descriptions are transcriptions of ceremonial songs. Black-and-white photographs. Color plates.

Grinnell, George B. *By Cheyenne Campfires*. New Haven, Conn.: Yale University Press, 1926.

More than sixty narratives of the Cheyenne Indians which, in addition to "their inherent interest . . . have a direct relation to the early history of our country." An introduction briefly describes the traditional lifeways of the Cheyenne and the importance of stories and storytelling in their culture. The selected narratives are arranged under the following headings: war stories, stories of mystery, hero myths, earliest stories, culture hero stories, and Wihio (trickster) stories.

Harrod, Howard L. *Renewing the World: Plains Indian Religion and Morality*. Tucson: University of Arizona Press, 1987.

Examines the religious and moral traditions of tribes living on the northwestern Plains as they existed from about 1850 to the turn of the century. Argues that the primary symbolic forms that encode the fundamental meanings contained in oral traditions and enacted in ritual provide clues to the religious and moral beliefs and dispositions. Concludes that vision, the gift of power, and the normative importance of kinship "were elements that constituted central features of Plains social worlds, formed the horizons of moral and religious experience, and deeply motivated their actions." Bibliography. Black-and-white diagrams.

Kroeber, Alfred L. *Gros Ventres Myths and Tales*. American Museum of Natural History, Anthropological Papers, vol. 1, pt. 3. New York: The Trustees, 1907.

Presents a representative selection of Gros Ventre myths and tales, collected on the Fort Belknap Reservation in northern Montana during 1901. An introductory note compares and contrasts themes found in Gros Ventre, Arapaho, and other Plains Indian narratives. The English translations of fifty narratives are then presented. Concludes with abstracts of the texts.

Lowie, Robert H. *Myths and Traditions of the Crow Indians*. Anthropological Papers of the American Museum of Natural History, vol. 25, pt. 1. New York: Order of Trustees, 1918.

A selection of eighty-one narratives from Crow oral tradition. An introduction first discusses the characteristics that Crow narratives share with those of other Plains peoples and those features which set them apart. It next deduces from a statistical analysis of shared motifs the former historical contact of the Crow with the Hidatsa, Arikara, and Gros Ventre. The introduction closes with the categories the Crow used to classify their narratives. The author uses the following subheadings to arrange the selected stories: old-man-coyote cycle; hero tales; tales of supernatural patrons; miscellaneous tales; and historical traditions. Bibliography.

__________. *The Religion of the Crow Indians*. Anthropological Papers of the American Museum of Natural History, vol. 25, pt. 2. New York: Order of Trustees, 1918.

A description of Crow religious concepts and ceremonial activities. Begins with a discussion of Crow religious terms and supernatural beings. It next describes the importance of visions and dreams in the life of the Crow. The characteristics and functions of Crow shamanism are then examined. Subsequent chapters deal with the practice of medicine; souls, ghosts, and afterlife; special medicine objects, including medicine rocks, medicine bundles, painted tipis, shields, and other objects of a sacred nature; magic; offerings and prayers; taboos; and miscellaneous data. An appendix presents the sacred narrative of the Five Brothers. Black-and-white drawings.

Malan, Vernon D., and Clinton J. Jesser. *The Dakota Indian Religion*. Bulletin 473, Rural Sociology Department Agricultural Experiment Station. Brookings: South Dakota State College, 1959.

Seeks, first, to describe and analyze the differences in the value systems of Dakota Indian and Western civilization, and, second, to test the hypothesis that those residents of the Pine Ridge Dakota (Sioux) Reservation who experience conflicts between traditional Dakota and modern American values will tend to participate in marginal religious activities. Defines marginal religious activities as "any spiritual belief or practice which combines elements of traditional and Christian religions." Contends that such beliefs and practices have provided an accommodation to the experience of conflicting values. Appendices contain the questionnaire used in the study and its findings. Bibliography. Black-and-white photographs.

Marriott, Alice L., and Carol K. Rachlin. *Plains Indians Mythology*. New York: Thomas Y. Crowell, 1975.

A collection of thirty-one narratives selected from the oral traditions of various Plains Indian groups. The texts are organized under the following categories: mythology—accounts of the supernatural, superhuman beings who have become embodied in the universe; legendary—explanatory stories and accounts of men and women who actually lived but who have become larger than life; and folklore—literally the lore or wisdom of the folk. Among the oral literatures represented are those of the Brule Sioux, Pawnee, Osage, Kiowa, Cheyenne, Shoshoni, Crow, Comanche, Mescalero Apache, and Arapaho. An introduction and epilogue review the culture history and contemporary status of Plains Indians, respectively. Bibliography. Black-and-white photographs. One map.

Murie, James R. *Ceremonies of the Pawnee*. 2 parts, edited by Douglas R. Parks. 2 vols. Washington, D.C.: Smithsonian Institution Press, 1981.

A highly detailed monograph on Pawnee ceremonial and cultural life authored by a tribal member who spent most of his life among his people. Part 1 describes the annual cycle of ceremonies practiced among the Skiri, northernmost of the four Pawnee bands. Part 2 presents Murie's eyewitness account of three remaining rituals of the southern groups: the White Beaver Ceremony of the Chawi and the Bear and Buffalo Dances of the Pitahawirata. An editor's introduction provides background on the manuscript, an overview of Pawnee society, and a biography of James R. Murie. Two appendices contain a discussion by anthropologist Clark Wissler and notes on songs and their composers. Bibliography. Indexed by name and subject. Black-and-white photographs.

Parks, Douglas R., et al., eds. *Earth Lodge Tales from the Upper Missouri: Traditional Stories of the Arikara, Hidatsa, and Mandan*. Bismark, N.D.: Mary College, 1978.

A bilingual presentation of twenty-five traditional narratives from North Dakota's Three Affiliated Tribes: the Mandan, Arikara, and Hidatsa. Places the English text and the Native text on opposing pages in order for the reader to correlate elements in the two renditions. The narratives are arranged in sections according to their tribe of origin. Each section is preceded by a brief note that presents information on the assembled texts. Bibliography. Black-and-white drawings by David J. Ripley.

Powell, Peter J. *Sweet Medicine: The Continuing Role of the Sacred Arrows, the Sun Dance, and Sacred Buffalo Hat in Northern Cheyenne History*. 2 vols. Norman: University of Oklahoma Press, 1969.

An account of Cheyenne history, customs, and religion covering the period from the tribe's arrival on the Plains to the late 1960's. Based on the testimony of tribal members and the author's participant observation of Cheyenne life. Volume 1 offers a historical narrative of the Cheyenne focusing on the importance of sacred beliefs and rituals to an understanding of their life and identity. Volume 2 provides a detailed presentation of the contemporary Sacred Arrow and Sun Dance ceremonies. Bibliography. Black-and-white photographs and drawings. Color plates. Maps.

Powers, William K. *Yuwipi: Vision and Experience in Oglala Ritual*. Lincoln: University of Nebraska Press, 1982.

An account of the contemporary Sioux curing ritual of *yuwipi* and its relationship with the practices of sweat bath and vision quest. The author has arranged his description of the three rituals into a meaningful sequence in which the major elements, functions, and experiential qualities of each are portrayed. Bibliography.

Voget, Fred W. *The Shoshoni-Crow Sun Dance*. Norman: University of Oklahoma Press, 1984.

Examines the Crow Indians' adoption of the Wind River Shoshoni Sun Dance in 1941 and its subsequent integration into Crow reservation life. The first two chapters present a brief history of the Crows and an extended description of their traditional culture and society. In chapter 3 the beliefs and practices of the traditional Crow Sun Dance, abandoned by them about 1875, are described. Chapters 4 and 5 recount the circumstances and individuals involved in the transmission of the Shoshoni Sun Dance to the Crow. Chapter 6 sets forth the ceremony and symbolism of the Shoshoni-Crow Sun Dance. A final chapter describes the integration and contemporary status of the ritual in Crow life. According to the author, "No other contemporary ceremony so thoroughly unites the past with the present in the service of both individuals and the Crow people.

The Sun Dance plays upon the full range of needs around which their ancestors built their worship and ceremonies. . . . These self same objectives are attainable in the present Sun Dance, though expressed in contemporary terms." Three appendices. Bibliography. Black-and-white photographs. Ten maps and figures.

Walker, James R. *Lakota Belief and Ritual*, edited by Raymond J. DeMallie and Elaine A. Jahner. Lincoln: University of Nebraska Press, 1980.

Ninety-two documents on Oglala Sioux religion compiled by James R. Walker during his assignment on the Pine Ridge Reservation as agency physician from 1896 to 1914. Part 1 contains a biography of Walker and an analysis of the basic assumptions that shaped his presentation of the collected materials. It concludes with a bibliographical essay on resources available for the study of Sioux religion. Parts 2 through 4 present the interrelated elements of Oglala religious thought and such major ceremonies as *Hunka* (Adoption) and the Sun Dance. Part 5 provides narratives on Sioux men's societies and warfare. Two appendices: a list of Walker's informants and a phonetic key for the pronunciation of Sioux terms. Bibliography. Black-and-white photographs and color plates.

__________. *Lakota Myth*, edited by Elaine A. Jahner. Lincoln: University of Nebraska Press, 1983.

Presents eighteen Oglala Sioux narratives recorded by James R. Walker during his tenure as physician on the Pine Ridge Reservation from 1896 to 1914. Contains three different types of literature: classic Lakota *ohunkakan* (folktales); sacred, esoteric narratives known only to a few holy men; and Walker's own literary systematization of all that he had learned concerning the Oglala narrative tradition. An extended introduction by the editor describes and assesses Walker's approach to the problem of transcribing and refashioning Sioux oral tradition.

Subsistence and Land Use

Bamforth, Douglas B. *Ecology and Human Organization on the Great Plains*. New York: Plenum Press, 1988.

Examines the relation between North America's central grasslands and the ways in which Paleo-Indian hunters and gatherers organized themselves to exploit this area's resources. Rejects the conclusions of earlier studies that find a continuity in Paleo-Indian lifeways despite substantial and continuous environmental changes. Argues that such puzzling findings are the result of research strategies that examine human adaptations to natural environment in terms of three variables: diet, technology, and settlement patterns; claims that adaptive changes are likely to have occurred during this period, and that these should have involved transformations in group organization. Bibliography. Maps.

Ewers, John C. *The Horse in Blackfoot Culture*. Bureau of American Ethnology, Bulletin 159. Washington, D.C.: U.S. Government Printing Office, 1955.

Documents the functions and significance of the horse within the nomadic, buffalo-hunting culture of the Blackfoot. Section 1 traces the diffusion of horses from the American Southwest up to their acquisition by the Blackfoot and other Plains peoples. The next twelve sections describe beliefs and practices related to the mid-nineteenth century Blackfoot "horse complex": customs of horse ownership, care, breeding, training, and social and ceremonial use. The first of two concluding sections discusses the impact of the horse on Blackfoot culture; the second details the phases of the horse complex in Plains Indian history and reviews two opposing theories regarding the influence of the horse on Plains Indian life. Bibliography. Black-and-white photographs and drawings. Tables.

Gilmore, Melvin R. *Uses of Plants by the Indians of the Missouri River Region.* Bureau of American Ethnology, Annual Report 33 (1911-1912). Washington, D.C.: U.S. Government Printing Office, 1919.

Examines the relation of Plains Indians to the flora of their indigenous environment. Provides a taxonomic list of plants which includes their scientific, Indian, and common English names as well as Native beliefs and uses associated with them. Concludes that the "large number of species used and their many uses show considerable development of practical plant economy, or economic botany." Bibliography. Black-and-white photographs. Tables.

Hellson, John C., and Morgan Gadd. *Ethnobotany of the Blackfoot Indians.* National Museum of Man Mercury Series, Canadian Ethnology Service Paper 19. Ottawa: National Museums of Canada, 1974.

An investigation of traditional Blackfoot uses for approximately one hundred species of plants. Discussion is organized according to the following informant-derived categories: religion and ceremony, birth control, medicine, horse medicine, diet, craft and folklore. The section on medicine includes an annotated list of Blackfoot medicinal plants. There is also an herbarium list of botanical specimens. Black-and-white photographs and diagrams.

Holder, Preston. *The Hoe and the Horse on the Plains.* Lincoln: University of Nebraska Press, 1970.

Examines the two major modes of Great Plains subsistence—hoe farming and hunting on horseback—within the context of European expansion in the New World. Focuses on the conflicts that arose between village gardeners and nomadic hunters after the latter acquired equestrian skills from the Europeans. The mounting of these hunters allowed them "to spread their nomadic life around the villages and on across the uplands in pursuit of bison herds." Uses Caddoan-speaking village peoples and Western Dakota Sioux groups to exemplify Plains horticulturalists and equestrian hunters, respectively. Bibliography. Black-and-white reproductions. Maps.

Wedel, Waldo R. *Environment and Native Subsistence Economies in the Central Great Plains.* Smithsonian Miscellaneous Collections, vol. 101, no. 3. Washington, D.C.: Smithsonian Institution, 1941.

Uses archaeological data to analyze the relationship between certain inferred climatic variations on the Great Plains and historic and prehistoric Native subsistence economies. Concludes that alternative settlement and abandonment of the western Great Plains was characteristic for Indian groups "just as it has characterized the subsequent white man's tenure . . . during periods of adverse climatic conditions." Bibliography of literature cited. Black-and-white photographs.

Will, George F., and George E. Hyde. *Corn Among the Indians of the Upper Missouri*. St. Louis, Mo.: William Harvey Minor Co., 1917.

Documents the cultural and economic importance of corn among Upper Missouri Indian tribes. Discussion includes how various groups planted and cultivated corn, their modes of harvesting and storing produce, the use of corn as a food and trade item, religious beliefs concerning the origins of corn, and corn ceremonies. Concludes with a list of the varieties of corn grown by the Arikaras, Mandans, Hidatsas, Iowas, Omahas, Otoes, Pawnee, Poncas, Sioux, Chippewas, Winnebagos, Iroquois, and southwestern Indians. Black-and-white photographs.

Wilson, Gilbert L. *Agriculture of the Hidatsa Indians, an Indian Interpretation*. University of Minnesota Studies in the Social Sciences 9. Minneapolis: Bulletin of the University of Minnesota, 1917.

A detailed account of pre-Columbian Hidatsa agriculture based on interviews with Buffalobird-woman, a representative agriculturist of that people. Allows the informant to detail her agricultural knowledge and experiences in her own way. Topics include preparing fields; the planting, tending, harvesting and uses of sunflowers, corn, squashes, and beans; the storage of produce; the construction of corn drying stages; the construction of agricultural tools, including hoes, rakes, and knives for slicing squashes; the layout and division of fields; postcontact crops; and the cultivation of tobacco. Black-and-white photographs and drawings.

Family and Society

Ahenakew, Edward. *Voices of the Plains Cree*, edited by Ruth M. Buck. Toronto: McClelland and Stewart, 1973.

An anthology of stories concerning the history and traditions of Plains Cree bands living in the area of the north Saskatchewan River. The texts in part 1, dictated to Ahenakew by Chief Thunderchild (1849-1927), provide vignettes of Plains Cree life during pre-reserve times. Part 2 contains the words of Old Keyam, a character created by Ahenakew to represent the confusion and despair of post-reserve Plains Crees exposed to Canadian civilization yet treasuring the lifeways and wisdom of the past. An editor's introduction provides biographical sketches of Chief Thunderchild and Ahenakew. One appendix. Bibliography.

Bowers, Alfred W. *Mandan Social and Ceremonial Organization*. Chicago: University of Chicago Press, 1950.

Sets forth the central assumptions, beliefs, and rituals of Mandan religious life. Part 1 reviews the fundamental features of the tribe's social organization, kinship system, and life cycle. Part 2 begins with an introduction to Mandan ceremonialism, then discusses the key ceremonies of the Mandan. Included among these ceremonies are the Okipa Ceremony, Vision Quests, Corn

Ceremonies, Eagle Trapping Ceremony, Catfish-Trapping Ceremony, Big Bird Ceremony, Small Hawk Ceremony, Snow Owl Ceremony, People Above Ceremony, Red Stick Ceremony, White Buffalo Cow Ceremony, and Adoption Pipe Ceremony. Four appendices: "Myths of the Okipa Ceremony"; "Nuptadi Shell Robe Bundle Myth Related by Ben Benson"; "Awatixa Shell Robe Bundle Myth Related by Bears Arm"; and "Additional Notes on Eagle Trapping." Bibliography. Black-and-white reproductions, photographs, and drawings.

Braroe, Niels, W. *Indian and White: Self-Image and Interaction in a Canadian Plains Community*. Stanford, Calif.: Stanford University Press, 1975.

Examines the conceptions of social self held by the Cree Indians living in a small Canadian Prairie community. Focuses on the problem of how these Indians, considered by many whites of the community as moral outcasts, sustain a morally defensible self-image. Examines this problem from the sociological perspective of symbolic interactionism. Part 1 begins with a discussion of the theoretical foundations of that perspective, then describes the community, traditional Cree lifeways, and historical circumstances surrounding white settlement in the area. Part 2 provides a detailed analysis of Indian-white interaction, concentrating on strategies Indians have adopted to deal with their outcast status. Bibliography. Black-and-white photographs.

Fowler, Loretta. *Arapahoe Politics, 1851-1978*. Lincoln: University of Nebraska Press, 1982.

Examines how Arapaho leaders have been able to legitimate their positions and mobilize political consensus through the creation and manipulation of political symbols. Argues that it is the capacity of symbols to gain and shed meanings that helped the Arapaho to cope successfully with crises of authority brought on by federal Indian policy. Arapahos interpreted new social realities in culturally acceptable and adaptive ways, thereby resolving problems of legitimization of authority. "Symbols emerged that worked to revitalize or reassert traditional values, yet at the same time assured whites that Arapahoes were neither dangerous nor uncooperative. At the same time, old symbols took on new meanings that both reinforced traditional understandings and motivations and made innovation culturally acceptable." One appendix. Bibliography. Black-and-white photographs. Maps and tables.

Goldfrank, Esther S. *Changing Configurations in the Social Organization of a Blackfoot Tribe During the Reserve Period (The Blood of Alberta, Canada)*. Monographs of the American Ethnological Society, vol. 8. New York: J. J. Augustin, 1945.

An analysis of how the Blood, a subdivision of the Blackfoot tribe, has adapted to life on its Alberta reserve. Focus is given to transformations in Blood social organization and the consequences of these changes for the individual and the group. Begins with an overview of Blackfoot economy and social organization in the pre-reserve period. Next considers Blood economy and social change from the beginning of the reserve period in 1877 to 1940. The following section describes additional changes in Blood life, including the nature of bands, men's societies, dance societies, the women's society, and religious belief and practice. Selected aspects of contemporary interpersonal relations are then considered. The monograph closes with a series of biographical sketches. Bibliography. Black-and-white photographs.

Hilger, M. Inez, Sr. *Arapaho Child Life and Its Cultural Background*. Bureau of American Ethnology, Bulletin 148. Washington, D.C.: U.S. Government Printing Office, 1952.

Examines the Arapaho customs, beliefs, and traditions that bear on the development and training of the child. An introductory section presents a historical and ethnographic sketch of the tribe. The following eleven sections describe specific ideas and practices relating to conception, birth, care, and socialization of children. Sections 12 through 19 discuss various aspects of the social and cultural environments in which the child lived. These include institutions of medicine and health, religion and supernatural powers, belief in life after death, domestic economy, tribal government, and marriage. Bibliography. Black-and-white photographs.

Hoebel, E. Adamson. *The Political Organization and Law-Ways of the Comanche Indians*. Memoirs of the American Anthropological Association 54. Menasha, Wis.: American Anthropological Association, 1940.

A study of Comanche legal institutions which focuses on techniques for adjudicating grievances and conflicts of interest. Examines legal actions in cases of adultery and wife-stealing; homicide; excessive sorcery; abnormal conduct such as incest, rape, theft, grave robbery, and suicide; and disputes arising from conflicts over inheritance and contract. Four appendices.

Llewellen, Karl N., and E. Adamson Hoebel. *The Cheyenne Way: Conflict and Case Law in Primitive Jurisprudence*. Norman: University of Oklahoma Press, 1941.

A description and analysis of Cheyenne law-ways which employs "a case method procedure of going in the first instance after cases of trouble and how they were handled." Focuses on Cheyenne norms and dynamics for resolving infractions of acceptable conduct, including homicide, sexual misconduct, unauthorized hunting, the appropriation of another's property, and bogus inheritance claims. Also examined is the role of military societies as a civil power and organ of government. Provides a "case finder," an index of abstracts for the longer or more frequently discussed cases appearing in the text. Black-and-white photographs.

Lopach, James J., et al. *Tribal Government Today: Politics on Montana Indian Reservations*. Boulder, Colo.: Westview Press, 1990.

An examination of the organization, legal principles, and political practices of seven contemporary reservation governments in Montana. Selected reservations include Crow, Blackfeet, Northern Cheyenne, Fort Peck, Fort Belknap, Rocky Boy's, and Flathead. Analyses are based on extended interviews with individuals on each reservation "selected because of their reputation of being politically knowledgeable and key participants in reservation politics." A concluding chapter identifies some basic elements, issues, and problems shared by these political systems. Bibliography.

Lowie, Robert H. *Social Life of the Crow Indians*. Anthropological Papers of the American Museum of Natural History, vol. 9, pt. 2. New York: Order of Trustees, 1912.

Describes the elements and operation of Crow social organization. Section 1 briefly sets forth the early history and tribal affiliations of the Crow. Section 2 focuses on the central place of matrilineal, exogamous clans in the tribe's social life. Next considered are the major categories and modes of Crow relationship, including those of kinspersons and comrades. The remaining sections examine names and naming, birth and childhood, beliefs and practices surrounding menstruation, courtship and marriage, the custom of warriors calling off the names of their mistresses, berdaches (men who take on patterns of behavior traditionally associated with women), death, customs of war, oaths, songs of praise, time reckoning, men's clubs, and miscellaneous customs. Bibliography.

Macgregor, Gordon. *Warriors Without Weapons: A Study of the Society and Personality Development of the Pine Ridge Sioux*. Chicago: University of Chicago Press, 1946.

Part of the Indian Education Research Project, the objective of which was "to investigate, analyze, and compare the development of personality in the Sioux, Hopi, Navaho, Papago, and Zuni tribes in the context of the total environmental setting—sociocultural, geographical, and historical—for implications in regard to Indian Service administration." Begins with a brief description of life on the Pine Ridge Sioux Reservation in southwest South Dakota. Next describes patterns characteristic of growing up on the reservation. Psychological sketches for ten Pine Ridge children, varying in amount of Indian blood from full-blood to three-sixteenths and ranging in age form three to sixteen, are presented in part 3. Uses the lives and personalities of these children to illustrate the group personality of Sioux children which was derived from the results of psychological tests given to a sample of 166. Argues that the lack of opportunity and satisfaction typifying reservation life "retards the growth of personality and prevents it from becoming positive, rich and mature. Life is lived on the defensive"; and that programs are needed to make of the reservation a secure place to grow up in and live. Two appendices: techniques used in testing and aggression in personality. Bibliography. Sixteen black-and-white illustrations. Two maps.

Mishkin, Bernard. *Rank and Warfare Among the Plains Indians*. Monographs of the American Ethnological Society, vol. 3. New York: J. J. Augustin, 1940.

Reexamines the interrelationships of rank and warfare and their place in Plains culture. Argues that students of Plains culture have tended to stress the individual psychological elements in warfare at the expense of economic factors. Submits that with the coming of the horse, economic motivations eclipsed revenge as the significant cause of war. War yielded property returns and the accumulation of wealth among men who achieved military status. "The adhesion of wealth to rank which no doubt previously had centered around war prowess alone changed the character and influence of rank." Based primarily on Kiowa materials. Bibliography.

Powell, Peter J. *People of the Sacred Mountain: A History of the Northern Cheyenne Chiefs and Warrior Societies, 1830-1879*. 2 vols. San Francisco: Harper & Row, 1981.

Documents the central position of the Council Chiefs and the warrior societies in Northern Cheyenne history from the early nineteenth century to 1974. The discussion, which is based primarily on the testimony of tribal elders, relates Cheyenne customs and religion, the capture of the Sacred Arrows in 1830, the tribe's tragic removal to present-day Oklahoma in 1878-1879, and their subsequent flight homeward under the leadership of Dull Knife and Little Wolf. Glossary. Maps. Black-and-white and color plates.

Powers, Marla N. *Oglala Women: Myth, Ritual, and Reality*. Chicago: University of Chicago Press, 1986.

Examines the relationship between gender and the social organization of the Oglala Sioux, a division of the Lakota or Western Sioux living on the Pine Ridge Reservation in southwestern South Dakota. Part 1 begins with a discussion of the traditional role of Lakota women, then investigates the central beliefs and values underlying the life cycle of women in pre-reservation days. Part 2 probes the meaning of growing up an Oglala woman in the contemporary world. Bibliography. Black-and-white photographs.

Schusky, Ernest. *Politics and Planning in a Dakota Indian Community*. Vermillion: Institute of Indian Studies, University of South Dakota Press, 1959.

Report has two goals: to serve as a guide for those interested in contemporary programs designed to alleviate certain economic and social problems on the Indian reservations of South Dakota; and to illustrate problems in the administration and development of Indian policy as they relate to present-day reservation conditions. Uses information from the Lower Brule Reservation in central South Dakota as the basis of the study. Two appendices: "Program for Use of Funds Appropriated to Lower Brule" and "Public Law 85-923, 85 Congress, H.R. 12663, September 2, 1958." Bibliography. Two maps, one chart, and eleven tables.

Secoy, Frank R. *Changing Military Patterns on the Great Plains (Seventeenth Century Through Early Nineteenth Century)*. Monographs of the American Ethnological Society, vol. 21. Locust Valley, New York: J. J. Augustin, 1953.

An analysis of various Great Plains military technique patterns of the Great Plains Indians as they developed from approximately 1630 to 1830. Divides the discussion among the following geographical regions, each possessing its own unique combination of historical, environmental, and cultural attributes: the Southern subarea, the Northwestern subarea, and the Northeastern subarea. Discussion includes the posthorse/pregun patterns on the southern and northwestern Plains; the development of the postgun/pregun pattern; and horse and gun patterns on the northwestern, northeastern, and southern Plains. A discussion considers these military patterns within the broader framework of Plains culture change. One appendix describes the use of the flintlock muzzle-loader on horseback. Bibliography. Maps.

Walker, James R. *Lakota Society*, edited by Raymond J. DeMallie. Lincoln: University of Nebraska Press, 1982.

Assembles thirty-one documents concerning traditional Lakota (Western Sioux) society by James R. Walker, agency physician on the Pine Ridge Reservation from 1896 to 1914. The papers in part 1, "The Structure of Society," describe the composition, operation, and interrelationship of Sioux bands and camps. Part 2, "History, War, Ceremony, and Art," contains essays on various aspects of Lakota daily life. Part 3, "Time and History," documents Lakota methods of measuring time and includes three Oglala "winter counts": calendars that chronicle band histories by means of pictographs and associated oral traditions. Bibliography. Black-and-white photographs.

Wissler, Clark, ed. *Societies of the Plains Indians*. American Museum of Natural History, Anthropological Papers, vol. 11., pts. 1-13. New York: The Trustees, 1912-1916.

A collection of seventeen essays which aims to present field data on the history, structure, and function of societies and comparable organizations among Indians of the Plains. Included in the volume are papers on societies and ceremonial associations in the Oglala division of the Teton Sioux; dance associations of the Eastern Dakota; military societies of the Crow Indians; societies of the Hidatsa and Mandan; societies and dance associations of the Blackfoot Indians; dancing societies of the Sarsi; political and ceremonial organizations of the Plains Ojibwa; political organizations, cults, and ceremonies of the Plains Cree; Pawnee societies; societies of the Arikara; societies of the Iowa; Kansa organization; Ponca societies and dances; dances and societies of the Plains Shoshoni; societies of the Kiowa; general characteristics of Plains Indian shamanistic and dancing societies; and a historical and comparative summary of Plains Indian age societies.

Material Culture and the Arts

Blish, Helen H. *A Pictographic History of the Oglala Sioux, Drawings by Amos Bad Heart Bull*. Lincoln: University of Nebraska Press, 1967.

An ethnographic analysis and album of more than four hundred ledger book drawings from the late nineteenth and early twentieth centuries by Oglala artist Amos Bad Heart Bull. Introductory chapters discuss the chief characteristics of Sioux art and the place of Amos Bad Heart Bull within that artistic tradition. The drawings depict scenes from both pre- and post-reservation Sioux life.

Densmore, Frances. *Cheyenne and Arapaho Music*. Southwest Museum Papers 10. Los Angeles: Southwest Museum, 1936.

Densmore's goal was to record the traditional songs of the Cheyenne and Arapaho. An introduction describes her field methods and major informants. The following two sections provide information on singers and Cheyenne musical instruments and their uses, respectively. The remaining discussion is concerned with various types of songs, including war songs, dance songs, songs medicine men use in treating the sick, Ghost Dance songs, Hand Game songs, Sun Dance songs, peyote songs, songs of social dances, and miscellaneous songs. Examples of each class of song are transcribed and subjected to musicological and cultural analyses. Bibliography of cited literature. Black-and-white photographs.

_________. *Mandan and Hidatsa Music*. Bureau of American Ethnology, Bulletin 80. Washington, D.C.: U.S. Government Printing Office, 1923.

A study of Hidatsa and Mandan songs collected on the Fort Berthold Reservation in North Dakota during the second decade of the twentieth century. Begins with a brief characterization of the author's singers-informants. Next presents information on the derivation of the names "Hidatsa" and "Mandan"; tribal histories and personality characteristics; selected aspects of society and culture; musical instruments; and dealings with the U.S. government. The body of the book provides transcriptions and ethnological and musicological analyses of selected social and ceremonial songs. Bibliography. Black-and-white photographs and diagrams.

_________. *Pawnee Music*. Bureau of American Ethnology, Bulletin 93. Washington, D.C.: U.S. Government Printing Office, 1929.

A study of Pawnee songs based on fieldwork conducted among the Skidi and Chaui Bands in 1919 and 1920. The introductory section contains a characterization of the author's singer-informants; a brief overview of Pawnee history, culture, and religion; and a tabular, melodic comparison of Pawnee songs with those of the Chippewa, Sioux, Ute, Mandan, Hidatsa, and Papago. The body of the monograph contains transcriptions and ethnographic and musicological analyses of selected ceremonial and social songs. Bibliography of authorities cited. Black-and-white photographs and diagrams.

_________. *Teton Sioux Music*. Bureau of American Ethnology, Bulletin 61. Washington, D.C.: Government Printing Office, 1918.

A collection and study of songs recorded among the Lakota (Western or Teton Sioux) of North and South Dakota's Standing Rock Reservation from 1911 to 1914. Begins with a tabulated melodic analysis of six hundred Chippewa and Sioux songs. The principle section of the book contains transcriptions and ethnographic and musicological analyses of 240 social and ceremonial and social songs. Bibliography. Black-and-white photographs. Drawings (one in color) by Sioux artists.

Ewers, John C. *Blackfoot Crafts*. Lawrence, Kans.: Haskell Institute Printing Department, 1945.

An examination of the four major crafts of the Blackfeet, "concerned primarily with the manufacture and ornamentation of articles fashioned from animal skins." An introductory section discusses Blackfeet Indians as warriors and craftsmen. Each of the next four chapters treats a major form of tribal craft: skin preparation and sewing, painting, quillwork, and beadwork. Minor

Blackfeet crafts, including pottery, tobacco pipe, wooden bowl, horn spoon, and feather bonnet making are then described. The monograph closes with a characterization of modern (circa 1945) Blackfeet crafts and craftsmen. List of selected readings in Blackfeet arts and crafts. Black-and-white photographs and diagrams.

__________. *Plains Indian Painting*. Stanford, Calif.: Stanford University Press, 1939.

A brief, though detailed, account of Plains Indian hide painting. Begins with an examination of technical aspects of the art including the sources, preparation, and application of colors, the fabrication and use of brushes, and the time required to paint a hide. Succeeding chapters discuss pattern and form in hide painting, the history of hide painting, other surfaces painted by Plains Indians, and the art of hide painting in other parts of aboriginal America. Bibliography. Forty-four black-and-white plates.

__________. *Plains Indian Sculpture: A Tractional Art from America's Heartland*. Washington, D.C.: Smithsonian Institution Press, 1986.

Seeks to demonstrate the importance of sculpture as a Plains Indian art; the creativity and skill evidenced by these carvings of human and animal forms in stone, wood, and other materials; and the many religious and secular functions such carvings served. Chapter 1 discusses forms of Plains Indian sculpture before 1830. Chapter 2 concerns the manufacture and varieties of effigy pipes and pipe stems. Chapter 3 examines the wide variety of religious, magical, and ceremonial effigies. Miscellaneous effigies, including those serving as children's toys, gaming pieces, and hair parters, are the subject of chapter 4. The conclusion identifies the major trends in Plains Indian sculpture for the period preceding 1830 to the present. An appendix lists named Plains Indian sculptors active during the nineteenth and twentieth centuries. Bibliography. Black-and-white reproductions, photographs, and diagrams. Color plates. One map.

Koch, Ronald P. *Dress Clothing of the Plains Indians*. Norman: University of Oklahoma Press, 1977.

Intended as a primer for those seeking to acquaint themselves with the costume heritage of the Plains. Organizes the text on the bases of materials used and clothing part rather than geography. Chapters treat the utilization of feathers; color and painted designs; quillwork; various kinds of Native ornaments; the use of beads, metals, and cloth obtained from whites in costuming; hair and headgear; skins and shirts; dresses; leggings; footwear; and dance and group costumes. A final chapter compares the clothing and designs of selected Plains tribes. Two appendices present the names and locations of suppliers for costume materials and museums. Bibliography. Black-and-white reproductions, photographs, and diagrams. Color plates. One map.

Lowie, Robert H. *Crow Indian Art*. Anthropological Papers of the American Museum of Natural History, vol. 21, pt. 4. New York: Order of Trustees, 1922.

An analysis of traditional Crow arts which examines their forms, decorations, and historical relationship to parallel arts of other tribes. The first section describes the painting of parfleches, rawhide bags, and robes. The subject of section 2 is the quill and beadwork decoration of pipe bags, soft pouches, cradles, clothing, moccasins, and ornamental riding gear. The remaining sections are devoted to discussions of realistic art and symbolism. Black-and-white photographs and drawings.

Lyford, Carrie A. *Quill and Beadwork of the Western Sioux*. Lawrence, Kans.: Printing Department, Haskell Institute, 1940.

Seeks to bring together a representative collection of designs found in Sioux quill and beadwork and to describe these designs so that they are easily reproduced. The first section discusses the modes of decoration practiced by the Sioux and the variety of materials to which they were applied. Section 2 details the preparation of skins and sinews, the major building blocks of Sioux material culture. In section 3, the dyes, techniques, and designs used in quillwork are set forth. The following section reviews the techniques of beadwork. The development of Sioux designs is the subject of the last section. Bibliography. Thirty-five sepia-toned photographs of finished pieces and forty-eight drawings of techniques and designs.

Netl, Bruno. *Blackfoot Musical Thought: Comparative Perspectives*. Kent, Ohio: Kent State University Press, 1989.

A study that attempts to describe Blackfoot concepts related to music and to discover adequate methods for describing and analyzing the musical culture of a group. Argues that musical culture is a coherent system of sound and ideas. Focus is on what the Blackfoot people think about music—"the conceptions, ideas, and assumptions that underlie the songs themselves and that govern the kinds of behavior that lead to the production and consumption of musical sound." Contains a discography, listing in chronological order recorded collections of Blackfoot music (1897-1986). Three appendices. Bibliography.

Petersen, Karen D. *Plains Indian Art from Fort Marion*. Norman: University of Oklahoma Press, 1971.

An analysis of selected drawings by twenty-six Plains Indian warriors held as prisoners at Fort Marion, Florida, during the last quarter of the nineteenth century. Part 1 describes the historical circumstances surrounding the Fort Marion incarcerations; the prisoners' motives for becoming artists; the media they used; the symbolic conventions characteristic of their drawings; and the fame the "Florida Boys" (as they came to be known) achieved. Part 2 presents extended biographies of eight of the artists and lists biographical data for sixteen others. Part 3 contains a pictographic dictionary intended to aid in interpreting drawings using pictographic conventions of nineteenth century Plains Indian art. Bibliography. Black-and-white photographs and reproductions. Color plates.

Wildschut, W., and John C. Ewers. *Crow Indian Beadwork*. New York: Museum of the American Indian, Heye Foundation, 1959.

Sets out to document the "quality, variety and originality of Crow [beaded] crafts and their relative independence of influences from neighboring tribes." Each of the first six sections considers a class of bead-ornamented articles: men's dress clothing, including shirts, leggings, feathered bonnets, vests, gauntlets, and feather fans; women's dress clothing, including dresses, leggings, and belts; robes and blankets; moccasins; riding gear, including saddles, head ornaments, horse collars, cruppers, and saddle blankets; and containers, including saddle bags, quivers, gun cases, sword and lance cases, cradles, belt pouches, mirror pouches, and pipe and tobacco pouches. Section 7 sets forth the major characteristics of Crow beadwork, describing in turn beadwork techniques, beadwork designs, and bead colors. Sections 8 and 9 concern the symbolism in Crow beadwork and the history of Crow beadwork, respectively. Bibliography. Color and black-and-white plates.

Wilson, Gilbert L. *The Hidatsa Earthlodge*, arranged and edited by Bella Weitzner. Anthropological Papers of the American Museum of Natural History, vol. 33, pt. 5. New York: Trustees of the American Museum of Natural History, 1934.

A study of the construction and layout of the Hidatsa earthlodge, utilizing information gathered on the Fort Berthold Reservation between 1906 and 1918. Begins with a description of the Hidatsa village at Like-a-fishhook-bend, the site of Old Fort Berthold. Part 2 discusses in detail the materials, strategy, and technology employed in building an earthlodge. Part 3 provides information on modern (circa early twentieth century) Hidatsa earthlodges. Part 4 describes the nature and fabrication of winter earthlodges, contrasting them with their summer counterparts. The final sections of the monograph discuss an aberrant form of earthlodge, types of temporary shelters used by Hidatsa hunters, and Hidatsa tipis. Black-and-white drawings.

Witmer, Robert. *The Musical Life of the Blood Indians*. National Museum of Man Mercury Series, Canadian Ethnology Service Paper 86. Ottawa: National Museums of Canada, National Museum of Man, 1982.

A description and analysis of the musical life of the Blood Indians of southwestern Alberta. Provides information concerning the considerable variety of musical forms and behavior currently found on the Blood reserve; the relation of this musical diversity to economic and social variables; and the continuity and change in Blood music, with particular attention to the effects of Euro-American music and values on its style and performance. Concludes that as of 1968, when the study was done, "there seemed to be little evidence in support of the notion that Blood-Blackfoot musical culture . . . was in imminent danger of being completely supplanted by white North American culture." Seven appendices. Bibliography of cited references.

Tribal Life

Baird, W. David. *The Osage People*. Phoenix: Indian Tribal Series, 1972.

Presents a brief tribal history of the Osage people. Begins with the tribe's traditional account of its origins and early migrations, precontact social and political organization, and religious belief and practice. Succeeding sections describe Osage encounters with French, English, and Spanish colonials from 1673 to 1803; contacts with the Americans, 1803 to 1839; settlement on the Kansas Reservation from 1839 to 1871; removal to Indian Territory and the allotment of Osage lands, 1872 through 1907; alterations in tribal life during the twentieth century; and prospects for the future. A list of suggested readings is provided. Black-and-white and color photographs. Three maps.

__________. *The Quawpaw Indians: A History of the Downstream People.* Norman: University of Oklahoma Press, 1981.

Traces the history of the Quapaw from prehistoric times to the mid-1970's. An early chapter follows the migrations of this Siouan-speaking people from the lower Ohio Valley to Arkansas. Subsequent chapters examine the effects of postcontact diseases and trade on the tribe's traditional patterns of subsistence and political organization; their forced removal from Arkansas and repeated resettlements because of federal mismanagement; and the persistence of Quapaw identity despite years of acculturation. Appendices. Bibliography. Black-and-white reproductions and photographs.

Berthrong, Donald J. *The Southern Cheyennes*. Norman: University of Oklahoma Press, 1963.

Traces the history of the Southern Cheyenne from precontact times to their last war with federal troops in 1874-1875. Chapter 1 chronicles Cheyenne migrations from the Minnesota River valley to the central and southern Plains during the late seventeenth to early nineteenth centuries. Chapters 2 and 3 discuss Cheyenne modes of subsistence, social behavior, religion, and government as they had evolved by the mid-nineteenth century. Subsequent chapters detail Cheyenne participation in intertribal warfare during the early and mid-1830's; clashes with white homesteaders and the U.S. cavalry in the 1860's; the massacres at Sand Creek and Washita; and treaty negotiations, land cessions, and removal to a reservation in Indian Territory. Bibliography. Black-and-white reproductions and photographs. Maps.

Blaine, Martha R. *The Ioway Indians*. Norman: University of Oklahoma Press, 1979.

Presents a history of the Ioway Indians, a people of the Siouan language family whose traditional homelands lay between the Mississippi and Missouri rivers. Chapter 1 draws on archaeological data to summarize the group's aboriginal lifeways. Chapters 2 through 5 treat Ioway-white relations from 1676 to the end of the eighteenth century in the context of competing economic and political interests of the French, British, Spanish, and Americans. The chapters that follow describe the devastating effects of the tribe's early nineteenth century land cessions to the American government on their traditional cultural and economic patterns; their assignment in 1836 to the Great Nemaha reservation in present-day Nebraska and Kansas; and the subsequent relocation of some tribal members to a reservation in Oklahoma. Bibliography. Black-and-white reproductions and photographs. Maps.

Boyd, Maurice. *Kiowa Voices*. 2 vols. Fort Worth: Texas Christian University Press, 1981.
Records the oral history and traditions of the Kiowa people. Volume 1 includes sections on Kiowa legendary origins, ceremonial dances, rituals, and songs. Volume 2 contains Kiowa versions of narratives depicting the exploits of the hero-trickster Saynday. Bibliography. Black-and-white reproductions, photographs, and drawings. Color plates.

Cash, Joseph H., and Gerald W. Wolff. *The Three Affiliated Tribes (Mandan, Arikara, and Hidatsa)*. Phoenix: Indian Tribal Series, 1974.
Provides a brief culture history of the Mandan, Arikara, and Hidatsa, the Three Affiliated Tribes of North Dakota. The first three sections treat the origins of each of the groups. Subsequent sections deal with traditional modes of subsistence, the effects of the fur trade, relations with the U.S. government up to 1870, the great smallpox epidemic of 1837, hostilities with the Sioux, the continual reductions of land base, settlement on the Fort Berthold Reservation, responses to government attempts at cultural assimilation, consequences of the Great Depression and Indian Reorganization Act of 1934, participation in World War II, forced relocations resulting from the building of the Garrison Dam, which flooded more than 25 percent of the reservation, and future prospects for the tribes. List of suggested reading. Black-and-white photographs and color plates. Maps.

Ewers, John C. *The Blackfeet: Raiders on the Northwestern Plains*. Norman: University of Oklahoma Press, 1958.
Provides a culture history of the Blackfeet Indians—a Plains confederacy composed of the Piegan (Pikuni), Blood (Kainah), and Blackfeet (Siksika) tribes—from prehistoric times to 1950. Chapter 1 describes aboriginal Blackfeet culture in the "dog days," before the introduction of the horse. Chapter 2 discusses first contact with whites, primarily British, Canadian, and French traders, during the eighteenth century. Chapter 3 focuses on Blackfeet responses to American explorers and traders during the first half of the nineteenth century. The following seven chapters reconstruct Blackfeet subsistence, camp life, arts, warfare, games, and religion as they existed in the mid-1800's. Subsequent chapters narrate how the strong, mobile, and independent Blackfeet were transformed into a sedentary, and dependent people from the mid-nineteenth to the mid-twentieth century. Bibliography. Black-and-white reproductions and photographs. One map.

Flannery, Regina. *The Gros Ventres of Montana*. Catholic University of America Anthropological Series, No. 15 and 16. Washington, D.C.: Catholic University of America Press, 1953, 1957.
Reconstructs the culture of the Gros Ventre, or Atsina, of Montana as it existed before the disappearance of buffalo around 1887. Part 1, "Social Life," provides information on Atsina tribal organization, patterns of subsistence, warfare and prestige, kinship behavior, and the life cycle. Part 2 describes beliefs and practices of traditional Gros Ventre religion, beginning with an account of

various categories of supernatural beings. Subsequent chapters concern tenets and rituals associated with the tribe's sacred Flat and Feathered Pipes, sacred dances, supernatural powers, curing practices, and other rites. A bibliography accompanies each volume. Black-and-white photographs.

Fletcher, Alice C., and Francis La Flesche. *The Omaha Tribe*. 2 vols. Bureau of American Ethnology, Annual Report 27 (1905-1906). Washington, D.C.: U.S. Government Printing Office, 1911.

A classic ethnography of Omaha lifeways based on the twenty-five-year collaboration between anthropologist Alice C. Fletcher and tribal member Francis La Flesche. Volume 1 begins with a discussion of the tribe's former affiliation with the Ponca, Osage, Kansa, and Quapaw. The next chapter focuses on the relation of the natural environment to Omaha social and religious evolution. The remaining chapters of volume 1 examine the socioreligious rites pertaining to the individual, tribal organization, tribal government, the ceremony of the Sacred Pole, and the quest for food. Volume 2 opens with a discussion of Omaha social life, including kinship, courtship and marriage, the care and socialization of children, etiquette, the sexual division of labor, personal adornment, clothing, and amusements. It then considers the topics of music, warfare, social and secret societies, disease and its treatment, death and burial customs, religion and ethics, and language. An appendix recounts the recent history of the tribe (from first contact with whites to the end of the nineteenth century). Numerous black-and-white illustrations and drawings.

Fowler, Loretta. *Shared Symbols, Contested Meanings: Gros Ventre Culture and History 1778-1984*. Ithaca, N.Y.: Cornell University Press, 1987.

An ethnohistory of the Gros Ventre of western Montana. Primary focus is given to processes of sociocultural continuity and change and their relation to the evolution of Gros Ventre identity. Among the topics discussed are variations in concepts of Gros Ventre identity and history among the generations and between Gros Ventre and Assiniboin, a Siouan-speaking people with whom they share the Fort Belknap Reservation.

Grinnell, George B. *The Cheyenne Indians: Their History and Ways of Life*. 2 vols. New Haven, Conn.: Yale University Press, 1923.

A highly detailed ethnography of the Cheyenne Indians based on a "half-century spent rubbing shoulders with them, during which [Grinnell] . . . had a share in almost every phase of their old time life." The chapters of volume 1 deal with early Cheyenne history; traditional ways of life; the yearly cycle of village life; certain customs of camp life; social organization; the training of children; courtship, love charms, marriage, relations between son-in-law and mother-in-law; women's quilling societies, decoration of dressed skins, and color symbolism; material culture, including weapons, musical instruments, riding equipment, tools, dress, the lodge and its furnishings, and pottery; subsistence and hunting; games and amusements; and political organization. Volume 2 is primarily concerned with warfare and religion. Separate chapters on methods of war; warrior societies; religious beliefs; disease and its treatment; the use of plants as food and medicines; selected rituals; the Massaum Ceremony; and culture heroes, including Sweet Medicine. Three appendices: sites of early Cheyenne villages, formation of the quilling society, and notes on Cheyenne songs. Black-and-white photographs, drawings. One foldout map.

Grobsmith, Elizabeth S. *Lakota of the Rosebud: A Contemporary Ethnography*. New York: Holt, Rinehart and Winston, 1981.

A portrait of the Lakota, or Western Sioux, living on the Rosebud Reservation in south-central South Dakota. Begins by tracing the history of the Lakota from precontact to the present-day. Next provides an overview of Rosebud's social structure, including its various communities, tribal government, and economic institutions. Subsequent chapters describe the dynamics of daily life, religious belief and ritual, issues of language use and bilingualism, and attempts at cultural revitalization. Includes a bibliography of references cited and a list of recommended readings. Black-and-white photographs, maps, and charts.

Hassrick, Royal B. *The Sioux: Life and Customs of a Warrior Society*. Norman: University of Oklahoma Press, 1964.

A description and analysis of Sioux life in the era of its greatest vigor, from about 1830 to 1870, based on oral testimony, accounts by early travelers and traders, and previous ethnographic and historical treatments. Includes discussion of social organization, the motives and practice of war, kinship and the family, relations between the sexes and the sexual division of labor, modes of hunting and production, and religious belief and practice. The material is organized around the dual psychocultural theme of self-expression and self-denial. "Using the Sioux way of life as a case study, an attempt is made to analyze the apparent conflict between self and selflessness by showing first that the need to resolve the conflict is one essential element of any way of life and then that, when the opportunity to resolve the conflict in one's own way is denied, the very reason for living may be lost." Two appendices. Bibliography. Black-and-white reproductions, photographs, and drawings. Maps.

Hoebel, E. Adamson. *The Cheyennes: Indians of the Great Plains*. New York: Holt, Rinehart and Winston, 1978.

An ethnography of the Northern Cheyenne as they existed from 1840 to 1860, "when their adaptation to nomadic horse culture was at flood tide, when white hunters had not yet exterminated the buffalo, nor had settlers preempted their lands, nor had the U.S. military beaten them into submission." Part 1, "Ritual and Tribal Integration," describes and analyzes the Cheyenne ceremonies of Arrow Renewal, the Sun Dance, and the Massaum, or Animal Dance. Part 2, "Social Structure," discusses selected aspects of Cheyenne social organization, including the family, kindred, and band; the military societies; the Council of Forty-four; and law and justice. A third section, "Subsistence and War," first examines the sexual division of labor within the tribe's hunting and gathering traditions, then turns to the values and traditions of warfare. Concludes with a consideration of Cheyenne worldview and personality. Bibliography of cited works and a list of recommended reading on the Cheyenne and other Plains Indians. Black-and-white photographs. One map.

Hoover, Herbert T. *The Yankton Sioux*. New York: Chelsea House, 1988.
Traces the history of the Yankton Sioux from the time preceding their contact with whites to the present-day. Begins with an overview of the place of the Sioux in the history of the United States. Subsequent chapters focus on the effects of changing eras of U.S. Indian policy on Yankton life. Demonstrates that in spite of the strong acculturative forces to which the Yankton have been subject, they have managed to preserve major elements of their traditional life. Bibliography. Black-and-white reproductions and photographs. Color plates. Maps and tables.

Howard, James H. *The Canadian Sioux*. Lincoln: University of Nebraska Press, 1984.
An ethnography of Santee and Yanktonais Sioux whose presence in Canada was the result of two military campaigns by the U.S. army in the latter part of the nineteenth century. Chapter 1 reviews Santee and Yanktonais ancestral culture before their escape to Canada. Chapter 2 describes tribal divisions, including traditional band names and the Canadian reserves. Chapter 3 traces the culture history of the Sioux since their arrival in Canada. In chapter 5, Sioux oral accounts of how they came to live in Canada are presented. Subsequent chapters deal with warfare, economy, social life, philosophy and religion, and Woodlands and Plains sources of Canadian Sioux ceremonialism. Closes with a section on the contemporary status of the Sioux of Canada. An appendix lists the author's informants. Bibliography. One map.

__________. *The Dakota or Sioux Tribe: A Study in Human Ecology*. Anthropological Papers 2. The Dakota Museum. Vermillion: University of South Dakota, 1966.
Presents, in three segments, ethnographic sketches of each of the three major cultural and dialectical divisions of the Dakota Indians: the Santee, or Eastern Dakota; the *wiciyela*, or Middle Dakota; and the Teton, or Western Dakota. The sketches, which focus on the social organization and cultural institutions of these divisions, are intended for those who know little or nothing about the Sioux. Bibliography. Black-and-white photographs.

__________. *The Ponca Tribe*. Bureau of American Ethnology, Bulletin 195. Washington, D.C.: U.S. Government Printing Office, 1965.
A history and ethnography of the Ponca, whose traditional homeland included northeastern Nebraska and south-central South Dakota. The focus of the first few sections is on tribal history. The book begins with a discussion of Ponca origins based on the findings of archaeology, ethnology, and ethnohistory. It then presents a version of the tribe's history by Ponca Peter Le Claire. Section 2 recounts the Poncas' first contacts with Americans and the tragedy of their forced removal in 1877. It describes how this removal eventually led to the division of the Ponca into two bands: the Northern Ponca of Nebraska and South Dakota, and the Southern Ponca of Oklahoma. The remaining sections detail

aspects of the tribe's society and culture, including economy; material culture and housing; dress and adornment; learning and art; social organization; religion, dances and ceremonies, sports and games; war and peace; life cycle; and the differential acculturation of the Northern and Southern Ponca bands. Bibliography. Black-and-white photographs and drawings. One chart.

Hoxie, Frederick E. *The Crow*. New York: Chelsea House, 1989.

Traces the history of the Crow Indians from prehistoric to modern times. Chapter 1 first presents the Crow story of creation and then compares and contrasts it with the biblical account. Chapter 2 reconstructs the tribe's early migrations, settlement on the western Plains, and emergence as a distinct people. Chapter 3 sets forth elements of traditional Crow social organization and culture. Chapters 4, 5, and 6 narrate the history of the Crow's relations with whites, from first contact through the reservation era. Concludes with a brief discussion of contemporary life on the Crow reservation. Bibliography. Glossary. Black-and-white and color photographs. Five maps and two charts.

Hyde, George E. *The Pawnee Indians*. Denver: University of Denver Press, 1951.

Seeks to fill the need for an extended history of the Pawnees. Begins with speculations concerning the tribe's origins, its early migrations into Kansas and Nebraska, and encounters with the Apaches (Padoucas) and other Indian groups in this region. Subsequent chapters deal with the relationship of the Pawnees with the Spanish, French, and Americans; the disastrous effects of epidemics on the Pawnee population; wars with the Sioux and Cheyenne; their removal from Nebraska to a reservation in Indian Territory; and the deleterious effects of this new environment and the federal government's policy of Christianization and civilization on Pawnee physical well-being and culture. Five appendices: the Padoucas, Pawnee stream names, white men among the Pawnee before 1850, miscellaneous notes, and tables of population. Black-and-white photographs. Two maps.

__________. *Red Cloud's Folk: A History of the Oglala Sioux Indians*. Norman: University of Oklahoma Press, 1937.

Seeks to provide a complete history of the Oglala tribe, a division of the Lakota or Teton Sioux Indians, "from the time of its origins until it came to the reservation and was broken to pieces by the policy then favored by the U.S. government." Part 1 discusses the migration and early history of the Oglala covering the period from 1650 to 1860. Part 2 deals with the hostilities arising between 1861 and 1870 from white encroachments on Oglala territories. Part 3, treating the years 1870 to 1877, includes descriptions of the Battle of the Little Big Horn, the stealing of the Black Hills by the federal government, and the establishment of the Pine Ridge agency. Appendices. Bibliography. Black-and-white reproductions and photographs. Maps.

__________. *Spotted Tail's Folk: A History of the Brule Sioux*. Norman: University of Oklahoma Press, 1961.

Traces the history of the Brule, a division of the Lakota or Teton Sioux, from the birth of the tribe's great leader, Spotted Tail, in 1823 to his assassination on July 4, 1881. Seeks to demonstrate the central importance of Spotted Tail in fashioning Brule responses to nineteenth century federal Indian policy and their forced abandonment of aboriginal freedom for reservation life. In one of his assessments of the leader, the author states that "frank, good-natured, shrewd, and witty, this Brule chief made friends of the high officials who held the fate of his people in their hands and obtained from them by friendly persuasion advantages for the Sioux that the fighting chiefs like Sitting Bull and Crazy Horse could not win by war and, indeed, did not value. These things were peace and time and aid to enable the Sioux to change from the hunting life to the ways of civilized existence." Bibliography. Black-and-white reproductions and photographs. Maps.

Kroeber, Alfred L. *The Arapaho*. Bulletin of the American Museum of Natural History, vol. 18, pt. 1. New York: Knickerbocker Press, 1902.

Describes the culture and decorative art of the Arapaho people. The first chapter presents an ethnographic sketch of tribal society and lifeways. Chapter 2 contains an examination of selected objects of Arapaho manufacture and use, focusing primarily on the ornamentation of these objects and their symbolic content. Concludes that there is "no fixed symbolism in Arapaho decorative art. Any interpretation of figure is personal. Often interpretation is arbitrary. . . . Where such a wide variability exists, and where every individual has a right to his opinion . . . it follows that it is impossible to declare any one interpretation of a given ornamental design as correct or as incorrect." Color and black-and-white plates.

__________. *Ethnology of the Gros Ventre*. American Museum of Natural History, Anthropological Papers, vol. 1, pt. 4. New York: The Trustees, 1908.

A description of Gros Ventre society and culture based on information collected at the Fort Belknap Reservation in northern Montana during 1901. Among the subjects discussed are tribal organization, food and hunting, decorative art, social customs, games, war and individual war experiences, personal supernatural powers, medicines and plants, tribal ceremonial organization and dances, modern ceremonial objects, religious customs, beliefs concerning the dead, and mythology. Black-and-white photographs and drawings.

Lowie, Robert H. *The Assiniboine*. Anthropological Papers of the American Museum of Natural History, vol. 4, pt. 1. New York: The Trustees, 1909.

An ethnography of Montana's Assiniboin Indians, a people belonging to the Dakota branch of the Siouan linguistic stock and originating from the Wazikute band of the Yantonai Sioux. The monograph opens with a brief history of the tribe. Following are chapters on material culture, amusements, art, war, social organization, religious beliefs and practices, and ceremonial organization. A concluding section on mythology contains the Assiniboin Trickster cycle and eighty miscellaneous folktales.

__________. *The Crow Indians*. New York: Farrar and Rinehart, 1935.

A classic account of traditional Crow lifeways. The first two chapters set forth the elements of the tribe's social organization and kinship system. Chapter 3 describes the stages of the life cycle. The sexual division of labor, amusements, and games are the subject of chapter 4. Chapter 5 discusses the literary characteristics and social functions of Crow narratives, and chapters 6 through 8 present representative myths and tales. In chapter 9, Crow men's societies are named and characterized. Chapter 10 concerns the place and practice of war in Crow society. Chapters 11 through 16 detail religious beliefs, ceremonies, and organizations, including the Bear Song Dance, the Sacred Pipe Dance, the Tobacco Society, and the Sun Dance. The final chapter discusses the Crow worldview. Two appendices: sources and clan names. Glossary. Black-and-white photographs and drawings.

McFee, Malcolm. *Modern Blackfeet: Montanans on a Reservation*. New York: Holt, Rinehart and Winston, 1972.

An ethnography of Montana's contemporary Blackfeet people which focuses on differential responses to the forces of white acculturation. Maintains that the tribe is made up of two contrasting groups—"white-oriented society" and "Indian-oriented society"—organized around distinctive values and characterized by radically different cultures, associational patterns, and internal organization. Begins with an overview of modern life on the Blackfeet reservation, then provides a tribal history encompassing the period before white contact to 1970. The remaining chapters detail the nature and separateness of the two orientation systems. Bibliography of references cited. List of recommended readings. Black-and-white photographs. Map.

Mandelbaum, David G. *The Plains Cree*. Anthropological Papers of the American Museum of Natural History, vol. 37, pt. 2. New York: Order of Trustees, 1940.

An ethnography of Plains Cree society and culture from the period 1870-1880, "before the buffalo disappeared and within the memory of the oldest informants." An introductory section, describes the traditional habitat and band divisions of the tribe. In the following section, the group's transition from a Woodlands to Plains people as well as their contacts with other Indian tribes and whites is set forth. Subsequent chapters concern Plains Cree subsistence and economy, manufactures and artifacts, social life, the life cycle, religious beliefs, ceremonies, warfare, and designations for segments of space and time. Bibliography. Black-and-white photographs and drawings.

Mathews, John J. *The Osage: Children of the Middle Waters*. Norman: University of Oklahoma Press, 1961.

Traces the culture history of the Osage people from aboriginal times to the mid-twentieth century. Part 1 considers Osage life before the coming of whites. Parts 2 through 5 treat the nature and effects of Osage contacts with various types of Europeans and Americans. Bibliography. Black-and-white reproductions and photographs.

Newkumet, Vynola Beaver, and Howard L. Meridith. *Hasinai: A Traditional History of the Caddo Confederacy*. College Station: Texas A&M University Press, 1988.

An overview of Caddoan history and culture organized around the traditional sequence of eleven ceremonial dances which serves to integrate the tribe's collective life and memories. A description of the drum dance, the initial dance of the cycle, precedes a discussion of Caddoan origins. Subsequent dances and topics include the Bear Dance: hunting; the Corn Dance: agriculture; the Duck Dance: architecture; the Alligator Dance: clothing; Women's Dance: family relationships; the Stirrup Dance: tribal relationships; the Quapaw Dance: foreign relationships; the Cherokee Dance: health; the Bell Dance: language; the Mourning Dance: contemporary affairs; and the Turkey Dance: historical perspectives. Glossary. List of suggested readings. Black-and-white photographs.

Stands in Timber, John, and Margot Liberty. *Cheyenne Memories*. New Haven, Conn.: Yale University Press, 1967.

A history of the Northern Cheyenne people based on the records and testimony of "one of the last Cheyenne to hear the tribal story from those who lived it." Discussion includes creation stories; the coming of the prophet Sweet Medicine and his miracles; chiefs, warriors, and military societies; sacred traditions, ceremonies, and power; the tribe's early history; battles with the Crow and Shoshoni; conflicts and treaties with the whites; the Battle of the Little Big Horn; early reservation life; the Ghost Dance; federal government attempts to assimilate the Cheyenne; and personal memories. According to coauthor Liberty, the value of Stands in Timber's history lies in three characteristics: "First, John has given us old material from new sources and new material from these same sources. . . . Second, [his] narrative provides white readers with a rare insight into the history and culture of his people. . . . And third, John has given us the history of the Cheyennes as they themselves recall and interpret it." Bibliography. Black-and-white photographs.

Unrau, William E. *The Kansa Indians: A History of the Wind People, 1673-1873*. Norman: University of Oklahoma Press, 1971.

Surveys the history of the Kansa Indians from ancestral times to the 1870's. Includes discussion of the tribe's origins and early migrations; their aboriginal social and cultural patterns; participation in the fur trade and its effects on their life; relations with the American government during the late eighteenth and early nineteenth centuries; the work of Catholic and Protestant missionaries among them; Kansa treaties and land cessions; their assignment to a reservation in Upper Neosho Valley of Kansas in 1846; and removal to Indian Territory beginning in 1873. Bibliography. Black-and-white reproductions and photographs and one color plate. Maps.

Wallace, Ernest, and E. Adamson Hoebel. *The Comanches: Lords of the South Plains*. Norman: University of Oklahoma Press, 1952.

An examination of Comanche culture focusing on the period of its zenith during the latter half of the nineteenth century. Chapter 1 discusses the emergence of the Comanche as a distinct people and their relations with other Indians of the southern Plains. Subsequent chapters provide a general overview of the tribe's participation in the Plains Indian horse-buffalo-tipi complex; their food, clothing, and dwellings; division of labor and forms of entertainment; life cycle; quests and uses of religious power; cosmogony and folk beliefs; political organization and law; and patterns of warfare. The book closes with a brief consideration of the effects of reservation life on the traditional patterns of Comanche lifeways. Bibliography. Black-and-white reproductions and photographs. One map.

Biography and Autobiography

Black Elk, as told to John G. Neihardt. *Black Elk Speaks*. New York: William Morrow, 1932.

The classic account of the life and teachings of Nicholas Black Elk, Sioux warrior and holy man. Black Elk tells of his boyhood, eyewitness to the Battle of the Little Big Horn, and travels in Europe as part of Buffalo Bill's Wild West Show. The most important sections contain the author's account of his sacred visions, including the great vision he received at nine years of age.

Eastman, Charles. *From Deep Woods to Civilization: Chapters in the Autobiography of an Indian*. Boston: Little, Brown, 1916.

The Dakota author traces the major events of his life in both the Indian and white worlds. Describes his traditional rearing as a Wahpeton Sioux, his primary education at the mission school of Alfred Rigss on the Santee agency, experiences at Beloit and Dartmouth colleges, medical training at Boston University, life as a doctor on the Pine Ridge Reservation during the Ghost Dance War, marriage to reformer Elaine Goodale Eastman, and disillusionment with the "civilized" ideal. In his final self-assessment he states: "I am an Indian; and while I have learned much from civilization, for which I am grateful, I have never lost my Indian sense of right and justice. I am for development and progress along social and spiritual lines, rather than those of commerce, nationalism, or material efficiency. Nevertheless, so long as I live, I am an American." Black-and-white photographs.

Jones, David E. *Sanapia: Comanche Medicine Woman*. New York: Holt, Rinehart and Winston, 1972.

A study of traditional modes of Comanche healing focused on Sanapia, the last of the tribe's Eagle doctors. Begins with a historical and ethnographic overview of the Comanche people. Then presents a biography of Sanapia, placing particular emphasis on her training and activities as a doctor. Subsequent chapters discuss the botanical and nonbotanical medicines used by Sanapia; Comanche beliefs and attitudes concerning ghosts, their relationship to illness, and treatments for those suffering from ghost sickness; and the symptoms and treatment of witch sickness. Bibliography and list of recommended readings. Black-and-white photographs. One map.

Marquis, Thomas B. *A Warrior Who Fought Custer*. Minneapolis: Midwest Co., 1931.

The recollections of a Northern Cheyenne warrior who participated in the Battle of the Little Bighorn, 1876. A valuable source of information on Cheyenne lifeways as they existed at the height of the tribe's buffalo hunting days, from the mid- to latter nineteenth century.

Michelson, Truman. *Narrative of a Southern Cheyenne Woman*. Smithsonian Miscellaneous Collections, vol. 87, no. 5. Washington, D.C.: Smithsonian Institution, 1932.
The descriptions and insights of a Southern Cheyenne woman concerning her own life and the traditions of her people. Stresses the highly disciplined morality and behavior expected of Cheyenne women.

Plenty Coups. *American: The Life Story of a Great Indian, Plenty-coups, Chief of the Crows*, edited by Frank B. Linderman. Chicago, N.Y.: World Book, 1930.
The autobiography of a Crow chief based on interviews in sign language which richly details the pre-reservation customs and values of the Crow people. Reflecting on the passing of his youth and the traditions of the Crow, Plenty Coups states, "I am old. . . . But I know justice and have tried all my life to be just, even to those who have taken away our old life that was so good. My whole thought is of my people. I want them to be healthy, to become again the race they have been. I want them to learn all they can from the white man, because he is here to stay, and they must live with him forever." Black-and-white drawings.

Standing Bear, Luther. *My People the Sioux*. Boston: Houghton Mifflin, 1928.
The autobiography of a Teton Sioux. The author weaves accounts of the major events in his life with commentaries on traditional Sioux culture and the crises caused by nineteenth century federal Indian policy. The book is particularly important for its insider's perspective on these traumatic years of enforced culture change; its portrayals of such famous personalities as Sitting Bull, Crazy Horse, and Spotted Tail; and for its depiction of life at Carlisle Indian boarding school. Black-and-white photographs and drawings by the author.

Sweezy, Carl. *The Arapaho Way: A Memoir of an Indian Boyhood*, edited by Althea Bass. New York: Clarkson N. Potter, 1966.
Sweezy, a Blue Cloud Arapaho born about 1881 ("[w]hen . . . most of the Cheyenne and Arapaho still lived in tipis"), recounts some of the major events of his youth and training in the traditional ways of his people. The editor stresses Sweezy's importance "as a link between the old, free-roaming, buffalo-hunting days of his forebears and the modern Indian who owns his home individually and eats and dresses and makes his living in much the same way as his white neighbors do." One black-and-white photograph and reproduction. Color plates of paintings by Sweezy.

Northwest and Plateau

General Studies and References

Bancroft-Hunt, Norman, and Werner Forman. *People of the Totem: The Indians of the Pacific Northwest*. New York: G. P. Putnam's Sons, 1979.

An oversized, profusely illustrated introduction to the Native American cultures of the Pacific Northwest. Chapter 1 succinctly reviews the area's natural environment and history of Indian-white relations. In chapter 2, patterns of village life, subsistence, architecture, arts, and social and tribal organization are described. The structure and functions of important social events known as potlatches are the subjects of chapter 3. Subsequent chapters address the topics of religious belief, myth and cosmology, and ceremonial songs and dances. Color plates.

Berreman, Joel V. *Tribal Distribution in Oregon*. Memoirs of the Anthropological Association 47. Menasha, Wis.: American Anthropological Association, 1937.

Sets as its aim to establish insofar as possible the tribal distribution of Oregon's aboriginal inhabitants "previous to the disturbing influences of exploration and settlement by the whites." Examines the movement and settlement of the Chinookan, Calapuyan, and Clatskanie tribes of the Columbia River and Willamette valley; the Hokan, Takelman, and Athapascan peoples of southwestern Oregon; the Kusan, Siuslawan, Yakonan, and Coast Salish groups of the north coast; and the Salish, Sahaptin, and Shoshonean tribes of eastern Oregon (before 1750). Argues that the introduction of the horse into the culture of the northern and western Plains groups was the major cause of tribal dislocations in prewhite days. Bibliography.

Drucker, Philip. *Cultures of the North Pacific Coast*. San Francisco: Chandler, 1965.

An overview of the Indian peoples and cultures of America's Northwest Coast. Part 1 begins with a survey of the region's habitat, then focuses on areawide patterns of economy and technology, social and political organization, and religion and ritual. Part 2 moves from a general consideration of Northwest Coast culture to an examination of regional specializations. It starts with a delineation of the area's linguistic, biological, and cultural subdivisions. Four cultural subdivisions are identified: the Northern, Wakashan, Coast Salish-Chinook, and Northwest California provinces. The remaining chapters provide sketches of tribes whose cultures were typical of the provinces to which they belonged. Bibliography. Color plates, black-and-white diagrams. Two maps.

__________. *Indians of the Northwest Coast*. New York: McGraw-Hill, 1955.

Presents the salient features of Indian cultures of the Northwest Coast. An introductory chapter provides background information on the area's natural environment, peoples, prehistory, physical anthropology, and history of European contacts. Subsequent chapters focus on areal patterns of subsistence, material culture, society, religion, ceremonials, life cycle, and art. Some of the dominant patterns include emphasis on woodcutting, garments principally of plant fiber, an economy built around fishing, lineage-based local groups, emphasis on the individual in social affairs, slavery, elaborate ceremonialism (including the potlatch and dancing societies), and rank-wealth correlation defining status. The discussion includes occasional references to local variations in these patterns and specialized local developments. Annotated bibliography. Black-and-white photographs and diagrams. Maps.

Duff, Wilson. *The Indian History of British Columbia.* Vol. 1: *The Impact of the White Man.* Anthropology in British Columbia Memoir 5 (1964). Provincial Museum of Natural History and Anthropology. Victoria: A. Sutton, 1965.

Summarizes the postcontact history of the Indian peoples of British Columbia. Includes a detailed classification of the province's tribes and bands, overviews of their population trends, and changes in tribal life that have resulted from Euro-American contact. Chapter 1 opens with a discussion of the problem of rendering Indian names in English. It follows with a classification of the major ethnic divisions, linguistic subdivisions, and tribes and bands. Chapter 2 presents information on Indian population for the periods before 1835, since 1835, and the present-day (mid-1960's). Chapter 3 traces the impact of the white man on Indian life in such areas as material culture, arts and crafts, economy, religion, social organization, and politics. Appendix: phonemes and phonetic key. Bibliography. Eight photographs; five maps; one graph; four tables.

Grumet, Robert S. *Native Americans of the Northwest Coast: A Critical Bibliography.* Newberry Library Center for the History of the American Indian Bibliographical Series. Bloomington: Indiana University Press, 1979.

A bibliographical essay that reviews 222 books and articles pertaining to the history and culture of Northwest Coast tribes. The essay is divided by the following subheadings: introduction; general works; the archaeology of the region; the history of the region; the art of the Northwest Coast; the Potlatch; the culture provinces, with sections for the northern culture province: Tlingit, Haida, Tsimshian, Northern Kwakiutl; the Wakashan culture province: Southern Kwakiutl, Bella Coola, Nootka; and the Coast Salish-Chemakun culture province: Coast Salish of British Columbia, Coast Salish and Chemukan of western Washington State. Lists recommended works for the beginner and for a basic library. One map.

Gunther, Erna. *Indian Life on the Northwest Coast of North America, As Seen by the Early Explorers and Fur Traders During the Last Decades of the Eighteenth Century.* Chicago: University of Chicago Press, 1972.

Seeks to add to our knowledge of the Native Northwest Coast cultures of the late eighteenth century by applying ethnohistorical method to documents authored by Spanish, British and Russian explorers and traders of that period. Among the peoples described are the Nootka, Chinook, Haida, Tlingit, Chugach of Prince William Sound, Athapascans of Cook Inlet, and Aleut at Unalaska. Where possible, the author attempts to relate information contained in the documentary sources to artifacts housed in various European museums. Two appendices: eighteenth-century objects in European museums and technological processes of the eighteenth century. Bibliography. Black-and-white reproductions and photographs.

Haeberlin, Hermann, and Erna Gunther. *The Indians of Puget Sound.* Seattle: University of Washington Press, 1930.

An ethnographic overview that focuses primarily on the social and cultural institutions of the Snohomish, Snuqualmi, and Nisqually peoples of Puget Sound. An introduction overviews the location, characteristics, and intertribal relations of the tribes described. Subsequent chapters provide information on villages and houses, economic life, crafts, dress and personal care, life cycle, social life of the group, and religious beliefs and ceremonies. Bibliography. Black-and-white diagrams.

Hays, H. R. *Children of the Raven: The Seven Indian Nations of the Northwest Coast*. New York: McGraw-Hill, 1975.

A summary of the history and culture of seven Northwest Coast nations: the Tlingit, Tsimshian, Haida, Kwakiutl, Bella Coola, Nootka, and Coast Salish. Part 1 provides a historical overview of the relationship of these peoples with whites from the early eighteenth through the mid-twentieth century. Part 2 describes selected aspects of Native society and culture, including arts and crafts, the life cycle, religious beliefs and ceremonies, and oratory. Closes with an overview of the recent history and contemporary status of Northwest Coast tribes. Bibliography. Black-and-white reproductions and photographs. One map.

Kirk, Ruth. *Tradition and Change on the Northwest Coast: The Makah, Nuu-chah-nulth, Southern Kwakiutl, and Nuxalk*. Seattle: University of Washington Press, 1986.

Documents the culture continuities of tribes belonging to the three major language divisions of central British Columbia and the adjoining northwestern tip of Washington State. Describes the worldviews and lifeways of peoples representative of these divisions: the Nuu-chahnulth (including the Makah of Washington State), the Southern Kwakiutl, and the Nuxalk. Part 1 contains the observations of tribal elders on their cultural heritage and its retention in the face of acculturative forces. Part 2 overviews the social and religious institutions characteristic of traditional Northwest Coast life. Part 3 presents a summary of the area's pre- and postcontact history, concluding with a chapter on the commitment of the present generation to ethnic survival. Bibliography. Black-and-white drawings and photographs; color plates.

McFeat, Tom, ed. *Indians of the North Pacific Coast*. Seattle: University of Washington Press, 1966.

An anthology of previously published essays on selected topics in Northwest Coast Indian society and culture. Part 1, "An Introduction to the Area," includes overviews of the area's tribes and primary forms of material culture. It also contains papers on boatsmanship and Nootka whaling. The articles in part 2 discuss various aspects and forms of social organization. Differing perspectives on the Potlatch are presented in part 3. Parts 4, 5 and 6 provide discussions of rank and class, ceremonialism, and deviance and normality, respec-tively. One appendix: cultural elements distribution. List of suggested readings.

Miller, Jay, and Carol Eastman, ed. *The Tsimshian and Their Neighbors on the North Pacific Coast*. Seattle: University of Washington Press, 1984.

An anthology of fourteen essays which examines cultural patterns shared by the

Tsimshian and other peoples of the Northwest Coast. The papers in part 1 focus exclusively on the Tsimshian and include treatments of their sacred narratives, totemic structures, modes of property inheritance, potlatch, kinship terms, symbols of wealth, and religious traditions. The essays in part 2 present discussions of selected cultural institutions found among such near and distant neighbors of the Tsimshian as the Haida, West Coast Nootka of Friendly Cove, Klallum, and Twana. One appendix. Bibliography. Black-and-white photographs. Tables, charts, and maps.

Ray, Verne F. *Cultural Relations in the Plateau of Northwestern America.* Publications of the Frederick Webb Hodge Anniversary Publication Fund, vol. III. Los Angeles: Southwest Museum, 1939.

Attempts to describe the distinctive features of Plateau social and cultural life. Focuses on patterns associated with political organization, social stratification, attitudes toward conflict, girls, puberty observances, disposal of the dead, religious life, and material culture. Argues that many elements paramount in Plateau culture are not to be found in adjacent areas and that although the peoples of the area borrowed from both Northwest Coast and Plains, "the importance of coastal influence has probably been overrated, and diffusion from the Plains is in large part recent and superficial." Bibliography. Maps.

Ruby, Robert H., and John A. Brown. *A Guide to the Indian Tribes of the Pacific Northwest*. Norman: University of Oklahoma Press, 1986.

An encyclopedic survey of 150 Indian tribes that now live or once lived in the states of Oregon, Washington, Idaho, and Montana. Most entries contain information on the ancestral homelands, languages, patterns of subsistence, populations, pre- and postcontact histories, federal claims, contemporary life and culture, and special events of the selected tribes. Descriptions vary in length from one paragraph to several pages. All end with a list of suggested readings. Includes a table listing the pronunciations of Pacific Northwest tribal names by M. Dale Kinkade. Black-and-white photographs and reproductions. Five maps.

__________. *Indians of the Pacific Northwest: A History*. Norman: University of Oklahoma Press, 1981.

A historical survey of the Indian tribes of Washington, Oregon, Idaho, and western Montana covering the period from the mid-1700's to the opening of the twentieth century. Begins with descriptions of Indian interaction with Spanish, British, and American explorers and traders. Succeeding chapters present a chronological treatment of the impact of trading posts established by the North West Company and Hudson's Bay Company on Indian life, the religious work of various Catholic and Protestant missionaries, the conflicts between settlers and tribes, treaty making and breaking, and the forced relocation of tribes on reservations as part of an overall policy to assimilate them into Euro-American society. Bibliography. More than one hundred black-and-white photographs and reproductions. Nine maps.

Schuster, Helen H. *The Yakimas: A Critical Bibliography*. Newberry Library Center for the History of the American Indian Bibliographical Series. Blooming-

ton: Indiana University Press, 1982.
A bibliographical essay that reviews 292 books and articles pertaining to the history and culture of the Yakima people. The essay is divided by the following subheadings: introduction; prehistory early influences, contacts, and change; explorers, fur traders, missionaries, and other early travelers; the treaty period; the Yakima War: 1855-1856; the Yakima War: 1858; the reservation period and the modern Yakima nation; general histories; biographies; general ethnographic sources; traditional social organization and customs; Yakima Indian religion; mythology; linguistics and language learning; related plateau tribal groups; and Yakima tribal publications. Lists recommended works for the beginner and for a basic library collection. Three maps.

Suttles, Wayne, ed. *Northwest Coast*. Vol. 7 in *Handbook of North American Indians*. Washington, D.C: Smithsonian Institution, 1990.
A compendium of fifty-eight essays by noted scholars. The first five papers overview the culture area and its environment, languages, human biology, and prehistory. Subsequent essays focus on the history of various subfields of Northwest Coast research; Indian contact with whites and its repercussions; the cultural prehistories of selected geographical divisions; the histories, languages, and cultures of particular tribes; mythology; art; and the Indian Shaker Church. Contains bibliography of references cited, photographs, maps and charts.

Underhill, Ruth M. *Indians of the Pacific Northwest*. Riverside, Calif.: Sherman Institute Press, 1945.
A basic introduction to Northwest Coast Indian culture, focusing primarily on the Salish peoples of Washington and Oregon. Includes discussions of subsistence, housing, tools and manufacture, social organization, government, religion, and contemporary (as of 1945) life. Bibliography. Black-and-white reproductions, photographs, and drawings. Tables. One map.

Zucker, Jeff, et al. *Oregon Indians: Culture, History, and Current Affairs. An Atlas and Introduction*. Portland: Oregon Historical Society, 1983.
A resource on the customs, history, and contemporary status of Oregon's Indian peoples. Part 1, "Traditional," includes discussions of the state's natural and cultural areas, the aboriginal tribes of Oregon, their food resources and subsistence patterns, demography, house types and family organization, trade networks, transportation, languages, social organizations, and first contacts with non-Indians. Part 2, "Historical," examines the phases of Indian policy in Oregon up to the present day; treaties and treaty making between the federal government and the state's tribes; the displacement of Oregon's Indians and their shrinking land base; the histories of the Warm Springs, Umatilla, Malheur, Burns, Klamath, Grand Ronde, and Siletz Reservations; and claims cases.

Archaeology

Fladmark, Knut R. *British Columbia Prehistory*. Ottawa: National Museums of Canada, 1986.
An overview of British Columbia prehistory intended for the general public as

well as professional archaeologists and their students. The majority of the book's twelve chapters are arranged chronologically, alternating between discussions of cultural developments on the coast and in the interior from 12,000 years ago to European contact. Includes a list of suggested readings. Black-and-white photographs and drawings. Color plates. Maps and tables.

Kirk, Ruth, and Richard D. Daughtery. *Exploring Washington Archaeology*. Seattle: University of Washington Press, 1978.

A survey of Washington State's natural and human prehistory. Part 1 begins with a summary of the continuity and change in the area's geology and climate during the past twenty-five million years. Subsequent sections discuss the cultural adaptations of prehistoric groups to Washington's various ecological zones. Most extensive coverage is given to the Ozette site, located fifteen miles south of Cape Flattery. Includes a guide to site locations. Black-and-white photographs and color plates. Maps.

MacDonald, George F. *Ninstints: Haida World Heritage Site*. Vancouver: University of British Columbia, 1983.

An account of the archaeological work being done at Ninstints, an abandoned Kunghit Haida village of the southern Queen Charlotte Islands. Provides brief descriptions of the ground plan of the village; the construction, characteristic arrangement, and decorations of its houses; the village's postcontact history, from earliest encounters with Europeans to its downfall resulting from epidemics; the argillite carvings of Tom Price, one of the last survivors of Ninstints; and the recent attempts of the scientific community to preserve the site. Bibliography. Illustrated with black-and-white drawings, reproductions, and photographs and several color plates.

Stewart, Hilary. *Artifacts of the Northwest Coast Indians*. Saanichton, British Columbia: Hancock House Publishers, 1973.

Surveys the material culture of coastal peoples of the prehistoric Northwest. Chapter 1 presents a case study of an archaeological dig. Chapter 2 briefly portrays the relationship between the area's tribes and their natural environment. Chapters 3, 4, and 5 describe the manufacture and functions of stone, bone and antler, and shell artifacts, respectively. The chapters are profusely illustrated with sepia-toned reproductions, photographs, and drawings by the author. Glossary of archaeological terms. Bibliography.

Folklore, Sacred Narrative, Religious Belief and Practice

Amoss, Pamela. *Coast Salish Spirit Dancing: The Survival of an Ancestral Religion*. Seattle: University of Washington Press, 1978.

An analysis of the persistence and growth of aboriginal-style spirit dancing among the Nooksack Coast Salish people of northwestern Washington. Chapter 1 provides a summary of life among the Nooksack before contact with whites. Chapter 2 examines the beliefs associated with the four semiautonomous systems constituting Nooksack religion: the guardian spirit complex, the ghost complex, the magic complex, and the High God complex. Chapter 3 describes how beliefs concerning supernaturals are dramatized in various ceremonies. Chapter 4 discusses the cultural and individual importance of the trance state in spirit dancing. Chapter 5 considers the ways in which contemporary spirit dancing benefits the individual and group. Bibliography. Black-and-white reproductions and photographs. Maps and tables.

Barnett, H. G. *Indian Shakers: A Messianic Cult of the Pacific Northwest*. Carbondale: Southern Illinois University Press, 1957.

A historical and cultural analysis of the Indian Shaker cult, a messianic religion still in practice among many of the tribes of Washington State. Chapter 1 presents an account of John Slocum, founder of the cult, and the earliest days of the Shaker church. Subsequent chapters deal with the addition of converts; opposition to the religion; stresses and dissension among church members; Shaker doctrines, ritual elements, and ceremonies; later accretions to the cult; and a summary of the social and psychological factors underlying the origin and spread of shaking. Bibliography. Black-and-white photographs.

Beckham, Stephen D., et al. *Native American Religious Practices and Uses in Western Oregon*. University of Oregon Anthropological Papers 31. Eugene: Department of Anthropoloby, University of Oregon, 1984.

A summary of the past and present religious practices of tribes living in the area neighboring western Oregon's Siuslow National forest. Seeks to serve as a sourcebook for evaluating the importance of Indian religious use sites located in the Forest. Chapter 1 outlines the project's methodology and goals. Chapters 2 through 6 provide ethnographic information on the Native Americans who occupied the region at the time of historic contact, including the Tillamook, Alsea-Yaquina, Coos, Lower Umpque, Siuslow, and Kalapuya tribes. Chapters 7 and 8 examine postcontact evolutions in Indian religious practices. Concludes with a description of five religious use sites in the Siuslow National Forest. Bibliography. Black-and-white photographs and reproductions. Maps, tables, and charts.

Clark, Ella A. *Indian Legends of the Pacific Northwest*. Berkeley: University of California Press, 1953.

A collection of more than one hundred sacred narratives and tales told by Indian peoples of Washington and Oregon. The author aims "to prepare a collection of Pacific Northwest myths and legends that the general reader will enjoy, either as entertainment or as information about an American way of living strange to him." Many of the texts concern the origin of natural features found in those states. The narrative are arranged according to the following subheadings: myths of the mountains; legends of the lakes; tales of the rivers, rocks, and waterfalls; myths of creation, the sky, and storms; and miscellaneous myths and legends. Bibliography. Glossary. Two maps. Black-and-white drawings.

Goldman, Irving. *The Mouth of Heaven: An Introduction to Kwakiutl Religious Thought*. New York: John Wiley & Sons, 1975.

Draws on the Kwakiutl and English-language manuscripts of anthropologist Franz Boas and his informant, George Hunt, to elucidate some of the central elements of Kwakiutl religious thought. Claims that anthropologists have misrepresented Kwakiutl life by failing to understand its fundamentally religious nature. Argues that "the main principles of Kwakiutl culture, those that govern lineage, rank, marriage, the distribution and exchange of property, and rivalries and antagonisms among chiefs, are also so closely identified with religion as to be conceived as religious expressions." Bibliography. Black-and-white illustrations.

Kan, Sergei. *Symbolic Immortality: The Tlingit Potlatch of the Nineteenth Century*. Washington, D.C.: Smithsonian Institution Press, 1989.

Describes and analyzes the rites comprising the nineteenth century mortuary cycle of the Tlingit Indians of the northern Northwest Coast. Part 1 provides a symbolic/sociological examination of aspects of Tlingit culture and society that directly relate to the tribe's mortuary/ancestral complex. Parts 2 and 3 contain analyses of the religious and political dimensions of the funeral ritual and memorial potlatch, respectively. The conclusion summarizes the study's findings and "examines the implications of this work for the anthropology of death, outlining a more comprehensive model of mortuary analysis, which combines attention to the political, religious, and often neglected but essential emotional dimensions of death-related rituals." Black-and-white photographs. Maps and tables.

Miller, Jay. *Shamanic Odyssey: The Lushootseed Salish Journey to the Land of the Dead*. Menlo Park, Calif.: Ballena Press, 1988.

A description and analysis of the Soul Recovery Ceremony, a ritual conducted by special shamans among the Southern Lushootseed of Puget Sound and neighboring Salish communities to cure someone whose soul had been carried away by ghosts to the land of the dead. Parts 1 and 2 provide generalized and specific accounts of the ceremony, respectively. Part 3 describes artifacts associated with the ritual on display or in storage at various museums. Subsequent sections compare aspects of the Lushootseed Soul Recovery Ceremony with those of other Native American cultures in order "to examine some of the important relationships binding together the Salish, the Northwest, and Native America in terms of beliefs about the afterlife, sacred potency, and shamanism." Bibliography. Black-and-white photographs. Two color drawings. One map.

Mourning Dove (Humishuma). *Coyote Stories*, edited by Jay Miller. Lincoln: University of Nebraska Press, 1990.

A collection of Interior Salishan tales concerning the exploits of Coyote (*Sin-ka-lip'*), "the ultimate negative example, sharing this distinction with other trickster-transformer characters such as Hare in the East, Raven in the Northwest, and Spider in the Plains." An editor's introduction provides a cultural context in which to interpret the narratives as well as a brief biography of Mourning Dove. Black-and-white drawings.

Ramsey, Jarold, comp. and ed. *Coyote Was Going There: Indian Literature of the Oregon Country*. Seattle: University of Washington Press, 1977.

Seeks to make accessible to the general public a representative selection of accurately rendered Oregon Indian myths. Included are myths of the Nez Percé, Cayuse, Chinook, Modoc, Wishram, Klammath, and northern Paiute. The texts are organized by the following subregions: northeastern Oregon, the Columbia, the Willamette Valley, the Coast, southwestern Oregon, and the Great Basin. An editor's introduction describes some of the important stylistic and thematic characteristics of the narratives. Bibliography.

Reichard, Gladys A. *An Analysis of Coeur d'Alene Indian Myths*. Memoirs of the American Folklore Society 41. Philadelphia: American Folklore Society, 1947.
A collection and analysis of sacred narratives belonging to the Coeur d'Alene people of northern Idaho. The first four chapters address the issues of narrative style, the aspects of culture and psychology reflected in the texts, and the distribution of whole tales, episodes, and themes. Following these discussions are forty-eight narratives, nearly half of which are drawn from the Coyote or trickster cycle. Bibliography.

Robinson, Harry, edited and compiled by Wendy Wickwire. *Write It on Your Heart: The Epic World of an Okanagan Storyteller*. Vancouver: Talonbooks/ Theytus, 1989.
A collection of Okanagan stories narrated in English by tribal elder and storyteller Harry Robinson. The texts are divided among four chronologically arranged sections. The first section contains stories of the creation of the world and its animal-peoples. Also included are narratives concerning the adventures of culture hero/trickster Coyote. Section 2 relates stories of human peoples, created after the time of animal-people. The stories in section 3 concern the relation of tribal ancestors with spirit helpers. The final section provides historical recollections from the period after contact with whites. An editor's introduction describes the characteristics of each period and presents a biographical sketch of Harry Robinson. Black-and-white photographs.

Slickpoo, Allen P., Sr. *Nu Mee Poom Tit Wah Tit (Nez Percé Legends)*. Nez Percé Tribe of Idaho, 1972.
A selection of forty-six legends from Idaho's Nez Percé tribe. An introduction describes the characteristics of these narratives and their functions in Nez Percé society. The texts are arranged under the following categories: "How Things Came to Be the Way They Are Today," "Tales of Disobedience," "Tales of Vengeance," "Tales of Shrewdness," "Tales of Greed," and "Tales of Bravery." Glossary. List of references. Black-and-white drawings.

Subsistence and Land Use

Gunther, Erna. *Ethnobotany of Western Washington*. Rev. ed. Seattle: University of Washington Press, 1973.
A study of plant knowledge and uses of selected tribes in western Washington, including the Chehalis, Cowlitz, Green River, Klallum, Lower Chinook, Lummi, Makah, Nisqually, Puyallup, Quileute, Quinault, Samish, Skagit, Skokomish, Snohomish, Snuqualmi, Squaxin, and Swinomish. An introduction

begins by briefly reviewing the literature on ethnobotany. It then discusses the geography and cultures of the study area, the study's methodology, informants, and arrangement of materials. The body of the monograph consists of a listing of plants organized according to botanical order, beginning with ferns. Information for each plant species includes Indian name(s) and uses as food, materials, or medicine. Indexed by the colloquial names of the plants. Two appendices. Bibliography. One map.

People of 'Ksan. *Gathering What the Great Nature Provided: Food Traditions of the Gitksan*. Vancouver: Douglas and McIntyre and Seattle: University of Washington Press, 1980.

Describes the traditional subsistence modes and culinary arts of the Gitksan, a Tsimshian people living in the Skeena River area of north- central British Columbia. Chapter 1 discusses general methods of cooking, preserving, and storing food. Chapter 2 presents traditional Gitksan preparations for a wide variety of fish, meat, fowl, berries and fruit, and tubers, bulbs, roots, bark, and greens. Also described is the rendering of Oolichan grease, an extremely important staple of the Gitksan and other Northwest Coast peoples. Chapter 3 contains cooking hints by tribal elders. Closes with discussions of Gitksan etiquette. Two appendices: the writing system and terminology. Black-and-white photographs and drawings by Hilary Stewart.

Stewart, Hilary. *Cedar: Tree of Life to the Northwest Coast Indians*. Seattle: University of Washington Press, 1984.

A detailed presentation of the central place of the cedar tree in the lives of Northwest Coast Indians. Stress is placed on the basic technologies and products associated with this tree. Part 1 presents an insider's perspective on the prominence of cedar work among the area's tribes. Part 2 contains a botanical description of the cedar tree; early evidence of its use by coastal peoples; and traditional narratives on the origins of Red and Yellow Cedars. Parts 3 through 6 examine the uses to which various parts of the tree—its wood, bark, withes, and roots— were put. The final part discusses the spiritual and healing powers Northwest Coast Indians attributed to the cedar. Bibliography. Black-and-white photographs, drawings, and maps.

__________. *Indian Fishing: Early Methods on the Northwest Coast*. Seattle: University of Washington Press, 1977.

A discussion of the traditional procedures Native Americans of the coastal Northwest used to catch, process, preserve, and cook fish. Begins with a Tlingit narrative which recounts how the fish came to be in the sea. Next describes the paramount place of fish and fishing in the cultures of Northwest Coast Indians. The following chapter discusses the wide variety of fishing gear, including lines, sinkers, hooks, lures, floats, clubs, spears and harpoons, nets and netting, and traps and weirs. Chapter 5 describes the customary modes of preserving, cooking, and feasting on fish. A final chapter presents the religious beliefs and practices associated with fish and fishing. The text is accompanied by carefully rendered drawings and black-and-white photographs of methods and equipment described. Bibliography. One map.

Family and Society

Codere, Helen. *Fighting with Property: A Study of Kwakiutl Potlatching and Warfare 1792-1930*. New York: J. J. Augustin, 1950.

Examines how changes in Kwakiutl life during the late eighteenth through early twentieth centuries served to strengthen the potlatch, a lavish ceremonial in which food and property are given away in exchange for the validation of the host's hereditary status. According to the author, "the binding force in Kwakiutl history was their limitless pursuit of a kind of social prestige which required continual proving to be established or maintained against rivals, and that the main shift in Kwakiutl history was from a time when success in warfare and head hunting was significant to the time when nothing counted but successful potlatching." Bibliography. Black-and-white drawings. Maps and tables.

Dauenhauer, Nora M., and Richard Dauenhauer, eds. *Haa Shuka, Our Ancestors: Tlingit Oral Narratives*. Seattle: University of Washington Press, 1987.

A bilingual presentation of fifteen Tlingit clan stories, reflecting the tribe's history, values, and culture. An introduction discusses the format and system of transcription, the characteristics of oral style, the wide range of themes and concepts displayed in the narratives, the editors' approach to translation, the nature of Tlingit grammar. Bibliography. Black-and-white photographs. Map.

Drucker, Philip, and Robert F. Heizer. *To Make My Name Good: A Reexamination of the Southern Kwakiutl Potlatch*. Berkeley: University of California Press, 1967.

A critique of writings that view the social functions of Southern Kwakiutl potlatching as fundamentally different from that of other Northwest Coast groups. Argues that the essence of the potlatch among all Northwest Coast societies, including the Kwakiutl, was to identify publicly the membership of the group and to define the social status of this membership. As such, it served as a formal procedure for social integration. Bibliography.

Garfield, Viola E. *Tsimshian Clan and Society*. University of Washington Publications in Anthropology, vol. 7, no. 3. Seattle: University of Washington Press, 1939.

Examines how clan and tribal affiliations structure the ongoing relationships of Tsimshian individuals. An introductory chapter identifies and describes the primary groupings of the tribe's social organization. Subsequent sections focus on patterns of relationship exhibited in the potlatch, life cycle, property rights and warfare, and secret societies. A concluding section identifies changes that have occurred in modern social and religious organization as a result of white contact. Bibliography. Glossary for Native terms appearing in the text. Black-and-white photographs and diagrams. Two maps.

Oberg, Kalervo. *The Social Economy of the Tlingit Indians*. Seattle: University of Washington Press, 1973.

Describes the economic and social life of southeastern Alaska's Tlingit Indians. Chapter 1, "The Tlingit and Their Country," includes sections on the tribe's natural environment, history, physical type, technology, and culture. Subsequent chapters discuss social structure and organization, property, the annual cycle of production, the organization of labor, the distribution of wealth, trade, and the consumption of wealth. One appendix. Bibliography. Black-and-white photographs. One map, charts, and graphs.

Material Culture and the Arts

Carlson, Roy L., ed. *Indian Art Traditions of the Northwest Coast*. Burnaby, British Columbia: Archaeology Press, Simon Fraser University, 1982.

Essays by nine authorities on Northwest Coast Indian cultural and artistic traditions. Topics include a general prehistory of the Northwest Coast, form in Northwest Coast art, meaning in Northwest Coast art, constraints that operated on production by Coast Salish artists, styles of coastal rock art, prehistoric art of the northern Northwest Coast, prehistoric art of the Lower Fraser region, Mid-Fraser and Thompson River area mobile art (art that is not fixed to any one location), and art from the Ozette site on the northern coast of Washington. Bibliography. Black-and-white photographs and diagrams. Maps.

Densmore, Frances. *Music of the Indians of British Columbia*. Bureau of American Ethnology, Bulletin 136. Washington, D.C.: U.S. Government Printing Office, 1943.

An analysis of Indian music from the Northwest Coast based on a sample of 2500 songs from widely dispersed peoples of the area. The ninety-eight songs presented in the text are categorized according to the following typology: songs with treatment of the sick, war songs, potlatch songs, dance songs, social songs, game songs, canoe songs, songs connected with stories, songs for children, love songs, divorce songs, and miscellaneous songs. A general description is presented for each category followed by the transcriptions and ethnological and musicological analyses of selected songs. Bibliography. Black-and-white photographs.

__________. *Nootka and Quileute Music*. Bureau of American Ethnology, Bulletin 124. Washington, D.C.: U.S. Government Printing Office, 1939.

A study of Nootka and Quileute songs collected at Neah Bay in Washington State during 1923 and 1927. Begins with a characterization of the author's singer-informants, followed by brief histories and ethnographies of the three tribes whose music is presented: the Makah and Clayoquot belonging to the Nootka branch of the Wakashan linguistic stock, and the Quileute, a Chimakuan tribe. The body of the book presents transcriptions and ethnological and musicological analyses of selected songs. Provides a tabular comparison of Nootka and Quileute songs with those of the Chippewa, Sioux, Ute, Mandan,

Hidatsa, Papago, Menominee, Yuma, and Yaqui. Bibliography. Black-and-white photographs and drawings.

Garfield, Viola E., et al. *The Tsimshian: Their Arts and Music*. Publications of the American Ethnological Society, vol. 18. New York: J. J. Augustin, 1951.
Three essays on the arts of Tsimshian Indians of the Northwest Coast. The first essay considers the tribe's artistic achievements within the wider contexts of its social and cultural institutions. Among the arts discussed are drama, dancing, music, painting, engraving, sculpture, metal work, and weaving. The second essay focuses on Tsimshian sculpture, especially as represented by masks and totem poles. The third essay reproduces and analyzes seventy-five songs. Included in this presentation are musical transcriptions of the songs, free and literal translations of the song lyrics, musical analyses by Marguerite Beclard d'Harcourt, and miscellaneous notes taken at the time the songs were recorded. Bibliography. Black-and-white drawings and photographs.

Inverarity, Robert B. *Art of the Northwest Coast Indians*. Berkeley: University of California Press, 1950.
An ethnological and stylistic examination of the Indian art of the Northwest Coast. The text first presents a summary of the pre- and postcontact histories of the inhabitants of that region. It next provides overviews of the material culture and social patterns traditionally shared by Northwest Coast peoples. A final section applies the categories of stylistic analysis to the art forms of the area. These categories include general style, medium, line, color, tones, form, texture, organization, pattern, development of design, and proportion. Part 2 contains nearly three hundred black-and-white and color plates accompanied by commentaries. Bibliography.

MacDonald, George F. *Haida Monumental Art: Villages of the Queen Charlotte Islands*. Vancouver: University of British Columbia Press, 1983.
A photographic essay and analysis of the architecture and monumental sculpture of the Queen Charlotte Haida. The first chapter of part 1 provides important data on Haida archaeology, history, and culture. Chapter 2 begins with a symbolic interpretation of the Haida house, then discusses house types, house buildings, house decorations (including crests and frontal poles), and monumental and architectural features (including mortuary sculpture and memorial poles). Chapter 3 profiles selected ethnographers who have worked among the Haida. Parts 2 and 3 contain photographs and commentaries on the monumental art and architecture of selected northern and southern villages, respectively. A brief history is also supplied for each village. Concludes with an essay entitled "Photography and the Haida Villages of the Queen Charlotte Islands: A historical Perspective" by Richard J. Huyda. Selected bibliography. Black-and-white drawings and photographs.

Merriam, Alan P. *Ethnomusicology of the Flathead Indians*. Chicago: Aldine, 1967.
A detailed analysis of Flathead music in its social and cultural contexts. Part 1, "The Ethnography of Flathead Music," begins by examining tribal conceptions

of music and musicianship. It next discusses the variety of Flathead sound instruments and ideas relating to their ownership. Subsequent chapters concern types and uses of music, including songs of personal power, songs of the life cycle, social songs and dances, songs and dances associated with war, and ceremonial songs and dances. The section closes with an analysis of continuity and change in Flathead music and a description of problems associated with the ethnographic interpretation of music. Part 2 contains a sample and analysis of Flathead songs. Four appendices. Bibliography. Charts.

Samuel, Cheryl. *The Chilkat Dancing Blanket*. Seattle: Pacific Search Press, 1982.
A technical, ethnological, and aesthetic analysis of the Chilkat blanket, a robe worn for dancing on ceremonial occasions by Indian nobility from Yakutat, Alaska, to Vancouver Island, British Columbia. Part 1 begins with traditional Tsimshian accounts of the origins of dancing blankets. It then discusses the ceremonial and social functions of such blankets as well as selected aspects of their manufacture and decoration. Part 2 describes the materials and techniques used in making these robes. Part 3 reconstructs the evolution of weaving styles. Part 4 provides highly detailed instructions for weaving a dancing blanket. Three appendices: map of major tribes of the northern Northwest Coast, dye recipes, and coloring guidelines. Bibliography. Black-and-white drawings and photographs; color plates.

Stewart, Hilary. *Looking at Indian Art of the Northwest Coast*. Seattle: University of Washington Press, 1979.
Intended to aid in appreciating and interpreting the two-dimensional art of Northwest Coast Indians. The first section identifies the basic forms through which Northwest Coast artists express design concepts. Section 2 describes and illustrates how these forms are combined to create the naturalistic and abstract animal designs typical of Northwest Coast graphic arts. The significance of each animal in aboriginal Northwest Coast culture is also discussed. Section 3 briefly examines the main characteristic of the following regional styles: Coast Salish, West Coast (formerly Nootka), Kwakiutl, 'Ksan, and Haida. Bibliography. Black-and-white photographs and diagrams. One map.

Waterman, T. T. *Notes on the Ethnology of the Indians of Puget Sound*. Indian Notes and Monographs, Miscellaneous Series 59. New York: Museum of the American Indian, Heye Foundation, 1973.
Studies the historical relationship between Puget Sound cultures and those of other regions of western North America. Focuses primarily on elements of material culture, including basketry and textiles, tools, and hunting and fishing implements. Presents brief discussions of games and the potlatch. Concludes that for certain specific traits, there is a clear influence from the Plateau. Bibliography. Black-and-white photographs and drawings.

Tribal Life

Boas, Franz. *Kwakiutl Ethnography*, edited by Helen Codere. Chicago: University of Chicago Press, 1966.

A posthumously published edition of Franz Boas' summary of Kwakiutl society and culture. An introduction briefly discusses the theoretical underpinnings of Boas' ethnography, his fieldwork among the Kwakiutl, and his relationship with informant George Hunt and his family. Chapter 1 provides a general overview of the Northwest Coast environment, languages, and cultures. Subsequent chapters concern technology and economic organization, social organization, the potlatch, war, religion, the Winter Ceremonial, mythology, the arts, and the life cycle. Five appendices present materials on gestures, medicine, games, the Northern Ceremonial, and the Winter Ceremonial of the $\mathrm{DE}^{\epsilon}\textit{na'x}{\bullet}\textit{da}^{\epsilon}\textit{x}^{\underline{u}}$. Bibliography. One map. Black-and-white photographs and drawings.

Colson, Elizabeth. *The Makah Indians: A Study of an Indian Tribe in Modern American Society*. Minneapolis: University of Minnesota Press, 1953.

A description of life on the Makah reservation at Neah Bay, Washington, as it existed in the early 1940's. Particular emphasis is given to the problem of assimilation with reference to the manner in which the Makah view themselves, how they interact with other Americans, and beliefs they hold regarding their relationship with one another. Concludes, on the one hand, that Makah have assimilated to the extent that forms of their contemporary culture are largely white derived and successfully manipulated in cooperation with whites. On the other hand, there "is a body of traditional associations or meanings common to Makah, but not shared with whites . . . [and] the Makah . . . continue to think of themselves as a distinctive people in contrast with whites." Bibliography.

Daugherty, Richard D. *The Yakima People*. Phoenix: Indian Tribal Series, 1973.

A summary of the history and culture of the Yakima Nation. Opening sections treat Yakima prehistory, language, traditional lifeways, and personal development. Subsequent discussion concerns the history of Yakima-white relations from the late 1700's to the present day (circa 1973). Provides a list of suggested readings. Black-and-white photographs and color plates. Maps.

Fahey, John. *The Flathead Indians*. Norman: University of Oklahoma Press, 1974.

Documents the changes in Flathead political, social, and economic institutions from the tribe's first contact with whites in the early nineteenth century through the opening of their reservation to homesteaders in 1910. Chapter 1 provides a conjectural reconstruction of tribal prehistory. Subsequent discussion reports on the Flathead's participation in the fur trade, which, "without intending it, largely destroyed the Indian way of life by depleting small game and speeding extermination of the buffalo"; the work of Jesuit missionaries beginning in 1841; the steady shrinkage of the tribe's traditional homelands in western Montana's Bitterroot Valley; their confinement to the Jocko (Flathead) Reservation; and the allotment of this reserve in the early twentieth century with the sale of "surplus" lands to whites. Bibliography. Black-and-white reproductions and photographs.

Gunther, Erna. *Klallam Ethnography*. University of Washington Publications in Anthropology, vol. 1, pt. 5. Seattle: University of Washington Press, 1927.

A detailed cultural description of the Klallum, a Salishan-speaking people whose traditional homeland lay on the northern coast of Washington State. After briefly describing the tribe's geographical setting, population, and linguistic and cultural relations, the monograph reports on various aspects of its traditional life. These include the nature of villages and houses, economic life, manufactures, measurements and time reckoning, dress and personal adornment, the life cycle, social life, religious life, the potlatch, and the singing of spirit songs. Bibliography. One map.

Haines, Francis. *The Nez Percé: Tribesmen of the Columbian Plateau*. Norman: University of Oklahoma Press, 1955.

A history of Idaho's Nez Percé Indians focusing on the period between their first contact with Americans (the Lewis and Clark expedition of 1805-1806) and the allotment of their reservation in 1895. The opening chapters sketch the tribe's aboriginal homelands; cultural patterns; and rapid transformation, following their introduction to horses and guns, from a sedentary, isolated group of fishing Indians living in small, permanent villages to seminomadic hunters of buffalo. Subsequent chapters examine Christian missionary work among the Nez Percé in the 1830's and 1840's; the creation of a Nez Percé Reservation at the Council on the Walla Walla in 1855; the internal dissensions and factionalism caused by the treaty; the invasion of miners on tribal territory after the discovery of gold; government attempts to "civilize" the tribe; the reduction of Nez Percé lands in 1863; events and conditions leading to the Nez Percé War of 1877; the removal of Chief Joseph and his followers to Indian Territory and later to the Colville Reservation after the war; and the application of the Dawes Allotment Act to Nez Percé lands from 1889 to 1895. Bibliographical essay. Black-and-white reproductions and photographs.

Hill-Tout, Charles. *The Salish People: The Local Contributions of Charles Hill-Tout*, edited by Ralph Maud. 4 vols. Vancouver: Talonbooks, 1978.

A compilation of scattered and long-unavailable reports by Charles Hill-Tout on Salishan peoples of the Pacific Northwest. Volume 1 contains information on the social and cultural traditions of the Thompson and the Okanagan Indians. Featured in volume 2 are Squamish and Lillooet lifeways. Ethnological studies and narratives of the Mainland Halkomelem are presented in volume 3. The series concludes with a volume on the oral traditions, beliefs, and practices of the Sechelt and the southeastern tribes of Vancouver Island. A biobibliography of the author concludes the final installment. Black-and-white photographs. Maps.

Josephy, Alvin M. *The Nez Percé Indians and the Opening of the Northwest*. New Haven, Conn.: Yale University Press, 1965.

Traces the history of the Nez Percé people from their first meeting with white Americans during the early nineteenth century through their war with the U.S. government in 1877. Part 1 begins with a brief overview of traditional Nez Percé society and culture. It then examines the effects of the tribe's participation in the fur trade on their customary lifeways. Part 2 describes Nez Percé-white relations up through the early 1870's, paying particular attention to missionary activity in the 1830's and 1840's and the Walla Walla Council of

1855, which both established the Nez Percé Reservation and gave rise to treaty versus antitreaty factions within the tribe. Part 3 discusses the causes and consquences of the 1877 Nez Percé War. Bibliography. Black-and-white photographs and drawings. Maps.

Powell, Jay, and Vickie Jensen. *Quileute: An Introduction to the Indians of La Push*. Seattle: University of Washington Press, 1976.

A concise, profusely illustrated ethnography of the Quileute, a Chimakuan-speaking people who live at the mouths of the Quillayute and Hoh rivers on Washington's Olympic Peninsula. Among the topics treated are the traditional lifeways of the tribe, myths and legends, the Quileute language, Quileute place names, tribal games, and food and recipes. Selected bibliography. Black-and-white photographs and drawings. Maps.

Ray, Verne F. *The Sanpoil and Nespelem: Salishan Peoples of Northeastern Washington*. University of Washington Publications in Anthropology, vol. 5. Seattle: University of Washington Press, 1933.

An ethnography of the Sanpoil and Nespelem, two Salishan-speaking peoples of the north-central Plateau. An introduction discusses the groups' linguistic and cultural affiliations, geography, villages, and population. Subsequent chapters examine the yearly cycle and daily round; architecture and household articles; clothing and personal adornment; subsistence modes including fishing, hunting, and gathering; food preparation; sociopolitical organization; the life cycle; amusements; religious beliefs and ceremonies; medical knowledge; and measurements and color classifications. Bibliography. Black-and-white photographs and drawings. One map.

Rohner, Ronald P., and Evelyn C. Bettauer. *The Kwakiutl: Indians of British Columbia*. Prospect Heights, Ill.: Waveland Press, 1986.

An ethnography of the Gilford Island band of Kwakiutl Indians. Part 1 attempts to portray the band's contemporary life, focusing on their manner of subsistence; religious beliefs and practices; normative standards, deviance, and modes of social control; political organization; health problems; and the experience of growing up Kwakiutl. Part 2 examines the major institutions of traditional Kwakiutl culture, including kinship, the potlatch, and the winter ceremonial. List of references and recommended readings. Tables. Black-and-white photographs.

Ruby, Robert H., and John A. Brown. *The Cayuse Indians: Imperial Tribesmen of Old Oregon*. Norman: University of Oklahoma Press, 1972.

Recounts the history of Oregon and Washington's Cayuse Indians from the days before white contact to the beginning of the twentieth century. Examines the impact of the fur trade, missionary work, and white settlement on the tribe's social and cultural patterns; the Whitman massacre in 1847 and the war between the Cayuse and white Oregonians which it ignited; the treaty of Walla Walla (June, 1855) in which the Cayuse agreed to cede their lands and relocate on the Umatilla Reservation; and the rejection of this agreement by many tribal members who nonetheless were eventually forced onto the reserve. Five appendices. Bibliography. Black-and-white reproductions, photographs, and drawings.

Ruby, Robert H., and John A. Brown. *The Spokane Indians: Children of the Sun.* Norman: University of Oklahoma Press, 1970.

An ethnohistory of the Spokane Indians, a Salish people of the Columbia Plateau "buffeted by massive cultural changes, seeking to accommodate to, then to resist, the tide of white encroachment, but in the end succumbing." Begins with an overview of the tribe's aboriginal society and culture. Subsequent chapters discuss the events and dynamics of Spokane-white relations from first contact in the late eighteenth century to the 1960's. Bibliography. Black-and-white reproductions and photographs. Maps.

Stearns, Mary Lee. *The Flathead Indians of Montana.* Memoirs of the American Anthropological Association 48. Menasha, Wis.: American Anthropological Association, 1937.

An ethnography of the Salish, or Flathead, Indians of western Montana. Begins with a consideration of what Flathead oral traditions and archaeology tell us of the tribe's history. Subsequent chapters concern Salish conceptions of the natural environment; religious belief and ceremony; the social environment, including discussion of forms of social control, kinship behavior and terminology, war; childhood; marriage and the family; subsistence; and medical treatment and ceremonies related to death. One appendix.

__________. *Haida Culture in Custody: The Masset Band.* Seattle: University of Washington Press, 1981.

Examines the changes that have occurred in Masset Haida society as a result of its political subordination to the Canadian government. Describes the Masset social condition as "structurally discontinuous," characterized by the segregation of institutions of governance from those which meet the psychobiological needs of individuals. Suggests that although structural discontinuity is a primary source of community disruption and normative confusion, the Masset case suggests that a "decapitated native community can maintain cultural continuity in those areas of social life that are relatively protected from external interference." Black-and-white photographs and tables.

Stern, Bernhard. *The Lummi Indians of Northwest Washington.* New York: Columbia University Press, 1934.

Describes the society and culture of the Lummi Indians, speakers of a Coast Salish dialect who inhabit a reservation near the Canadian border in northwestern Washington State. Part 1, "The Cycle of Life," includes sections on childbirth, the socialization of boys, girls' puberty ceremony, marriage, the household, and death. Part 2, "Tribal Culture," discusses modes of subsistence, festivities, social distinctions, medicine men, magic, *xunxanital* (a secret society that punishes those using magic to injure others), weaving and woodworking, and conflict. Part 3, "Legend and Lore," contains a selection of sacred narratives. Black-and-white photographs. One map.

Stern, Theodore. *The Klamath Tribe: A People and Their Reservation.* Seattle: University of Washington Press, 1966.

Provides a history of the Klamath Indians of south-central Oregon from aboriginal times to the termination of their reservation in 1954. Chapter 1 first presents an overview of the cultural patterns of the Klamath and closely affiliated Modoc before contact with whites. It then examines the relations between the Klamath-Modoc and Anglo-Americans up to the signing of the treaty of 1864, which established the Klamath reservation. Subsequent chapters examine the effect of various eras of federal Indian policy on the tribe. Bibliography. Black-and-white photographs. Maps.

Teit, James A. *The Salishan Tribes of the Western Plateau*, edited by Franz Boas, Bureau of American Ethnology, Annual Report 45 (1927-1928). Washington, D.C.: U.S. Government Printing Office, 1930.

A collection of papers describing the lifeways of the Coeur d'Alene and the various groups of Okanagan and Flathead peoples. Information on the following topics is presented for each group: history, geographical distribution and population; manufactures; house and household; clothing and ornaments; modes of subsistence; travel, transportation, and trade; warfare; games and entertainments; sign language; social organization; the life cycle; religious beliefs and ceremonies; and medicines and current beliefs. Bibliography. Black-and-white photographs and drawings. Tables and charts.

Turney-High, Harry H. *Ethnography of the Kutenai.* Memoirs of the American Anthropological Association. Menasha, Wis.: American Anthropological Association, 1941.

Describes the society and culture of the Kutenai Indians, a widely dispersed people inhabiting interior British Columbia, the northern Idaho panhandle, and northern Montana west of the Rockies. Includes sections on the origin and meaning of the tribal name, the Kutenai bands and their histories, the nature and scope of aboriginal territories, modes of subsistence, housing, transportation and domestic animals, technologies and manufactures, dress and ornamentation, knowledge and the arts, the life cycle, kinship and social organization, religious beliefs and ceremonies, language and communication, and principles of economics. Bibliography. Black-and-white photographs. One map.

Biography and Autobiography

Blackman, Margaret B. *During My Time: Florence Edenshaw Davidson, a Haida Woman.* Seattle: University of Washington Press; Vancouver, Toronto: Douglas and McIntyre, 1982.

Davidson, a Haida woman born in the village of Masset, Queen Charlotte Islands, in 1896, tells of her childhood, marriage and family, and later years. According to Blackman, "[h]er narrative provides commentary on the cultural themes and values governing her life, the options and choices open to the Haida individual, male and female roles, culture change, and the processes by which cultural information is lost." One appendix. Bibliography. Black-and-white photographs. One map and a chart.

Chief Joseph. *Chief Joseph's Own Story*. Reprinted by permission from the *North American Review*, April, 1879, and "Northwestern Fights and Fighters" by Cyrus Townsend Brady. n.p., n.d.
Chief Joseph (In-mut-too-yah-lat-lat/Thunder-traveling-over the mountains) tells of the U.S. government's unjust treatment of the Nez Percé people and how this injustice resulted in their conflict with federal troops in 1877. Chief Joseph states that "[w]hen I think of our condition my heart is heavy. I see men of my race treated as outlaws and driven from country to country or shot down like animals. . . . Whenever the white man treats the Indian as they treat each other, then we shall have peace."

Mourning Dove. *Mourning Dove: A Salishan Autobiography*, edited by Jay Miller. Lincoln: University of Nebraska Press, 1990.
The recollections of a Salishan Indian who was the first Native American woman to publish a novel. The work contributes a feminine perspective on life on the Colewille Reservation in the late nineteenth and early twentieth centuries. The first section discusses the typical life stages of a Salishan woman. Section 2 describes the tribe's traditional patterns of subsistence. The concluding section provides a tribal history. An editor's introduction presents a biographical sketch of Mourning Dove and the significance of her autobiography. One appendix. Bibliography. Black-and-white photographs.

Nowell, Charles J. *Smoke from Their Fires: The Life of a Kwakiutl Chief*, edited by Clellan S. Ford. New Haven, Conn.: Yale University Press, for the Institute of Human Relations, 1941.
Nowell, a member of a high-ranking Kwakiutl family, relates the major events in his life and traditions of his people. The narrative moves from the author's birth at Fort Rupert, Vancouver Island, in 1870 through discussions of his childhood, schooling at Alert Bay, teenage years, experiences with girls, marriage, participation in potlatches, adult life, and later years. Color reproductions. One map.

Spradley, James, ed. *Guests Never Leave Hungry: The Autobiography of James Sewid, a Kwakiutl Indian*. New Haven, Conn.: Yale University Press, 1969.
A chief of the Nimpkish band of Alert Bay Kwakiutl details his many experiences and accomplishments in both the Indian and white worlds. The editor's analysis examines the factors underlying the subject's successful adaptation to two radically different ways of life. Bibliography. Black-and-white photographs.

Arctic and Subarctic

General Studies and References

Damas, David. *Arctic*. Vol. 5 in *Handbook of North American Indians*. Washington, D.C.: Smithsonian Institution, 1984.

An anthology of essays on Arctic prehistory, history, and cultures. An editor's introduction applies the concept of culture area to Eskimo peoples. The essays in part 1 treat the history of Arctic archaeology and ethnology, the Arctic physical environment and ecosystems, Eskimo and Aleut languages, human biology in the Arctic, and Arctic archaeology. Parts 2, 3, and 4 contain articles on the history and cultures of the western Arctic, Canadian Arctic, and Greenland, respectively. Part 5 provides perspectives on the contemporary status of Arctic Natives and issues affecting their lives.

Denkin, Albert A., Jr. *Arctic Archaeology: A Bibliography and History*. New York: Garland, 1978.

A listing of resources on Arctic archaeology designed to facilitate access to a widely scattered literature. Part 1 contains an extended bibliographical essay with discussions of the following topics: explorers and ethnographers, expeditions and pioneers, chronologists and prehistorians, archaeologists and anthropologists, recent developments, and current trends and problems. The entries in the bibliography are alphabetically arranged by author. One appendix: additional sources of information.

Graburn, Nelson, and B. Stephen Strong. *Circumpolar Peoples: An Anthropological Perspective*. Santa Monica, Calif.: Goodyear, 1973.

Provides brief ethnographic portraits of Arctic and Subarctic native peoples. An introductory chapter presents information on climate and geography, ecology and demography, physical anthropology, some common cultural characteristics of circumpolar tribes, linguistics, and white-Indian relations. Subsequent chapters examine distinctive cultural and social features of specific groups, including the Samek (Lapps), Northern Yakuts, Northern Evenk (Tungus), Chukchi, Naskapi, Aleuts, and Eskimos. Concludes with a discussion of modern conditions among Siberian, Alaskan, Canadian, and Greenlandic Natives. An annotated bibliography accompanies each chapter. Black-and-white reproductions, photographs, and drawings. Maps and charts.

Helm, June. *The Indians of the Subarctic: A Critical Bibliography*. Newberry Library Center for the History of the American Indian Bibliographical Series. Bloomington: Indiana University Press, 1976.

A bibliographical essay that reviews 272 books and articles pertaining to the history and culture of Subarctic Indians. The essay is divided by the following subheadings: introduction; basic reference works: identifications and classifications; major ethnographies; prehistory; histories and historical materials; Indian accounts and personal histories; contemporary conditions; native newsletters and newspapers; traditional Indian culture and society; language; and bibliographies and series. Lists recommended works for the beginner and for a basic library collection.

__________, ed. *Subarctic*. Vol. 6 in *Handbook of North American Indians*. Washington, D.C.: Smithsonian Institution, 1981.

A compendium of sixty-six essays by noted scholars synthesizing what is currently known concerning the prehistory, history, languages, and cultures of

Subarctic Native peoples. Part 1 contains broad discussions of such topics as the Subarctic environment, fauna and economy, the histories of ethnological and archaeological research in the Subarctic, the prehistories of the area's various regions, Northern Athapascan and Subarctic Algonquian languages, and museum and archival resources. Essays on tribes are organized according to the area's four major physiographic-ecological zones: the Subarctic portion of the Canadian Shield and the Mackenzie borderlands, the Subarctic Cordillera, the Alaska Plateau, and the region south of the Alaska Range. The remaining papers examine postcontact Indian settlements, modern Subarctic Indians and Métis, and expressive aspects of Subarctic Indian culture. A sixty-three-page bibliography lists all references cited in the essays. Black-and-white reproductions, photographs, and diagrams. Maps and charts.

Helm, June, and John R. Wood. *The Subarctic Athabascans: A Selected Annotated Bibliography*. Fairbanks: Institute of Social, Economic, and Government Research, University of Alaska, 1974.

An annotated listing of materials on the Northern Athapascan Indians intended as a research tool for those concerned with Native peoples of North America's Subarctic. Section 1 provides an alphabetical list of Athapascan literature by author. Section 2, also arranged alphabetically by author, contains complete bibliographic information for these titles and annotations. Section 3 organizes the entries by tribal group or area of Canada and Alaska. Tribal subheadings for the Alaskan Athapascan groups include the Atna, Eyak, Ingalik, Koyukon, Kutchin, Tanaina, and Tanana. Those for the Canadian Athapascan groups are the Bearlake, Beaver, Carrier, Chilcotin, Chipewyan, Dogrib, Hare, Nahane, Sarsi, Sekani, Slave, and Yellowknife. The section concludes with citations for general Alaskan, Canadian, and Subarctic Athapascan references. Section 4 lists the Athapascan literature according to the following "times of observation: "precontact and early white contact, early 1700's through 1800; 1801-1900; 1901-1940; and contemporary, 1941 through the present. Two appendices: partial list of unpublished Athapascan literature and partial list of Athapascan references in foreign languages. One map.

Jones, Dorothy M., and John R. Wood. *An Aleut Bibliography*. Fairbanks: Institute of Social, Economic, and Government Research, University of Alaska, 1975.

An annotated listing of English-language materials on the Aleut intended for those interested in sociological aspects of Aleutian history and culture. Section 1 provides an alphabetical list of Aleut literature by author. Section 2, also organized alphabetically by author, contains complete bibliographic information for these titles and annotations. Section 3 arranges the entries according to "time of observation" within four periods of Aleutian history: precontact and aboriginal, Russian administration to 1867, American administration from 1867 through 1940, and the contemporary period, including the World War II years. In Section 4, materials are organized according to the subject and type of publication, including accounts of explorers, scientists, and travelers; formal history; cultural anthropology; material culture; archaeology and prehistory;

physical and medical anthropology; linguistics; and postcontact economic development. Appendix: bibliographical works. Two maps.

Oswalt, Wendell H. *Eskimos and Explorers*. Novato, Calif.: Chandler and Sharp, 1979.

Traces the history of Eskimo encounters with European and Euro-American explorers from A.D. 1000 through the late 1800's. Begins with chapters on Norse-Eskimo relations in Greenland during the early eleventh century, the Forbisher expedition of 1576, and Eskimo-white contacts resulting from the "perfect craze" to find a northern sea route to the Far East. Subsequent chapters, which are arranged geographically, treat the West Greenlanders, Polar Eskimos, East Greenlanders, Canadian Inuit, Alaskan Inuit, and Alaskan Yuit. A concluding chapter compares and contrasts Eskimo life before and after contact with explorers. The author states that "[i]f aboriginal Eskimo life is best characterized as a constant struggle for survival, the aftermath of discovery has been nothing less than a battle against extinction." Two appendices. Bibliography. Black-and-white reproductions. Maps.

Simeone, William E. *A History of Alaskan Athapaskans, Including a Description of Athapaskan Culture and a Historical Narrative, 1785-1971*. Anchorage: Alaska Pacific University Press, 1982.

Traces the important events affecting the lives of Alaska's Athapaskan peoples from their first contact with whites in the late eighteenth century to the Alaska Claims Settlement Act of 1971. Part 1 offers an account of Athapascan subsistence, trade, kinship, ceremonialism, leadership, and warfare as they existed in the early to mid-nineteenth century. Part 2 contains a historical narrative of Athapascan-white relations focusing on the following topics: the Russian occupation (1785-1867), the Russian Orthodox church, the Hudson's Bay Company, the American fur trade (1867-1886), the Gold Rush period (1886-1867), Anglican and Catholic missions, and U.S. government Indian policy.

Archaeology

Bandi, Hans-Georg. *Eskimo Prehistory*, translated by Ann E. Keep. Fairbanks: University of Alaska Press, 1972.

Outlines Eskimo prehistory for various parts of the Arctic. The first two chapters present preliminary information on contemporary Eskimo culture, the earliest movements of population into the New World, and milestones in Arctic archaeology. The body of the book provides an extended discussion of sites, artifacts, and prehistoric cultures in the Eskimo area, including various regions of Alaska, Canada, and Greenland. A conclusion summarizes the author's reconstruction of the origin, development, and dissemination of Eskimo culture. Appendix. Bibliography. Black-and-white photographs and drawings. Maps and tables.

Dumond, Don E. *The Eskimos and Aleuts*. Rev. ed. London: Thames and Hudson, 1987.

Summarizes the physical, cultural, and linguistic evolution of the Eskimo and Aleut peoples from about 23,000 B.C. to A.D. 1500. Chapter 1 discusses early encounters between the Norse, English, and Russians and various Eskimo-Aleuts peoples. The chapters that follow overview archaeological findings for the Aleutian Islands, Pacific Coast and Kodiak islands, southwest Alaska, Chuckchi Peninsula, north Alaska, north Canada, and Greenland. Bibliography. Black-and-white photographs and drawings. Maps.

Maxwell, Moreau S. *Prehistory of the Eastern Arctic*. Orlando, Fla.: Academic Press, 1985.

Attempts to arrange in chronological sequence "descriptions of the adaptive technologies, tactics, and strategies devised by the prehistoric Eastern Arctic Eskimo over a nearly 4000-year period." Begins with the entrance of Paleoeskimo peoples into the eastern Arctic during the third millennium B.C. Subsequent chapters identify and describe the various expansions and modifications of pre-Dorset, Dorset, and Thule cultural traditions, which preceded the arrival of Norse settlers in the eleventh century A.D. Bibliography. Black-and-white photographs and drawings. Maps and tables.

Tuck, James A. *Maritime Provinces Prehistory*. Ottawa: National Museums of Canada, National Museum of Man, 1984.

Summarizes what is currently known regarding human prehistory in Canada's Maritime Provinces, which include Nova Scotia, New Brunswick, Newfoundland, and Prince Edward Island. Organizes the discussion around three periods, that are easily blocked by the presence or absence of certain elements in the archaeological record: Paleo-Indian, dating from 11,000 to 9000 B.P. and distinguished by a particular type of spear or dart point; Pre-Ceramic, 9000 to 2500 B.P., characterized by the absence of clay pots; and Ceramic, beginning about 2500 B.P. and continuing to the time of European contact. Bibliography. Black-and-white photographs and drawing. Maps.

Wright, J. V. *Ontario Prehistory: An Eleven-Thousand-Year Archaeological Outline*. Ottawa: National Museums of Canada, National Museum of Man, 1972.

Seeks to inform the general public of the principal prehistoric events during the 11,000 years of human presence in Ontario. Considers these events under four periods: the Paleo-Indian period, 9000 to 5000 B.C.; the Archaic period, 5000 to 1000 B.C.; the Initial Woodland period, 1000 B.C. to A.D. 1000; and the Terminal Woodland period, A.D. 1000 to the historic period. These periods are applied to the province's two principal regions, northern and southern Ontario, whose environments and prehistoric cultures vary in significant ways. Bibliography. Black-and-white and color photographs. Maps.

Folklore, Sacred Narrative, Religious Belief and Practice

Goddard, Pliny E. *The Beaver Indians*. Anthropological Papers of the American Museum of Natural History, vol. 10, pt. 4. New York: The Trustees, 1916.

A collection of eighty-one myths and tales from western Canada's Beaver

Indians. Preceding these narratives are a selection of ethnological notes on shelter, transportation, food, clothing, industrial arts, social organization, burial customs, and religion. Bibliography. Black-and-white photographs and drawings.

Hallowell, A. Irving. *The Role of Conjuring in Saulteaux Society*. Publications of the Philadelphia Anthropological Society, vol. 2. Philadelphia: Philadelphia Anthropological Society, 1942.

Seeks to make intelligible Saulteaux magicoreligious beliefs by describing the role of conjuring in that society. Defines Saulteaux conjuring as "an institutionalized means for obtaining the help of different classes of spiritual entities by invoking their presence and communicating human desires to them." Describes the characteristics and distribution of the Saulteaux type of conjuring, the means by which individuals become conjurers and an estimate of their number, economic compensation for conjurers, the elements of a conjuring performance, the conditions under which conjuring ceremonies are held, different types of skepticism concerning conjurers and conjuring, and the social functions of conjuring. Bibliography. Black-and-white photographs.

Kleivan, I., and B. Sonne. *Eskimos: Greenland and Canada*. Iconography of Religions, Section 8: Arctic Peoples. Leiden: E. J. Brill, 1985.

Overviews the central beliefs and ceremonies of Inuit religion. Among topics discussed are rites of passage, including those associated with birth, development, puberty, and death; hunting rituals; ritual behavior in relation to social conflict; the training and practices of shamans; and Inuit spirits and deities. Black-and-white photographs.

Lantis, Margaret. *Alaskan Eskimo Ceremonialism*. Monographs of the American Ethnological Society, vol. 11. New York: J. J. Augustin, 1947.

A survey of the ceremonial life of the Alaskan Eskimo. Defines ceremonialism as "any standardized public procedure of magico-socio-religious character, consisting of songs, prayers, offerings and sacrifices, mimetic dances, processions, games, feasts, and other traditional ritual objects and acts." The first three sections of part 1 describe rites associated with individual life crises. Sections 4 through 6 discuss building rites, war ritual, and rites for sun, moon, and weather. The conclusion of part 1 concerns ceremonialism connected with hunting. Each of the eight sections of part 2 focuses on one aspect of ceremonialism as a whole—for example, shamanism and purification. Bibliography.

Norman, Howard, ed. *Northern Tales: Traditional Stories of Eskimo and Indian Peoples*. New York: Pantheon Books, 1990.

A collection of 116 folktales from 35 different tribes of the Arctic and Subarctic. The narratives are arranged according to the following headings: "Stories of Village Life," "How Things Got to Be the Way They Are" (creation stories), "Tricksters and Culture Heroes," "Stories About Animals," "Shaman Stories," "Stories of Strange and Menacing Neighbors," "Hunting Stories," and "Stories About All Sorts of Marriages." Among the peoples represented are the Montagnais, Aleuts, Tanainas, Dogribs, Chukchees, Hares, and Naskapis. Bibliography. Black-and-white drawings.

Speck, Frank G. *Naskapi: The Savage Hunters of the Labrador Peninsula.* Norman: University of Oklahoma Press, 1935.

A detailed description of the religious beliefs and ceremonies of the Montagnais-Naskapi Indians. Identified and discussed are important spiritual beings and forces; the concept of soul; mythological personages and themes; the relationship of the Montagnais-Naskapi to the animals of the forest, tundra, and waters of the interior and coast; concepts and forms of divination; magical practices; and medicinal practices and charms for hunting. Glossary of Montagnais-Naskapi terms. Black-and-white photographs and drawings. One map and one table.

Subsistence and Land Use

Gubser, Nicholas J. *The Nunamiut Eskimos, Hunters of Caribou.* New Haven, Conn.: Yale University Press, 1965.

An analysis of the ecological adaptations of the Nunamiut, an Eskimo group that lives in Anaktuvuk Pass in the central Brooks Range of northern Alaska. Seeks to document how the group's ideas and concepts concerning the world of nature contribute to the maintenance of their society. The monograph begins with a brief tribal history. The following four chapters outline Nunamiut household and community organization and activities. Next treated are ideas and cognitive processes essential to the tribe's experience of geography and plant and animal life. The final chapters examine the Nunamiuts' exploitation of the caribou and other elements of their environment. Two appendices. Bibliography. One table.

Henriksen, Georg. *Hunters in the Barrens.* Newfoundland Social and Economic Studies 12. Institute of Social and Economic Research, Memorial University of Newfoundland. Toronto: University of Toronto Press for the Memorial University of Newfoundland, 1973.

Examines how seasonal shifts in Naskapi modes of subsistence affect their social, ecological, and ideological patterns. Argues that the Naskapi alternate between two life spheres: a winter sphere centered on hunting caribou in Labrador's interior and a summer sphere, characterized by village life on the coast of Labrador. Demonstrates that the Naskapi "hold the same values in both worlds, but the opportunities to maximize these values differ in the two worlds." Bibliography. Tables and charts.

Krech, Shepard, III, ed. *The Subarctic Fur Trade: Native Social and Economic Adaptations.* Vancouver: University of British Columbia Press, 1984.

A collection of six papers by anthropologists, geographers, and historians concerned with Indian social and economic adaptations to participation in the fur trade. The tribes discussed include the Western James Bay Cree, Chipewyan, Slavey, and Dogrib. A bibliography accompanies each essay. Maps and tables.

Leighton, Anna L. *Wild Plant Use by the Woods Cree (Nihithawak) of East Central Saskatchewan.* National Museum of Man Mercury Series, Canadian Ethnology Service Paper 101. Ottawa: National Museums of Canada, 1985.

Provides information on 123 wild plants used by Saskatchewan's Woods Cree Indians. Part 1 discusses plants employed as herbal remedies, food, teas, building materials, and for other needs. Briefly compares Saskatchewan Woods Cree plant uses with those of the Chippewa, Mistassini Cree, Attikamek, Alberta Cree, and Slave Indians. Part 2 includes an annotated list of data concerning plant species used by the Woods Cree of Saskatchewan. Black-and-white drawings. Maps and tables.

Nelson, Richard K. *Hunters of the Northern Forest*. Chicago: University of Chicago Press, 1973.

Examines modes of environmental exploitation among the Kutchin, an Athapaskan-speaking people of interior Alaska. Part 1 first summarizes the topic and methodology of the study, then provides a general description of Kutchin culture, their natural environment, and subsistence cycle. Part 2 is concerned with Kutchin knowledge and techniques associated with hunting, fishing, and gathering. Part 3 reports on the logistics of trapping the wide variety of fur-bearing animals of the region. Concludes with a history of changing patterns of Kutchin settlement, from the time of their first contact with Europeans to the emergence of villages. Bibliography. Black-and-white photographs. Maps.

_________. *Hunters of the Northern Ice*. Chicago: University of Chicago Press, 1969.

A study primarily concerned with traditional and modern forms of knowledge, techniques, and equipment employed by Eskimos of northwest Alaska in hunting, traveling, and surviving on the sea ice. Begins with a detailed portrait of the region's climate and geography. Next considers, in turn, the assorted resources of the sea-ice environment in relation to Eskimo hunting behavior and methods of exploitation. A concluding chapter discusses how the forces of acculturation have rendered hunting an endangered art among these Eskimo. Bibliography. Black-and-white photographs and drawings. Maps.

_________. *Make Prayers to the Raven: A Koyukon View of the Northern Forest*. Chicago: University of Chicago Press, 1983.

Seeks, first, to present a detailed account of Koyukon Athapaskan theories and relations with the natural world and, second, to contribute a Native natural history of the northwestern Subarctic that will afford biologists, naturalists, and environmental scientists "an alternative view on the nature of nature, together with a different concept of humanity's proper role in the environment." Finds that the basic assumption underlying Koyukon beliefs about nature is that the natural and supernatural worlds are inseparable, each being an intrinsic part of the other. This basic presupposition, in turn, encompasses three broad precepts: Explanations for the origin, design, and functioning of nature, and for proper human relationships to it, are found in stories of the Distant Time; natural entities are endowed with spirits and with spiritually based power; humans and natural entities are involved in a constant spiritual interchange that profoundly affects human behavior. Four appendices: the study, the boreal environment, Koyukon terms for natural entities, and uses for selected major species. Bibliography.

Spencer, Robert F. *The North Alaskan Eskimo: A Study in Ecology and Society*. Bureau of American Ethnology, Bulletin 171. Washington, D.C.: U.S. Government Printing Office, 1959.

Examines the relation between economy and society for the coastal and inland Eskimos of northern Alaska. Includes discussions of geography and ecological adaptations; language; houses and settlements; customary law; economy and society; property, wealth, and status; competition and cooperation; voluntary associations; trade; the life cycle; religious belief and practice; culture change; and folklore. Finds that the North Alaskans represent a basic Eskimo type with roots in antiquity. The differences that exist between the social institutions of coastal and inland groups are of degree only and in large measure "predicated on adjustments to the terrain and the business of making a living within it." For appendices. Bibliography. Black-and-white photographs and drawings. Maps.

Tanner, Adrian. *Bringing Home Animals: Religious Ideology and Mode of Production of the Mistassini Cree Hunters*. New York: St. Martin's Press, 1979.

Examines the relationship between the hunting and trapping system of the Mistassini Cree of the Canadian Subarctic and their social and religious customs. Among the book's key arguments are that the organization of space within the hunting camp is a reflection of the social organization of the hunting group; certain rites express symbolically ideas about spatial organization; and various elements of Cree religion relate directly to the practical reality of material production. These elements include divination, rites that take place during the killing of animals, and feasting. Bibliography. Black-and-white photographs and drawings. Tables.

VanStone, James W. *Athapaskan Adaptations: Hunters and Fishermen of the Subarctic Forests*. Chicago: Aldine, 1974.

Provides an ecological perspective on the Athapascan cultures of North America's Subarctic. Focus is on the variety of adaptive strategies these tribes have devised in order to survive in their extensive and diverse environment. Argues that "[t]raditional Athapascan culture must be thought of as essentially an accommodating culture, and accommodation, in turn, greatly facilitated survival in a demanding environment." Bibliography. Black-and-white photographs.

Wenzel, George W. *Clyde Inuit Adaptation and Ecology: The Organization of Subsistence*. National Museum of Man Mercury Series, Canadian Ethnology Service Paper 77. Ottawa: National Museums of Canada, 1981.

Analyzes the role of socially prescribed patterns of kinship behavior in shaping the subsistence activities and material adaptations of Inuit hunters in the Clyde River area of eastern Baffin Island. Argues that "the structural features associated with Clyde Inuit social relations also function as a discrete set of regulators which bring about, on a wider scale, the interactions occurring between the cultural system and the environment."

Family and Society

Briggs, Jean L. *Aspects of Inuit Value Socialization*. National Museum of Man Mercury Series, Canadian Ethnology Service Paper 56. Ottawa: National Museums of Canada, 1979.

Examines the role of play and playfulness in the creation, maintenance, and internalization of the central values of Inuit society. One of the author's conclusions is that "games present problems—often in the form of value conflicts—and dramatize them, so that they are made conceptually clear and emotionally vivid; they involve the child by making him solve the problems and by making the latter of dangerous—thus, crucial—importance. In this way they charge each value with complex emotional meaning, such that motivations—commitments—intrinsic to each are created." Bibliography.

Condon, Richard G. *Inuit Youth: Growth and Change in the Canadian Arctic*. New Brunswick, N.J.: Rutgers University Press, 1987.

Examines the social, psychological, and ideological responses of Inuit people of Holman Island to the psychobiological changes that occur during adolescence. The discussion is organized around several themes essential to understanding adolescent life on Holman: the rapid rate of social change experienced by that island's population during the last few decades, the strong influence of seasonal variation on all aspects of local social and economic life, and the high degree of autonomy allowed Inuit youngsters in structuring their lives. Three appendices. Maps, tables, and charts.

Giffen, Naomi M. *The Roles of Men and Women in Eskimo Culture*. Chicago: University of Chicago Press, 1930.

Examines the divisions in Eskimo social life that are based on sex. Finds the "division between men's and women's lives to be clearly defined, though the distribution is exclusively a practical one. Besides the tasks regularly apportioned by custom, others are done by either sex, according to the exigencies of the occasion." Discussion includes sexual divisions in relation to the procuring of food, food preparation, transportation, building and care of houses, manufacturing, property and inheritance, clothing and ornament, and nonmaterial culture. Bibliography.

Honigmann, John J., and Irma Honigmann. *Eskimo Townsmen*. Canadian Research Centre for Anthropology. Ottawa: University of Ottawa, 1965.

A study of Eskimo town life at Frobisher Bay, a Baffin Island community of sixteen hundred persons and administrative center for the region stretching one thousand miles north to Ellesmere Island. Focuses on the origins and patterns of social organization extending beyond the family; values directing the Eskimo way of life, including satisfaction or dissatisfaction with town life; the psychodynamic aspects of personality; patterns of child rearing; and alcohol abuse and rehabilitation. One appendix provides demographic information. Black-and-white photographs, drawings. Tables.

Lips, Julius E. *Naskapi Law*. Transactions of the American Philosophical Society, New Series, vol. 37, pt. 4. Philadelphia: American Philosophical Society, 1947.

A discussion of the principles and processes of law and order among the Lake St. John and Mistassini bands of Naskapi Indians. Begins with an outline of Naskapi economy. Next discusses the tribe's lawways as they relate to sociopolitical organization, the individual, the family, property and inheritance, contracts and tradeways, crime and methods of punishment, and law-enforcing agencies. Argues that in the case of Naskapi law, equity is "not only an ethical obligation but a jural one as well and is enforced by the sanctions of positive law." Bibliography. Black-and-white photographs. Tables.

Osgood, Cornelius. ***Ingalik Social Culture***. Yale University Publications in Anthropology 53. New Haven, Conn.: Yale University Press, 1958.

Depicts the social institutions and mores of the Ingalik, an Athapaskan people living on the lower Yukon River in Alaska. Part 1 presents a brief summary of Ingalik country, cultural setting, and historic contacts followed by a description of the author's method. Part 2 begins with data on village activities, including group hunting and fishing, sports and games, shamanistic practices, trade and warfare, various important ceremonies, and practices surrounding death. It next considers the activities of family life, focusing on activities at the house, activities away from the house, and the life cycle. The third and fourth sections of part 2 deal with categories of interpersonal relations and individual behavior, respectively. Part 3 provides a summary and analysis of the data. One appendix. Bibliography. Black-and-white drawings.

Savishinsky, Joel S. *The Trail of the Hare: Life and Stress in an Arctic Community*. New York: Gordon & Breach, 1974.

Examines stress and the mobility patterns of the seminomadic Colville Lake band of Hare Indians. Identifies the environmental and social sources of tension and ways of coping with these as they participate in the six major phases of band movement during the course of the year. The author comments that "[b]y taking up the specific social and ecological tensions which characterize each season in the same rhythmic manner in which the people experience them, we thus receive a diachronic and existential perspective on stress and mobility." Bibliography. Black-and-white photographs and drawings. Maps and tables.

Material Culture and the Arts

Duncan, Kate C. *Northern Athapaskan Art: A Beadwork Tradition*. Seattle: University of Washington Press, 1989.

An in-depth examination of Northern Athapaskan beadwork, "focusing on the turn-of-the-century period, when the art flourished in its most diverse and creative variants." Chapter 1 provides information on Athapaskan origins, geography, territorial-linguistic divisions, subsistence, and relations with whites. Chapter 2 discusses modes of Northern Athapaskan decoration prior to European contact. Chapters 3 and 4 concern the history of beadwork styles and technology. Subsequent chapters identify and describe five regional styles in Northern Athapaskan embroidery. Bibliography. Black-and-white reproductions, photographs, and color plates. Maps.

Osgood, Cornelius B. *Ingalik Material Culture*. Yale University Publications in Anthropology 22. New Haven, Conn.: Yale University Press, 1940.

A description of the arts and manufactures of the Ingalik, an Athapaskan-speaking people of the lower Yukon River in Alaska. Includes entries for items listed under the following categories: primary tools; containers; weapons; fishing implements; snares, deadfalls, and other traps; clothing, cradles, and personal ornaments; shelters, caches, and racks; travel implements; dyes and paints; toys and games; puberty paraphernalia; funerary objects; religious and ceremonial objects; and miscellaneous manufactures. Entries present information on the following subjects: materials used, construction, variations in construction, where made, sex typically responsible for manufacture, when made, utility, variations in use, where used, when used, user, length of life, and ownership. Five appendices. Bibliography. Black-and-white photographs and drawings. One map.

Ray, Dorothy Jean. *Aleut and Eskimo Art: Tradition and Innovation in South Alaska*. Seattle: University of Washington Press, 1981.

An investigation of Aleut, Yupik, and Pacific Eskimo decorative and sculptural arts for the historical and contemporary periods. Part 1 begins with descriptions of Native artifacts found in the journals of early explorers and whalers. It next describes the materials and coloring agents used by Native artists. Sections 3 and 4 discuss traditional and new art forms, respectively. Part 2 contains 219 black-and-white reproductions and photographs of Aleut and Eskimo artworks with commentaries. Two appendices. Glossary of words of non-English derivation. Bibliography of references used.

__________. *Eskimo Art: Tradition and Innovation in North Alaska*. Seattle: University of Washington Press, 1977.

Documents the continuity and change in North Alaskan Eskimo arts from 1778 to the mid-1970's. Argues that during the past two centuries, transformations have occurred not only in style, form, and material of these arts but in the reasons for their creation. The main chapters of part 1 identify, compare, and contrast traditional forms of Eskimo art and more recently evolved "market" varieties. Part 2 contains 307 black-and-white reproductions and photographs of Eskimo works with commentaries. Glossary of special terms. Bibliography.

Roberts, Helen H., and Diamond Jenness. *Songs of the Copper Eskimo*. Report of the Canadian Arctic Expedition 1913-18, vol. 14: *Eskimo Songs*. Ottawa: F. A. Acland, 1925.

A collection and analysis of songs recorded primarily at Copper Eskimo settlements in the Dolphin and Union straits between 1914 and 1916. Section 1 begins with discussions and transcriptions of the music from numerous Copper dance songs. It then repeats this exercise for the music of peoples in the neighboring regions of the Mackenzie River, Inland Hudson, and Point Hope. Section 2 supplies the texts and translations of these songs. Black-and-white photographs.

Tribal Life

Balikci, Asen. *The Netsilik Eskimo*. Garden City, N.Y.: Natural History Press, 1970.

An ethnographic description of the traditional lifeways of the Netsilingmiut, a tribe of hunters living on North America's Arctic coast. Primary emphasis is given to those sophisticated and specialized aspects of their technology, social organization, and religion which allow them to survive in one of the world's harshest environments. Argues that "[e]ssential aspects of Netsilik life and culture seem to address themselves in some way to the problem of the survival of the individual and the group in an extremely hostile environment." Bibliography. Black-and-white photographs and drawings.

Boas, Franz. *The Central Eskimo*. Bureau of American Ethnology, Annual Report 6 (1884-1885). Washington, D.C.: U.S. Government Printing Office. 1888.

A cultural description of that division of the Eskimo people who inhabit the northeastern Arctic and the eastern islands of the Arctic-American Archipelago. Begins with discussions of the geography of northeastern Arctic, the distribution of Central Eskimo tribes, and the influence of geographical conditions on this distribution. The next six chapters concern economic patterns and material culture. Following these are treatments of social and religious life, tales and traditions, and science and arts. One appendix. Glossary. Black-and-white drawings.

Chance, Norman A. *The Eskimo of North Alaska*. New York: Holt, Rinehart and Winston, 1966.

A description of modern Eskimo life based on fieldwork in Barrow, Kaktovik, and Wainwright, Alaska, between the years 1958 and 1962. Begins with a summary of Eskimo culture as it existed before and after white contact. The chapters that follow examine child-rearing practices; patterns of subsistence; kinship and family relations; legal and political organization; ethos, ethics and worldview; the dynamics of change as expressed in village integration, regional patterns, the quest for identity, and government policy; and the continuity and change in Eskimo life. Glossary. Bibliography of references. List of recommended readings. Black-and-white drawings. One map.

Fitzhugh, William W., and Susan A. Kaplan. *Inua: Spirit World of the Bering Sea Eskimo*. Washington, D.C.: Smithsonian Institution Press, 1982.

A "visual ethnography" of the Bering Sea Eskimo based on the artifacts, photographs, and notes collected by Edward William Nelson during his residence in western Alaska between 1877 and 1881. The text and images are organized around the following topics: modes of subsistence, village life, life in the *qasgiqs* (large, semisubterranean structures that function as men's houses and ceremonial centers for the community), direct and indirect contacts with other tribes, prehistory, ivory engravings, and continuity and change in Eskimo art. Bibliography. Sepia-toned photographs and color plates. Maps and tables.

Honigmann, John J. *Ethnography and Acculturation of the Fort Nelson Slave*. Yale University Publications in Anthropology 33 and 34. New Haven, Conn.: Yale

University Press, 1946.
A culture history of the Fort Nelson Slave, an Athapascan people inhabiting the northeastern portion of British Columbia. Seeks to reconstruct the patterns of aboriginal Slave culture and the changes those patterns have undergone as a result of European contact. An introductory section provides information on geographical setting, demography, and social history. Sections 2 and 3 discuss the tribe's pre- and postcontact modes of subsistence, technology, and social institutions. Finds that the forces of acculturation have little affected the Slave's traditional stress on individualism. Other aspects of culture were found to have changed through time. Four appendices. Bibliography. Black-and-white drawings. Maps and tables.

Hughes, Charles C. *An Eskimo Village in the Modern World*. Ithaca, N.Y.: Cornell University Press, 1960.
A study of culture change at Gambell, an Eskimo village on the northwestern tip of Lawrence Island in the northern Bering Sea. Analysis is based on information gathered during two periods of field research, the first in 1940 and the second in 1954-1955. The goal was to document the effects of increased white contact on village life as well as the historical and cultural roots of some of those effects. Pays particular attention to changes in demography, health and medical care, subsistence and material culture, and social institutions. A final chapter evaluates the nature of these changes and their implications for the future of the village. Bibliography. One appendix. Glossary of frequently used Eskimo terms. Black-and-white photographs. Maps, tables, and charts.

Jenness, Diamond. *The Life of the Copper Eskimos*. Report of the Canadian Arctic Expedition 1913-18, vol. 12. Ottawa: F. A. Acland, 1922.
A description of the society and culture of the Copper Eskimos, a Central-Greenlandic-speaking people who live principally on the mainland shores of Coronation Gulf, Bathurst Inlet, and on Banks and Victoria islands. The first three chapters are concerned with the tribe's natural environment and demography. The next several sections contain discussions of subsistence and diet, dwellings, social organization, and patterns of winter and summer life. Concludes with accounts of the life cycle, religious beliefs and shamanism, amusements, and psychology and morality. Bibliography. Black-and-white photographs and drawings. One map.

__________. *The Sacree Indians of Alberta*. Ottawa: National Museums of Canada, 1938.
A description of the traditional customs and beliefs of the Sacree Indians of Alberta based on fieldwork performed in 1921. The first chapter traces Sacree history from first encounter with whites to their settlement on a reserve near Calgary. Subsequent chapters provide information on social organization, the life cycle, male societies or clubs, the Sun Dance, Grass Dances, religious beliefs and ceremonies, and medicine bundles and other sacred objects. Black-and-white photographs and drawings.

_________. *The Sekani Indians of British Columbia*. Ottawa: National Museums of Canada, 1937.
A reconstruction of the traditional lifeways of northern British Columbia's Sekani Indians based on research carried out in 1924. The initial chapter presents a description of the tribe's natural environment. Chapter 2 briefly summarizes their history and social divisions. Following are discussions on conflicts with neighboring tribes, physical appearance and material culture, social organization, the life cycle, and religion. One appendix. Black-and-white photographs and drawings.

Jones, Dorothy M. *Aleuts in Transition: A Comparison of Two Villages*. Seattle: University of Washington Press, 1976.
Probes the contrasting effects of acculturation on two Aleut villages. Although both communities exhibit relatively high levels of acculturation to the dominant society, "they differ dramatically . . . in the extent to which they are able to realize their values and aspirations due to the varying structure and power in the two villages. These variations in opportunity and power, in turn, give rise to pronounced differences in behavior and life-styles." Bibliography. Tables.

Lantis, Margaret. *The Social Culture of the Nunivak Eskimo*. Transactions of the American Philosophical Society, New Series, vol. 35, pt. 3. Philadelphia: American Philosophical Society, 1946.
An ethnography of the Eskimo of Nunivak Island, located off the southwestern coast of Alaska in the Bering Sea. Part 1, "Non-Material Culture," contains information on the natural environment, ceremonialism, religion, recreation, the life cycle, and social organization. A conclusion and summary addresses the topics of Nunivak as an example of generic Eskimo and local Bering Sea cultures, the antiquity of Nunivak culture, and Nunivak culture as an integrated whole. Part 2, "Mythology," presents English translations of forty-five Nunivak sacred narratives. Three appendices. Bibliography. Black-and-white photographs and drawings.

Laughlin, William S. *Aleuts: Survivors of the Bering Land Bridge*. New York: Holt, Rinehart and Winston, 1980.
A study of the Aleut people, integrating data from ethnography, archaeology, history, physical anthropology, and demography. Includes discussion of Aleut physical characteristics and biology, ecosystem and modes of subsistence, origins and prehistory, language and culture, relations with Russian explorers and colonials, and responses to challenges from contemporary Western culture. Glossary. Bibliography and list of recommended readings. Black-and-white photographs. Maps and tables.

Osgood, Cornelius B. *Contributions to the Ethnography of the Kutchin*. Yale University Publications in Anthropology 14. New Haven, Conn.: Yale University Press, 1936.
An ethnography of the Kutchin Indians of Yukon Territory, Canada, and Alaska based on fieldwork carried out in 1932. Seeks to present a description of aboriginal Kutchin customs at the period prior to permanent European contact.

Begins with a discussion of the tribe's geography and ethnohistory. The next section contains information on the material culture of various Kutchin communities, including modes of subsistence, food preparation, dress, shelter, means of transportation, and manufactures and tools. Part 3 describes various aspects of Kutchin social culture including patterns and technology of warfare, arts and amusements, the units of social organization, the life cycle, religious belief and ceremony, and sacred narratives. The monograph closes with a brief account of culture changes among the tribe resulting from historic influences. One appendix: "Tabulation of Aboriginal Kutchin Culture Traits." Bibliography. Black-and-white photographs and drawings.

__________. *The Ethnography of the Tanaina*. New Haven, Conn.: Yale University Press, 1937.

Describes in detail the lifeways of the Tanaina, an Athapaskan-speaking people living on the south coast of Alaska. An introduction quickly surveys the subdivisions of the Tanaina nation, their natural environment, historic contacts and source literature, the character of the author's informants, and the purpose of the monograph and its presentation. The text's body is divided into three sections: material culture, including discussions of food, dress, shelter, travel, and manufactures and implements; social culture, containing information on war, arts and amusements, social organization, social customs, and religion; and mythology, presenting fifteen of the tribe's sacred narratives and histories. A conclusion considers changes in Tanaina culture resulting from historic influences. Three appendices. Bibliography. Black-and-white photographs and drawings. Maps.

__________. *The Han Indians*. Yale University Publications in Anthropology 74. New Haven, Conn.: Department of Anthropology, Yale University, 1971.

A compilation of ethnographic and historical information on the Han Indians of the Alaska-Yukon boundary area. The first section presents the culture of the tribe as it existed at the time of initial white contact, circa the mid-nineteenth century. Includes in this discussion patterns of religion and ceremonial practices, social organization, the life cycle, arts and amusements, war, tool making and use, subsistence, dress, and mythology. Section 2 portrays the continuities and changes in Han culture for the period preceding 1847 to that following 1947. Considers as well Han attitudes toward change. Two appendices. Bibliography. Black-and-white photographs.

__________. *Ingalik Mental Culture*. Yale University Publications in Anthropology 56. New Haven, Conn.: Yale University, Department of Anthropology, 1959.

A description of Ingalik ideas concerning the external world. Begins with the Native views on the realm of nature, including anatomy and physiognomy, animal life, plant life, and the physical world and measurement. Parts 2 and 3 treat Ingalik conceptions of the social and spiritual worlds, respectively. Part 4 examines ideas through which the Ingalik attempt to mediate discrepancies between the sphere of spiritual things and their own natural and social worlds. Involved here are the perceived needs to create good relations between the tribe and the spirits of fish and animals on which they depend and prevent those spirits that prey on human beings from making overwhelming demands on the lives of the Indians. Concludes with an analysis of the material presented. Six appendices. Bibliography. Black-and-white drawings. Two maps.

Speck, Frank G. *Beothuk and Micmac*. Indian Notes and Monographs, no. 22, pts. 1 and 2. New York: Museum of the American Indian, Heye Foundation, 1922.
An ethnographic survey of the eastern Subarctic's Micmac and Beothuk (or Red) Indians. Part 1 furnishes the scant information available on the Beothuk, who were exterminated during the early colonial era, and offers speculations concerning their origins and ethnic relations with neighboring tribes. More extensive attention is given to Micmac material culture, society, narratives, and ceremonies. Part 2 concerns the distribution and organization of Micmac hunting territories in Nova Scotia and Newfoundland. Black-and-white photographs. Maps and tables.

VanStone, James W. *Point Hope: An Eskimo Village in Transition*. Seattle: University of Washington Press, 1962.
Examines the effects of acculturation on subsistence, social structure, and individual life in Point Hope, an Eskimo village on the north coast of Kotzebue Sound. Among the author's conclusions are that despite the continued importance of the traditional round of subsistence activities, almost every villager is involved with two separate economic systems, a money and a subsistence economy; in spite of the decline in the importance of the extended family head in village social structure, leadership patterns do not seem to have experienced as great a change as might be expected; individuals do not find it necessary to associate themselves with indigenous attitudes in order to maintain their cultural identity; and though greatly modified from aboriginal times, the family structure is still a focal aspect of communal solidarity. Bibliography. Black-and-white photographs. Maps.

Wallis, Wilson D., and Ruth S. Wallis. *The Micmac Indians of Eastern Canada*. Minneapolis: University of Minnesota Press, 1955.
An ethnohistory of the Micmac Indians based on documentary sources and fieldwork expeditions in 1911-1912 and again in 1950 and 1953. Part 1, "Tribal Life," provides information on economic patterns; shelter, food, clothing, and crafts; concepts of the natural world; ethnozoology and ethnobotany; concepts of physiology and curing; dreams and dreaming; religion; supernatural powers; social and political organization; dances, songs, and games; intertribal relations; kinship and marriage; the life cycle; and the contemporary (circa 1950) Micmac. Part 2, "Folktales and Traditions," contains a large and diverse sample of Micmac folklore and stories.

Biography and Autobiography

Blackman, Margaret B. *Sadie Brower Neakok: An Inupiaq Woman*. Seattle: University of Washington Press and Vacouver: Douglas and McIntyre, 1989.
Neakok, an Eskimo woman born in Barrow, Alaska, in 1916, recounts the

highlights of her private and public lives. Included in her narrative are her childhood in Barrow; attendance at a BIA school in San Francisco and the University of Alaska, Fairbanks; activities as a teacher, volunteer public health aide, and welfare worker; marriage and family; election as the first woman elder in the Barrow Presbyterian church; and selection as community magistrate in 1960. One appendix. Bibliography. Black-and-white photographs.

Senungetuk, Joseph E. *Give or Take a Century: An Eskimo Chronicle*. San Francisco: Indian Historian Press, 1971.

Senungetuk, an Inuit artist from Wales, Alaska, chronicles the major events in his life. During the opening chapters, he fondly recalls his childhood in a traditional Eskimo village, "one of the few places on earth where Western civilization is not the primary concern of the inhabitants." He then describes the culture shock and prejudice he and his family experienced upon moving to Nome. Includes a chronology of Alaskan Native history and lists of inventions and contributions by Alaskan Natives, Alaskan Native organizations, and a brief Alaskan Native's who's who. Black-and-white and color reproductions of illustrations by the author.

CONTEMPORARY LIFE

Family and Family Services

Johnston, Patrick. *Native Children and the Child Welfare System.* Toronto: Canadian Council on Social Development in association with James Lorimer and Co., 1983.

Examines the effects of the child welfare system on Canadian Native peoples. Chapter 1 discusses the history and contemporary policies of child welfare services provided to Canada's Native populations. Chapter 2 presents statistical data on Native participation in provincial and territorial child welfare programs.

National Indian Council on Aging, Inc. *American Indian Elderly: A National Profile.* Albuquerque, N.M.: Cordova Printing, 1981.

The results of a two-year study designed to present a nationwide assessment of the social and economic conditions of Indian/Alaskan Native elderly; to accumulate data on service delivery systems serving Native elderly; and to formulate policy recommendations and strategies for serving Indian elderly in an efficient, effective, and culturally sensitive manner. Four preliminary chapters offer an introduction to the research, a summary of findings, the project background, and the research design. A needs and a service analysis compose the two main sections of the book. Each contains a brief discussion of how the research was conducted and its findings. The last chapter lists conclusions and recommendations. Two long appendices present the responses to instruments and surveys used in the research.

Red Horse, John, et al. *The American Indian Family: Strengths and Stresses.* Isleta, N. Mex.: American Indian Social Research and Development Associates, 1981.

A collection of papers, discussions, and recommendations from a conference on the strengths and coping skills of the American Indian family sponsored in 1980 by the American Indian Social Research and Development Associates. Among the conference's primary objectives were, first, to "review relevant research concerning Indian families, identifying those areas where little is known or little has been done and prioritizing those areas which suggest themselves as basic or most in need of investigation"; and, second, "to identify resources for stimulating improved and meaningful research by Indian researchers, and for examining the most appropriate major methodologies to mount significant research."

Unger, Steven, ed. *The Destruction of American Indian Families.* New York: Association on American Indian Affairs, 1977.

An anthology of essays which examines the destructive consequences of federal Indian child welfare policy. Sees in this policy a "continuing bias . . . to coerce Indian families to conform to non-Indian child-rearing standards." The essays in each of the five sections focus on a particular aspect of the Indian child welfare crisis. Those appearing in sections 1 and 2 present contemporary and historical overviews, respectively. The theme of section 3 is the human costs of federal policy. Section 4 contains a paper contrasting parent-child relationships in the law and in Navajo custom. The collection concludes with two articles on recent attempts by certain tribes to gain control over child welfare and placement.

Religion

Deloria, Vine, Jr. *God Is Red*. New York: Grosset & Dunlop, 1973.

Contrasts the basic assumptions and practices of the Judeo-Christian tradition with those of Native Americans and other tribal people. Argues that Christianity is unable to address many of the contemporary crises of meaning facing humanity. Recommends the development of new religious doctrines inspired by the spirits of the world's respective lands. The traditions, beliefs, and customs of Indian peoples offer the basic categories for such a religious revolution in North America, and, in this sense, its god should be red. Five appendices, including key documents in modern Indian-white relations and a list of tribal names and their meanings.

Steltenkamp, Michael F. *The Sacred Vision: Native American Religion and Its Practice Today*. Mahwah, N.Y.: Paulist Press, 1982.

First-person reports by a Catholic priest which explore contemporary religious practices and attitudes of the Lakota (Sioux) and other Native North Americans. The first of three sections examines the meaning of the Sacred Pipe among the Sioux. The second part describes the beliefs and ceremonies of the Native American church. The last section addresses the theme of cultural variations in God: self-revelation. An appendix provides an eighty-six-item list of plants and their uses by North American Indians. Short bibliography.

Vecsey, Christopher, ed. *Religion in Native North America*. Moscow: University of Idaho Press, 1990.

Eleven studies that "represent the contemporary state of scholarly understanding regarding the religious dimensions of American Indians' lives a half millennium since the first Columbus meeting." The first four essays focus on central beliefs and rituals of selected religious systems, including those of the Omaha, Lakota, and Inuit. The second group of papers examines how and to what extent certain tribes have maintained their aboriginal religious patterns in the face of Euro-American contact. The third section contains articles that critically examine non-Indian study and use of Native American religious forms. Concludes with an overview by Ake Hultkrantz on Native American religious studies during the past decade. Bibliography. Black-and-white photographs and drawings.

Resources and Economic Development

Ambler, Marjane. *Breaking the Iron Bonds: Indian Control of Energy Development*. Lawrence: University Press of Kansas, 1990.

Examines the attempts being made on fifteen western reservations to increase tribal control over energy development. Chapters 1 and 2 summarize the history of federal policy regarding tribal mineral leasing. The remaining seven chapters describe the recent strategies tribes have employed to increase their say over the development of energy resources on their lands. Concludes that "reservation economic development is necessary because most Indian peoples would like to continue to live on their reservations without remaining dependent upon federal subsidies. . . . The public must reconcile its impulses to decry Indian dependency while trying to defeat their efforts toward independence." Four appendices: the first presents an Indian land and mineral time line (1862-1986); the second, a listing of Council of Energy Resource Tribes Reservations (1988); the third, Charles Lipton's Eighteen Points for evaluating oil and gas contracts; the fourth, suggestions for industry. Selected bibliography. Twenty-eight black-and-white photographs; two maps; two tables.

Jorgensen, Joseph G., et al. *Native Americans and Energy Development*. Cambridge, Mass.: Anthropological Resource Center and Seventh Generation Fund, 1978.

An anthology of papers directed at supplying Native American and Anglo communities in the West with information on development of their energy resources. An introductory essay first presents a hypothesis for explaining the processes of development and underdevelopment in the region; next examines the effects of recent energy developments on rural Anglo populations and Indian tribes; and considers the responsibilities of social science research with reference to Western energy development. The remaining four essays focus on particular issues or the struggles of selected communities. Bibliography. Black-and-white photographs; charts and maps.

__________, ed. *Native Americans and Energy Development II*. Boston: Anthropology Resource Center, 1984.

A sequel to the anthology published in 1978. Examines the problems encountered by tribes attempting economic development through the exploitation of their energy resources. The lead essay discusses the positions of corporations, Indian tribes, and the federal government in regard to tribal energy development. States that "in the past four years, very little has changed. . . . As before, corporation profit, urban areas gain energy and water resources at the expense of Indian societies, Indian tribes lose their resources, few Indians gain steady employment, Indian communities are disrupted and Indian beliefs are often ridiculed by white employees of energy corporations. The federal government has served more as the handmaiden of corporate desires than as the protector of Indian interests." The next three essays discuss the origins, operations, and limitations of CERT, Council of Energy Resource Tribes. The remaining papers cover the choices, dilemmas, and struggles faced by selected Indian peoples, including Pueblos, Navajo, Chippewa, the Three Affiliated Tribes of Fort Berthold (Mandan, Hidatsa, and Arikara), California tribes, and Northern Cheyenne.

Stanley, Sam, ed. *American Indian Economic Development*. The Hague: Mouton, 1978.

Seven case studies that provide Indian perspectives on the economic development of Native North American communities. Reports emphasize the historical and cultural factors in terms of which the economic situations of these communities must be understood and recommendations for their development assessed. Communities include the Navajo, Lummi, Morongo, Pine Ridge Sioux, Passamaquoddy, Cherokee of Oklahoma, and Papago. Indexes of names and subjects.

Health/Alcoholism

Leland, Joy. *Firewater Myths: North American Indian Drinking and Alcohol Addiction*. New Brunswick, N.J.: Publications Division, Rutgers Center of Alcohol Studies, 1976.

Examines the opposing theses that Indians are "constitutionally prone to develop an inordinate craving for liquor and to lose control over their behavior when they drink" and that alcohol addiction occurs less frequently among Native Americans than in the general population. Finds no evidence in support of the first hypothesis (the "firewater myth") and a lack of substantiating or discrediting data for the second (the "reverse-firewater doctrine"). Argues that disagreement as to whether or not alcohol addiction occurs among Native Americans is due largely to confusion concerning what constitute valid indicators of alcoholism. Recommends an application of ethnoscientific methods to alcohol research. By investigating the set of categories and diagnostic signs of alcoholism native to each culture, researchers might discover that such concepts are entirely culturally relative or that there exist cross-culturally shared definitions for the "alcohol addict." Bibliography. Tables and charts.

Torrey, E. Fuller, et al. *Community Health and Mental Health Care Delivery for North American Indians*. New York: MSS Information Corp., 1974.

An anthology of previously published essays on topics related to Native American mental health, including patterns of disorder, treatment, and care delivery for both reservation and urban Indians. The book is divided into two parts. Part 1, "Psychiatric Studies," begins with an editor's overview of mental health services for Indians and Eskimos. It is followed by fourteen articles dealing with the mental health problems and needs of specific groups.

Part 2, "Health Services for Indians," presents six papers on mental health programs and research. Charts and tables.

U.S. Congress, Office of Technology Assessment. *Indian Health Care*, OTA-H-290. Washington, D.C.: U.S. Government Printing Office, 1986.
An assessment of health care for those American Indians and Alaska Natives who qualify for medical and health-related programs available from the federal government. Chapter 1 contains a summary and conclusions of the study. Chapter 2 overviews federal-Indian relations. Chapter 3 presents data on Indian population and demographics. Chapter 4 provides information on the history of Indian health, health problems and needs of particular relevance to Native Americans, and regional differences in Indian health status. Chapter 5 examines direct and contract health care delivery programs for Indians. Concludes with a chapter on the implications of recent changes in federal Indian policy for Native American health services. Six appendices. Maps, charts, and tables.

Indian Law and Government

Brakel, Samuel J. *American Indian Tribal Courts: The Cost of Separate Justice.* Chicago: American Bar Foundation, 1978.
An introduction to the history, structure, and function of the separate and semiautonomous Indian court system. Introductory sections overview the evolution, jurisdiction, and current status of tribal courts; the political context in which they operate; and contemporary reservation life, of which they form a part. Subsequent sections present a general description of the courts; statistics on crimes and disputes; the problems of overcriminalization and summary justice; case studies from the Standing Rock, Blackfeet, and Navajo court systems; theoretical perspectives on the nature of Indian courts; and conclusions and recommendations.

Flowers, Ronald B. *Criminal Jurisdiction Allocation in Indian Country.* Port Washington, N.Y.: Association Faculty Press, 1983.
Attempts to clarify the complex division of criminal jurisdiction and jurisdictional disputes among federal, state, and tribal governments in Indian country. Chapter 1 offers definitions for the terms "Indian" and "Indian country." Chapters 2 through 4 present a historical overview of Indian-white relations as well as early legislation and treaties.The federal recognition of tribal sovereignty is the subject of chapter 5. Chapters 6 through 8 discuss civil and criminal jurisdiction. Chapter 9 returns to the issue of tribal sovereignty. Chapter 10 proposes solutions for problems in the jurisdictional scheme. A concluding chapter discusses whether or not Native Americans have been treated fairly.

French, Laurence, ed. *Indians and Criminal Justice.* Totowa, N.J.: Allanheld, Osmun, 1982.
A collection of fifteen essays focusing on selected aspects of Indian crime, justice, and correction. An introduction presents a historical analysis of Indian justice. The papers in part 1 focus on the social, economic, and political dimensions of Indian criminality and the law. Part 2 contains discussions of the

basic Indian legal doctrines, Native American crime in the United States, Indian law enforcement, the incidence and causes of violent crimes among Native Americans, and American Indian tribal courts. The volume concludes with articles related to Indian correctional treatment and facilities. A bibliography of references accompanies each essay.

Levitan, Sar A., and William B. Johnston. *Indian Giving: Federal Programs for Native Americans*. Baltimore: Johns Hopkins University Press, 1975.

A critical review of federal Indian policy as it pertains to the socioeconomic conditions of Native Americans living both on and off reservations. Includes descriptions and statistical data on Indian demography, economic status and development, education, health and family, and social services. Sees the history of federal Indian relations as "a chain of mistakes and tragedies extending almost to the present." Suggests leaving the resolution of the "Indian question" to Indians and recommends shifts in Indian policy that will facilitate this process.

O'Brien, Sharon. *American Indian Tribal Governments*. Norman: University of Oklahoma Press, 1989.

An introduction to the history and contemporary structure and operation of Native American tribal governments. Part 1 describes the traditional governmental forms and processes of the Haudenosaunee (Iroquois League), Muscogee (Creek), Lakota (Teton Sioux), Pueblo, and Yakimas. Part 2 presents a historical overview of the effects of Indian-white relations on tribal governments. Part 3 returns to the five peoples discussed in part 1, this time with an eye to their contemporary governmental forms and powers. In part 4, the relations between tribes and federal and state governments are analyzed. Includes a chart of important events in the history of Indian-white relations and a glossary. Bibliography. Illustrated with black-and-white photographs.

Rosen, Lawrence, ed. *American Indians and the Law*. New Brunswick, N.J.: Transaction Books, 1976.

An anthology of nine papers which seeks "to clarify the implications that might follow in the wake of any attempt to restructure federal Indian policy, and to help establish criteria on the basis of which Indians and whites can reach greater accord on their common legal problems." The essays in part 1 concern the historical and administrative context of American Indian policy. Those in part 2 deal with Indian resources and tribal self-determination.

Education

Fuchs, Estelle, and Robert Havighurst. *To Live on This Earth*. Garden City, N.Y.: Doubleday, 1972.

Draws on data from the 1971 National Study of Indian Education to describe and analyze various aspects of Native American education. Topics include the demographics of Indian schooling; the achievement of Indian students; the mental health of Native American youth; evaluations of Indian education by students, parents, teachers, and community leaders; curriculum; boarding schools; new educational approaches; post-high school education for Indians; Indians in large urban areas; criticisms of Indian education; and the authors' evaluation of Indian education. Two appendices: "Overview of the National Study of American Indian Education" and "Summary and Critique of Research Methods for Study of Indian Education." Figures and tables.

Henry, Jeannette, ed. *The American Indian Reader: Education*. San Francisco: American Historian Press, 1973.

A collection of previously published and newly commissioned articles on various aspects of Native American education. The essays in part 1 articulate a philosophy of education in which cultural differences among all peoples act "as an aid to learning, a higher awareness of human responsibility, and a way to develop human beings capable of functioning in any society." Part 2 contains papers on the evolution of Indian education. Part 3 presents articles on problems facing contemporary Indian education. Part 4 contains critiques and evaluations of curricula and educational materials dealing with Native Americans. Part 5 provides a sample of reviews of films and books concerning American Indians. Part 6 considers the issue of relevancy in education. Part 7 offers a selection of course and curriculum outlines. One appendix: "Organizing and Maintaining a Native American Reference Library."

Kadge, Gerda. *A Comprehensive View of Indian Education*. Toronto: Canadian Association in Support of the Native Peoples, n. d.

A concise overview of the history and contemporary status of Indian education in Canada. Begins with a brief examination of the development of Canadian Indian education. Discerns three distinct phases in this development: "Before the whiteman," "Pre-confederation," and "Post-confederation." Subsequent sections examine the basic philosophy behind the Indian education system; church influence on Indian education, various types of schools that have been offered to Canadian Indians, changes in government and public attitudes toward Indian education, the nature and problems of integrated schools, and the problem of Indian school "dropouts." Bibliography. Charts.

Paquette, Jerry. *Aboriginal Self-Government and Education in Canada*. Kingston, Ontario: Institute of Intergovernmental Relations, 1986.

Provides a comprehensive policy analysis of Canada's policy on aboriginal education. Aimed at providing a framework against which to assess programs designed to improve the quality of aboriginal education and the control exercised by Native parents over their children's education.

Reyhner, Jon, ed. *Effective Language Education Practices and Native Language Survival*. Choctaw, Okla.: Native American Language Issues, 1989.

An anthology of eleven papers, presented at the Ninth Annual International Native American Language Issues Institute, which seeks to "add to the growing support for a multilingual, multicultural World where Native languages are respected, encouraged, and taught." The keynote address argues the importance of maintaining Native languages. Subsequent topics include the "English Only" threat to Native languages, the efforts of various Indian groups to develop standardized written formats for their languages, a model for bilingual education, and attempts to gear modes of instruction to Native students. Bibliographies accompany each paper. Tables.

Thompson, Thomas, ed. *The Schooling of Native America*. Washington, D.C.: American Association of Colleges for Teacher Education in collaboration with The Teacher Corps, U.S. Office of Education, 1978.

A collection of essays, drawn from the first Native American Teachers Corps Conference in 1978, that seeks to "contribute to the analysis and clarification of issues attendant to improving the educational opportunities of Indian children everywhere." Among the topics addressed are the failures of American Indian education; multicultural teacher education at the Rough Rock Demonstration School on the Navajo Reservation; the reasons Indians drop out of college; the ideal school system for American Indians; the relation of educational and political reform; and Indian "Head Start" programs. Four appendices. Select bibliography. Sepia-toned photographs and drawings.

Images, Self-Identity, and Protest

Akwesasne Notes. *B.I.A. I'm Not Your Indian Any More*. 2d, rev. ed. (Mohawk Nation) Rooseveltown, N.Y.: Akwesasne Notes, 1974.

Chronicles the experiences of the "Trail of Broken Treaties" Caravan, a group of nearly one thousand Native Americans which arrived at Washington, D.C., in November of 1972 with a set of twenty demands for change in U.S. Indian relations. Describes the origins of the caravan, its journey to the nation's capital, and the betrayals and frustrations that led to its takeover of the Bureau of Indian Affairs headquarters. Organized as a day-to-day report that incorporates numerous newspaper articles and editorials incorporated into its narrative. Illustrated with photographs, editorial cartoons, and pen-and-ink drawings.

__________. *Native Peoples in Struggle*. Bombay, N.Y.: E.R.I.N. Publications, 1982.

A selection of speeches from the Fourth Russell Tribunal on the Rights of the Indians of the Americas, held at Rotterdam in November of 1980. The collection's primary goal is to document the thinking of present- day Native peoples on their political histories, contemporary situations, and aspirations. Among the recurrent problems voiced in the speeches are "1) the defense and recovery of traditional lands and resources; 2) the recognition of rights to exist as distinct peoples with different cultures and beliefs; 3) equal rights before, and access to the functions and services of the state; 4) the denunciation of all forms of repression and violence." One group of papers is specifically concerned with Native North Americans.

__________. *Voices from Wounded Knee*. Rev. ed. Rooseveltown, N.Y. (Mohawk Nation): Akwesasne Notes, 1973.

Documents the 1973 occupation of Wounded Knee on the Pine Ridge Sioux Reservation by members and supporters of the American Indian Movement. Uses interviews with individuals involved in the takeover to give an insider's view of its structure, operation, and significance. Also supplies information on Teton Sioux history, Pine Ridge society and economy, contemporary tribal politics, and federal Indian relations essential for placing the occupation within the context of Indian activism in the 1970's. Concludes with a Wounded Knee chronology, 1868-1973. Black-and-white photographs; 1 map.

Barsh, Russel L., and James Y. Henderson. *The Road: Indian Tribes and Political Freedom*. Berkeley: University of California Press, 1980.

Discusses the problem of Native American political liberty as it concerns the relationship between Indian tribes and the U.S. government. Argues that in terms of an effective voice in national government and their right to establish local governments that exercise any and all powers they have reserved to them, Native Americans have suffered a century's erosion of their political freedom and sovereignty. Chapters discuss the concept of political liberty in America, the evolution of the doctrine of tribal sovereignty, and the divestment of Indian political liberty and possible means of its restoration.

Bataille, Gretchen M., and Charles L. P. Silet, eds. *The Pretend Indians: Images of Native Americans in the Movies*. Ames: Iowa State University Press, 1980.

Essays on Hollywood's distorted portrayal of Native American peoples and cultures. The essays in part 1 concern the origins and forms of Native American stereotypes. Those in parts 2 and 3 present early and more recent views on the Indian in film. Part 4 offers a photographic essay on the American Indian as portrayed by Hollywood. Part 5 contains reviews of *Cheyenne Autumn, Little Big Man, Tell Them Willie Boy Is Here, Buffalo Bill and the Indians*, and other movies that deal with Indian personalities, themes, and issues. Part 6 is an annotated checklist of articles and books on the popular images of the Indian in American films. Black-and-white photographs.

Berkhofer, Robert, Jr. *The White Man's Indian*. New York: Alfred A. Knopf, 1978.

Traces the continuity and change in white ideas and images of Native Americans. The essays in each of the book's four parts concentrate on a major theme. The author believes that taken together, these themes "constitute the heart of White understanding of the Indian in the past and the present." They include the invention and perpetuation of the idea of the Indian; the evolution of the scientific understanding of the Indian; the ideological components of the portrayal of Indians in literature, art, and philosophy; and imagery and federal Indian policy. Black-and-white reproductions and photographs.

Beuf, Ann H. *Red Children in White America*. Philadelphia: University of Pennsylvania Press, 1977.

Compares and contrasts the racial attitudes of Indian and white preschool children. Focuses on whether the perspectives of Indian youngsters regarding race differ significantly from those of their white peers and, if so, the social factors that may account for these differences. The first part of the study supplies basic background on Native North American history. Part 2 describes the perceptions of Indian preschoolers on race and the social order. The results of the study are the subject of part 3. Part 4 provides a new theory, based on several sociological and psychological principles, to explain the development of racial attitudes. Bibliography.

Cornell, Stephen. *The Return of the Native: American Indian Political Resurgence*. New York: Oxford University Press, 1988.

An examination of the nature and evolution of *The New Indian Politics*, "a far-reaching attempt by Native Americans to regain some measure of control over their lives, their future, and their place in American society." The chapters provide both a broad historical narrative and an analysis of the political and economic relations that have linked Native Americans to Euro-American society and "the effects those relationships have had on their opportunities and abilities to act." Tables and charts.

Deloria, Vine, Jr. *Behind the Trail of Broken Treaties: An Indian Declaration of Independence*. New York: Delta, 1974.

In November of 1972, a caravan of nearly one thousand Native Americans calling itself the Trail of Broken Treaties arrived in Washington, D.C. The group's major purpose was to present the federal government with a twenty-point agenda for reorganizing U.S. Indian relations. This book describes the social and historical factors that led to Indian politicization and protests during the 1970's. Argues that Indian tribes should be restored to the status of quasi-international, independent entities under the protection of the U.S.

Hertzberg, Hazel W. *The Search for an American Indian Identity: Modern Pan-Indian Movements*. Syracuse, N.Y.: Syracuse University Press, 1971.

Seeks to identify, examine, and trace the history of various forms of Pan-Indianism: organized, nationwide movements stressing common Indian interests, identity, and accommodation to the dominant society. Identifies the first third of the twentieth century as the formative period for the major types of contemporary Pan-Indianism. Focuses on the origins of these movements; their principal ideas; their understanding of Indianness; their leaders, membership, and organization; their interconnections; and the wider social and historical contexts in which they evolved. Bibliographical essay. Black-and-white photographs.

Josephy, Alvin M., Jr. *Now That the Buffalo's Gone: A Study of Today's Indians*. New York: Alfred A. Knopf, 1982.

An examination of contemporary Indian affairs and their historical background which seeks to help explain the feelings, viewpoints, and aspirations of present-day Native Americans. The book is divided into three parts, concerning the past, present, and future of Indian white relations, respectively. Within each part, one or more case studies highlighting a particular theme in this relationship are presented. Among these themes are the will of Native Americans to endure, the continuing racial stereotyping of Indians, efforts by Indians to retain their spirituality, and the modern quest for Indian self-determination. Bibliography.

__________, ed. *Red Power: The American Indians' Fight for Freedom*. New York: McGraw-Hill, 1971.
An anthology of essays and documents, arranged in chronological order, which seeks to illustrate the "Indians' present fight for self-determination, self-government, and the right to make their own decisions and manage their own affairs." An editor's introduction briefly sets forth the social and historical background of the Red Power movement. The twenty-five selections that follow focus on various aspects of recent Indian politicization, including affirmations of Native American ethnicity and the struggles of tribes to reclaim rights and resources of which they have been deprived. Preceding each selection is a note explaining the issues it addresses.

Roscoe, Will, ed. *Living the Spirit: A Gay American Indian Anthology*. New York: St. Martin's Press, 1988.
An anthology of essays, poems, and images concerned with the history, traditional roles, and contemporary experiences of Native American homosexuals. Part 1, "Artists, Healers, and Providers: The Berdache Heritage," is composed mainly of ethnohistorical and ethnographic treatments of the subject. The selections in part 2, "Gay Indians Today: Living the Spirit," portray the status and feelings of modern-day gay Indians. Part 3 identifies agencies and services of particular interest to the gay Indian community. It also lists tribes with berdache roles. Bibliography.

Steiner, Stan. *The New Indians*. New York: Harper & Row, 1968.
Vignettes of contemporary reservation life in which "the survival of the old Indian and the emergence of the new Indian are told in their own words." Focuses on the increasing use of political organizing and protest among Native Americans to redress the past and present wrongs committed against them. Ten appendices. Selected bibliography. Black-and-white photographs. One map.

Urban Indians

Stanbury, W. T. *Success and Failure: Indians in Urban Society*. Vancouver: University of British Columbia Press, 1975.
Examines the social and economic conditions of urban Indians in British Columbia. Identifies as its objectives to supply Native Americans, policymakers, and the Canadian public with data on the problems and opportunities encountered by Indians living in cities; to provide information for testing hypotheses concerned with various aspects of urban Indian life; and to understand the "process of change and adjustment as it affects Indians who move from largely isolated rural enclaves into the midst of the dominant society's urban environment." Glossary. Bibliography. One map, tables, and graphs.

Waddell, Jack O., and O. Michael Watson, eds. *The American Indian in Urban Society*. Boston: Little, Brown, 1971.
An anthology of essays concerned with the character, dynamics, and experience

of urban Indian life. Organizes the papers around the following questions: What is the character, historically and currently, of the urbanization trends in America as they have affected Indians? What is the character of Indian participation in the social institutions found in the city? Why do some Indians "succeed" in adapting to urban life while others decide to return to their largely rural home community? Contributors include nine anthropologists and one Native American.

Contemporary Art and Literature

Allen, Terry, ed. *The Whispering Wind: Poetry by Young American Indians*. Garden City, N.Y.: Doubleday, 1972.
An anthology of 104 works by fourteen young Native American poets from the Institute of American Indian Arts at Santa Fe, New Mexico. Features the poems of Alfonso Lopez, Liz Sohappy, Grey Cohoe, Janet Campbell, Ramona Carden, Ted Palmanteer, Donna Whitewing, Calvin O'John King D. Kuka, Patricia Irving, Ronald Rogers, Emerson Blackhorse "Barney" Mitchell, Agnes T. Pratt, and Phil George. Introduction by Mae Durham.

Geiogamah, Hanay. *New Native American Drama: Three Plays by Hanay Geiogamah*. Norman: University of Oklahoma Press, 1980.
A trilogy of dramas by Kiowa playwright Hanay Geiogamah. The plays are entitled *Body Indian*, *Foghorn*, and *49*. An introduction by Jeffrey Huntsman provides a brief analysis of each of the works and comments on their significance for the American theater. Black-and-white photographs.

Highwater, Jamake. *The Sweet Grass Lives On: Fifty Contemporary North American Indian Artists*. New York: Lippincott and Thomas Y. Crowell, 1980.
Seeks to portray the breadth of visual imagination and achievement characteristic of contemporary Native American arts. An introductory section summarizes some of the major trends in the history of Indian art in North America. Part 2 presents black-and-white and color reproductions of works by fifty contemporary Indian artists. Accompanying the reproductions are biographical sketches and statements by these artists concerning the creative process. Bibliography.

Hobson, Geary, ed. *The Remembered Earth: An Anthology of Contemporary Native American Literature*. Albuquerque: University of New Mexico Press, 1979.
A collection of poetry, short stories, and essays by contemporary Indian authors. Seeks to include as wide a spectrum as possible of "those of Native American blood and background who affirm their heritage in their individual ways as do writers of all cultures." The volume's integrative theme is that of the power of remembering the land and that the land is people. An introductory essay by the editor reflects on the renascence of contemporary Native American literature. Illustrated with black-and-white illustrations and photographs.

Katz, Jane, ed. *This Song Remembers: Self-Portraits of Native Americans in the Arts*. Boston: Houghton Mifflin, 1980.
Autobiographical sketches by twenty contemporary Native American men and

women active in the visual, performing, and literary arts. Contributors include Pitseolak and Kenojuk, two Eskimo graphic artists; Kwakiutl woodcarver Tony Hunt; Dakotah Sioux pipe carver Amos Owen; Navajo painter-sculptor-lithographer R. C. Gorman; Cecilia White, a Tlingit dancer; and writers Gerald Vizenor, Simon J. Ortiz, Leslie Silko, and N. Scott Momaday. An editor's introduction compares and contrasts Native American contributions to the arts with those of artists of Euro-American descent. Black-and-white photographs.

McNickle, D'Arcy. *The Surrounded*. New York: Dodd, Mead, 1936.

This novel begins with the return of Archibald Leon, an Indian-Spanish mixed blood, to his home on the Flathead reservation in Montana. Intending only a brief visit, he is involved in a series of events which first delay then make his departure impossible. Victimized by the destructive forces of white culture and law, Archibald embodies the fate suffered by his surrounded people.

Momaday, N. Scott. *House Made of Dawn*. New York: Harper & Row, 1968.

A densely structured novel concerning the cultural, psychological, and spiritual dislocation of modern Native Americans. Abel, a World War II veteran, returns to his reservation in New Mexico only to be engulfed by an intense sense of alienation. The novel, told in four parts from various points of view, graphically depicts Abel's downward spiral into and victory over existential despair.

Niatum, Duane, ed. *Carriers of the Dream Wheel: Contemporary Native American Poetry*. New York: Harpers, 1975.

An anthology of contemporary Native American poetry which includes the works of Liz Sohappy Bahe, Jim Barnes, Joseph Bruchac, Gladys Cardiff, Lance Henson, Roberta Hill, N. Scott Momaday, Dana Naone, Duane Niatum, Simon J. Ortiz, Anita Endrezze Probst, W. M. Ransom, Wendy Rose, Leslie Silko, James Welch, and Ray A. Young Bear. Illustrated with black-and-white portraits of each poet and sixteen color drawings by Wendy Rose. Prefaced with a "Note on Contemporary Native American Poetry" by N. Scott Momaday.

__________, ed. *Harper's Anthology of Twentieth Century Native American Poetry*. San Francisco: Harper & Row, 1987.

A collection of recent poetry by thirty-six Native Americans. Features the work of Frank Prewett, Louis (Little Coon) Oliver, George Clutesi, Mary Tall Mountain, Nora Dauenhauer, Maurice Kenny, Elizabeth Cook-Lynn, Carter Revard, Jim Barnes, N. Scott Momaday, Gerald Vizenor, Peter Blue Cloud, Duane Niatum, Paula Gunn Allen, Jimmie Durham, James Welch, Simon J. Ortiz, Emma Lee Warrior, Gladys Cardiff, Lance Henson, Barney Bush, Gail Tremblay, Linda Hogan, William Oandasan, Roberta Hill Whiteman, Wendy Rose, Steve Crow, Earle Thompson, Ray A. Young Bear, Joy Harjo, Daniel David Moses, Anita Endrezze, Nia Francisco, Robert H. Davis, Louise Erdrich, and A. Sadongei. An introduction by Brian Swann provides a brief survey of Native American literature and addresses such issues as the distinctive features of Native American poetry, the contexts surrounding recent trends in Native American verse, and the importance of oral tradition, ancestors, myths, and the search for wholeness to the works of Indian poets. Provides biographical sketches of the artists. Indexes of first lines and titles.

Peyer, Bernd C., ed. *The Singing Spirit: Early Short Stories by North American Indians*. Tucson: University of Arizona Press, 1989.

An anthology intended to "introduce some of the major Indian authors of the late nineteenth and early twentieth centuries by way of one of the more elusive genres in the history of Indian writing: the short story." Contributors include Susette La Flesche, Pauline Johnson, Angel DeCora, William Jones, Francis La Flesche, Gertrude Bonin, Charles Eastman, Alexander Posey, John M. Oskison, John Joseph Mathews, and D'Arcy McNickle. Biographical sketches of the authors precede their works.

Rosen, Kenneth. *The Man to Send Rain Clouds: Contemporary Stories by American Indians*. New York: Viking Press, 1974.

Seeks to "bring to the surface a small but important and growing body of literature that has until now been virtually ignored." Contains nineteen short stories, most of which written by young American Indian writers. Authors include: Leslie Silko, Simon J. Ortiz, Anna Lee Walters, Joseph Little, R. C. Gorman, Opal Lee Popke, and Larry Littlebird and the members of the Circle Film. Notes by the contributors. Black-and-white reproductions and photographs.

Silko, Leslie M. *Ceremony*. New York: Viking Press, 1977.

In this novel Tayo, a young World War II veteran from Laguna Pueblo, struggles to regain his sanity and place within his tribe after being released from a psychiatric ward of an army hospital. Realizing that his cure must be rooted in something larger and more inclusive than white medicine, he eventually seeks and finds restoration in the beliefs and ceremonies of his people.

Welch, James. *Winter in the Blood*. New York: Harper & Row, 1974.

The narrator of this novel, an unnamed, thirty-two-year-old Blackfeet Indian, floats aimlessly in the spiritual void of modern reservation life. His loneliness and indifference, punctuated by self-destructive binges of drunkenness, fighting, and unconnected sex, are both rooted in and reflective of the tragic circumstances of his people.

NATIVE AMERICANS

Index